ZHOU ZUOREN

AND AN ALTERNATIVE CHINESE

RESPONSE TO MODERNITY

Harvard East Asian Monographs, 189

# Zhou Zuoren

# and an Alternative Chinese

# Response to Modernity

## Susan Daruvala

Published by the Harvard University Asia Center
and distributed by Harvard University Press
Cambridge (Massachusetts) and London, 2000

© 2000 by the President and Fellows of Harvard College

Printed in the United States of America

The Harvard University Asia Center publishes a monograph series and, in coordination with the Fairbank Center for East Asian Research, the Korea Institute, the Reischauer Institute of Japanese Studies, and other faculties and institutes, administers research projects designed to further scholarly understanding of China, Japan, Vietnam, Korea, and other Asian countries. The Center also sponsors projects addressing multidisciplinary and regional issues in Asia.

Library of Congress Cataloging-in-Publication Data
Daruvala, Susan, 1949–
    Zhou Zuoren and an alternative Chinese response to modernity / Susan Daruvala.
        p. cm. -- (Harvard East Asian Monographs ; 189)
    Thesis (Ph.D.)--University of Chicago, 1989.
    Includes bibliographical references and index.
    ISBN 0-674-00238-5
    1. Chou, Tso-jen, 1885–1967--Criticism and interpretation. 2. Modernism
    (Literature)--China. I. Title. II. Series.
    PL2754.T75 Z665 2000
    895.1'85109--dc21                                        00-24706

Index by the author

 ⊗   Printed on acid-free paper

Last figure below indicates year of this printing
10 09  08  07  06  05  04  03  02  01  00

*This book is dedicated to my mother*

E. D. Daruvala

*who taught me to value independence*

*and to the memory of my father*

Fali R. Daruvala

# Acknowledgments

This book began in 1989 when I started work on a dissertation at the University of Chicago. My first thanks are to Leo Oufan Lee, always a truly encouraging and inspiring teacher. I am deeply grateful for his generous and unfaltering support through the years. I am also very grateful to David T. Roy and Antony C. Yu, the other two members of my dissertation committee, for their expert guidance, generosity, and the example of their outstanding teaching and scholarship. Without these three teachers, this book would not have taken the shape it has.

In the decade it has taken to produce this book, I have incurred numerous other scholarly and intellectual debts. Michel Hockx has aided me in numerous ways, most importantly by making detailed comments on the first draft, which helped enormously with revisions. Francesca Orsini, David Pollard, Roger Thompson, and David Der-wei Wang also read the first draft in full and made many stimulating criticisms and suggestions. I am grateful to David Der-wei Wang for letting me know he supported the book and to David Pollard for his pioneering research on Zhou Zuoren. The conversations I had with Lawrence and Pushpa Surendra inspired me to refine my arguments in the first chapter. My warmest thanks to them for their friendship, which I cherish deeply.

I owe especial thanks to Yang Yi for sending me books I needed to complete my research. I am also grateful to Rana Mitter, Han Weimin, Joe McDermott, Hans van de Ven, Henry Y. H. Zhao, and Cathrin Zondler for helping me to obtain materials and to Sy Ren Quah for help with the Character List. Much of the research and writing for the dissertation was done in Taiwan. I am indebted to Li Shuyuan for giving me a hand with Chinese poetics and to Lin Sufen for helping me to locate books and materials. The actual writing of the book began only after I started teaching in the Faculty for Oriental Studies at Cambridge in 1995, where I am fortunate in having many fine colleagues. I want to thank them for their confidence in me. Many thanks also to my students for their support in the classroom and the pleasure and challenge of teaching them. Since last year a fellowship at Trinity College has speeded the writing of this book.

Before Chicago, my debts go back a long way, to my teachers at the University of Leeds, where I studied Chinese as an undergraduate, especially Don Rimmington, who stayed in touch after I had left. I also want to thank Stuart Schram for his thought-provoking teaching at the School of Oriental and African Studies, London, and John Dolfin, who let me work at the Universities' Service Center in Hong Kong even though, at the time, I had no institutional affiliation.

Thanks also to the University of Chicago for a dissertation writing grant from the National Taiwan University endowment. My thanks are owed to those who made it possible for me to present materials at seminars or conferences: Gregory Lee, who organized the Conference on Chinese Writing and Exile at the University of Chicago in 1989; the organizers of the British Association of Chinese Studies conference in Leeds in 1994; the European Association of Chinese Studies Conference in Prague in the same year; and Hans van de Ven and Robert Bickers for the China History Workshop at Nuffield College Oxford in 1996.

John Ziemer of the Harvard University Asia Center has been rigorous, patient, and knowledgeable about the field and lived up to his reputation as the kind of editor dreamed of by academic writers. His queries, suggestions, and meticulous editing have greatly improved the book. Needless to say, I bear full responsibility for any errors and shortcomings.

Finally, I want to thank my family and friends. Among friends, Roman and Joasia Rollnick showed special grace and warmth even when the demands of writing made it hard to reciprocate. My parents-in-law, Sidney and Lois Robbins, have given me unfailing love and support throughout the years. My husband, Neal E. Robbins, has been a constant source of loving encouragement and good counsel. I could not have written this book without him. Our children, Joel and Anna, have grown up with this book, and their humor, resilience, and sterling character have been a huge source of strength. Last but certainly not least, none of us would have managed so well without my mother, E. D. Daruvala. Although now nearly eighty, she has shared the burdens of childcare and household management in our family, held the fort during long periods of intensive writing, and, with her sharp wit, continues to keep us on our toes.

S. D.

# Contents

ZHOU ZUOREN

AND AN ALTERNATIVE CHINESE

RESPONSE TO MODERNITY

# ONE

~

# Modernity and the Rupture

# with the Past

This is a study of the modern Chinese writer Zhou Zuoren (1885–1967) and of alternative responses to nationalism and modernity. Zhou was an important early contributor to the watershed May Fourth New Culture movement (1917–23), which set the direction for the subsequent development of modern Chinese literature.[1] Zhou represented the humanistic strand of thinking concerned with defining an ideal life. A founding member of the Literary Association of China (Wenxue yanjiu hui), set up in 1920, he initially advocated the creation of literature to foster humanitarian values.[2] However, two years later he broke with the idea that literature had a part to play in reforming individual consciousness and so, by extension, in saving the nation. Since the late nineteenth century, concern for the future of the nation, which was widely shared by Chinese intellectuals across the political spectrum, had underpinned all discussions of modernity. The May Fourth movement magnified this trend. But now, for Zhou, respect for the writer as an individual took precedence over the needs attributed to the nation, an idea that was to have important consequences.

Zhou promoted the essay, rather than realist fiction or poetry, as the form most suited to expressing a writer's individuality. He was recognized early on as the foremost prose stylist of the day and published collections of his essays regularly until 1945. Although he remained a staunch defender of individual human rights, his underlying assumptions were radically at odds with those of many of his contemporaries, including his elder brother, Zhou Shuren (1881–1936), better known under his pen-name of Lu Xun. (A third brother, Zhou Jianren [1889–1984], trained as a biologist, translated Darwin's *On the Origin of Species* in 1947 and held several important government posts after 1949.) A brilliant pioneer of the modern Chinese short story, Lu Xun, who eventually embraced Marxism out of a profound sense of national and cultural crisis, was raised to the level of cultural icon by Mao Zedong in 1940.[3] Although scholars have since stripped away the distortions of Maoist hagiography, Lu Xun is still the paradigmatic figure in modern Chinese literature.

Quite early in his essay-writing career, Zhou made his allegiance to broadly based Confucian values clear. This, and his air of detachment from the mounting political crisis in the 1930s and the fears of an impending war with Japan, made him seem out of step with the times. But it is, above all, his collaboration with the Japanese after 1939 that has continued to confound assessments of him. This book does not, however, seek to explain his collaboration either as the logical terminus of its argument or as its denouement, for this would imprison us in the teleological narratives that have, as I hope to show, kept Zhou's work from being properly understood. In these narratives, a writer's biography, his literary production, and China's national history are entwined in such a way that the first two must be judged in terms of the third. Up until a decade ago, for Chinese and Western scholars alike, however attracted they were to Zhou's gentle, erudite style, he was an anachronistic figure out of step with history, a self-proclaimed Confucian humanist who ended up a traitor. In the mid-1980s, Chinese literary scholars who sought to recuperate the May Fourth legacy from Communist Party historiography hailed Zhou as a proponent of liberalism and individualism.[4] Biographical information on Zhou Zuoren is readily available elsewhere, but for the sake of convenience I begin with a brief sketch of

Zhou's life, before discussing the new evaluations made possible by the passing of the Maoist era (and in Taiwan by the repeal of martial law).[5]

Born into a gentry family in Shaoxing prefecture in Zhejiang, Zhou was eight in 1893 when corruption charges against his grandfather, a high-ranking official, sent the family fortunes into decline. Zhou Zuoren received a traditional education but in 1901 followed Lu Xun's footsteps by entering the publicly financed Jiangnan Naval Academy in Nanjing, where English was an important part of the curriculum. By the time of his graduation, he had won a government scholarship to study in Japan, where he joined Lu Xun in Tokyo in 1906. There, in addition to studying Japanese, Zhou became involved with his brother's literary projects and took courses in European literature and classical Greek. He read widely in English, laying the foundation for a lifelong interest in anthropology and mythology.

In 1909, Zhou married a Japanese woman, Hata Nobuko (1887–1962). Lu Xun returned to China the same year, and Zhou turned his energies to reading Japanese literature. Zhou returned to Shaoxing with his wife in autumn 1911. Between 1912 and 1917, while employed as a school inspector and then an English teacher in Shaoxing, Zhou published a number of translations and short essays introducing foreign literature. In April 1917, at the urging of Lu Xun, who was working in the Ministry of Education in Peking, Zhou moved to the capital. His involvement in the May Fourth New Culture movement and his break with it are treated later in this chapter. In July 1923, for reasons that were never made public, a bitter quarrel flared up between Zhou and Lu Xun, who moved out of the residence in which they had run a joint household.[6] From then on, they apparently had no private contact, although they did collaborate in setting up the journal *Yusi* (Threads of talk) in November 1924. Both brothers were blacklisted by the government in March 1926 after unrest in which the troops of warlord Duan Qirui (1865–1936) massacred fifty students, and Lu Xun left Peking. Unlike Lu Xun, who stopped teaching and devoted himself to writing after 1927, Zhou maintained both his literary and his academic career.

After these events, Zhou's essays focused on his reading of history and literature rather than touching directly on public affairs. In 1930 he set up the short-lived magazine *Luotuo cao* (Camel grass), announcing that it would deal not with politics but with literature, ideas, antiquities, and "leisurely conversation." He published in a variety of magazines, and through his practice of republishing his work in thematically linked essay collections, he was able to reach a much wider and more enduring readership. Since the 1980s, Zhou has come to be seen as a key figure of the literary grouping now known as the Peking School (Jing pai), which included Shen Congwen (1902–88), Feng Wenbing (1901–67), Yu Pingbo (1900–1990), Liang Shiqiu (1902–87), and other Peking-based writers and academics.[7]

After the Japanese occupation of Peking in July 1937, despite public appeals for him to leave, Zhou did not join the exodus of intellectuals, explaining in a letter to the editor of *Yuzhou feng* (Cosmic wind) that he had too many family dependents. He accepted the position of head librarian at Peking University in January 1939, shortly after an apparent assassination attempt in which he was slightly wounded. Zhou claimed that the Japanese had engineered the assassination attempt to persuade him to collaborate; the Japanese accused the Guomindang. In 1941 Zhou became a member of the State Council in Wang Jingwei's (1883–1944) pro-Japanese government in Nanjing. After World War II, Zhou was tried and sentenced to fifteen years imprisonment for collaboration by the Guomindang government but released shortly before the Communist takeover. He returned to Peking, where during the 1950s he translated Greek and Japanese classics and wrote books about Lu Xun. He also published essays under pseudonyms in newspapers in China and during the early 1960s in Hong Kong, but for most of the reading public in China he might as well have been dead.[8] On August 24, 1966, during the Cultural Revolution, Red Guards invaded the Badaowan residence where he had lived since 1919 and made him their captive. After being severely beaten, Zhou was confined to a shed in appalling conditions for the rest of his days. He died on May 6, 1967, at the age of 82.

Such are the bare bones of Zhou's life. It is easy to pick out the elements that have become tropes when placed against the narrative of national history. The family decline caused by the accusation of corruption becomes a synecdoche for the failure of late Qing China. Zhou's quarrel with Lu Xun becomes symbolic of his refusal to assent to the "progressive" course for China. Since the two brothers had the same class and educational background, Marxists and those writing within the national history paradigm can only explain Zhou's attitudes as a failure of character. This is confirmed by his invocation of Confucian values (the main target of May Fourth iconoclasm), which in turn is seen to foreshadow his turn toward "leisurely pursuits" and, later, his collaboration with the Japanese. His marriage to a Japanese woman is often held to suggest a cultural ambiguity that is the key to his future betrayal.[9]

Writing in the mid-1980s, Shu Wu, one of the most perceptive and sympathetic scholars working on Zhou, spoke for the majority when, after praising his contributions to the New Culture movement, he continued:

His later failure was due to the foundation of his intellectual structures, which was the aristocratic style of superior, cold, and detached "Mean-ism" [i.e., the Confucian Doctrine of the Mean]. Chinese culture is self-regulating and is thus the best soil for the Doctrine of the Mean. When the question is the survival of the race, what is needed are earth-shattering shocks to thoroughly reform the culture and realize a cultural revolution. This is what Lu Xun did. But Zhou embarked in the frail boat of the Mean to navigate history's waves.[10]

Contrast this assessment from a mainland scholar with a contemporary American opinion:

Because the warlord government would not tolerate his agitational activities, Lu Xun left Peking . . . a few months after the [March 1926] massacre [of students]. Zhou Zuoren stayed on and wrote highly personal essays; he drifted deeper into a mood of emotional privacy. His May Fourth concern for "mankind" became vanquished by "society," a force he had always deemed hostile. . . . A would-be rebel, Zhou Zuoren gradually drifted deeper and deeper into a hermit's life. His personal sadness could no longer embrace the magnitude of China's social affliction.[11]

By the late 1980s, Chinese scholars had begun to write of Zhou as a proponent of individualism and liberalism. This standpoint enabled a more balanced view of Zhou's contributions to emerge and also changed the basis on which he was judged. His failure was now attributed to the fact that at the time of the New Culture movement the material conditions—freedom of publishing, creative freedom, and economic guarantees—for "enlightenment" did not exist.[12] When, for want of these conditions, Zhou did not succeed, the argument continues, he lost his sense of duty toward the people and his faith in them.

However, in terms of *significance*, some scholars came to see Zhou as Lu Xun's equal. Lu Xun represents the awakened Chinese people's march toward Marxism-Leninism, and Zhou symbolizes in tragi-comic fashion the complexity and tortuousness of this awakening. Together the two embody the necessary historical lesson.[13] One can sense that behind this assertion lay the wistful hope that the Communist Party would soon perceive the necessity of "material conditions" for enlightenment, such as publishing and creative freedom. There was also the desire to recuperate Zhou's contribution to the understanding of man and sexuality, which both Qian Liqun and Shu Wu admire.[14] During the 1990s, Zhou's previously uncollected writings were published, and others were reissued. The national interest in traditional culture together with the trend toward promoting China's Confucian heritage no doubt contributed to the growth of publishers' interest in him.

These views still did not come to grips with Zhou's real importance—namely, that he saw with great clarity that the intellectual and moral freedom of the individual was profoundly threatened by the discourse on the nation in terms of which Chinese intellectuals were embracing modernity. The term "discourse" is familiar in its broadly post-structuralist sense as the range of meanings attached to a concept shared by institutions (power) and intellectuals (knowledge). Discourses cohere not because they possess an internal logic but because their constituent elements coexist at one particular historical moment. The notion of discourse is very useful since it contains the insight, owed principally to Foucault, that the ideas and assumptions that make up discourses, or discursive practices, are linked to and productive of forms of power.[15] It is possible to accept this insight, without accepting the airtight view of some post-structuralists that individuals are *constituted* by discourses of power.[16] Because some discourses persist in ways that make nonsense of the idea of historical moment, I also invoke Patrick Tort's concept of "discursive complexes," complexes of logically related ideas that can survive apparent historical breaks.[17]

A key element in the discursive construction of modernity, which links it to the modern nation-state, is the view developed in the

eighteenth-century European Enlightenment of history as a linear progress toward the triumph of reason. This view was expressed most clearly
in Hegel's *Philosophy of History*. In his attempt to raise history to the level
of philosophy, Hegel drew extensively on James Mill's *History of British
India*. Mill's book had used India as a testing ground for the utilitarianism of his friend Jeremy Bentham, to which he added his own understanding of political economy, and was subsequently used as a text for
India-bound British civil servants until the 1850s.[18]

Absorbing Mill's view of India as barbaric and immoral, Hegel was at
the same time eager to question the French Enlightenment construction
of China's "benevolent despotism."[19] He contrasted the healthy rationality of Western civilization, which knew how to balance state and civil society, with its absence in China (where the state devoured society) and
India (where social organization precluded the political). As Ronald Inden points out, these propositions were to become fundamental to both
Indian and Chinese studies.[20] China and India were conceived as static,
stagnant societies, ahistorical in that History had not worked itself out as
the cunning of Reason, the dialectical process by which men come to
consciousness as subjects who find freedom in being citizens of a state.
This vision, as is well known, underlies Marx's idea of the Asiatic mode
of production. What in terms of linear time was "present" and "past" was
represented spatially as "Europe" and "Asia." For Asian (and other) nationalists during the twentieth century, the drive to overcome this divide
fueled the dream of an independent nation-state.

Prasenjit Duara, referring to this reified narrative as Enlightenment
History ("designate[d] with a capital H to distinguish it from other
modes of figuring the past"), has argued that

> it allows the nation-state to see itself as a unique form of community which finds its
> place in the oppositions between tradition and modernity, hierarchy and equality,
> empire and nation. Within this schema, the nation appears as the newly realized
> sovereign subject of History embodying a moral and political force that has over-
> come dynasties, aristocracies and ruling priests and mandarins who are seen to rep-
> resent themselves historically. In contrast to them, the nation is a collective histori-
> cal subject poised to realize its destiny in a modern future.[21]

As the nineteenth century progressed, this discourse became reinforced by evolutionism and Social Darwinism. It is impossible to exag-

gerate how profoundly the *scientific* credentials of these two ideas affected Asian elites, who gained ample evidence of Western technical prowess in the process of Western expansion (later replicated by Japan following the Meiji decision to pursue modernity).

Wah-kwan Cheng has shown that, in China, acceptance of the superiority of science as a way of understanding the world convinced the reformer Yan Fu (1854–1921) that Chinese tradition, exemplified by the Confucian moral order, was no longer viable.[22] Cheng distinguishes Yan's epistemologically radical espousal of scientific universality from merely institutionally radical policies such as "Western learning for use, Chinese learning for the essence" put forward by Zhang Zhidong (1833–1909) and Kang Youwei's (1858–1927) bold plan for top-to-bottom governmental reform. Unlike Yan's, these policies were articulated from within Confucian discourses. Following Japan's victory over China in the 1894–95 war, Yan called for the replacement of all these merely modernizing discourses by the "ethic" of modernity.[23] His proposals centered on three fundamental tasks: cultivating the people's strength, nourishing their intelligence, and uplifting their morality.[24]

Similarly, Liang Qichao's (1873–1929) rejection of traditional historiography was coupled with the impulse to provide China with a "scientific" history in the Enlightenment mode.[25] Philip Huang has noted the significance of Liang's adoption of the Japanese term *bunmei* (Chinese: *wenming*) in place of *fuqiang*—wealth and power—to express the reformist goal:

> Before 1898 he had spoken of reforms invariably in terms of their relevance to *fuch'iang*. His overriding concern had been to borrow Western political institutions to strengthen China. But now he spoke instead of *wenming*, not in its classical sense of a civilized cultural condition but in its Meiji Japanese meaning of "modernity"—it signified for him the desirable attributes of modern civilization, particularly the advancement of science, technology, material well-being and liberal democracy.[26]

In the course of human history, Liang held, only the "white peoples," particularly England with its liberal polity, had been able to spread *wenming*.

It is helpful to see this distinction between modernization (i.e., selective institutional reforms) and modernity (an outlook) as paralleling that made by historians between "state-making" and "nation-building." Here, state-making refers to "the impulse towards bureaucratization and ra-tionalization," whereas nation-building refers to "the identification of the citizen with the nation-state."[27] The effort at state-making thus came to be paralleled and in some ways driven and superseded by the effort at nation-building. This is very clear, in China's case, from the fact that Yan and Liang turned their attention to promoting fiction written in the ver-nacular, rather than literary Chinese, as part of the project of national salvation.[28]

Yan Fu's discovery of the people as the source of Promethean energy in Europe had led to their incorporation into the discourse of late Qing reformers as both the symbol of and the means toward the nationhood that was the reformers' goal.[29] They were convinced that if the people could be educated in science and rational thinking and their bodies strengthened, the Chinese nation could be constituted and take its place in the world. The people thus became the raw material of nationhood. They needed to be shaped into citizens, a process through which they would come to reveal the qualities of modernity, which paradoxically they contained hidden within them.[30] Such a vision required an outside consciousness, which in Yan Fu's original vision was the state, but which, after the aborted 1898 Reform movement, devolved on the intellectuals.[31] The quest for the people soon became an overriding ideological impera-tive for both reformists and revolutionaries.[32]

Within this discourse, and against the background of the political events in the first decade and a half of the century, there developed a his-torical consciousness centered on the newness of the present and a Social Darwinian reading of the promise and threat of the future. Intellectuals saw themselves in a messianic role, standing "outside" the people and re-sponsible for pushing them into the twentieth century.[33] Incensed by gov-ernment complicity with external aggression and domestic reaction, they became ever more vocal after 1915. By 1917, they were able to join forces, and the New Culture movement and its iconoclastic assault on "Confu-cian tradition" were under way. The political events of May 4, 1919, accel-erated the movement to bring "enlightenment" (qimeng) to the people, in the belief that post-Cartesian rationality would lead to patriotism.[34] The demand for revolution was articulated around the issues of language (i.e., the demand for the vernacular) and literary realism, which was intended, among other things, to effect the transformation of society and the individual.[35] The May Fourth intellectuals achieved one of their most far-reaching successes in 1921 when the government agreed that the vernacular should be the medium of instruction at all levels of education, replacing the literary language used hitherto for serious writing. At the same time, intellectuals sought to tap the creative energy of the people and to find answers to China's problems in popular culture.[36] The issues of national salvation and the construction of the people (either through enlightenment or through the discovery of values congruent with modernity within popular culture) were thus perceived as tightly bound together.

To be sure, the dominant position of the May Fourth movement in the historiography of modern Chinese literature is being modified in important ways. It is now a commonplace that the popular literature known pejoratively as "Mandarin ducks and butterflies" (from traditional motifs for romantic love) was far more important than its marginal position in literary histories would imply.[37] A recent study by David Wang speaks eloquently for the many repressed modernities of late Qing fiction and takes Chinese literary modernity back to the mid-nineteenth century, half a century earlier than the calls for Enlightenment fiction of Liang Qichao and Yan Fu.[38] Moreover, it can be argued that privileging the nation-building discourse allows one to ignore the intellectual and literary heterogeneity of the May Fourth movement and that of intellectuals in the subsequent years.

While fully acknowledging this, I remain convinced not only that, on the discursive level, the May Fourth movement was crucial to the shape of modern Chinese literature but that it had a profound effect on subsequent Chinese history. The May Fourth movement, it has been noted, although "unthinkable" without the narrativization of Enlightenment history, was itself "immensely productive of subsequent history."[39] Consequently, although I date the May Fourth movement from 1917 to 1923, I conceive of the May Fourth period as stretching to 1942, when Mao's speech at the Yan'an Forum on Literature and Art summed up and codified ideas and practices that had been prevalent among writers, especially on the Left.

My use of Mao's speech as the end point for this period should not be seen as implying that the Left prevailed over the Right. In fact, the

Guomindang produced its own, remarkably similar, set of strictures for writers around the same time.[40] The difference was that the Communist Party made far more effective use of techniques such as the rectification campaign to control writers and, through its claim to speak for the workers and peasants, had a stronger moral hold over them. The May Fourth movement inherited and enlarged on the Qing reformist discourse on the people, and its dominant discourse constituted the Chinese response to modernity most congruent with those historical narratives in which modernity is ineluctable. The two political parties who struggled so bitterly to control China were in agreement on the fundamental goal of making China strong and modern.[41]

Zhou Zuoren addressed many of the same issues of culture and nation as his contemporaries, but unlike his contemporaries he did not accept the assumption, prevalent since the late Qing, that in certain crucial epistemological respects, Chinese civilization was inferior to the modern civilization of the West. Consequently, he rejected the idea that the mission of literature was to help usher in the new forms of scientific thinking and political power that would overcome this inferiority and enable the constitution of a modern Chinese nation.

In the chapters that follow, I argue that this assumption of civilizational inferiority within the Chinese discourse of modernity emerged at times and in ways that were profoundly distorting for literature and for the modern nation and the modern selves who were imagined and produced in that literature. It is seen in emblematic form, for example, in Lu Xun's negative depictions of China, and it is still part of the currency of intellectual discourse. This sense of cultural and national crisis accounts for the eagerness with which many Chinese intellectuals were later to support the Communist Party, feeling that it alone could save the nation. We should not forget, though, that this discourse was shaped by the reality of China's position in a world dominated by imperialism. What we find in Zhou, however, is a remarkably original attempt to rethink the relations between individual and nation, nation and modernity. He would find ways other than the dominant ones of constructing the notion of the individual and affirming the individual's importance. Zhou constructed his alternative response to modernity in three interrelated ways: first, by his use of traditional aesthetic categories; second, by the importance he ascribed to locality in a writer's identity and self-representation; and third, by constructing a literary history in opposition to the dominant one.

The most important of the traditional aesthetic categories Zhou promoted were *quwei*, "flavor" or "taste," and *bense*, the "true colors" found in a writer's work. A writer's work was to be valued to the extent that it evoked the true "flavor" of the human and natural worlds, and that depended on his or her ability to perceive and convey it through imagery. *Bense* referred to the ability to develop and impart one's own independent insights and depended on sensitivity to language. By claiming the relevance of these aesthetic categories for modern Chinese writing, Zhou was trying to create a space free from political or other types of dogma. Early critics hailed Zhou's essays on such mundane subjects as frogs, boats, street foods, and tea as a respite from the stridency of contemporary fiction and criticism. In promoting these aesthetic categories, Zhou was also speaking for the admissibility, as sources in the construction of the self, of the philosophic traditions from which they came. In fact, Zhou's aesthetics drew on late Ming Neo-Confucian ideas that the individual had an innate capacity to make moral judgments. This translates into a rejection of the notion, underpinning the dominant May Fourth discourse, that the values of Chinese civilization had no meaningful place in the modern world. Zhou showed by example that it was possible for a modern Chinese literary sensibility to deploy traditional aesthetics, without indulging in the nostalgic gesture of essentializing tradition. Moreover, since these late Ming ideas had arisen in opposition to the then dominant orthodoxy, Zhou's use of them contradicted the notion that Chinese civilization lacked the resources for self-criticism.

The second plank of Zhou's approach was to make the locality, rather than the nation, into a salient part of a writer's identity and self-representation. It was by writing about the locality (defined in terms of social customs and natural conditions) that a writer was best able to realize the demands of the aesthetics of flavor. Zhou's invocation of the locality, which did not necessarily signify native place, served as a buffer against the demands that literature should serve the ideological interests of the modernizing nation-state. The dreams, myths, material culture, social relations, and scholarship of a locality gave it its particular flavor.

The author whose work best reflects Zhou's prescriptions is Shen Congwen, whose writing on West Hunan made him a serious contender for the Nobel prize in the 1980s. However, the locality was articulated within the wider area of China, not in opposition to it. Chinese identity in Zhou's thinking was based on shared access to the fullest resources of the language and on intersubjective relationships. It was beyond good and bad and functioned as an irreducible shared minimum against which the localities produced infinite variety and difference.

The production of literary histories is one way of attempting to determine the future direction of creativity. In Zhou's version, periods of openness to outside influences and individualism are equated with cultural confidence and periods of strong central control with didacticism and impoverished creativity. This history, produced in 1932 as nationalist sentiment was on the rise, implicitly rejected the idea that there could be only one homogeneous Chinese identity and explicitly pronounced the May Fourth movement heir to the intensified didacticism of the Qing dynasty Tongcheng literary school. Zhou also reiterated his longstanding rejection of the May Fourth idea of a linear progression from dead classical Chinese to the living vernacular.

This book sets out this reading of Zhou's thinking, with aesthetics and the philosophic view of human beings on which they were predicated as its core. Aesthetic concepts are immensely important for literature, because they shape the expectations and sensibilities of readers and writers. More than that, they also proceed from assumptions about subjectivity. The great importance of Zhou's placing of traditional aesthetic concepts at the center of his work is that he showed it was possible to remain untouched by the key claim of modernity that the present is superior to past. His act was a statement about how the resources of Chinese civilization could be deployed in the construction of a Chinese modernity.[42]

I use the term *civilization* rather than the term *culture* in order to stress what is at issue: I am not saying that Zhou worked from a set of propositions that could have been assimilated as an option into the rationalistic framework of nation-building. Rather, the point I am trying to make is that Zhou's literary construction of the way the individual subject and the locality relate to the nation challenged the very way in which the nation was being imagined. What emerges is a much more flexible, tolerant mode of ordering human relationships. From this, it should be clear that in using the term *civilization*, I do not have in mind the monolithic blocks ("Confucian," "Islamic," "Hindu") that have recently been projected as dominating the twenty-first century.[43] To my mind, these imagined entities are products of the logic of ideologies of nationalism dominant since the nineteenth century. I shall argue that because the nation-state is the distinguishing feature of modernity, Zhou's literary voice represents an alternative response to modernity, one that suggests significant ways of altering its most dangerous feature, the conceptual separation of the individual as a moral subject from reality.

## Nationalism and Modernity

My reading of Zhou proceeds from a particular reading of modern Chinese history, which in turn depends on a set of assumptions about modernity and nation that need to be explained. So far I have spoken of modernity and nationalism in terms of one another, "the discourse on the nation in terms of which Chinese intellectuals were embracing modernity." The fact that, despite the porosity of national boundaries to international capital and global culture, it is practically impossible to conceive of the world divided in any way other than into nation-states suggests the inseparability of modernity and nation-states. Yet the exact nature of the relationship between them remains anything but settled. In this section, I consider these terms separately and show how I think they are related. One of my underlying assumptions is that modernity has been produced and experienced in the historical context of imperialism and colonialism over the past 200 years.

Why name imperialism and colonialism as the makers of modernity's context rather than, say, industrialization, capitalist accumulation, or scientific advance? These can, perhaps even more plausibly, be argued to have "made" the modern world, especially if they are considered together as overlapping categories. I have picked imperialism and colonialism for two reasons. First, in Asia, which is my focus, modernity was often experienced most forcibly through the encounter with expanding European empires, notably the British. Second, it has been argued convincingly by Christopher Bayly that the global crisis of 1780–1830 produced the modern world and that the emergence of the modern nation-state and the ideologies of nationalism in both the metropolitan areas and the colonies were an integral part of that dynamic.[44] This analysis removes the economic motive for imperialism, expressed in the idea that the British had to become imperialists because they needed to protect trade, from its hitherto pre-eminent position as an explanatory factor. However, that is not to say that just because capitalist commercial developments were not always the main impetus in the spread of empire, imperialism was not intimately related to the spread of certain capitalist forms. Imperialism and colonialism are what tied the processes of nation-building, industrialization, and commercial and extractive capitalism together in large parts of the world. A number of questions arise: Was the context formed by imperialism/colonialism the only possible matrix of modernity? Should the nation-state be understood as part of the imperialism/colonialism matrix? Is the nation-state the inevitable outcome of modernity, or was it instead its vehicle? How does understanding the nature and origins of nationalism and nations help us to come to grips with modernity? What part does capitalism play? Does the nation-state exhaust the possibilities for the organization of human societies under conditions of modernity, or is there room for maneuver?

I cannot hope to answer these questions. But in what follows I argue that the distinct set of historical contingencies that saw the simultaneous emergence of the modern nation-state and the establishment of colonial empires, from the late eighteenth century through the nineteenth century and into the twentieth, represents a specific development of modernity, which I call, for heuristic purposes, "second-order modernity." This contrasts with first-order modernity, a much more general, somewhat Braudelian, set of processes of socioeconomic change in different parts of the world that led to higher levels of global economic integration. Some of these sets of processes comprise institutions and practices arising from various cultural and technical developments in Western Europe, which can be intuitively dated to the Renaissance. But they are not the only ones.

The case has been made that Asian economies were linked by commercial manufacturing production and long-distance trade and that they supported complex consumer societies long before the advent of European interests.[45] Recent scholarship by Yoshinobu Shiba shows emerging in Asia a variety of economic, social, and cultural practices that, if not identical to later developments that can be inserted directly into the global economy, are its precursors. These include rationalized bureaucracies, commercialization of some sectors of the economy, and the development of urban leisure culture. Intra-Asian trade is increasingly seen as an integral part of these developments. This dilutes the European cultural specificity often associated with modernity.[46] Certain practices once thought to exist only in "the West" are now found to have had a wider distribution, such as, for instance, double-entry bookkeeping.[47] "Modernity" (here, first-order modernity) becomes instead a function of the processes of global economic integration dating, for example, from the point when Mexican silver routed through the Philippines by Spain began impinging on East Asian economies. On this level, we could posit that some early condition of modernity is responsible for the similarities in urban expansion and intellectual life of sixteenth-century China and late Renaissance Europe noticed by some scholars.[48] Having said this, we must beware of giving incipient global economic integration too much weight as a causal factor, because such a sweeping paradigm would obscure the empirical facts of local realities. The society that Timothy Brook describes in his history of commerce and civilization under the Ming dynasty seems undeniably "modern" in its pursuit of sophisticated pleasures, including travel, but generated an alternative to European capitalism.[49]

With Bayly's date of 1780–1830 in mind, we can assert that by the mid-nineteenth century, most of the practices and institutions that we recognize as distinctively modern—sanitary hospitals, professional armies, expanded government bureaucracies, big cities with urban proletariats—(in my terms, second-order modernity) were making inroads in various parts of the globe, where features of first-order modernity may or may not have already been present. Most commonsense descriptions of modernity come from sociology—tautologically, the study of modern society—which by definition stands apart from premodern, or, as the loaded term has it, "traditional" society. Thus, modernity in these texts is understood principally as the condition resulting from "modernization," made possible by technological innovations—electricity, telephones, trains—and expanded bureaucracies to run transport systems, schools, and government offices. These, according to modernization or development theories current in the 1960s and 1970s, led to the breakdown of "premodern" or "traditional" modes of relationships and thinking. The superficial empirical sense in which this seems true glosses over the temporal implications of modernity—the idea that the "modern" is always more adequate to reality than what is (or was) in the past. This sociological approach can be expanded to include the notion that modernity brings with it a self-consciousness and capacity for reflection impossible in "traditional" societies. In this sense, modernity is perceived as ineluctable and irreversible. Once people begin to think as moderns, there is no going back to traditional modes of thought and relationships.

The simplistic dichotomy between modern and traditional has been challenged many times since it was first proposed in the development studies literature, and the recognition that the traditional can exist with, and promote, the modern is widespread.[50] At the same time, poststructuralist approaches have forced us to recognize the extent to which categories such as "tradition" can be essentialized and rendered ahistorical. Literary and cultural studies focusing on the entry of modernity into non-modern societies seek to answer how modernity as discourse, or even an aesthetic, becomes translated, appropriated, and transformed at a particular time in a particular place. In this mode of enquiry, the disjunctures and tensions inherent in a text or set of practices become revealing of historical specificities and possibilities that may or may not have been exploited or remarked on before.

Although modernization theory forms a natural starting point for the understanding of modernity, two antithetical viewpoints growing out of modernization need to be acknowledged. Marshall Berman's celebratory *All That Is Solid Melts into Air* seeks to link the critical insights of aesthetic *modernism* to the world created by *modernization*. Nineteenth-century modernists like Baudelaire and Dostoevsky, he writes, understood the danger and destructiveness of modern forms of living in large, anonymous cities but had the vision to embrace the possibilities they brought for the growth of human sensibilities, knowledge, and understanding. Berman's project is to reclaim both their critique of modernity and their optimism about it. He sees a dialectical movement between the two that leads to new ways of envisioning human community and thus frees modern man from nostalgia for the past. Marx is his archetypal thinker, for Marx, he holds, understood better than anyone the endless, restless creativity of the bourgeoisie, who cause "all that is solid to melt into air" through their constant revolutionizing of the means of production.

The longest section of Berman's book concerns the Russian experience of the "modernity of underdevelopment"—Petersburg contrasted with Paris. Analyzing both the forms of the city and the literature produced there beginning with Pushkin in the 1840s through Zamyatin in the 1920s, Berman argues that yearnings for self-transformation and social transformation went hand in hand to produce a distinct type of modernism. Although it arose in Russia, this form of modernism has spread, along with modernization, through the Third World.[51] Berman's passionately written work provides many insights into literary modernity and literary modernism, which can be particularly valuable for students of Chinese literature.[52] Berman, however, makes no reference to nation-states—another demonstration of how difficult it seems to be to confront the analytical categories of modernity and the nation-state together.

At the opposite pole from Berman's ebullience is Zygmunt Bauman's disturbing study, which argues that modernity was the decisive factor among the conditions that made possible the Holocaust.[53] A sociologist driven to reconsider the key assumptions of his discipline by his wife's account of life in a concentration camp, Bauman argues that the organization of modern society on rational, technical principles has made moral actions and values an essentially private matter. Moreover, all modern societies possess similar strategies for turning moral action into a matter of indifference and by such means containing the disruptive impact of moral behavior. These strategies work, not by condoning evil, but by making technical (purpose-oriented, procedural) goals the only yardstick for social action.[54] For instance, a bureaucracy presented with a particular problem thought up concentration camps as a rational, workable solution. No individual was required to take moral responsibility for actions carried out as part of the solution. Bauman's arguments have relevance for my claim, made above, that Zhou Zuoren resisted the propensity of modernity to separate the individual as a moral subject from rationality. However, my argument is made within the context of Zhou's resistance to a dominant discourse on the nation. Although Bauman refers to the reliance of modern societies on ideological mobilization carried out by the state, he does not specifically engage the concept of nation or nationalism.[55]

The study of nationalism encompasses a wide spectrum of concerns, from the institutional business of state-making to the nation-building processes that lead to the creation of a subjective sense of self as a member of a national community. The distinctions between state-making and nation-building neatly parallel those between modernization and modernity. But the origins of the nation-state are as complex as those of modernity. The view that the nation-state was called into existence by the emergence of industrial society, because only a nation-state could provide the education and common culture required in modernized or modernizing post-agrarian societies, has been put forward most trenchantly by Ernest Gellner.[56] Similarly, Benedict Anderson argues that it was print capitalism—the invention of new printing technologies and the subsequent rise of a mass market for novels and newspapers—that enabled societies to imagine themselves as a particular kind of community: the modern nation-state.[57] Despite Anderson's focus on the subjective dimensions of nation-building, both he and Gellner see nationalism as a "more or less inevitable outgrowth of a modern industrial society."[58] Their views are, in fact, most consonant with the commonsense account of modernity I sketched out initially and arguably remain the dominant explanations today.

But the opposite case has been argued with equal brilliance and much more detail by Liah Greenfeld, whose daring insistence on the power of ideas redresses Gellner's dismissal of nationalist thought as "hardly worth analysing."[59] Her careful semantic inquiries and detailed forays into national histories illuminate issues of class, status, and the subjective interactions of people with their worlds that are omitted by Gellner and rendered unproblematic by Anderson. Greenfeld seeks to explain why the emergence of nationalism predated every significant component of modernization.[60] Her five-country study illustrates her thesis that nationalism arose initially in sixteenth-century England with the idea of the sovereign people. By the mid-eighteenth century, as the idea was being appropriated in France, Germany, Russia, and what would shortly become the United States of America, the idea of nation came to stand for the uniqueness of a given people. The success of elites in these countries in propagating this view fueled the envy or, in her Nietzschean term, *ressentiment* of elites elsewhere in the world, who felt denied the same dignity by the condition of their societies and, more important, by their own precarious positions within them. Nationalism thus gave elites an extremely powerful, open-ended symbolic resource with which to effect the creative transformation not only of their own identities but of the social realities (social structures) with which they lived. Accordingly, Greenfeld concludes that the idea of the "nation" is the constitutive element of modernity, instead of the other way round.

What are we to make of these conflicting claims? Gellner's account (and to a lesser extent, Anderson's) are masterful iterations of still dominant discursive practices in which industrial modernization and its culture of nationalisms occur together so ineluctably that they constitute a fact of nature and thus take on the character of a sovereign good. I find much to distrust about the claim of goodness, as my discussion of Bauman makes clear. On the other hand, industrial modernization is a historical process, whose results have demonstrably done much to make the world "modern" in the commonsense use of the term. In studying any particular time and place, the task is always to see how the force of ideas and the force of processes such as industrialization galvanize human agents and are appropriated by them. The chicken-and-egg question is perhaps less important than the sort of omelette produced as the result of their interaction.

The absence of capitalism from Gellner's schema is quite arresting, and he himself points out the differences between his model and the Marxist one. "Identity of culture, access to power, and access to education were the only elements fed as premises into the model. . . . Capital, ownership and wealth were simply ignored and deliberately so." They were specifically replaced by "access to the acquisition of the bundle of skills which enable men to perform well in the general conditions of an industrial division of labour."[61] Gellner's dismissal of capital is troubling for two reasons. One is that it denies the contribution of capital to the industrialization he sees as the *raison d'être* for the nation-state. Second, it makes it easier to ignore imperialism, which is also absent from his account. I am not suggesting a single-strand, monocausal relationship between imperialism and capitalism, nor do I wish to echo Lenin's dictum that "imperialism is the highest form of capitalism" and apply it in blanket fashion to the past two centuries of world history. Indeed, it would be wrong to suggest that the entities "capitalism," "imperialism," and "industrialization" remained unchanged abstractions, always taking the same forms, representing the same processes, and having the same relationships with one another.[62] But it would be equally wrong to deny *any* validity to Lenin's comment, which developed the commonsense understanding of imperialism of his time, and refuse to consider the ways in which they may have been implicated together.[63] (Interestingly, Lenin contrasted the desire of bourgeois politicians between 1840 and 1860 to get rid of colonies with the late nineteenth-century recognition that colonies provided a way of exporting surplus labor and so "avoiding civil war." This supports Bayly's idea that the desire to offset working-class radicalism at home was central to British colonial policy.)

One feature common to imperialism and capitalism is the tendency to spread beyond the boundaries of the societies in which they originate. What then, accounts for such boundaries as do exist? Noting that "from its early origins, capitalism is international in scope," Anthony Giddens argues that "a capitalist society is a society only because it is a nation-state." He does not tie the institution of the nation-state to capitalism, holding that "the administrative system of the capitalist state, and of modern states in general, has to be interpreted in terms of the coordinated control over delimited territorial arenas which it achieves."[64] In other words, capitalism is not the reason for the existence of the nation-state; rather, the nation-state, which differs from previous societal organizations in the immensely increased degree of administrative control it commands over populations and resources, plays an important role in guaranteeing the environment needed by capital. If capital is inherently international in tendency, it is the nation-state that makes possible access to the competitive labor and product markets in whose context capital accumulation can take place.[65]

Eighteenth-century thinkers who produced the discursive framework for the emergence of a system of nation-states focused on the way commerce would enable men everywhere to become brothers in the global fraternity of "humanity."[66] But they recognized that "the only kind of international political order that would allow the market to exercise its natural benevolence was one in which empires had been transmuted into international federations of states, united, not politically or militarily, but by common cultural ties and economic interests."[67] French and German Enlightenment thinkers envisaged a cosmopolitan system within which, through commerce broadly understood to include intellectual exchange, peoples would develop their capacities and become fully civilized.[68] This teleological slant—commerce as training in civilization—alerts us to the way in which even as universal civilization was being imagined as constituting an emporium of world products, discursive notions of rationality and scientific inquiry were becoming necessary prerequisites for admission.

Greenfeld contributes much more than Gellner to our understanding of the emergence of nation-states because of her awareness of the rhetoric of civilization in the development of nationalisms. The logic of her account is also supported by historians such as Bayly who want to make ideological and institutional changes in Britain—that is, the development of British nationalism—central to explanations of the spread of British power.[69] Similarly, in his study of the Macartney mission to China in 1793, James Hevia demonstrates the ideological importance to the participants in the mission of the notions of public sphere and public opinion that had helped constitute the sense of English nationhood. These concerns loomed far larger than the desire to initiate trade between equals.[70] Bayly notes that as Englishness gained sharper definition, racism became entrenched. In the last twenty years of the eighteenth-century notions such as "native depravity" became generalized to include whole populations, in contrast to the "moral independency" characteristic of Britons and, tellingly, deemed to be dependent on free trade.[71]

Unlike Gellner's stark industrialization model, which discounts every other factor, Greenfeld's modular model of nationalism recognizes that the process took place within an incipient international arena or, as she puts it, a "supra-societal system of which the West was the centre."[72] Yet her account nowhere mentions either imperialism or colonialism. Consequently, it does not address the role of Franco-British rivalry and the fear of Napoleon in fostering a vigorous, conservative, British nationalism in the late eighteenth century. Nationalist thought in her account operates on the domino principle, with one society after another tumbling into nation-building discourse, two hundred years after sixteenth-century England established the pristine example.[73] More important, Greenfeld's account fails to address the *relations of power* involved in the spread of the concept of nation-state, which the work of the political philosopher Partha Chatterjee has made commonplace.[74]

Chatterjee works from the Foucaultian premise (made influential by Edward Said's study of orientalism) that thought itself can subjugate and that consequently any field of discourse should be studied as a battleground of political power. The idea of nationalism entered the colonial world as part of the discourse about knowledge that justified and validated European post-Enlightenment rationality and epistemology while buttressing European economic and military power. This is the Hegelian discourse of history as progress toward the rationality expressed in the nation-state.

Chatterjee argues that when elites in the colonial world appropriated the discourse of nationalism in order to challenge European domination, they remained imprisoned in the same post-Enlightenment rationalism, even after independence. In this sense, nationalist thought constitutes a derivative discourse. Chatterjee is also concerned to show that theorists of nationalism such as Gellner and Anderson replicate the same structures of domination in that the non-West is still expected to conform to supposedly universal Western norms of progress (e.g., a unitary state, industrialization), which are raised to the level of an ethic. With few exceptions, Indian historians had worked within the same categories, he observes. However, Chatterjee does not want to dismiss the nation-state. Particularly in his more recent work, he focuses on the historically specific circumstances in which instances of this appropriation took place. He finds that, in their struggles with one another as well as with the colonial powers, elites confronted historical possibilities and political practicalities that created opportunities for a genuinely different, nationalist discourse.[75]

For the moment what I find valuable about Chatterjee's argument is, first, the idea that nationalism entered the non-West in tandem with imperialism and, second, the related idea that it constitutes a "derivative discourse." Two caveats are necessary here: I do not intend to essentialize the category of the non-West; neither do I want to assert homogeneity within it or to suggest that the disparate societies that made up the non-West were passive. Similarly, in speaking of a derivative discourse, I do not want to downplay the importance of the space nationalism comes to provide for developing alternative possibilities "located on the terrain of politics," which Chatterjee ascribes to "the historical effectivity of nationalism."[76] I am interested in Chatterjee's schema because it helps to answer the question of why modernity and nationalism come to occupy so much of the same discursive space, for the post-Enlightenment rationality and epistemology to which he refers are the markers of modernity.

Nationalism's "historical effectivity"—the fact that in the hands of leaders as different as Gandhi and Mao it brought to an end an exploitative imperialist order made immoral by the racism and instrumentalism that underpinned it—coexists with a paradox. Namely, in the post-imperial world of nation-states postcolonial modernization replicates many of the same forms of economic and cultural domination. Hence Chatterjee's acute question, "Why is it that the non-Western colonial countries have no historical alternative but to try to approximate the given attributes of modernity when that very process of approximation means their continued subjection under a world order which only sets their tasks for them and over which they have no control?"[77]

Chatterjee's answer to this question is that Reason traveled piggyback around the world on capital. This is a convincing answer in many respects, since the parallels between the practices of extractive capital under colonial regimes and the outcomes of socioeconomic practices (development) promoted under international trade and financial arrangements arrived at since de-colonization are very suggestive. However, this does not explain the humanly dismal outcome of the modernizing efforts of the socialist countries, which were supposed to be a genuine alternative. The answer to this question can, I think, be found by seeing what it is about modernity that may have led to the suppression of other historical alternatives to the nation-state, which, in Gellner's view, is the form of organization necessary for industrialization. For the philosopher Charles Taylor, one of the hallmarks of modernity is a "stance of disengaged reason" toward the world, which calls for its rational mastery. It is best exemplified by science and technology but spreads beyond it. It is also allied to a disengaged, disciplinary attitude toward the self, which leads to an ideal of rational self-responsibility, of individuation. One of the marks of the stance of disengaged reason is its ability to *foreclose all options*, to negate or ignore those of its philosophical antecedents it has superseded. In my view, this insight is crucial. Taylor notes that this stance is responsible for the inarticulateness about ethics that haunts the modern world and is experienced as a sense of rupture with the past.[78]

In the context of the non-West, what is being foreclosed, negated, ignored, and otherwise delegitimized here are the civilizations that existed on the sites currently occupied by the new nation-states.[79] This may seem to contradict the fact that the claim to nationness rests precisely on the demonstration of uniqueness, which comes from possession of a unique cultural heritage with its unique traditions. The point is, though, that this heritage must be naturalized to fit within the parameters of the particular type of rationalization that accompanies the modern nation-state. Nation-building is the process by which such rationalization is infused into the level of interpersonal relationships and individual subjectivity. Hence the evocation and the invention, or reinvention, of markers of cultural identity in the nation-building process. Anything, putatively or genuinely from the past, which serves to define membership in the national entity and promote national homogeneity gains legitimacy. This is not to say that this is a smooth process, for nationalists may disagree among themselves and compete to infuse cultural forms and practices with conflicting meanings. However, the *full* civilizational repertoire of answers to questions about human existence with which these cultural forms can be identified cannot be invoked, thanks to the ability of the stance of disengaged reason to negate anything that preceded it. Forms of knowledge and models of selfhood that fall outside the basic rationalizing drive of modernity are ipso facto delegitimized as inappropriate and as constituting the same sort of epistemological break or rupture that is taken to exist between modernity and the past. Gellner's broad contrasts between agrarian society, characterized above all by ignorance, and industrial society illustrates this approach clearly.

It is precisely because the epistemological claims of the stance of disengaged reason have been expanded into moral ones that this is possible. We sense this very clearly, for example, in Taylor's careful explication of how the stance of disengaged reason functions as a moral imperative. This is an important part of his defense of modernity. What Bauman sees as modernity's fatal flaw, Taylor celebrates. This is important for my argument, because I believe that the propensity of the stance of disengaged reason to sunder people from prior moral sources has been amplified with enormous consequences in China during the twentieth century. Chatterjee's discussion of how the universal claims made for rationality in contemporary debates in anthropology resulted in essentializing Western culture is most illuminating. Rationality is wider than mere scientific truth, he says.

It is seen as incorporating a certain way of looking at the properties of nature, of ordering our knowledge of those properties in a certain consistent and coherent way, of using this knowledge for adaptive advantage vis-à-vis nature. It is, as Max Weber would have put it . . . an ethic. Rationality becomes the normative principle of a certain way of life which is said to promote a certain way of thinking, namely science.

Once the stricter definition of scientific truth is contained within the wider notion of rationality as an ethic,

the ethic of rationality is . . . seen to be characteristic of 'scientifically-oriented' or 'theoretically-oriented' cultures . . . by a conceptual sleight-of-hand, the epistemic privilege which is due to 'scientific truth' is appropriated by entire cultures. What results is an *essentialism*: certain historically specific correspondences between certain elements in the structure of beliefs in European society and certain, albeit spectacular changes in techno-economic conditions of production are attributed the quality of essences which are said to characterise Western cultures as a whole.[80]

The epistemic privilege Chatterjee identifies as being claimed for rationality, which now functions as "the last bastion of global supremacy for the cultural values of Western industrial societies,"[81] is identical with the epistemic privilege Taylor grants the stance of disengaged reason in the emergence of modernity. It is this epistemic privilege that produces a constant dual pressure to discount other civilizations and to essentialize Western civilization as coterminous with rationality and hence modernity.

The tensions involved here are expressed particularly clearly in an article by Paul Ricoeur entitled "Civilization and National Cultures." Ricoeur takes the idea of rationality and divides it into premodern and modern phases. Thus, he argues compellingly, from time immemorial world civilization has been experienced at the level of *techne*, because man is a rational creature and rationalization at the level of *techne* becomes the property of humanity over time. This is how discoveries and inventions such as agriculture and agricultural implements spread. But world civilization now is the result of the spreading of rationality brought about by advances in science and technology—modernization. Counterpoised to this world civilization are mere national cultures, and this has resulted in the creation of a meaningless world in which "it becomes possible to wander through civilizations as though through vestiges and ruins."[82] He sees as the solution to the malaise engendered by this situation a process in which "civilizations confront each other more and more with what is most living and creative in them." But this, he feels, can happen only at some time in the future when Western culture will have met other civilizations "by means other than the shock of conquest and domination."[83]

Ricoeur's plea seems strangely outmoded to contemporary readers, not only because we are rightly anxious to escape from the binarism of the West and its Other but because in the view of postmodernist critics of that binarism all other civilizations seem already to have been erased by the global condition of modernity. Yet this does not solve the issue at all, of course, since the idea of a global (post)modernity—which is often seen as leading to the supersession of the nation-state—is still deeply indebted to the Enlightenment mode of history. Postmodernity and modernity are conjoined, in that both are posited on a rupture with the past. More suspiciously, capitalism is still the beneficiary of whatever changes may have taken place.

But why do we still seem to be trapped in the Enlightenment version of history, even though we are aware of its origins? Patrick Tort's development of the idea of transhistorical discursive complexes suggests a solution to the puzzle.[84] According to Tort, the Enlightenment view of history is underwritten by the ideology of evolutionism and growth, which he refers to as a *para-scientific ideology*—a dominant ideology that is represented as scientific and that functions more as a typology than a narrative. As a result, while the details of the scientific ideas invoked may change, the import remains the same.[85] The assumptions of evolutionism remain enormously important in shaping social philosophies today, as shown by the perennially resurfacing "nature versus nurture" debate, no matter how discredited individual thinkers (e.g., Spencer) may become.

Tort argues that in the context of the nineteenth-century rise of in-dustrialization and liberal socioeconomic practices, which valorized the sciences as tools and as the keys to education, it was natural that these same sciences should structure the ideological grid through which society was represented.[86] The various crises brought about by the growth of in-dustrial capitalism (the melting of everything solid into thin air, which Berman represents so effectively with his various dizzying figures of speech) could be met most effectively by an ideology of progress. Such an ideology had already been partly formed in the preceding century, as a range of Enlightenment thinkers developed a historical anthropology to account for the origins and progress of human language and knowledge, which they conceived as an upward evolutionary spiral in which ideas, cultural acquisitions, and needs interacted together. Tort demonstrates the continuity between the eighteenth-century notion of progress and nineteenth- and twentieth-century appeals to evolutionism, distinguish-ing most clearly between Darwin's specific contribution to the biological sciences and the evolutionary philosophy elaborated by Herbert Spencer. Most important, he demonstrates that contemporary sociobiology func-tions in the same way, borrowing and reworking ideas from the sciences but totally unable to contribute to the sciences themselves.[87]

This is where the heuristic device of first- and second-order moderni-ties becomes useful. Second-order modernity, in which human societies are uniformly organized as nation-states, is distinguished by the central-ity of certain notions of rationality and linear progress for which science becomes the "regime of truth." In this connection I have already men-tioned the "stance of disengaged reason," which Taylor sees as the hall-mark of modernity *tout court*. To me, this propensity of modernity is re-lated to and reinforces nationalism's famous selective memory, noted by Ernest Renan when he said, "Forgetting . . . is a crucial factor in the crea-tion of a nation."[88]

In other words, both second-order modernity and the nation-state share in common the gesture of forgetting, with its concomitant negation of civilizational antecedents and the cutting off of moral sources. But, if second-order modernity, the matrix of the nation-state, is identified as the outgrowth of specific historical circumstances, then it should not be essentialized to stand for the whole of modernity. On this basis, I would modify Greenfeld's contention that the nation is constitutive of modernity by making the nation constitutive of second-order modernity. The critique of modernity undertaken by thinkers such as Bauman could then be redirected as a critique of nationalism. This is justified, I think, by Bauman's discussion of how to approach the Holocaust, which can be considered as either "evidence of the fragility of civilization, or evidence of its awesome potential."[89]

The fact that most people (including many a social theorist) instinctively choose the first, rather than the second, approach, is a testimony to the remarkable success of the etiological myth which, in one variant or another, Western civilization has deployed over the years to legitimize its spatial hegemony by projecting it as temporal superiority. Western civilization has articulated its struggle for domination in terms of the holy battle of humanity against barbarism, progress against degeneration, truth against superstition, science against magic, rationality against passion. It has interpreted the history of its ascendance as the gradual yet relentless substitution of human mastery over nature for the mastery of nature over man. It has presented its own accomplishment as first and foremost, a decisive advance in human freedom of action, creative potential and security. It has identified freedom and security with its own type of social order: Western, modern society is defined as *civilized* society, and a civilized society in turn is understood as a state from which most of the natural ugliness and morbidity, a well as most of the immanent human propensity to cruelty and violence, has been eliminated or at least suppressed.[90]

The "etiological myth" is the logical outcome of the Enlightenment mode of history buttressed by evolutionism, and "Western, modern society" cannot be anything other than the nation-state. Note that all the distinguishing marks of second-order modernity, as I am trying to establish it, exist at the level of ideas: "the stance of disengaged reason," "the Enlightenment mode of History," the "etiological myth." In other words, the interface between first- and second-order modernity is at the level of ideas, of ideology. Ideas and ideologies are extremely powerful in shaping the world, especially when they come to constitute discourses that seem to explain social experience and the world, because they then produce the categories in terms of which the world can be acted on.

One intriguing thing about Berman's, Bauman's, and Greenfeld's accounts of modernity and nationalism is their fascination with the Russian and German experiences, whether their focus is modernity or nationalism. In many respects, Greenfeld's argument is close to Bauman's, but she is saved from Bauman's pessimism because she distinguishes sharply between two basic kinds of nationalism. One is the benign, civic nationalism of England, cognate with Yankee political culture in the United States, which is based on the sovereignty of the people and hence promotes democratic principles. In contrast, the collectivist, authoritarian nationalisms of continental Europe based on the uniqueness of the people led to the reification of the "general will" and the concept of the state as an ethical totality, from which the people derived their dignity, instead of the other way around.

Eventually, Greenfeld is able to blame the Holocaust on German Romanticism. Out of *ressentiment* at Germany's place in the world, she argues, intellectuals in the early nineteenth century denounced Gallic instrumentalist rationality in favor of organicist views of human beings and society in which the "whole" man would find fulfillment. They also excoriated British capitalism and embraced the idea of violent revolution or war to transform society and man together, believing that intellectuals would give a particular lead to this process.[91] Finally, German nationalism found a scapegoat in the Jews.

Greenfeld's claim for the uniqueness of the Holocaust does not seem a tenable proposition, however, in view of the mass killings of civilian populations in the name of the nation (and in practice often in the interests of the ruling national apparatus) in such disparate places as the former Soviet Union, Cambodia, Rwanda, and the former Yugoslavia. At one point Greenfeld does seem ready to concede this. "Why," over the past two hundred years, she asks, "have intellectuals of the West been so taken up with [the] fantasy" of "the never-never land of perfect Community?"[92] In fact, Greenfeld leaves the door open to a repeat performance of the Holocaust elsewhere by arguing that Marxism is the twin of Nazism. In a compelling analysis of two articles by Marx, Greenfeld contends that as a Jew, Marx had to resolve the question of how to arrive at the perfect society without it being German. He did so by replacing Germany by the proletariat and "the West" (i.e., Britain and France) by capitalism.[93] This vision, she concludes, had international appeal for all those societies struggling with their own apparent inferiority.

Stimulating though Greenfeld's discussion is, the sharpness of her division between civic and authoritarian nationalism is questionable, because ideas and institutions cannot be easily divided into variant exemplars of the civic and authoritarian modes. Hegel, the philosopher of the state as an ethical totality, drew for some of his ideas on a British historian of India and made History into the expression of human rationality. Moreover, Hegelian ideas came to have widespread currency in areas under the sway of the English version of civic nationalism. (These considerations are part of the reason for my reservations regarding Greenfeld's failure to see imperialism as more central in the development of nationalism.)

By stressing the irrationality of *German* nationalism, Greenfeld overlooks the rationality (in the Weberian sense) that the Third Reich shared with nation-states generally. In contrast, Bauman characterizes modern culture as a garden culture that "defines itself as the design for an ideal life and a perfect arrangement of human conditions."[94] Every garden involves a struggle against weeds, and Bauman finds the two most extreme examples of this pursuit in the regimes of Stalin and Hitler. Their victims were killed, he notes, not in order to settle conquered lands, but "because they did not fit, for one reason or another, the scheme of a perfect society. Their killing was not the work of destruction, but creation. They were eliminated so that an objectively better human world—more efficient, more moral, more beautiful—could be established. A Communist world. Or a racially pure, Aryan world."[95] The Russian and German experiences of totalitarianism show "what the rationalizing, designing, controlling dreams and efforts of modern civilization are able to accomplish if not mitigated, curbed or countered."[96]

How the "dreams and efforts of modern civilization" are implicated in its institutions is an enormously complex question, but the end product is the particular modernity structured by the nation-state, which I call second-order modernity. This is the modernity before which all the preexistent civilizations are said by Ricoeur to have become "vestiges and ruins." But we need to accept that all other civilizations have been reduced in this way only if we accept the Enlightenment version of history, which was a historically specific discourse, and its attendant ideologies of rationality and evolutionism. Although second-order modernity has a tremendous capacity to displace other civilizations, this displacement has not necessarily been complete or irrevocable. Nor is the only acceptable model of selfhood the modern one. Civilizations are not closed structures that have to compete for hegemony over meaning. Here, I am following Ashis Nandy in seeing civilizations as great, baggy wholes, each containing many strands, some inimical to human dignity and happiness, and some furthering them. Different civilizations may possess different values, but all possess the resources for self-criticism and for producing different visions of themselves.[97] It is important to add that the view of civilizations as open structures means not only that are they heterogeneous, but also that it is possible for them to coexist in the same geographical space.

It was this view of civilizations that initially gave me some insight into the work of Zhou Zuoren and prompted me to account for the eclipse of civilizations in the rhetoric of nationalism and their replacement with culture and cultural nationalism. Although my source for the idea that it is possible to separate civilization and nation is Nandy, his concerns clearly echo those of Rabindranath Tagore (1861–1941) in his book *Nationalism*, published in 1917 after a visit to Japan the previous year. The difference is that whereas Nandy blames modernity (which he terms an excrescence of Western civilization) for the dehumanizing aspects of modern life, Tagore directs his criticism at the modern nation. The modern nation is the result of the transformation of the political side of society, "with the help of science and the perfecting of organization," into an expansionist entity that "goads all its neighbouring societies with greed of material prosperity," thus destroying the "higher life" based on moral autonomy. In a passage remarkably reminiscent of Bauman, Tagore wrote, "When a society allows itself to be changed into a perfect organization of power, then there are few crimes which it is unable to perpetrate. Personal man becomes eliminated to a phantom, everything becomes a result of policy carried out by the human parts of the machine, with no twinge of pity or moral responsibility."[98] Tagore does not oppose "Western civilization" but the idea of "the Nation," which he treated separately from the question of the British presence in India. "This government by Nation is neither British nor anything else. It is an applied science and therefore more or less similar in its principles wherever it is used."[99] Asserting that "the spirit of conflict and conquest is at the origin and in the centre of Western nationalism," he concluded that "the Western nation acts like a dam cutting off the free flow of Western civilization into the country of the No-Nation."[100] To paraphrase Tagore's argument here, nationalism and imperialism, which he saw as linked through trade, greed, and aggression and mutually productive of each other, denied the possibilities of modernity to humanity.

Mention of Tagore here may well seem surprising, for he is perhaps best known to students of China for the strong negative reaction he aroused among many Chinese intellectuals during a visit in 1923, but, as we will see in a later chapter, there is also a connection between Tagore and certain Japanese thinkers on these issues, most notably Okakura Tenshin.[101] Zhou Zuoren drew on ideas common among Japanese thinkers who contributed to oppositional discourses, which were often articulated in pan-Asianist terms. I do not intend to suggest any direct "influence" of either Tagore or Okakura on Zhou Zuoren. However, Tagore's general appraisal of the way nation-building discourses function is similar to Zhou's, as we will see. My quotations from Tagore are taken from a speech he made to a Japanese audience, and while he claimed that it was to the extent that Japan had been able to resist the idea of the nation that it had been able to acquire the fullest benefits of Western civilization,[102] he was clearly worried about the effect of nationalism on Japan:

I have seen in Japan the voluntary submission of the whole people to the trimming of their minds . . . by their government, which regulates their thoughts, manufactures their feelings, becomes suspiciously watchful [and wants to] meld them into one uniform mass. The people accept this all-pervading mental slavery with cheerfulness and pride because of their nervous desire to turn themselves into a machine of power called the Nation.[103]

Tagore's argument is original and noteworthy for the distinction it makes between nation and civilization, since this creates a space for an alternative response to modernity.

It might be objected that there is no need for such a space and that if we are going to talk about Indian thinkers, the example of Gandhi, who led the Indian nationalist movement and also voiced a radical critique of modernity, would suggest that alternative modernities can be imagined within the framework of the nation-state. However, although I acknowledge the importance of Gandhi's quest to build an inclusive moral basis for a national community and to his creative commitment to exploring religious truth, there seems to have been no room in Gandhi's project for any kind of modernity.[104] Perhaps, as Duara has suggested, it was because Gandhi's "utopianism was so radically oppositional that it reproduced the essentializing quality of modernity which he sought to fight."[105] And perhaps for this reason, despite Gandhi's personal vision and heroism (and that of many of his followers), he did not succeed in deflecting the Indian national imaginary from being founded on a monological (Hindu culturalist) construction of history in the Enlightenment mode from which Muslims were structurally excluded.[106]

Tagore's distinction between civilization and nation is important for my argument about Zhou Zuoren, because Chinese *nationalism* was far too close to the Social Darwinist, Enlightenment mode of history to offer a space for dissent from the instrumentalist underpinnings of second-order modernity. Duara makes a similar point when he says that "in the hands of Chinese intellectuals, social Darwinism began to produce the very categories through which the world could be seen and acted upon in its terms: race, nation and History."[107] The result of this was to collapse the (imagined) category of nation into the state, by which I mean that when the nation was imagined, it was imagined as a state, rather than, say, a congeries of cultures.

The distinction between civilization and nation makes it easier for us to see that the twin gestures of forgetting need not be complete. Nandy, writing about India, finds examples of Europeans who opposed colonialism without condescension or guilt and Indians who attempted to create a critical awareness of Indian realities and the Western presence without accepting all the normative and institutional goals of modernity, such as nation-building, that followed from acceptance of utilitarian or Social Darwinist thinking.[108] This contrasts with the more common response of Indian elites to modernity, which was to aggrandize those strands in Indian culture that were most congruent with the ideology of the colonialists and to disavow the others.[109] Their reactive critiques of their own society demonstrate a profound sense of inferiority. These aggrandized strands provided what continues to exist today as the dominant discourse of Indian nationalism.

Nandy's insight can be applied to May Fourth literature (by which I mean literature produced within the May Fourth discursive framework).

Indeed, the sense of Chinese inferiority fed the despair that led to the "obsession with China" blamed by C. T. Hsia in a celebrated article for the "parochial" nature of modern Chinese literature.[110] Theodore Huters's comment that the obsession was "less a marker of sentiment and more a deep-seated perplexity about how to overcome powerful sets of norms from the past" is a helpful insight. But the experience of China as an obsessive moral burden or a source of deep-seated perplexity are both responses to the proposition of civilizational inferiority.[111]

In the first respect, Lu Xun, who depicted Chinese civilization as an iron house suffocating its inmates and its history as one long cannibalistic banquet, peopled with self-deluding individuals typified by Ah Q, is the paradigmatic figure.[112] His work, while often seeming to go against May Fourth optimism, expressed the inner logic of the dominant May Fourth Enlightenment discourse and its late Qing reformist roots. It was part of his genius to bring to the realist literary project a "particular quality of moral introspection,"[113] which undoubtedly contributed further to his status as a paradigmatic intellectual. Moral introspection can result in clarity, which is what the proponents of Lu Xun as a fearless Marxist claim. Contemporary scholars are more apt to see it as resulting in crippling anguish. But even a Lu Xun read as weak, cowardly, and self-hating is still seen by critics as representing "the active, critical half of the Chinese cultural soul."[114] Indeed, for the purposes of this book, the chief interest of Lu Xun lies in what the paradigm he represents can tell us about the underlying discourse of modernity and nation.

### Lu Xun: The Paradigmatic May Fourth Intellectual

Lu Xun added to the nation-building endeavor a heroic Nietzschean subjectivity, which emerged very clearly in his years in Japan. His intellectual and literary ventures there have been amply discussed elsewhere. Lu Xun went to Japan in 1902, preoccupied with the questions "What is the ideal life of man?," "What does the Chinese national character most lack?," and "What is the root of China's sickness?" and came to the conclusion that "what the Chinese most lacked was sincerity and love."[115]

Lu Xun's problematic, with its concern for the ideal life and the moral side of man, went considerably beyond the stance of either constitutional reformists like Liang Qichao or republican revolutionaries like Sun Yat-sen (1866–1925).[116] On the other hand, the questions themselves are formed within the discourse of civilizational inferiority that Yan Fu had admitted into his reformist platform. Lu Xun's concern with the moral health of China was inextricable from this discourse, expressed in perceptions of the body centering on health and disease. Thus, his decision to study medicine and his switch two years later to literature were two sides of the same coin. In his conflicting accounts, the issue became a trope for his own struggle to come to grips with the denial of Chinese civilizational viability as well as its remedy—the nation-building project implicit in the late Qing reformist discourse. Needless to say, this discourse cannot be separated from the context of the imperialist world order of the late nineteenth century. Reformist elites throughout Asia had quite similar preoccupations with exercise and diet as a way of getting their populations to "measure up" to the (mainly Anglo-Saxon) norm.

Lu Xun narrativized his initial decision to go to Japan and study medicine in the context of his father's sufferings at the hands of traditional Chinese doctors during his lingering terminal illness. The failure of Chinese medicine thus becomes the wellspring of his distrust of Chinese culture. Eventually there occurs the famous incident during the Russo-Japanese War, in which Lu Xun and his classmates at the Sendai Medical School were shown a newsreel slide of a Chinese prisoner being beheaded in front of a group of unconcerned, but rudely healthy, compatriots. According to this account, Lu Xun decided that "medical science was not so important after all" because physical sturdiness was obviously no use to people of "a weak and backward country" if they could serve only as spectators at such tragedies. Consequently he went to Tokyo with plans to "launch a literary movement."[117]

In the autobiographical account in "Mr. Fujino," however, Lu Xun's focus is on the Chinese intelligentsia, represented by the loafing, effeminate, empty-headed Chinese students in Tokyo who frame his text. Because he despises them so much, he leaves Tokyo for Sendai, where he meets the kindly teacher Mr. Fujino. Much of the narrative, which leads to an abbreviated account of the slide show, focuses on the unkindness of some of Lu Xun's Japanese fellow students, who accuse him of having been informed of examination questions in advance. From this the conclusion is drawn, "China is a weak country, therefore the Chinese must be an inferior people, and for a Chinese to get over sixty marks could not be due to his own abilities. No wonder they suspected me."[118] Here, Lu Xun seems to be assimilating to himself, albeit in the voice of others, the moral and intellectual inferiority of the Chinese students in Tokyo. The decision to study medicine in this text thus expresses a more general desire to exert control over the physically unmanly and spiritually unhealthy Chinese intelligentsia. A similar process of assimilating this discourse to himself is at work in the slide show incident. Thus one can agree with the reading suggested by Ozaki Hideo of Lu Xun as "someone who simultaneously becomes the Chinese who was shot *and* the people watching."[119] To Wendy Larson's observation that Lu Xun combined the stances of victim and passive audience into "an ultimate Chinese 'nature' that becomes his motive for writing,"[120] we could add that the part of him which agrees "no wonder they suspected me" takes on the stance of the actively cheering Japanese audience of which he is a part.

The spiritual overcoming stressed in the essays Lu Xun published after leaving Sendai appears as a solution to the conflict thus engendered. He predicted that the twentieth century would bring forth "brave individuals of superhuman willpower" to overcome the excesses of the nineteenth-century materialism.[121] He also called for "Mara poets"—literary geniuses who heroically brought about the national rebirth of their countries. Lu Xun's examples were Byron, Shelley, Pushkin, Mickiewicz, and Petöfi. The "love" the Chinese lacked was perhaps the love Zarathustra expresses for "the great man who is willing to be a bridge to the future" and who "justifies the men of the future and redeems the men of the past."[122]

But Lu Xun's elitist concern after 1906 with the figure of the Mara poet is complicated by a contradiction. Although he seems to have excluded the people from his vision of the nation to which the poet gives voice, he also internalized within himself the image of that passive, victimized people. When Lu Xun's attempt to set up a magazine titled *New Life* (*Xin sheng*) foundered in 1909, with it ended "our discussions of a future dream world"[123] as well as Lu Xun's dream of being a Mara poet and consequently his hope of self-transcendence. Lu Xun fell into a deep depression that lasted nearly a decade.[124] When finally he was persuaded to write during the New Culture movement, his metaphor for Chinese civilization was not disease but cannibalism.

Perhaps Lu Xun was impelled to move beyond the metaphor of disease in his fiction to counter the optimism of the New Culture movement that the sickness of Chinese society could be cured. Hu Shi (1891–1962), for example, wrote of the role of progressive individuals, "The health of the society and the nation depends on a few tenacious, unrelenting white blood cells who battle the wicked and depraved elements of society; only through them is there hope of reform and progress."[125] It was actually Zhou Zuoren who penned the essay published under Lu Xun's name[126] that equated the "dark and confused elements" of the Chinese heritage with a case of syphilis that had penetrated every sphere of activity and tradition.[127] The essay quoted the view of the Frenchman Gustave Le Bon (1851–1931) that most of our movements and activities were controlled by hundreds of generations of dead ancestors, who far outnumbered their descendants.[128] This made the struggle to be "humans" instead of dead ghosts much harder. Yet just as it was to be hoped that medicine would find a cure for syphilis, so the spiritual medicine "science" would cure minds. The important thing was to work for change.

Lu Xun, on the other hand, adopted a stance of extreme skepticism. This is suggested by his story "Medicine," which recounts efforts made to procure a piece of bread dipped in the blood of an executed revolutionary in the belief it will cure consumption. The protagonists are completely oblivious to the meaning of the revolutionary's sacrifice. According to Lu Xun, the hopeful symbolic ending of the story was written in "obedience" to the leadership of the New Culture movement: "I, for my part, did not want to infect with the loneliness that I had found so bitter, those young people who were still dreaming pleasant dreams, just as I had when young."[129]

Lu Xun's refusal to hope made him, paradoxically, the voice of the New Culture movement's totalistic assault on Chinese civilization. But the New Culture movement also involved another turn toward the people who were to become the nation, a turn we find expressed in the 1920s and 1930s in the work of folklorists and historians and in the literary representation of the masses.[130] Here, Lu Xun's depiction of the shame and worthlessness of the intellectuals whose literacy connected them to the cannibal culture served to connect him with the later valorization of the laboring masses as the true representatives of the nation. As perceptively noted by W. K. Cheng, this valorization is prefigured in his story "A Small Incident" in which the *wenren* persona shrinks beneath his fur gown as he realizes his moral insignificance before an ordinary rickshaw-man.[131] Thereafter the incident often returns to him, "teaching me shame, pushing me to reform, and increasing my courage and hope."[132]

After his turn to the left, Lu Xun began to translate Soviet literary theory and Russian literature. His insistence on doing "hard" (i.e., literal) translation has been seen as an expression of extreme humility toward foreign thinkers.[133] He was probably also working on the theory, put forward by May Fourth leader Fu Sinian (1896–1950) in 1919, that the Chinese language lacked "precision" and that the way to make Chinese thought more precise was to impose "precise" Western linguistic structures on it.[134] Turning the metaphor of cannibalism inward, Lu Xun described this as a process of "stealing fire from foreign countries to cook my own flesh."[135] In the early 1930s, in tune with his political commitments, Lu Xun developed the combative "dagger and spear" style he felt necessary for the times.[136] The works of this period make chilling reading thanks to their similarity to the *ad hominum* attacks that became a feature of political campaigns, particularly after 1949.

If Lu Xun is regarded as the foremost modern writer and thinker, it is perhaps because he managed to embrace two extremes found in the philosophical underpinnings of modernity—the Nietzschean view of the self and the Hegelian mode of history found in Marx. The Nietzschean "will to overcome" is predicated on a view of the self as a self-created aesthetic subject.[137] Basing his conception of man on a dubious theory of psychological "drives," Nietzsche held that it is to the extent that the creator-self has undertaken the discipline of rejecting everything that makes him like other men that he succeeds in becoming the superman.[138] Marxism offers a supposedly scientific basis for the role of the will in transcending evolutionism, for revolution expresses the will of the most advanced parts of the social organism.[139] Moreover, the painful acquisition of the scientific knowledge necessary to foster that project (in Lu Xun's case, by doing "hard" translation) also symbolizes "overcoming." In his philosophical allegiances, Lu Xun represented both what he wanted to overcome and his aspirations for the future, and as a result his literary self-identity was circumscribed by "the nation."

In his response to Marxism, Lu Xun prefigured the way the discourse on the people at the core of the late Qing response to modernity was to lead to the Maoist Marxist state. The irony is that whereas Lu Xun clung tenaciously to a moral view of the world, the Chinese response to modernity had replaced the traditional conception in which the people, as moral beings, were subject to renovation (*xin min*)[140] with an aggrandized view in which they were subject to instrumental manipulation. Because Lu Xun had no hope that a moral consciousness could be awakened in Ah Q or the cannibal culture regenerated, he could only gesture in the direction of whatever force might be able to impose a "self-overcoming" on China. The aggrandized, distorted version of traditional didacticism formed a perfect fit with the utilitarian idea of the malleability of man. Its legacy can be seen in extreme form in the Maoist belief that "the poor and blank" could be transformed by instrumental policies into signifiers of national regeneration.

Mao Zedong's accolade of Lu Xun in 1940 as "the major leader in the Chinese cultural revolution . . . not only a great writer but a great thinker and a great revolutionist" is thus not surprising.[141] It merely shows that Mao recognized the extent to which Lu Xun's work articulated the inner logic of the discourse on the people-as-nation that is part of the project of (second-order) modernity. At a more pragmatic level, Mao must have recognized the value of Lu Xun's mix of personal integrity, patriotism, and pronounced self-distrust as a model for intellectuals. Ever since Mao delivered the Yan'an Talks on Literature and Art in 1942, intellectuals have been called on to show their patriotism through the repeated acts of "self-overcoming" with which they were required to demonstrate submission to the Communist Party's ideological control.

### Zhou Zuoren's Alternative Response to Modernity

The discourse on the people and the nation that crystallized in the May Fourth period and can be recovered in paradigmatic form in Lu Xun's writing represents what Nandy calls a "dominant response to modernity." Implicit in the argument is the assumption that the dominant re-

sponse, built as it is on feelings of inferiority and an instrumental philosophy, is inherently problematical. The dominant civilizational strand
that emerged from this encounter was precisely the authoritarianism Enlightenment historians take as the target of Enlightenment thinking.[142]

This authoritarianism derives from the habits of mind fostered by the
concern with institutional and philosophical orthodoxy of the Cheng-
Zhu school of Neo-Confucianism.[143] The basic texts of this school—
which claimed to propound the only orthodox tradition of Confucian
learning (*daoxue*)—had been adopted as the basis for the state examinations by the early Ming. It thus "became integrated into the framework of
educational institutions capable of reproducing an ideologically cohesive
ruling class through the civil service examinations."[144] Not surprisingly,
the school had "a tremendous impact on education and profoundly
shaped the nature of literati culture for five hundred years."[145] Thus,
when Yu-sheng Lin sees the "totalistic anti-traditionalism" of the May
Fourth discourse as having evolved "under pressure of socio-political realities after 1911" from a "deep-seated, traditional . . . mode of thinking,"
he is corroborating the intensification of the exclusivist, totalizing cultural strands described by Nandy.[146] This was, in fact, the substance of
the charge Zhou was to make in the 1930s against the Tongcheng literary
school.

However, Lin's contention that "even if Confucians wanted to look
beyond their own framework of ideas and assumptions, they were hardly
provided with any alternative way of thinking within the range of Chinese culture" is contradicted by Zhou Zuoren, who drew on the late
Ming Neo-Confucian counter-tradition associated with thinkers like Li
Zhi (1527–1602) and Jiao Hong (1540–1620).[147] Specifically attacking
Cheng-Zhu orthodoxy, counter-traditionalists stressed that the individual had an innate capacity for making moral judgments and need not depend on received opinion to know what was right or wrong. This counter-tradition arose in the context of massive social changes under way in
late Ming China, which, Kai-wing Chow has recently argued, provoked a
crisis in the Confucian order.[148] The gentry response, which aided the
Manchus in consolidating their hold over China and so received state
sanction during the Qing, was to promote ritualism and familism and to
attack counter-traditional thinking. Chow's work is relevant here because

it shows the ritualism and familism targeted by May Fourth elites to have been a specific, and comparatively recent, historical development. But for many May Fourth intellectuals and much subsequent scholarship, these "evils" have been generalized as "Chinese feudal tradition."

In many essays, Zhou stigmatized contemporary nation-building discourse as inheriting the worst features of Cheng-Zhu Neo-Confucianism, which he held responsible for blighting Chinese intellectual and cultural life since the Song dynasty. He claimed to have begun disliking *daoxue* as a boy when he discovered the book *Hanxue shangdui* (An assessment of Han Learning) by Fang Dongshu (1772–1851) in the family library. Fang's book, written just before the Opium War, blamed Han Learning, the Qing school that advocated a return to Han dynasty interpretations of the Classics and opposed those of Neo-Confucianism, for fostering moral passivity and useless erudition and thus allowing the chaotic situation in Canton to develop.[149] His aim was to revive both the philosophy and literary style of Zhu Xi (1130–1200).[150]

The centrality of this late Ming influence in Zhou's thinking is reflected in his aesthetic categories of *quwei* and *bense*, which were predicated on a particular philosophic view of the self that owes much to late Ming thought. Based on this philosophic view, Zhou's interests in anthropology, mythology, and human sexuality, which began during his years in Japan, became a way of gaining knowledge of the human mind and its potential. Indeed, the concept of the "childlike heart" (*tongxin*) that Li Zhi equates with innate moral capacity may be seen as informing and linking Zhou's preoccupation with anthropology (given Victorian anthropology's ontogenetic approach to human societies) and children. This cluster of interests meshed with the salience he saw in locality in a writer's self-representation and literary production. Locality, defined in terms of the social and natural worlds, became the space in which *quwei* was to be found. The nonlinear literary history he formulated was structured around the poles of "literature to convey the Way" (*wen yi zai dao*) and "literature to express the intent" (*shi yan zhi*). In his view, works in the first category fell under the intellectual sway of orthodoxy and those in the second depended, in his reading, on the recognition of the intent of the innately moral individual.

Zhou's alternative response to modernity, presented in outline here and to be developed in the body of this book, was not (and, by definition, could not be) a nativist effort to supply an essentialist civilizational "other" to the West. It was developed in the course of his own critical engagement with contemporary realities and discourses. Zhou's participation in the New Culture movement illustrates the way his own practice and experiences led him to change his positions on some issues. The "break" with the May Fourth discourse did not take the form of an ideological conversion to a newly discovered truth. Rather, it unfolded as a creative intellectual process by which Zhou discarded some approaches, including didacticism and idealism, and refined and strengthened ideas and attitudes that he had brought to the New Culture movement.

Zhou arrived in Peking in April 1917 to join the faculty at National Peking University (Beida), which under the bold, innovative leadership of Cai Yuanpei (1876–1940) was becoming the intellectual center of the country and a forum for free academic debate between progressive and conservative scholars.[151] Cai had assumed the presidency of the university in December 1916, and shortly thereafter brought in Chen Duxiu (1879–1942), editor of New Youth (Xin qingnian), on the recommendation of the Japanese-trained linguists Qian Xuantong (1887–1938) and Shen Yinmo (1887–1964). The following summer, Hu Shi returned from the United States, where he had trained with John Dewey, to teach philosophy. Also attracted to Beida were the poet Liu Bannong (1891–1934) and Li Dazhao (1888–1927), appointed chief librarian in February 1920.

Zhou notes in his memoirs that all these men were among the colleagues from the humanities who, like him, had offices in the same building.[152] They became variously involved in writing for and editing the radical journals of the day: New Youth and Weekly Critic (Meizhou pinglun), which was set up principally by Chen Duxiu and Li Dazhao to be more timely and pointedly political than New Youth.[153] The journals were a platform for the expression of the mounting intellectual ferment and political dissatisfaction, which finally spilled over on May 4, 1919. This story is too well known to require recapitulation here. Zhou's articles, including "A Literature of Man" ("Ren de wenxue") (December 1918), earned him recognition as a leading May Fourth theorist. His poem "The Rivulet" ("Xiao he"), published in *New Youth* in February 1919, was widely hailed as the first "outstanding work" of new poetry.[154]

Zhou's organizational contribution to the New Culture movement was also important. His influence on students such as Yu Pingbo, Fu Sinian, and Gu Jiegang (1895–1980) who set up the New Tide Society (Xin chao she) in November 1918 made him a bridge between students and the older generation of progressive intellectuals at Beida.[155] The New Tide students sought to take the tide of "new thought" into Chinese society in order to further the "spiritual emancipation" of the country. Zhou joined the organization in May 1920, the only faculty member to do so, and became editor in chief of its journal in October 1920.[156] He was also, along with Liu Bannong and Gu Jiegang, one of the pioneers of the movement to collect Chinese folk literature and do research on it.[157]

Zhou's radicalism at the time cannot be doubted. At the same time, his refusal to accept the basic demand of modernity that all options which preceded it should be denied or negated emerges quite clearly in his writing (although he never articulated it explicitly). The recollections of the New Culture movement presented in Zhou's memoirs are structured around a fundamental divergence between his aims and understandings and those of Hu Shi and Chen Duxiu. Since Zhou provides textual evidence for his claims, which center on the issue of language, we need not regard his assertions as the justifications of hindsight.

When Zhou arrived in Peking, Hu Shi and Chen Duxiu had been corresponding publicly for several months on language reform (vernacularization) in the service of a literary revolution. The idea of radical language reform had been mooted as early as 1906 in the draft program of the Alliance in Shanghai of Students from All Provinces (Gesheng liu Hu xuesheng zonghui). These returned students from Japan called for the publication of magazines in the vernacular in every province and nationwide training in the national language (*guoyu*) in order to eliminate provincial dialects.[158] Their goal was the eventual establishment of a national parliament, but the alliance soon disappeared. Nearly a decade later, in November 1915, Chen Duxiu published an article calling for the introduction of realism into Chinese literature. Realism and naturalism had developed in European literature, Chen argued, because "due to the rise of science since the end of the nineteenth century, the real nature of the universe and human life has been discovered."[159] As is well known, this elicited an enthusiastic letter of support from Hu Shi, published in October 1916, in which he put forth his programmatic "eight don'ts" (e.g., "Don't use classical allusions"; "Don't avoid vulgar diction") for literature, which were to serve as the basis for a "literary revolution" (*wenxue geming*).[160]

Encouraged by Chen, Hu followed this up with his "Tentative Proposals for the Reform of Chinese Literature" ("Wenxue gailiang chuyi"), which appeared on January 1, 1917. in *New Youth*.[161] Although he avoided mention of revolution, Hu, on the analogy with Luther and Dante whose "living literature" (*huo wenxue*) replaced the "dead literature" (*si wenxue*) written in Latin, pronounced vernacular literature (*baihua wenxue*) to be the orthodox (*zhengzong*) literature of China. Chen immediately published "On the Theory of Literary Revolution" ("Wenxue geming lun"), in the February 1 issue. In this article, he praised revolution as the foundation of Europe's brilliance and called for revolutions to wash away the dirt in all spheres of Chinese life, including literature.[162] He announced three principles for the Revolutionary Army of literature:

1. To overthrow the painted, powdered, and obsequious literature of the aristocratic few and create the plain, simple, expressive literature of the people;

2. To overthrow the stereotyped and over-ornamented literature of classicism and create the fresh and sincere literature of realism;

3. To overthrow the pedantic, unintelligible, and obscurantist literature of the hermit and recluse and create the plain-speaking and popular literature of society in general.[163]

With this article, the debate started to attract widespread attention. Qian Xuantong and Liu Bannong wrote letters to the editor affirming their support.

Zhou Zuoren started buying *New Youth* soon after he arrived in Peking and was shown back issues by Lu Xun, but according to his account, neither he nor Lu Xun was particularly impressed by it. "Although it was edited by Chen Duxiu, it did not seem anything special," he later wrote.[164] What really had an impact, in Zhou's estimation, was the abortive attempt to restore the boy emperor Puyi by the Manchu loyalist general Zhang Xun in July 1917.[165] These events left Zhou with the feeling that "China's reforms had never succeeded in the past, because what had been needed was a "revolution in thought" (*sixiang geming*).[166]

To help bring about such a revolution, Zhou resolved from then on to write and translate into the vernacular. His first effort was a translation of the Tenth *Idyll* of Theocritus (fl. 3rd century B.C.E.) under the title "A Modern Translation of an Ancient Poem" ("Gu shi jin yi"), completed on September 18, 1917, and published in *New Youth* the following February. In an introductory note, Zhou said he believed translations could only be done into the vernacular, otherwise it would be impossible to be faithful to the original.[167] Zhou makes the contrast between his stance and that of Chen Duxiu and Hu Shi very plain by discussing his translation just after recalling his impressions of *New Youth* as lackluster. Talk of "literary revolution" was just a fancy way of talking about genre reform (*gaige wenti*), because, Zhou said, "the joke was, they still used classical Chinese (*guwen*) in their own writing."[168] To underline his point, Zhou quotes a sentence by Chen Duxiu, written in literary Chinese, in answer to a point of Hu Shi's: "The idea that the central principle of the reform of Chinese literature is for it to be in the vernacular is incontrovertible. We cannot allow opponents any room for discussion on this. We have to take what we have advocated as absolute truth and not allow others to correct it."[169]

What is important here is not Zhou's assessment of the impact of the Hu-Chen proposals but the implicit contrast he then made between their motivation for using the vernacular and his own. His stand was for a "revolution in thought"; for him, a "literary revolution" by itself was "not enough."[170] From Chen Duxiu's three principles quoted above, however, the iconoclastic intent of the revolution in literature is apparent, and it is clear that the revolution was intended to extend far beyond literature. These gigantic tasks could reasonably be supposed to require a revolution in thought. In what sense, then, could Zhou, writing in the 1960s, suggest that talk of literary revolution was "not enough"?

The answer lies in the proposition that the demand for the creation of a new national language and literature in the vernacular, or as Chen put it, "the plain, simple expressive literature of the people," represented a major step in the nation-building process. It was, in effect, a continuation of the discourse on the people; they were to constitute the modern nation in which the vernacular stood for the people, although the aim was now not simply to educate the masses but to invent them in the image of the new nation.[171] This invention took place within the matrix of perceived Chinese inferiority vis-à-vis the West.

Thus for Chen Duxiu:

All our traditional ethics, law, scholarship and customs are survivals of feudalism. When compared with the achievement of the white race, there is a difference of a thousand years in thought, although we live in the same period. [Unless we improve,] our people will be turned out of this twentieth-century world, and be lodged in the dark ditches fit only for slaves, cattle and horses. . . . I would much rather see the past culture of our nation disappear than to see our nation die out now because of its unfitness for living in the modern world.[172]

Chen suggested that youth (whom he likened to the new, healthy cells of the body) should follow six principles: to be independent instead of servile, progressive instead of conservative, aggressive instead of retiring, cosmopolitan instead of isolationist, utilitarian instead of formalistic, and scientific instead of imaginative.[173]

Zhou's suggestion that this is "not enough" implies a fundamental difference with the pervasive premise of the worthlessness of traditional culture that lay behind the smokescreen of language reform.[174] The difference was precisely that Zhou was not so much preoccupied with the intrinsic inferiority of Chinese culture and character as he was concerned to bring ideas from abroad to Chinese society—hence the value of translation. Thus the first author he translated into the vernacular was not a modern realist but an ancient Greek.

Moreover, he introduced his use of the vernacular by referring to Kumārajīva (fl. 385–409), whose life's work had been to render Buddhist sutras into Chinese and who had equated translating books with "chewing food [to make it digestible] to feed people."[175] This represents an attempt to draw a parallel between the contemporary influx of new ideas and a successful example of the same in the past (the entry of Buddhism). Zhou's tactic contrasts with the assertion by most of those in the New Culture movement of the complete bankruptcy of Chinese civilization and the need to embrace modernity. Zhou's use of the example of Kumārajīva is significant, because the issue of whether to regard the influx of Buddhism as cultural enrichment or cultural disaster has surfaced from time to time in the elite discourse of Chinese cultural identity for over a thousand years. As will become evident in this book, Zhou favored the

argument that Chinese civilization was capable of absorbing and benefiting from outside influences. To name but one example, Hu Shi regarded Buddhism as a harmful cultural influence, and in this he was
drawing in part on traditional views.[176] In his autobiography, Hu describes how as a boy he came to reject his mother's Buddhist beliefs after
stumbling on the anti-Buddhist passages in the *Zizhi tongjian* (The com-
prehensive mirror for aid in government) of Sima Guang (1019–86) and
the writings of Zhu Xi.[177] Is there a link between Hu Shi's affinity as a
boy for the more culturally conservative view and his implicit acceptance
in adulthood of the view that Chinese civilization had failed? No one can
say for sure, but it seems plausible to suggest one.

Thus, at the very beginning of the New Culture movement, the
meaning Zhou ascribed to the use of the vernacular was significantly
different from that of Hu Shi and Chen Duxiu. After he broke with the
dominant May Fourth discourse, Zhou was able to call on a native critical tradition that had developed in response to the totalizing elements in
Chinese culture. This tradition was distinguished by its lack of hostility
to Buddhism and critical openness to it. Zhou's own openness to Buddhism had led him while studying in Nanjing to seek instruction from
the lay Buddhist scholar Yang Wenhui (1837–1911), who had become
aware of European progress in studying the Buddhist canon and who
subsequently brought many lost texts back to China from Japan. But
Zhou never developed a religious affiliation with Buddhism.

This does not mean that Zhou did not share the feeling of cultural
crisis—the lesson he had drawn from the attempted restoration of Puyi
was precisely that China was socially and morally in dire straits. Zhou
developed his notion of a "revolution in thought" (*sixiang geming*) in an
article of that title first published in March 1919.[178] The literary revolution was almost a *fait accompli*, he said, with the vernacular (*baihua*) increasingly being used. However, literature was more than language; it was
a fusion of language and thought. If the language used to express thought
was poor, that would hinder the development of literature, and if the
quality of thought was poor, what was the point of having language for it?
"We oppose *guwen*, mainly because it is obscure and difficult to understand and fosters a generalized mode of thinking in the nation (*yangcheng
guomin longtong de sixiang*), as a result of which expressivity and compre-

hension are not developed. But it is also because the thought expressed in it is harmful to people." Zhou continued that "this unnatural thinking, which results from a fusion of Confucianism and Daoism, is lodged within *guwen* itself and cannot be separated from it." This seems a rather uncompromising rejection of key elements of Chinese civilization, but the example Zhou gave of the way "unnatural thinking" inheres in *guwen* was of immediate political relevance following the attempted restoration. This referred to the style of dating in which 1912 was named as the first year of the Republic (*minguo zhengnian*). However, "some contemporaries felt this did not sound suitably classical and used the term *chunwang*" (an alternative form for the first year of a reign used in the *Spring and Autumn Annals*). This usage had about it the smell of the Imperial Clan Party (Zongshedang—a faction in the Qing court that opposed abdication), Zhou said. Eliminating *guwen* and getting rid of the implements used to express this kind of absurd thinking could be an effective method. But this left the problem that people's thinking remained unchanged, and they could express the same rubbish as easily in the vernacular as in literary Chinese. Was a monarchist wearing a foreign suit and holding up a placard for *weixin* (reform in a renovative sense, used by Kang Youwei's movement for a constitutional monarchy) advocating democratic government? he asked. "How can a reform in which just language and not thinking has been changed be considered a complete victory for the literary revolution?" Zhou gave several examples of new usages in the vernacular that conveyed the old orthodox morality of loyalty to the emperor or head of the family and expressed the fear that popularization of the vernacular would make it easier, not harder, for these ideas to spread without a genuine change in modes of thinking.

The juxtaposition of Chen Duxiu's text and his own article in Zhou's memoirs reminds the reader of the charge Zhou would later make in his lectures on the origins of the new literature that Hu Shi and Chen Duxiu had inherited the didacticism of the Tongcheng school (see Chapter 2 for a fuller discussion). In fact, the authoritarianism of the dominant May Fourth discourse is apparent in the exchange between Hu and Chen. In a letter to Chen, Hu had written that the correctness of the various views expressed by Qian Xuantong and others in response to his "eight don'ts" could not be decided in a day or by one or two people. He hoped this would lead to ardent debate. "We have deployed the flag of revolution, and although it would be impermissible to retreat, we also would not dare to take what we have advocated as absolute truth and not allow others to correct it," he wrote.[179] Chen's reply, printed just after Hu's letter, contains the comment, "My humble opinion is that acceptance of dissenting views and free debate are assuredly principles for the development of scholarship, [but] the idea that the central principle of the reform of Chinese literature is for it to be in the vernacular is incontrovertible." On this point, there was to be no discussion. Scholarship, in Chen's view, could work only within certain ideological parameters. And despite Hu's expressed reservations, by April 1918 he had spelled out the aim of the literary revolution as nothing less than the creation of "a literature in the national spoken language and a national spoken language able to produce literature" (*guoyu de wenxue, wenxue de guoyu*) and denounced everything written in the literary language as "lifeless museum pieces."[180]

Although sharing the premise of Chinese cultural sickness, Zhou's search for a cure did not take him along quite the same paths as it did his contemporaries. At the time of the New Culture movement, Zhou was intellectually deeply involved with the Japanese utopian-socialist New Village (Atarashiki mura) movement established by the writer Mushakōji Saneatsu (1885–1976) in 1918. Mushakōji was a leading member of the Shirakaba literary group, founded in 1910 to bring optimism and beauty to a literary scene dominated by naturalism. Zhou had been one of the earliest readers of the group's journal.[181] Life in the New Village was intended to promote "a humane life" (*ren de shenghuo*) for each individual, based on equality, shared labor, and the peaceful resolution of differences. Mushakōji believed that this ideal was shared by millions and would inevitably be realized. His concern was to bring it about peacefully by helping to transform individual attitudes through the practice and example of the New Village. Otherwise, he feared, humanity would have to undergo the bloodshed, destruction, and loss caused by revolution.[182]

Shirakaba idealism is clearly visible in Zhou's "A Literature of Man" and "A Literature of the Common People" ("Pingmin de wenxue"), both written in December 1918.[183] Of these, "A Literature of Man" is regarded as Zhou's major theoretical contribution to the New Culture movement and was praised in 1935 by Hu Shi as having shown the direction the "new literature" should take.[184] The article argues that humanity is one and that each individual is a part of it. Literature should foster this ideal by advocating the new scientific view of man as an evolved creature, better than animals and free of the superstition of a spirit. Man's body and spirit should be seen as being in harmony, not in conflict, and customs and teachings that oppose man's natural instincts should be rejected. The touchstone for judging literature should be whether it promoted a human or an inhuman view of life; this was an issue not of content or literary method but of the author's moral standpoint. Consequently, much of China's traditional literature, including vernacular novels such as *Water Margin* (*Shuihu zhuan*), should be rejected.

Seven months later, in July 1919, Zhou visited the New Village and returned very moved and excited by the "dream come true" it represented of the power of the "love of humanity" in action.[185] His enthusiastic reports of his visit in the October 1919 issue of *New Tide* and elsewhere led to the formation of "New Village" organizations in Peking and outside Shanghai. Although Zhou does not seem to have become more than briefly involved in their activities, he was recognized as the movement's intellectual mentor; among those who discussed it with him was the young Mao Zedong.[186]

Opposition came from an unexpected quarter, however. Lu Xun wrote to Qian Xuantong that Zhou's articles on the movement needed reworking and were not worth being carried in *New Youth*.[187] Lu Xun also put his criticism of Zhou's utopianism in the mouth of a fictional character who exclaims, "Reform? Where are the weapons? Work and study? Where are the factories?"[188] Hu Shi also opposed Zhou, charging him with following Mencius' injunction to "attend to one's own virtue in solitude" (*du shan qi shen*), and equated the New Village experiment with the self-cultivation of the traditional recluse (*yinyi*).[189] Hu Shi's criticisms reveal that his conception of the individual (which served the dominant May Fourth construction) differed from Zhou's in regard to the presumption of the individual as primarily a moral subject.

This is in keeping with Hu's view of society as the "greater self" (*dawo*) to which the individual is hierarchically subordinate as a "small self" (*xiaowo*).[190] Hu argued that the type of individualism that "attended to one's own virtue" (*du shan de geren zhuyi*) was dangerous because it led those discontented with society to withdraw from it rather than to struggle within it. This tactic had been understandable when people did not know the strength of organized individuals, but there was now no place for such thinking. Furthermore, Zhou was wrong to think that the individual was the starting point for changing society. The individual could not exist apart from society and was a product of social forces. Consequently, it was these forces, which included language, habits, thinking, and education, that had to be changed, not the individual. Hu envisaged a process of piecemeal tinkering with the social organism ("those who want to do anything must be continually researching, thinking, investigating, solving practical problems") as part of the process of struggle. As a social experiment analogous to Zhou's but worthy of the present, he recommended the "social settlements" programs in U.S. cities, which brought culture, childcare, and general social uplift to the poor. Despite this gradualism, with his opposition of a "social" present and an ineffectual (yet dangerous) "individualist" past, Hu Shi constructed modernity as immanent. He delegitimized "humanity" as a meaningful category (presumably because it would transcend the nation-state) by noting that individualists always claimed to worship it.

Given Chen Duxiu's and Hu Shi's differences with Zhou Zuoren, how are we to account for the prestige of "A Literature of Man"? The most important factor is probably that Zhou's construction of "individual" was opposed to "tradition" and so could be used in the iconoclastic assault on the past. Perhaps the article's many ambiguities (such as the condemnation of vernacular novels) were overlooked in the general relief of the literary reform camp that someone had produced a set of concrete proposals for the content of the new literature. Moreover, Zhou wrote with lucidity and passion. It was only when Zhou's articles on the New Village movement appeared that basic differences of approach began to be obvious.

Zhou was aware that his focus on the individual constructed as moral agent and his prescriptive approach to literature involved him in a serious contradiction.[191] In a talk given in January 1920, he tried to reconcile the idea that the value of a work of art lay in its expression of the writer's personal emotions and thoughts with the belief that society needed a literature that would enlighten even as it gave pleasure. The idea that art should exist for its own sake he dismissed as hindering self-expression or making life serve art.[192] Zhou began by recognizing that "art in the service of life" could easily slip into utilitarianism, but at the same time he argued that the historical background and the contemporary environment called for "a literature of human life" (*rensheng de wenxue*). Uneasy with his invocation of social and historical conditions, however, Zhou then reformulated this in universal terms: all humans understand the fear of death, but they do not all desire freedom and happiness to the same extent. Consequently when those of more advanced consciousness express themselves, they speak for all. He concluded in a quite didactic vein, "The artists of this new epoch are 'iconoclasts,' but they hold to a new religion—the ideal of humanitarianism is their belief; human aspirations are their god."[193] However, the problem represented by didacticism, which was inherent in the summons to create a "literature of man," was common to the entire May Fourth project, and Zhou soon began to turn away from it in his theoretical formulations.

### The Break with the May Fourth Discourse and Afterwards

From January to September 1921, Zhou was sick with pleurisy. In June he went to recuperate at the Biyun Buddhist temple outside Peking. This was a period of great mental turmoil for Zhou. In a letter to Sun Fuyuan (1884–1966), a member of the New Tides Society and later of the Literary Research Association, he described his struggle to find his own direction:

The recent confusion and trouble in my thoughts has . . . already reached a peak. Tolstoy's selfless love and Nietzsche's superman, communism and eugenics, the teachings of Christianity, Buddhism, Confucianism, and Daoism, and the example of science: I like and respect them all, but at the same time, I cannot synthesize them into one to create one path along which to walk. I can just keep them heaped in my head, like the goods in a village general store. Or perhaps there simply isn't only one "national highway" in the realm of thought.[194]

This last line perhaps indicates the beginning of the resolution of Zhou's struggle. At around the same time, he wrote a short essay promoting a literary form and an aesthetics that cut right across the May

Fourth demands for realist fiction or a poetry of self-expression divorced from the strictures of tradition. "There are many thoughts that, since they cannot be turned into fiction and are not easy to turn into poetry, can be put into the essay form." Zhou had belles lettres in mind, for he named this type of essay *meiwen*. However, he was not willing to allow the content to be dictated by the form, for "if we discuss its character, then belles lettres are also fiction, and fiction is also poetry." The prerequisites for the genre, "as for all other literary works," were simply "genuine simplicity and clarity," Zhou said.

On January 22, 1922, in his first public act since his illness, Zhou began writing a column for the *Morning News* (*Chenbao*) paper, under the title "In My Own Garden" ("Ziji de yuandi").[195] This marked a turning point. He had lost the New Culture movement's basic instrumentalist belief that people could be shaped by literature. In his opening essay, he explained the reasons for the title of his column:

One hundred and fifty years ago, France's Voltaire wrote his novel *Candide*, in which he narrated the sufferings of this world and ridiculed Dr. Pangloss's philosophy of optimism about heaven's designs. After many misfortunes, Candide and his teacher, Dr. Pangloss, finally settle in a corner of Turkey and make their living by cultivating their garden. Candide uttered the following comment about Dr. Pangloss's never-renounced conviction that everything always happened for the best: "All that is very well, but let us cultivate our garden."[196]

Having suggested his distrust of overarching theories about life with his reference to *Candide*, Zhou indicated that he intended to expand the metaphor of the garden. In his view, there were no restrictions on what one could grow, whether fruit or vegetables, medicinal plants or flowers. As long as one acted according to one's own lights and exerted oneself in cultivating one's acknowledged plot of land, that would completely fulfill one's responsibilities.

What I especially want to announce with these bland and ordinary words is only that growing roses and violets[197] also constitutes cultivating our own garden. They differ from fruit, vegetables, and medicinal plants only in being a different type of crop, but they have the same value.

His own garden, by inclination and aptitude, was literature, and he did not regret this, Zhou said.

To follow the aspirations of one's heart and grow roses and violets is the right way of respecting one's own individuality. Even if, as others say, a person must repay his or her debt to society, I believe that I have already done so. Because society does not need only fruit, vegetables, and medicinal plants, it also has a pressing need for roses and violets. A society that despises these things must be extremely obtuse. It is a society only in form, lacking any spiritual life. There is no need for us to pay such a society any attention.

If, in the name of some cause or other, people were forced to sacrifice their individuality in the service of an obtuse society—or, in prettified language, if people were forced to meet society's expectations—that would be quite as unreasonable as enforcing loyalty to a ruler in the name of the [Confucian] prescribed relationships or forcing people to go to war in the name of the nation.[198]

The question of whether literature should serve life or art, he now saw as pointless. Of course, literature belonged to life, because it was the living expression of the feelings of an individual.[199]

"In My Own Garden" was the starting point for Zhou's post–May Fourth career as an essayist, which he pursued while continuing to teach Chinese literature at Beida and then through the war years. The persona he projected in his essays is remarkable for its resilience and flexibility. Rather than denouncing his May Fourth past, when in 1926 he republished many of his articles from the previous decade, he claimed that although the thinking in them was immature, this did not matter, since he was publishing them not to edify his readers but to give them an idea of what sort of person he was. Maturity in any case was a kind of terminus, and what he loved about life was its movement. He still cared for the humanitarian ideals he had held, but he regarded them as his personal predilection rather than a workable political program.[200] Despite this stance, many of Zhou's articles in the 1920s were biting comments on current events and won him a reputation as an outspoken critic. Thus he attacked the Japanese-sponsored *Shuntian ribao* newspaper for denigrating the sacrifice of Communist Party founder Li Dazhao, who was executed after the warlord Zhang Zuolin (1873–1928) came to power in Peking. He also bitterly criticized Cai Yuanpei and Hu Shi, then in Shanghai, for appearing unperturbed by the bloodletting.

Zhou's importance lies not so much in his social criticism as in his grasp of the wider issues underlying Chinese experience this century and in the way he articulated his position through his aesthetics. Some of these issues returned to the surface in the mid-1980s, with the emergence of a group of young writers who became known as the "searching for roots" (*xungen*) literary movement. Their stories broke through the language and discourse that had straitjacketed literature since the 1942 Yan'an Forum by creating remote, myth-laden settings and characters for whom Maoist politics and state-run culture seemed irrelevant. In this they were sometimes inspired by the example of Gabriel García Márquez, winner of the 1982 Nobel prize for literature.[201]

In 1987, Li Tuo suggested that the *xungen* writers had brought back into fiction a certain structural use of imagery (*yixiang*) that had almost disappeared in the May Fourth realist literary project.[202] "Imagery," however, does not convey the relationship between the component parts *yi* (meaning, idea, intent) and *xiang* (image) of the binome, which is, as Li points out, a traditional aesthetic category. In its locus classicus, *yixiang* is what directs the writer in the creative process and is dependent on stillness of mind as well as learning.[203] Li Tuo's crucially important insight enabled him to link the *xungen* writers to Wang Zengqi (1920–97), whom he saw as their immediate predecessor. Although Wang began his writing career in the 1940s, literary critics regard him as within the tradition of the 1930s Jing pai literary group, which included Shen Congwen. In other words, with Wang as the link, we can now posit a very loose lineage of fiction writers from Shen Congwen to the *xungen pai*. What unites these writers, whose lives span three generations, is the refusal to allow writing to serve politics and a keen desire to discover, recover, and recreate the local.

However, it is very hard to formulate what is entailed in their disinclination to follow political guidelines and their regionalism without turning attention to Zhou Zuoren, the mentor of the Jing pai writers. This enables us to take the May Fourth movement and its antecedents into account in framing our questions. If we start from the premise that the May Fourth discourse on literature was part of the discourse on the nation, it becomes clear that the invocation of locality and positing of a politically independent authorial presence that runs through the otherwise extremely heterogeneous work of these writers signified, at least potentially, a different way of constructing the self and its relation to the nation.

But how could one assume that this different way of constructing the self and the nation is anything more than a series of coincidences in the work of individual, unrelated writers? In other words, what would enable us to raise it to the level of discourse? Here, Li Tuo's insight that the common denominator in the work of Wang Zengqi and the *xungen* writers is the re-emergence of imagery as a structurally important aesthetic category has far-reaching implications. In Zhou Zuoren the use of traditional aesthetic concepts underpinned his turn away from politics to culture and, paradoxical as it may seem, fruitfully identified ways of constructing identity in relation to the nation-state. These can clarify some of the major issues that continue to confront Chinese writers and our reading of them.

Making this claim means going beyond the nation as a given, a linguistically naturalized trope of belonging, to question the nation itself.[204] Here, aesthetics becomes the thin end of the wedge that prises "nation" away from its accustomed position as the emblem of modernity in order to question the totalizing claims of that modernity itself. The notion that a traditional aesthetics can make a fruitful contribution to modern literature is paradoxical only if we assume that the civilization that produced it has nothing more to say to or about modernity.

The reading of Zhou Zuoren that I present in this book is in some ways an abstraction. It does not lie neatly on the surface of Zhou's texts. In order to arrive at it, I have had to alternate theoretical, textual, and contextual approaches to Zhou's work, and this is reflected in the structure of this book. Chapter 2 contrasts the constructions of culture found in Zhou and Lu Xun, examines Zhou's use of work on mythology and anthropology by J. G. Frazer, Andrew Lang, and Jane Harrison, and discusses Zhou's debt to Japanese constructions of culture. Chapter 3, which is the centerpiece of the book, focuses on Zhou Zuoren's aesthetic choices and shows how they served to distance literature from the state. Chapter 4 analyzes how Zhou's decision to use the essay form and the controversy in which he became involved in the 1930s over the origins of the modern Chinese essay are related to the literary construction of the self and, by extension, the kinds of self tolerated in the modernizing nation-state. In Chapter 5 I argue that Zhou's nonlinear literary history in which Han Yu's construction of China and the Tongcheng school's

ideological prescriptions are explicitly linked to the nation-building project contains an alternative vision of nation, community, and individual.
Zhou refused to use writing to serve politics, but politics, in the sense of
current affairs and contemporary debates, often served his writing. In
this chapter I seek to correlate the developments in Zhou's thinking with
wider events. I conclude with a discussion of the aesthetics of the Roots
writers.

Like all readings, this reading of Zhou Zuoren's work is arrived at
through the filter of my own particular concerns and interests. I believe
that my reading of Zhou is valid, but not that it is exclusive. Indeed, with
such an intriguing, complex, and richly rewarding subject as Zhou Zuoren, how could this not be the case?

# TWO

～

# Constructions of Culture

On a late autumn evening in 1906, when dusk had already fallen over the city, Zhou Zuoren arrived at a modest boarding house in the hilly Yushima ni-chōme section of Hongo district in Tokyo. Lu Xun had moved to Tokyo six months earlier, after deciding to abandon his medical studies and pursue a career in literature. He was now returning, this time with his brother, from a two-month trip home to Shaoxing. Zhou Zuoren, for whom everything was new, felt a mounting sense of anticipation as they entered the building. Like others of his generation he was attracted by Japan's success in transforming itself, but the details of Japanese life most excited his curiosity.[1]

The Fushimi boarding house was a small, unpretentious, family-run place, and the first person who came to help the travelers with their luggage and brought them some tea was a girl of fifteen or so, named Inui Shigeko. Zhou eagerly took in the tatami-matted room, so simple and spacious compared with the oppressive, furniture-crammed Chinese interiors he knew. Then, as he watched Shigeko moving about the room, he noticed with astonishment that the feet peeping out from beneath her kimono were bare. Almost sixty years later, Zhou was to describe how the girl's bare feet provided him with "my first and most lasting image of Japan . . . [an] impression both ordinary and profound. In a few words, it was Japan's love of naturalness and worship of simplicity."[2]

This little vignette from Zhou's memoirs can be placed beside Lu Xun's account of the slide show at the Sendai Medical School. Like Lu Xun, Zhou sought to distill the complex, sometimes inchoate, emotional, intellectual, and experiential factors that shaped his creativity into a powerful, retrospective literary account of a "moment of truth." But where Lu Xun's account opens onto a vista of despair, Zhou's moves into a long string of associations. Originally among the women of the Jiangnan area (which includes Shaoxing), bare feet had been a common sight, as lines from the nineteenth-century poet Zhang Ru'nan attest. Zhou next mentions his abhorrence of footbinding and his admiration for the qualities of "cleanliness, politeness, and untrammeledness (satuo)" in Japanese culture. By "untrammeledness," Zhou meant merely the absence of "the hypocrisy of religion or orthodox Confucianism (daoxue)," which concealed prurience with phony respectability and which gave itself away by its dislike of nudity.

Havelock Ellis, pursuing his own campaign against Victorian prudery, had called the Japanese "the Greeks of another age and clime," for both civilizations prized physical cleanliness and accepted nakedness, and Zhou enlisted his aid.[3] Zhou cited Li Bai's (701–62) line "two feet as white as frost, not confined by duckhead stockings" as an example of charm, rare among the ancients. In footwear, Zhou observed, the ancient Greek sandal could be considered the most beautiful, the Japanese geta the most comfortable, and the southern Chinese straw sandal the most economical. Leather shoes did not meet the criteria for naturalness and absence of concealment or adornment. "I have not seen ancient Greece, but at least I could experience Japan"; even if he had gained nothing else, he could go out among crowds of "ordinary people" without being distressed by the sight of bound feet. But in China, even at the time he was writing in 1940, one could see saddening things.[4]

Whereas for Lu Xun China was symbolized in the slide-show incident by strong, healthy bodies tragically deficient in national consciousness, Zhou signifies the "jarring and unpleasant" aspect of China with bound feet and hypocritical minds, both deformations brought about by

Confucian orthodoxy and superstition. However, these things are aberrations against the happier Chinese cultural past testified to by the poets. Even in the present, the virtues of simplicity and frugality can be found among the Chinese, as illustrated by their use of straw sandals. The quotation from Havelock Ellis conjoining Greece and Japan constructed acceptance of the "natural," and hence "innocent," body as an ahistorical, universal civilizational ideal, against which not only bound feet but also leather-shod ones could be found wanting. The evocation of bare feet in Zhou's anecdote provides a focal point for several of the most important ideas in his thinking.

Zhou Zuoren followed his brother into literature, but the literary world he created was very different, shaped in many ways by his fondness for Japanese culture and the interests he acquired or nourished in Japan. Unlike many of his contemporaries, Zhou did not see Japan as either a conduit for Western technology or a cultural junior from whom China was being forced by unfortunate circumstances to learn the trick of copying.[5] Cheng Ching-mao notes the comment of the Japanese scholar Imamura Yoshio that Lu Xun was "cold and indifferent" to Japanese literature, with the exception of Natsume Sōseki (1867–1916), and that "he cared for it only as a means of introducing foreign literature to China. To put it more harshly, he only acknowledged its utility."[6]

Why did Japan play such a major role in Zhou's life, when it apparently had little effect on so many of his contemporaries? Why did he value the qualities he perceived in Japan when few others did? His marriage to a Japanese woman, Hata Nobuko, in 1909 has little explanatory value here, for other Chinese intellectuals with equally strong personal ties to Japan, such as Guo Moruo, were far less captivated by it. There is, of course, no one simple answer, but one important factor must be the fact that the values Zhou found so attractive in Japan had themselves been articulated in opposition to a bureaucratic regime identified with its own variant of Neo-Confucian orthodoxy. These values were expressed in languages derived from Buddhist and Neo-Confucian ideals, and thus they meshed with Zhou's cultural criticism while enriching its idiom. So although the discursive construction of values such as cleanliness and spontaneity sprang from a Japanese nativism that would eventually serve

Japanese militarism, Zhou read them in a larger Buddhist and Confucian context that bolstered his own constructions. To be sure, as his mention of Havelock Ellis and Greece suggests, such constructions had also been appropriated into other, quite different discourses, including those of late Victorian dissent.

Writing in 1935, after a two-month visit to his wife's family, Zhou gave two reasons why Japan had attracted him so much.

The first was a matter of personal temperament, the second we could call a delight in things of the past. I grew up in the southeastern riverlands, where life is plain and frugal. In winter we had no heating and chilly drafts blew right through the bedclothes, and very salty pickled vegetables or very salty pickled fish appeared at meals throughout the year. With this kind of training, naturally, life in Tokyo boarding houses could not fail to suit me.[7]

Significantly, in what seem to be matters of "personal temperament," Zhou does not refer to his own personal tastes but invokes his place of origin, the implication being that his temperament had been formed and molded by the chilly weather and salty food of home. This gives his attachment to Tokyo a double meaning: he is not just marking his sojourn abroad with the triumphant expatriate claim of adjustment. He is suggesting that the similarities of geography and custom that functioned as the foundation for his affection for Tokyo[8] encompassed other similarities of austerity and simplicity with which his personal temperament, formed by his homeplace, resonated. Indeed, Zhou was to describe Tokyo as his "second home" (di'erge guxiang); in a poem penned shortly before he left Japan in 1911, he wrote: "I have traveled far, but do not long to return / A long-term guest, I love this once-alien place."[9]

Zhou was always careful to insist on the partial nature of his knowledge, and in one essay he stressed that his viewpoint could never be the same as that of a Japanese writer, who would find more to criticize.[10] He made a clear distinction between Tokyo (even more cautiously, during the war, "a part of Tokyo"),[11] where he had lived six years, and Japan, pointing out that he had had very little opportunity to travel outside the capital. He was consequently familiar with late Meiji life as lived in Tokyo and the literature of the period. Moreover, the Japanese literature and art he most admired was that of Edo, the forerunner of modern Tokyo.[12] Thus, Zhou's admiration for things Japanese was tied to his admiration for the genius of a particular locality at a particular period.

This approach is intriguing for the way in which, by focusing on the locality, it seeks to sidestep the notion of an inherited *national* character created by environment that had become part of the nineteenth-century discourse of nationalism. In representing his relationship to his native place and Tokyo in these terms, Zhou aligned himself with a particular range of Chinese and Japanese thinking on place. One notion he deployed was the Chinese articulation of the idea of *genius loci*: the view that art reveals a relationship between temperament, the geographical features and customs of a locality, and cultural and moral attributes.[13] In the preface to his second book, written in 1925, Zhou says that he has made two discoveries about himself. One is that although he hates moralists, he is himself a moralist intent on establishing a new morality. The second is that he cannot rid himself of his East Zhejiang (Zhedong: east of the Zhe river) temperament. "Although our family has lived there only fourteen generations, the four hundred years of influence from the *fengtu* (social customs and natural conditions) there has been very strong."[14] This is the reason, he adds self-mockingly, that he cannot avoid sounding like a typical Shaoxing legal assistant and reprimanding others. The early date of this statement (1925) shows that his construction of his relationship with Tokyo in these terms must be seen as more than a strategy to avoid having to confront the issue of nation (and national loyalty) as tensions rose in the mid-1930s.

*Genius loci* should not be understood in Chinese cultural history as a primarily literary phenomenon. As suggested by the term *fengtu*, it is also the expression of a pervasive correlative cosmology in which the human being replicates the natural world[15]—thus the well-known comment "the men are outstanding and the land numinous" (*ren jie di ling*) from the early Tang writer Wang Bo (649–76).[16] This cosmology extended not only into elite literary and artistic practice but also into the fabric of everyday life, influencing, among other activities, food preparation, medicine, and geomancy. Consequently, when Zhou Zuoren invoked it, he was tapping into a symbolic and affective world of enormous dimensions, not easily displaced even by the decline of the cosmology itself.

Zhou could not, of course, be innocent of the Herderian notion of belonging to a group formed by natural forces that so deeply informed the discourse of the nation. Moreover, one of the first books he read in Japan was the English translation of Hippolyte Taine's (1828–93) *History of English Literature*.[17] For Taine, as for the majority of his contemporaries, "a nation is like a man . . . for it has its own character, both mental and moral, which manifests itself from the beginning and develops from epoch to epoch," without ever changing its "fundamental qualities."[18] Nations were a product of race, surroundings, and epoch. Race (coterminous with linguistic families) was the primordial given, but differences in climate, food, and so on produced different sets of habits, aptitudes, and instincts, and it was their interaction with dominant ideas or events that were reflected in religions, philosophy, and art. Reflecting the tremendous confidence in empiricism of his time, Taine resolved to "write the history of a literature and seek in it the psychology of a people."[19] Zhou commented in his memoirs that "amusing as it may seem . . . this was the first book I ever saw on what is called literary history. I was very struck by the fact it discussed the social background [to literature], and it taught me a lot."[20]

One can, of course, find many similarities between Taine's synthesis of race, surroundings, and epoch and Zhou's invocation of temperament and climate, but the differences are more significant. One is that in his attribution of similarity to Tokyo and Shaoxing, geography (climate) and the material culture (food) it gives rise to are privileged over race. Also, although Zhou sometimes referred to Chinese and Japanese as members of the "yellow race," he did not (and obviously could not) see language as genetically related to race, as Taine did in his discussion of the Aryans. Writing in 1925, he scoffed at the idea that China and Japan represented "the same language and the same race" (*tong wen tong zu*). It was just that "cultural exchange" had made each other's thinking a little easier to understand and the written language (*wenzi*) easier to learn, despite the fact that the Chinese characters used in Japanese often hindered rather than helped Chinese understanding.[21] What is most significant in Zhou's formulation is that culture, by which he means the material culture of everyday life, is being privileged over nation, which is not even mentioned. For Taine, the nation was a fundamental unit of organization.

Under the rubric of "personal temperament," Zhou has slyly led us to one of the most important areas of his thinking. We will return to the question of why Japan entered into Zhou's construction of locality after discussing the other half of Zhou's explanation of why he was attracted to Tokyo.

## Archaism and Revolution: The Legacy of Zhang Binglin

The second reason Zhou gives for his initial interest in Japan is directly related to the political debates of the time. In the end, it also leads back to the idea of locality:

> At that time, I was a believer in national revolution (*minzu geming*), and every nationalism inevitably contains some archaism (*fugu* [lit. "return to / of antiquity"]) in its makeup. We opposed the Qing, and we felt nearly everything before the Qing dynasty [1644–1911] or the Yuan dynasty [1279–1368] was good, and that still more would this be the case for even earlier things.[22]

Xia Huiqing (1863–1924) and Qian Nianqu (1855–1927) had noticed admiringly that Tokyo shop signs had a Tang flavor. Huang Zunxian (1848–1905) wrote that whereas some Japanese writing could be found that resembled that of the Jin era (265–420), for "freshness and directness," nothing similar had been produced in China since the Song (960–1279) and the Yuan. The Meiji sinologue Oka Senjin (1833–1914) noted a similar comment from a Chinese visitor. Japanese calligraphy to this day, Zhou continued, had not only preserved the traditions of Tang calligraphy but even the techniques, whereas in China these were no longer used.

On the "archaicizing" level, then, Japan appealed to Zhou and his contemporaries as a repository of qualities China had once had, because its material culture expressed a legacy of Chinese craftsmanship and aesthetics. Zhou's comment on nationalism and archaism functions rhetorically to close the issue of nationalism by relegating it to his student days and so leaves the ground clear for what he regards as far more important—the cultural and artistic practices shared by China and Japan. The figure behind Zhou's reference to the concept of national revolution was Zhang Binglin (1868–1936), the fellow provincial with

whom the Zhou brothers studied classical Chinese in Tokyo in 1908 and
1909.[23] A formidable scholar trained in evidential scholarship (*kao-zhengxue*) at the Gujing Academy in Hangzhou, Zhang was able to claim
an intellectual pedigree leading back to the late Ming figure Gu Yanwu
(1613–82).[24] He left the Gujing Academy in 1896, just after China's defeat
in the Sino-Japanese war of 1894–95, and joined Liang Qichao's *Shiwubao*
journal in Shanghai, although he was later to quarrel with the reformers.
When Zhang arrived in Tokyo in June 1906, he was immediately asked
to become editor of *Min bao* (People's journal), the propaganda arm of
the *Tongmenghui*, (Revolutionary Alliance) headed by Sun Yatsen. The
newspaper quickly gained enormously in influence, challenging the constitutional reformism of Liang Qichao and his *Xinmin congbao* (New citizen journal).[25]

As part of his revolutionary activities, Zhang lectured Chinese students on "national learning" (*guoxue*), which he held to be the site of the
"national essence" (*guocui*).[26] As is well known, both terms entered the
Chinese lexicon from Meiji Japan. Since the eighteenth century in Japan,
*kokugaku* (the Japanese reading of *guoxue*) had designated the nativist
learning that developed in opposition to Chinese learning, and *kokusui*
(*guocui*) stood for the national spirit held by certain Tokugawa Neo-
Confucians to have been eclipsed by Buddhism.[27] The term was revived
in the 1880s by publicists such as Shiga Shigetaka, Miyake Setsurei, and
Kuga Katsunan intent on promoting a "sense of nation" based on the
morality and mores of a shared Japanese realm of human feeling.[28]
Zhang invoked these categories in a parallel fashion to designate a recovery (*guangfu*) of the cultural vitality that, he held, the alien rule of the
Manchus had destroyed in China. Zhang brought to *guoxue* the categories of learning in which he had been trained, in particular history and
evidential scholarship.

In Zhang's account, having inherited Ming loyalist traditions through
family and teachers, he had developed a racial awareness of Han identity,
but it was only through his extensive reading after the defeat of 1895 that
he became able to theorize it.[29] In other words, the defeat brought home
to him the fact he lived in the modern world of nation-states of which
race was a primordial characteristic. His progression from reformer to

revolutionary was completed after the catastrophe of the Boxer Rebellion, when he declared that the only solution for China was to overthrow the Manchu dynasty and restore China to Han Chinese rule.[30] He became concerned with defining China as a nation of a "historical race" (*lishi minzu*) and believed scholarship would make this possible.[31] Unlike the reformer Kang Youwei, who construed the Manchus as Chinese by acculturation (*jiaohua*), Zhang came to invoke Ming loyalist racist constructions of Manchus as irremediably different.[32] The categories of history and race were mutually reinforcing: knowledge of history would stimulate love for the race (*minzu*) and would serve to make the revolution against the Manchus more profound. But this gave Zhang's anti-Manchuism an instrumentalist, less-than-primordial twist: it existed to reinforce Han national identity, obviously necessary for survival in the new world order, which Zhang pragmatically evaluated as having come to stay. In 1908 he described the imperial powers as far more harmful to the Chinese than the Manchus, adding, "So long as there are nation-states, we must uphold nationalism. . . . We are concerned not just for our own Han race but for other victimized nations."[33]

Undeniably, Zhang was caught up in the discourse of national identity that accompanied the Western presence and in the sense of crisis engendered by the 1895 defeat. Yet he was also able to distance himself from the Enlightenment mode of history in important ways. The most likely source of this resistance is his adoption, while in prison in 1903, of a Buddhist worldview based on the doctrines of the Yogacara (Weishi) school, particularly the Faxiang sect, that enabled him to reject Western theories of materialism and social evolutionism.[34] He was thus definitively able to reject the view of Western civilization as superior, but this did not stop him from reading widely in Western philosophy. Buddhist nominalism also led Zhang to reject the idea of any human group or entity, such as the state, as having a reality of its own and to recognize only individual human beings as real.[35] On the other hand, Buddhist philosophical beliefs about the equality of beings and the goal of relieving suffering—including the suffering of unjustly oppressed groups—enabled Zhang to justify his political activism.

Although Zhang's later political choices were to disappoint the Zhou brothers and most of their generation, there are two ways in which he was important for Zhou Zuoren. First, the center of gravity of his historiography lay in the locality, and this gave it an anthropological cast. Second, his instruction in classical Chinese made it possible for Zhou (and Lu Xun) to make new, radical choices in language and break away from the then-dominant Tongcheng literary style.

Zhang defined history as, "broadly speaking, divisible into the three categories: the spoken and written language, laws and institutions, and the records of great men."[36] This expansion of the scope of history to include all written records had been established in the eighteenth century by evidential studies, as had the use of its methods to examine philosophic issues. Zhang saw himself as inheriting living historiographical traditions; he scornfully rejected the religious view of Confucius embraced by Kang Youwei and the New Text school as attempts to accommodate European preconceptions.[37] For him, the greatness of Confucius lay in the fact that by reordering the classics, he had given the Chinese people their history.[38] History, moreover, flowed into the present. Pursuing the idea that knowledge of the historical record would increase love for the people (*minzu*), Zhang called for the study of "personages, institutions, geography, customs, and so on" (*renwu zhidu dili fengsu zhi lei*). These things were to be found in China, "the place where we eat, sleep, sit, and act," and were as necessary as "food, drink, and clothing."[39]

The people have become an important component of the nation, in Zhang's formulation, but in a direction opposite of Yan Fu's. The reformist discourse saw the people as an undiscovered, and desired, constituent of a modern nation, who were to be imbued with the qualities of modernity by the outside agency of the state. But for Zhang, the people embodied a national past, which, provided the obstacle of alien Manchu rule was removed, could come into full cultural flower again. Love of the people and esteem of the nation and its history went together. Judging from the stress on institutional continuity in Zhang's thinking, it is obvious that the meeting place for the people and the elite, that is, the "site" of the uncovering of history, must primarily be the locality. It is within the locality that the variations of custom, language, and history—the stuff of scholarship and patriotism—are to be found.

Locality can be understood as a subjective and social construct that is based on a series of objective, often institutional or historical referents. Shaoxing, for example, is the name of a prefecture comprising eight counties, but Zhou once remarked that when he said he collected books from Shaoxing he really meant just those written by people from the two counties of Shanyin and Kuaiji.[40] James Cole notes that although there were differences between the periphery and core areas of Shaoxing, in the context of Qing bureaucratic politics it tended to function as a unit. Shaoxing had an unusual relationship with the political center (through its dominance of bureaucratic networks), but in terms of trade it was part of the rich fertile Jiangnan region, celebrated in literary and cultural imagination for centuries. In terms of academic affiliation, Shaoxing was identified with Zhedong (East Zhejiang) as against Zhexi (west of the river and including some parts of Jiangsu.)[41] When Zhou spoke of his Zhedong temperament, he was probably thinking of himself as the inheritor of a certain intellectual style. Cole notes that "Shaoxing natives contrasted what they considered the overrefined frippery of [Zhexi's] cultural centers, Hangzhou and Suzhou, with the supposedly 'pure,' simple and unadorned customs of their own [Zhedong]."[42] In his article "Place and Literature" (discussed in Chapter 3), Zhou took as his reference the whole of Zhejiang province. But another delineation used by Zhou was the historic one of the Wu Yue *yilao*—the Ming officials from Jiangsu and Zhejiang who refused to serve the Qing. He also used the term *Yuezhong*, used for Shaoxing in the late Ming, in the appropriate historical context.[43]

In Zhang Binglin's view of history, we see foreshadowed many of the categories into which Zhou organized his own thinking and interests.[44] Ultimately we can even credit Zhang's conception of history with having helped to structure the May Fourth idea of "going to the people" among the Peking University academics, including Zhou, who became one of the leaders of the folklore movement.[45] By grounding the people in the locality, scholarship ensures their continuity with history, a continuity that is in some ways mediated by the locality. The locality thus also mediates the relationship between the scholar and the people because it contains them both, since they share a common origin there. The relationship of the intellectual to the locality in Zhang Binglin's theory of revolution played an important part in shaping Zhou's subsequent constructions of locality. Although Zhou was to renounce the linguistic practices he had derived from Zhang's archaism, he never came to see the past as decisively severed from the present and consequently was not impelled to see himself as cut off from the locality. In this, he contrasts with the intellectual who accepts modernity as rupture and who sees the people as the material out of which a modern nation will be wrought. Such thinkers are unable to see continuity between past and present or between themselves and their native place.

This was one of the major differences between Zhou Zuoren and Lu Xun. Lu Xun even disliked identifying himself as coming from Shaoxing, preferring to say that he came from Zhejiang.[46] In those of Lu Xun's stories that are structured around the return of the protagonist to his old hometown, the main impact comes from the depiction of the despair of the protagonist, who can neither re-enter the past nor see any way out of the plight of those who remain there.[47]

Interestingly, the different attitudes of the Zhou brothers to past and present are illustrated to some extent by their perception of their relationship with Zhang Binglin. When in 1926 Zhang supported the use of force against the Chinese Communist Party, Lu Xun remained silent. Several years later, he told a friend he felt that the relationship between teacher and disciple demanded that, whatever his misgivings, he say nothing.[48] Zhou, on the other hand, publicly parted company with Zhang.[49] However, he always acknowledged his debt of gratitude for the knowledge of Chinese literature he had gained from Zhang (through his lectures on the *Shuowen jiezi*) and asserted that Zhang's greatest contribution had been to phonology and philology.[50]

Zhang's most important contribution to the intellectual development of the Zhou brothers was to teach them the terse Wei-Jin style of *guwen*. This was of revolutionary significance, for it gave them a new language, in place of the late Qing *guwen* of the translator Lin Shu (1852–1924) and Yan Fu, which was heavily influenced by the conservative Tongcheng literary school. Lu Xun's rejection of the Tongcheng style was "a major step of intellectual orientation," for it aligned him with the potential radicalism of Zhang Binglin and thus in opposition to the Tongcheng-using constitutional reformers.[51] Qian Xuantong praised Zhou Zuoren for "opening a new era" with his translations from foreign literature in 1909, for unlike Lin Shu and Yan Fu, he was faithful to the original texts and did not seek to edit them to suit political aims.[52]

The suggestion here is that the Tongcheng style was more than a style, it was a discourse (in the Foucauldian sense), a suggestion that certainly seems justified by the school's involvement in political institutions in the nineteenth century. This was indeed the point Zhou Zuoren insisted on (although not, of course, in the same terms) in his 1932 lecture series on the origins of the new literature.[53] Zhou's lectures were structured around the dichotomy between the use of "literature to convey the Way" (*wen yi zai dao*) and its use to "express one's intent" (*shi yan zhi*), terms that we will consider in detail in Chapter 3. The didacticism of the first Zhou held to be inherently wrong, since it ignored the expressivist function of art, which flourished in China only when the government was weak.[54] Strong government inevitably led to didacticism. Zhou felt that Han Yu (768–824) had infused a particularly strong didactic strain into the culture with his notion of "succession of the Way" (*daotong*), which came into full flower in the Song as the one system of texts through which orthodox Confucian teachings were transmitted.[55] Han Yu's shadow had stretched over the writing of the Ming and Qing, with brief expressivist interludes.

The rise of the Tongcheng school in the Qing brought another qualitative change, according to Zhou. The canon developed by this school drew on the *Zuo zhuan* and Sima Qian, gave pride of place to Han Yu, and added the works of Gui Youguang (1507–71) and Fang Bao (1668–1749). Thus they were in the *guwen* tradition of the Eight Masters of the Tang and Song, but with a major difference, Zhou said:

The Eight Masters advocated "literature to convey the Way," but they still concentrated on the [stylistic] aspects of *guwen*. It was just that they wanted to put the Way into their writing as content; so they were still just literary men. But the members of the Tongcheng school were not just literary men; they wanted to be "moralists" at the same time. They thought Han Yu's essays were all right, but his achievements in moral philosophy were not far-reaching; whereas Cheng-Zhu Neo-Confucianism was all right, but the literary style of its founders rather poor. Since they wanted to take the achievements of each side and combine them into one, they made it their ambition to "follow Cheng-Zhu in learning and action and write in the manner of Han Yu and Ouyang Xiu." They believed that "literature is the Way," and that the two should never be separated. . . . They did not see themselves as writers but as a combination of moral philosophers, evidential scholars, and literary stylists.[56]

As the medium became the message, didacticism was transformed into a much subtler instrument. Zhou's view is corroborated by others. As one scholar put it, Tongcheng thinkers (or more specifically, Fang Bao) "did not mean that the substance of prose must be moral and didactic in nature. Rather the ideas and feelings a writer expresses in his work, whatever its subject matter, must not go contrary to the Confucian (and Neo-Confucian) moral principles."[57] Yao Nai's (1732–1815) innovation was to extend this from prose writing to "the entire realm of literary art, including poetry."[58]

In literary terms, Zhou did not find much that was innovative in Tongcheng school stylistics, although he felt they were better than those of the Ming archaists. In fact, he asserted, their *guwen* was so close to *ba-guwen* that he could describe them as "writing informal essays (*sanwen*) in *bagu*."[59] Their importance in Zhou's history stems from the fact that the Hunanese statesman Zeng Guofan (1811–72) revived the Tongcheng system, although he felt that it was lacking in substance and needed the injection of content in the form of statecraft (*jingshi*). In fact, in advocating that a concern for statecraft replace the Tongcheng emphasis on moral principles, Zeng essentially expanded the concept of prose literature to include politics and economics.[60]

After that, [statesman and educationist] Wu Rulun (1840–1903), Yan Fu, and Lin Shu all emerged, introducing foreign literature and at the same time introducing scientific thought, so that the Tongcheng school, which had been greatly enlarged in scope by Zeng Guofan, gradually drew closer to the newly established literature. Afterward, those taking part in the new literary movement like Hu Shi, Chen Duxiu, and Liang Qichao were all greatly influenced by them. That is why we can say that the beginning of the present literary movement was touched off by people in the Tongcheng school.[61]

Although Zhou went on to differentiate Hu Shi and Chen Duxiu from Yan Fu and Liang Qichao, "who became reactionary forces" and opposed the New Culture movement, the identification of Hu and Chen with the Tongcheng school is clearly a way of pointing to the didacticism inherent in the May Fourth discourse.

Zhou's reason for attributing this affiliation to Hu and Chen is that they shared with Yan Fu and the others the aims of introducing Western literature and science. Since many of the essays in which Zhou explored his interests in anthropology, mythology, and biology also effectively did the same thing, we have to read his comments in light of his dismissal of their rhetoric of language reform. Their project was inherently didactic, and in its attitude toward readers it was just a variation on Tongcheng moralism.

From this viewpoint, Zhou had kept alive the revolutionary significance of Zhang's gift of Wei-Jin *guwen*, even though he stopped using it when he found its archaism incompatible with contemporary needs.[62] Lu Xun had, it is true, acquired from Zhang the means to refine his use of language but had not accepted the potential for individual expressive freedom to be found within it. On the contrary, Lu Xun's study of the Wei-Jin literati led him to the conclusion that "the discovery of the values of art proved to be, instead of a road to spiritual emancipation and artistic transcendence, a double burden on the individual psyche" and thus to the denial of "the autonomous status of literature together with its claim to immortality and transcendence."[63] Perhaps having already lost faith in the viability of Chinese traditions when he came to study with Zhang Binglin, Lu Xun could conceive of literature only as a massive effort at self-overcoming in the Nietzschean sense. What Lu Xun valued in Zhang Binglin was his revolutionary temper, which he may have considered akin to the spirit of the Mara poets. In an article written after Zhang Binglin's death and shortly before his own, Lu Xun called Zhang's polemic essays his greatest and most lasting contribution to the world and confessed to having completely forgotten the philology Zhang taught. With a characteristically belligerent flourish, he concluded that the essays should be collated and republished so as to live on in the hearts of "fighters" in the present and future generations.[64]

Lu Xun's silence in regard to Zhang's later conservatism can be explained as his way of protecting his emotional attachment to Zhang's fiery rhetoric and to the symbolic traditional teacher-disciple relationship. The content imparted in the course of that relationship had become meaningless to him.

## Two Ways of Seeing Time and Culture: Lu Xun and Zhou Zuoren

The diverging appreciations of locality and history that I have imputed to the Zhou brothers naturally led to different ways of constructing culture, both textual and material. In Lu Xun's volume of reminiscences, *Zhao hua xi shi* (Dawn blossoms picked at dusk), the reader is drawn into the ever-expanding imaginative world of the child as he grows up. As a very small boy, he listens to his grandmother's stories. The warmth and pleasure with which Lu Xun describes his introduction to the strange and fantastic denizens of the *Shanhaijing* (Classic of the hills and seas) and the ghostly messenger Wuchang from the folk *Jade Calendar* are well known. But these were pleasures won with difficulty in a harsh, barren world in which children were punished for reading picture books. The crushing weight of traditional education is conveyed with great pathos in Lu Xun's description of how he was forced to memorize a passage from a history primer before being allowed to go to a fair. When he is finally allowed to go, "the scenery along the river, the snacks in the hamper, the . . . bustle of the fair . . . none of these seemed to me very interesting." He concludes, "Now everything else is forgotten, vanished without a trace: only my recitation from the history primer remains as clear as if it had happened yesterday."[65]

As an adolescent attending the Jiangnan Naval Academy, he feels that something is not quite right, that he is living under a pestilential cloud. But then he comes across Yan Fu's translation of *Evolution and Ethics* and comes to the astonishing realization: "Oh! So this world contains a man called Huxley who sits in his study and thinks and comes up with such fresh ideas!" Eventually he is forced to the conclusion that knowledge is unobtainable in China. "There is only one way out: go abroad."[66]

The textual world presented in Zhou's recollections of his early youth is much richer. Having received the same basic education as Lu Xun, including encouragement from their grandfather to read novels, he found that by about the age of fifteen he "could appreciate the flavor of *wenyan* (literary Chinese)."[67] He read the two major Qing dynasty *wenyan* story collections, the *Liaozhai zhiyi* (Strange tales from the Leisure Studio) by Pu Songling (1640–1715) and Ji Yun's (1724–1805) *Yuewei caotang biji* (Jottings from the Thatched Abode of Discriminating Observations).[68] Later Zhou decided that he disliked the former for its diction and the latter for its didactic style—they were, he said, like the fishtrap after you've caught the fish. But from there he moved on to Tang collectanea, which were his entry into *zaxue* (miscellaneous learning).

In his memoirs, Zhou lists one of the most famous of the Tang collectanea, the *Youyang zazu*, along with an English-language children's edition of *The Arabian Nights*, as one of the "new books" that opened his mind. Because it was truly diverse and broad, he said, "it touched on every one of the subjects I felt to be interesting, including myths and legends, popular sayings and nursery rhymes, tales of the marvelous and accounts of flora and fauna. There was nothing it did not contain, and it was an introduction to every kind of interesting knowledge."[69] Zhou quoted from a verse he had written praising it as "better than the novel *Shuihu* at transporting the reader to marvelous places." Indeed, he asserted, three-fourths of his *zaxue* derived from it.[70] Inspired by his reading of the British mythologist Andrew Lang (1844–1912), when he returned to Shaoxing from Japan, he wrote an article introducing two stories from the *Youyang zazu* in order to refute the prevalent belief that China had no children's stories.[71]

There is a marked contrast between Zhou's enthusiastic representation of the world he found in his reading and the tragic sense of deprivation in Lu Xun's recollections, even if we make allowances for the generic differences between Zhou's memoirs and Lu Xun's powerful, compressed recollections. Lu Xun's engagement with the literary tradition is exemplified by his enormous scholarly achievements, directed toward the field of fiction,[72] but his attempt to rework myths and legends to convey a radically modern sensibility has been seen as flawed.[73]

We have seen how Zhou's early encounter with Fang Dongshu's *Hanxue shangdui* sparked his dislike for the Tongcheng school and no doubt provided him with the impetus to find alternatives to the Neo-Confucianism inspired by Zhu Xi. He always felt, he added, that Song learning in the Qing dynasty was closely geared to the examination system and that scholars studied it as a route to success. His own schooling had been in preparation for the examinations, and in the course of achieving a thorough grounding in Chinese, he had discovered "two stinks"—orthodox Confucianism and the Eight Masters of prose, whose writings he felt produced an effect similar to that of *baguwen*.[74]

This account shows that the groundwork for Zhou's literary attitudes and for his development of his own vision of Confucianism was laid in his youth. Undoubtedly his dislike of the Tongcheng school was stimulated by reading Fang's book. No doubt Zhou's search for alternatives to orthodox Neo-Confucianism led him to ask for instruction in Buddhism from Yang Wenhui.[75]

In his own writing, Zhou was able to move without constraint between the Qing dynasty and his own time. One function of his continual exploration, recovery, and re-presentation of Qing dynasty literati was to attenuate the break with literati culture experienced with the abolition of the examination system. Moreover, many of the writers Zhou quoted, if not actually from Shaoxing, were from Zhejiang or the Lower Yangtze region. In this context, it is interesting to note that one of Zhou's major contributions to the study of folklore was to report on the legends surrounding the figure of Xu Wei (Xu Wenchang; 1521–93), a Shaoxing literatus who had become a ribald, anti-establishment folk hero. The legends, which turned out to have counterparts all over China, provided the folklore movement with plenty of material with which to analyze popular attitudes to authority. They could also be read as providing an alternative image of the literatus. It has been argued that this image was closer to "the folk" than the hidebound traditional scholar of May Fourth rhetoric, and certainly the scatological nature of the stories bears this out.[76]

By themselves, the essays Zhou devotes to late Ming and Qing literati figures sometimes seem abstruse. However, his essays should always be read in the context of the collection in which they appear, for the collection is the artistic and thematic unit.[77] The concerns of figures from earlier times are thus woven into a much wider, more diverse context. The *Talks in Wind and Rain* (*Feng yu tan*) collection is a case in point. The book can be seen as an exploration of the relationship of language, thought, and generic modes of expression. Less abstractly, it is about the writing of essays, but this is never made explicit. Rather, each essay takes the discussion a little further or gives an opportunity for digression. Whereas some essays provide an appreciation of one individual or commentary on him (e.g., "About Fu Qingzhu," "About Wang Nüe'an"), others discuss particular texts or genres (e.g., "Japanese Comic Stories [*Rakugo*]," "*Hao-an xianhua*" [Leisurely jottings of Hao-an; i.e., Zhang Erqi (1612–78)], "Preface to an Outline of Shaoxing Nursery Rhymes," "Four Fairy Tales by Andersen"). The last two (which occur together in the book) are an example of a train of thought being pursued across two essays. The collection also includes essays such as "Springtime in Beiping," a reminiscence in a much more lyrical mode, and "Copied from an Old Diary." Not only is the collection about writing, we can see Zhou hard at work in it too, and we are privy to his thinking in "The Future of Literature" and the seminal "True Colors" ("*Bense*"), which is discussed in Chapter 3. Holding together the collection and drawing it into the present are the preface and postface. In the first, Zhou cites various allusions to "wind and rain" and then relates the phrase indirectly to the political situation; in the second he comments that having finished proofreading the collection, written in the five months between November 1935 and April 1936, he was left feeling that his writing was "still so poor."

After I shut up the literature shop [a reference to his decision to devote himself to the study of history and philosophy in 1928], it seems that I have come to understand a little more about what is good and bad in writing and thinking. This naturally has had an effect on my ability to evaluate others. But when I look at myself, I am filled with shame, and can never find . . . satisfaction. However, I do the best I can, and what is beyond my ability can't be helped. I am now a teacher, and writing is something I do for pleasure outside my work, it is not a heaven-ordained task or a means of livelihood. But because I am a teacher, I feel the same sense of responsibility as when I am in the classroom.[78]

Part of the interest of the collection for the reader comes from the insights it gives into the guiding intelligence behind it. Moreover, we become involved, as his readers, in the ongoing drama of his own attempts to wrestle with writing and language. The contemporary world, and Zhou's place in it, also seeps into the book. Appended to the collection are two short essays recording the misappropriation and misuse of his name.[79] These throw another kind of light on the issues of careful and correct naming—a major concern of Qing scholarship—which runs like a thread through some of the most esoteric texts in the collection. Just before the appendix is an even more important essay, one of a series of four re-evaluations of Japan Zhou wrote just after his visit there.[80] It is important to note that Zhou never cites his Ming or Qing sources as authorities to buttress a single viewpoint. Zhang Erqi, for instance, was highly critical of the individualism of the late Ming.[81] Zhou's essay collections, then, were never mere strings of marginalia; rather, they were the products of his active engagement with texts and events.

It was often on the basis of literati memoirs of local material culture that Zhou constructed his own lyrical evocations of it. Lu Xun did sometimes do so too, but with a demurral; for instance, when he quoted the Shaoxing scholar Zhang Dai (1599–1684), he ended with the comment that "Ming writers tend to exaggerate."[82] His sense of loss in relation to his locality is apparent in the preface to Zhao hua xi shi:

There was a time when the vegetables and fruits I ate as a child in my old home kept coming into my mind: caltrops, horsebeans, water bamboo shoots, muskmelons. So succulent, so delicious, were they all, like a magic potion they bewitched me into longing for my old home. Later, after a long absence, I tasted them again and found them nothing special. It was only in memory that they kept their old flavor. Perhaps they will continue to cheat me for the rest of my life, making my thoughts turn continually to the past.[83]

In his memoirs, Zhou quoted this passage of his brother's and added: "[Lu Xun] said this when he was forty-six, and although over thirty more years have since passed, I think I can also borrow it. But perhaps I was not quite so cheated." As if following this train of thought, Zhou recalls some lines from a fu describing local fish and vegetable markets by the Shaoxing writer Li Ciming (Li Yueman; 1830–94) and compares the passage favorably with other examples. Then he adds, "But what makes me pursue memories of the past is even more inconsequential and trifling. It is the night candy and toasted pastry children eat."[84]

Despite the seeming modesty of this statement, it is crucially important. Most of Zhou's readers would probably catch the reference to his essay "Mai tang" (Candy selling), which appeared in 1938.[85] Zhou is drawing attention to a fundamental difference between his brother's text and his own: in Lu Xun's evocation of fruits and vegetables there is little to suggest commensality, but Zhou's essay celebrated street foods, thus calling to mind the society in which they were produced. The reader of the memoirs is also aware, probably, that the essay was written during the Japanese occupation but before Zhou had begun to collaborate.

"Mai Tang" demonstrates with what moving effect Zhou could combine erudition and lyricism. It begins in typical fashion, quoting from two *biji* references to the vendors who beat their gongs as they peddled *ye tang* (night candy). Then he continues:[86]

There is not a word about it in the section on foods in the *Yueh-yen*,[87] there is even nothing about *li-kao-t'ang* (pear sweetmeat), which is rather disappointing. If there were no "night candies" in Shaoxing, how much duller life would be for the little ones, because this candy and *chih-kao* (toasted pastry) are two great favorites with the children; they all have to have them, whether street urchins or the children of the rich. The name "night candy" cannot be explained; it is just a round, hard candy, also commonly known as "longan candy," because it looks like the longan fruit. There are also some with pointed corners, which are called *tsung-tzu-t'ang* (candy like Dragon Boat festival dumplings), some red, some yellow, and each used to cost one cash. At the larger street corner candy store, you might have gotten ten candies for seven or eight cash, but this was the price thirty years ago, which I'm sure must have greatly changed.

Next follow descriptions of the preparation of eggplant and plum candies, and descriptions of the candy-vendor's basket, which had a glass lid on it. To the great excitement of the children, the candy vendors would bang on their gongs, of which we learn:

The gong was quite different from other gongs. It had a diameter of less than a foot, a narrow rim and no strings. When hitting it, one finger would press against the inner rim, completely different from the brass gongs that are held by a string and hit with a stick. The people used to call it a *t'ang-lo gong*, the *t'ang* pronounced as in the word for soup, in the fourth tone, indicating the sound it gave off.

A little later we come to the subject of the sellers of toasted pastry:

[They] came mainly in the afternoon. They had a fire going in a bamboo crate, with a cooking pot on the fire. Pastry made of brown sugar and rice flour was cut into bits and roasted; each piece cost one cash. They also had *ma-tzu* (pastry) and would call out loudly "Ma-tzu ho chih-kao." The word "ho" was only an expletive . . . but in the Zhejiang dialect it was more guttural than anywhere.

After more descriptions of pastries, Zhou comments, "Since I came to Peking I have not seen these pastries anymore, because in the South rice is the staple food and these pastries were made with rice flour; the situation is completely different [in the North]." He then makes the same point about the passage of time as Lu Xun, but to exactly the opposite effect: "The things we ate when we were small were not always so tasty but later they seem to become extremely delicious and unforgettable. This is exactly the reason why I keep remembering all these candies and sweetmeats."

Whereas for Lu Xun, his present experience and mood contradict his memory and accuse it of deception, Zhou celebrates the power of memory to bring things back into being even more sharply and vividly than they may originally have appeared. The essay concludes:

> In observing the peculiarities of a locality, its foods are very important. Not only its everyday staple foods, but also the tidbits and sweets are very interesting. It is a pity that few people have given these things their attention. The literati, native to the district, consider these things too trivial to talk about; outsiders give only slight attention to foods, but instead write about men and women. . . . Actually the affairs of men and women are more or less the same and not worth that much effort. On the other hand the various foodstuffs are full of "flavor" and could be talked about much more.

The locality, then, does not exist in the private affairs of men and women but in the shared culture—shared to the extent that the children of the rich and the poor alike clamor for the same sweets, that all understand the same local usages of language, that all may observe the hand-held gong and the glass-lidded box, and that literate men take the trouble to record them, thereby demonstrating their continuity through time. These may not be exactly the "people, institutions, geography, and customs" Zhang Binglin had in mind, but the locality as the site of history and the relationship of the intellectual to it are the same. By referring to "flavor" in the last sentence, Zhou is bringing us to the heart of his aesthetics, which was also centered on the locality.

The essay also makes a reference to Japan:

> Some years ago, I read the *Sentetsu sōdan* by the Japanese Hara Kōdō.[88] In the third volume some paragraphs deal with Chu Shun-shui,[89] and one part reads:
>
>> Shun-shui had become quite assimilated throughout these years. He could speak Japanese; however, when he fell seriously ill, he talked again in his native tongue

and none of the servants could understand him. (The original text is in Chinese writing.)

I felt a great pity when I read this. The language that Shun-shui spoke must have been the dialect of Yu-yao. Though I am from the neighboring district, I can understand the dialect and would have understood him. Yu-yao also has the "night candies" and *chih-kao* (toasted pastry). It is a pity that Shun-shui did not mention them, probably because no one would have understood him anyhow.

What role does Japan play in this celebration of locality, written several months into the Japanese occupation of Peking? On the surface it seems to confirm the ironic mode of reading Zhou's texts, in which the irony is a function of the reader's prior knowledge of Zhou's life. Zhou's decision to remain in Peking was greeted with dismay. Thus the presence of Japan in this text has the effect of upsetting any presumption on the part of a reader that loyalty to native place and loyalty to nation were identical by bringing to mind Zhou's disloyalty.

Like most of Zhou's texts, however, this one presupposes an educated reader. As it turns out, the ironies of the passage are on Zhou's side, for Zhu Shunshui was a Ming loyalist who ended up in Japan in 1659 after many hardships, trying to win support for the anti-Manchu cause. Befriended by a samurai, Zhu eventually spent the rest of his life there, in the court of the famous Mito domain scholar and daimyō Tokugawa Mitsukuni, where he was lionized as a teacher and authority on state worship of Confucius. One of Zhu's anti-Manchu writings was particularly popular among revolutionary Chinese students in Japan at the turn of the twentieth century.[90] Zhu's status as an unimpeachable Chinese patriot who was treated with utmost respect and friendship in Japan (and even arranged to be buried there) complicates contemporary readings through the prism of nationalist sentiment. It reproaches Japanese claims to be teachers of China and suggests to both that the link between them has been scholarship rather than enmity.

The insertion of Japan into "Mai tang" reflects Zhou's relationship with a pan-Asian sentiment that developed at the turn of the century, exemplified by the writings of the Japanese art historian Okakura Tenshin (1862–1914). "Asia is one," Okakura proclaimed, united by "two mighty civilizations, the Chinese with its communism of Confucius, the Indian with its individualism of the Vedas."[91] Okakura's nicely alliterative construction of Asia certainly replicated the Hegelian discourse on India and China. The introduction to the book, written by Sister Nivedita (Margaret Noble; 1867–1911), a British woman from Ulster resident at the Vivekananda Ramakrishna mission in Calcutta, shows how attractive a reworking it could be for nationalist elites and their sympathizers.[92]

In Okakura's text, Japan is given a privileged position, as the Asian country that has received and consecrated the genius of China and India and has made the most headway in assimilating modernity. It is up to Japan to lead Asia to "return to itself" and to counterpoise Asian spirituality to the problems of Western society. This line of reasoning appears so thoroughly compromised by its similarity to the rhetoric of the Greater East Asian Co-Prosperity Sphere, not to mention its underlying orientalism, that it is easy to dismiss it outright. Indeed, from its very inception, pan-Asianism has been one of those ideas that can attract heterogeneous and contradictory sets of meanings. It can easily be assimilated into a nationalist, or indeed imperialistic, discourse. Zhang Binglin, whose pan-Asianism was part of his anti-imperialism, was quick to denounce the opportunism of Japanese public figures who sought to cultivate Asian revolutionaries and European politicians at the same time.[93]

Yet although pan-Asianism did come to be harnessed to Japanese militarism by the late 1930s, Okakura's plea that Japan ought to "return to Asia" rather than uncritically emulate the West developed within the context of popular Japanese skepticism about the goals and methods of the bureaucratic Meiji government.[94] This particular government followed the injunction of Fukuzawa Yukichi (1834–1901) that Japan should "part from Asia" and join the Western imperialist nations in intervening against "barbarous" Asian lands because it represented Enlightenment civilization. Ten years after his appeal, Fukuzawa hailed the victory over China in 1895 as proof that Japan had achieved this goal.[95] For Okakura, the severing of Japan's ties with the East Asian cultural sphere constituted "the loss of . . . a universe."[96] In seeking to revive this universe, he was placing himself against what his friend Tagore was later to call "the voluntary submission of the whole people to the trimming of their minds" in the name of the "machine of power called the Nation."

Where pan-Asianism becomes oppositional is where it brings to the surface a particular idea of locality: "Asia knows, it is true, nothing of the fierce joys of a time-devouring locomotion," writes Okakura, who produced the English version of the book while visiting India,

but she still has the far deeper travel-culture of the pilgrimage and the wandering monk. For the Indian ascetic, begging his bread of village housewives, or seated at evenfall beneath some tree, chatting and smoking with the peasant of the district, is the real traveller. *To him a countryside does not consist of its natural features alone. It is a nexus of habits and associations, of human elements and traditions, suffused with the tenderness and friendship of one who has shared, if only for a moment, the joys and sorrows of its personal drama.* The Japanese peasant-traveller, again, goes from no place of interest on his wandering, without leaving his *hokku*, or short sonnet, an art form within reach of the simplest.[97] (italics added)

It is in this aestheticized locality, with its aestheticized subject, that we find much common ground between Zhou and Japanese intellectuals; just why this was so is the subject of the rest of this chapter. What the freight of twentieth-century political history attached to the pan-Asian label obscures is the possibility that habits and intersubjective relationships (as a random example, acceptance of the presence of individuals not engaged in productive labor, such as begging ascetics) could continue to hold something of value. Unfortunately, the fact that such possibilities are regarded as so inimical to modernity results in their symbolic value being co-opted by the far right and aligned with more extreme versions of nationalism.

Politically, Zhou was no pan-Asianist. He saw the relationship between China and Japan as one of regional affinity, based on a shared Buddhist-Confucian heritage. His reference to Zhu Shunshui both particularizes it and gives it temporal depth.[98] But Zhou's construction of this heritage was oppositional: against orthodox Confucian morality, against Japanese expansionism, and sometimes against both at the same time. In an essay written in 1925, he demolished the idea that "loyalty to the ruler" was a quintessential Japanese quality, citing Naitō Konan to the effect that before the entry of the term *zhongxiao* from China for the virtue of "loyalty and filial piety," there did not appear to be any equivalent Japanese term. But this explanation, he warned, was not intended to bolster Chinese pride or comfort the upholders of National Essence.[99]

Zhou was outspoken in his condemnation of Japanese militarism and urged Chinese intellectuals to do everything possible to dissuade their fellow countrymen from trusting Japan. The Japanese slogan about shared glory and coexistence (*gong rong gong cun*) between the two countries could equally as well be applied to pork once it had been swallowed and absorbed into someone's body, he wrote in June 1927.[100] But he also felt it a matter of unassailable fact that "an unbreakable cultural relationship" existed between the two countries based on a millennium of exchange. Those from either country who wanted to understand their own national history, culture, literature, and aesthetics would be ill advised to ignore the other in their research.[101]

## Anthropology, Mythology, and the Affective Life of the People

Tokyo, which Zhou Zuoren claimed as his second home, was more to him than a repository of the legacy of Chinese civilization. He also experienced it in its own right as a specific locality with its own material culture and was aware of contemporary attempts to explore and preserve it. Zhou's Japanese experience was an important precursor to his leading role in the Chinese movement to collect folk literature.[102] Moreover, at the same time that Zhou was learning about Tokyo and Edo popular culture, he was devouring books in English on cultural anthropology, which provided him with a key for understanding social life. In addition, Zhou also began to learn Greek and to study Greek mythology while in Tokyo.[103]

Anthropology and Greek mythology became closely related intellectual resources for Zhou. The first provided a means of understanding a society's rituals and social conventions as expressions of culturally shaped fears of sex and death. The second stood as a shining example of the way art, having broken free of ritual and dogma, could help purge life of the fear of the unknown.

While in Shanghai on the way to Tokyo, Zhou bought a copy of Edward Tylor's (1832–1917) *Anthropology*, translated as *On Evolution* (*Jinhua lun*). The title is not as surprising as it may seem, if we consider that Darwin himself had made "cultural studies the legitimate heirs of evolutionary biology."[104] Although he did not understand the reason for the title, Zhou said, this was a good introductory text by "England's founder of anthropology," the man who had written *Primitive Cultures*.[105] But Zhou probably did not read Tylor's book right away. His introduction to cultural anthropology came by way of C. M. Gayley's (1858–1932) *Classic Myths in English Literature*, which was part of a consignment of books Lu Xun had ordered. It was one of the first books Zhou read in Japan. Gayley's many references to the interpretative theories of Andrew Lang prompted Zhou to buy Lang's *Custom and Myth* and *Myth, Ritual and Religion*.[106]

Lang's work was part of the Victorian anthropological project dominated by Tylor and Sir James Frazer (1854–1941). These men held diverse views, but they shared a commitment to building a scientific, evolutionary view of the culture of the human species and thus illuminating a branch of natural science. All human customs and mythologies could be unraveled and fitted into the story of human progress, they held, the principal fact about human culture being that it was unitary and characterized the species as a whole. Closely related to this was the notion of the psychic unity of human beings, which explained the similarity of widely dispersed practices.[107] In this schema, the ultimate explanation for human thought and action was to be found at the level of individual biology and psychology.

However, mankind had not progressed at the same rate from savagery through barbarism to civilization around the world. There was "a mental evolution and a ladder of progress in mankind's history," as demonstrated among other things by the "evidence of survivals" of primitive customs among civilized peoples.[108] Lang set himself the task of tracing this mental evolution in the domain of myth and religion. "Our object," he explained, "is to prove that the 'silly, savage and irrational' element in the myths of civilized people is, as a rule, either a survival from the period of savagery, or has been borrowed from savage neighbours by a cultivated people, or lastly, is an intimation by later poets of old savage ideas."[109] Basing his argument mainly on Greek examples, which he compared to those from other parts of the world, Lang went on to argue that myths survived mainly among the peasantry and conservative priesthoods, who had shared least in the general civilizational advance. Moreover, even among the Greeks who had the most beautiful mythology of all, a very large proportion of legends was "practically on a level with the myths of Maoris . . . and Bushmen." In fact, "the whole of Greek life yields relics of savagery when the surface is excavated."[110]

By making the "survivals" so pervasive and widespread and producing examples from the modern world, Lang's argument almost overturned the notion of the steady, upward ascent of man. He muddied the evolutionary waters still further at the end of his book by warning that "man can never be certain that he has expelled the savage from his temples and his heart"; on the other hand, "even the lowest known savages" would pray to "their Father and ours" in their hour of need.[111]

In *Custom and Myth* Lang proposed a method for what he now called "folklore studies": if the apparently meaningless customs and rituals of civilized peoples were compared with similar practices for which savages had an explanation, their significance would be revealed. This was because similar psychological states produced similar actions.[112]

Zhou eagerly seized on the notion of a ubiquitous "savage mind" that, once understood, provided the key to customs, children's stories, legends, and myths.[113] He found confirmation for this in Frazer's social anthropology. The synchronic view of man Zhou found in these two writers must have contributed significantly to his anti-evolutionary thinking (for which he may also have been indebted to Zhang Binglin). It provided him with the means to make a critical analysis of Chinese cultural practices without having to acknowledge the superiority of Western culture.

Frazer's work went farther than Lang's, however. Zhou described it as dealing with the ethical code (*lijiao*) as well as customs and being more useful than the study of mythology. It enabled one to pierce for a moment the mystery, and consequently the oppressive terror, surrounding "sacred or profane facts," he claimed.[114] It has been argued that *The Golden Bough*, with its immense catalog of sacrificial rites to promote fertility and avert chaos and death, made civilization seem "no more than a veneer over an inferno of primitive terrors and passions."[115] And yet it was the triumph of reason and science that had made this apparent. *The Golden Bough* thus contained "a dual perspective of intelligence and hopelessness, of rational dreams and tragic awareness."[116] Frazer thus stands with Auguste Le Bon in bolstering the view we find in Zhou of a handful of rational men in each generation having to struggle against the accumulated weight of "ghosts" from the past. Invoking Frazer, Zhou lamented that China might claim to be sustained by the teachings of Confucius, Mencius, Laozi, and Zhuangzi, but for most of the Chinese people, they might as well never have existed. In reality, primitive Northeast Asian shamanism lay just below the surface of everyday life.[117] Although Frazer provided the conceptual framework, Zhou may have found the notion of a "Northeast Asian shamanism" in the writing of a Japanese anthropologist he identifies as Dr. Torii.[118]

Frazer's explorations of the power of sexuality more or less paralleled Freud's discovery of the subconscious.[119] Frazer thus fitted the dangerous aspect of sexuality into a communal context rather than an individual one. This insight of Frazer's enabled Zhou to identify the sexual overtones in acts of oppression and reaction. When a Sichuan student convicted of adultery was executed "to maintain public morality" and Hunan governor Zhao Hengti (1880–1971) slept apart from his wife to bring on rain, Zhou discussed both cases in terms of primitive beliefs in the power of sexuality to threaten society or influence nature.[120] Zhou wrote one of his most biting castigations of Chinese savagery after learning of the sadistic voyeurism of crowds who attended the public decapitations of young women.[121] Frazer's displacement of the power of sexuality away from the individual psyche may explain Zhou's lack of interest in Freud, who made the aggression born of thwarted desire the root of the ego. Havelock Ellis (1859–1939), not Freud, was Zhou's mentor here: Ellis abstracted individual sexual behavior to an innocent realm governed by "nature" and shared by animals and primitive (in this case, socially unconstructed) humans. For Zhou, Ellis's primary message was that sexuality was part of a continuum linking "human feelings and the natural order of things"—renqing wuli in the phrase Zhou used.[122] As such, Ellis held, it should be neither aestheticized nor scientized, both of these being "cold, abstract" perspectives entirely inappropriate to the relations between the sexes.[123] A proper appreciation of "human feelings and the natural order" was the hallmark of the civilized individual for Zhou, who, as we shall see, conceived of the self as grounded in knowledge. Thus in Zhou's mental world, Ellis provided a space in which sexuality was a function of knowledge of a proper way of being, and Frazer held up to daylight the oppressive, self-opaque, primitive world of the "false Confucians" and shamanists.

Lang's contribution to Zhou's thinking, though sharing much with Frazer, was on a less abstract level, for it focused more on myth as the deployment of the imagination. As such, myth represented knowledge at a certain pleasurable stage shared by children and primitives but also available in literature. Although literature may have evolved with great variation, "since basic human nature has not changed," the best of each literature can still move men, Zhou wrote. The barriers of time and space just added a layer of "strange, colorful patterns" behind which the myths still "pulsate."[124] He scorned "materialists" who rejected the "monstrous creatures and supernatural beings" of romance (chuanqi) literature as valueless. Such people did not understand how to use their intuition and emotions. They did not realize that animism may have hindered the development of culture, but it had enabled literature to express our common fears and sorrows.[125] Zhou argued forcefully against the belief that allowing children to read myths—a category including fairy tales and legends—would encourage superstition. It could only nourish their imaginations and interest (quwei), he said. Imagination did not have to be destroyed in order to preserve the thirst for knowledge, which only science could fill.[126]

In 1926 Zhou remarked that of all his interests, myth was the one that had not changed, and that the myths he loved best were Greek ones, for they were the most beautiful.[127] What Zhou meant by myth was the anthropological explanation of myth—that is, the method pioneered by Lang.[128] It is also important to note that his knowledge of the Greek myths had come from the same sources, that is, through the work of the popularizers of European antiquity who had been inspired to new ways of looking at the classics by Frazer.[129] Of these, Zhou was probably most familiar with Jane Harrison's (1850–1928) writings.

Harrison's starting point (as presented by Zhou) was that religious ritual and myth are two sides of the same coin, in that both are the expression of basic human hopes and fears. In the early stages of the development of religion, men see the world as populated by numina, a hazy multitude of forces for life and death. The great contribution of the Greeks, rather late in the development of their religion, was to clarify and individualize all these forces. Numina became gods when Homer and Hesiod wrote their works and the Greeks took to representing them in sculpture. Not only was religious terror driven out of life, but poets replaced the priests.[130] Zhou's translation of Harrison's work came with a revealing addendum: he had been moved to begin this long-planned project on an oppressively hot day as gunfire from some unknown source resounded outside. His translation itself became a performative act imbued with longing for a time when the frightening, stupefying "shamanistic" culture of warlord China would be transformed by poets into myths. By that time, of course, the process of purging the warlords from social and mental life would be under way. Myth, then, in Zhou's thinking, represented the taming and bringing to light of the cultural unconscious. Moreover, because Greek mythology owed its special beauty to its creation by poets, not priests, it also reiterated the superiority of expressive over didactic literature. It thus functioned at the deepest level as an organic link between social life and art.

Zhou's endorsement of myth rested on the condition that it not be exploited for propaganda purposes, a possibility of which he was always aware. In his essay in defense of myth, he claimed that there is nothing wrong with finding beauty in superstition, provided we realize it is not true. By the time myths enter literature, people have already come to disbelieve them. But then he quickly added, "We will not allow mythmakers to write myths as though they were true and turn them into religious propaganda," although "we will approve their creating false myths" because the mythmaker in contemporary times is a poet.[131]

Zhou's deep interest in cultural anthropology and the power of myth does not by itself account for the richness of his literary evocations of culture. This depends to a considerable extent on his experience of Japanese culture, and here his emotional involvement with Tokyo is a crucial factor. He himself commented that what he had gained from Japan was mostly in the domain of sentiment (qing); it involved the country itself and so had "local color." In this way, he said, it differed somewhat from the Western knowledge he also gained in Japan. As he put it, "When we become interested in Japan, even after grappling with [its] literature and art for a long time, we find we have only got the half of it. We have to get into the affective life of the people."[132]

Both aspects—the anthropological study of myth and Japanese constructions of "the affective life of the people"—came together to illuminate Zhou's thinking on the locality and the nation.

## Japanese Constructions of Place

Although Zhou Zuoren received less formal instruction in Japanese than he had in English, the language soon became much more familiar to him than English. Commenting on the difference, Zhou likened his Japanese to a hardy, well-rooted potted plant and his English to a bouquet of flowers in a vase. He had used his English to gain access to knowledge but had not tried to understand English literature. But, "when I read Japanese, I am not just looking for knowledge, but I am interested in what I am reading about. The language gives me pleasure, and sometimes it is difficult to separate it from the subject."[133]

By mid-1909, after his marriage and as Lu Xun was preparing to return home, Zhou began a course of independent reading to improve his Japanese. There was another reason for his efforts: the Japanese writing system had just been reformed, reducing the number of kanji, and Zhou found that he could no longer rely on his eyes alone to understand what he read. He needed to begin to use his ears. Not knowing what to choose in contemporary fiction and drama (or perhaps not caring to), Zhou decided to start with inexpensive anthologies of kyōgen plays and kokkeibon (joke books) and the short senryū verse form, which often contained a humorous twist.[134] Zhou later praised senryū for expressing truths about existence with humor, or sometimes pathos, and lamented the lack of humor in Chinese life.[135] He also read rakugo—stand-up comic routines that relied not only on wordplay but also on an understanding of folk customs and daily routines for their humor. The examples that Zhou quotes center on the visitations of ghosts at special times of the year, although as he notes these spirits differ from Chinese ones.[136] Two of the authors Zhou cites are Shikitei Sanba (1776–1822) and Jippensha Ikku (1765–1831). Their novels, loose and episodic in form and often drawing on kyōgen, centered on the brothels, teahouses, and bathhouses of Edo encountered by the lower strata of chōnin (merchant) society.[137] Zhou made frequent visits to watch kyōgen, rakugo, and other forms of popular entertainment and quoted Mori Ōgai (1862–1922) to the effect that a visit to the theater provided the education necessary for visiting the red-light district in Yoshiwara.[138]

He also read histories of the theatre, noting that the plays of Chikamatsu (1653–1725) and other Tokugawa dramatists had highlighted the clash between human sentiment and duty. "Japanese popular culture, unlike China's, is good at using beautiful forms to embody deeply felt tragic sorrows," he remarked. He also collected popular songs from the Edo period and in 1920 translated sixty of them, because "although vulgar, they were full of artistic feeling."[139]

The literary and performing arts that interested Zhou undoubtedly contributed to his aesthetic and emotional experience of Tokyo as a specific locality with parts of its Edo heritage very much alive. He read the writings on Japanese and Korean material culture of Yanagi Muneyoshi (1889–1961), the recognized leader of the Japanese folk art movement. Yanagi was a founder of the Shirakaba group and concerned with the twin questions of the meaning of life and aesthetics.[140] Zhou enjoyed reading his "sincere and simple yet splendid writing" on mysticism and the beauty of common utensils and Japanese paper. Long after he had returned to China, he kept up with the writings of the folk arts group.[141]

Zhou's fascination with Tokyo led him to want to learn about the "human sentiments and material aspect" (renqing wuse) of the city in the pre- and post-Restoration periods, and he collected books produced by the Japan Photography Society of disappearing Musashino scenes and reprints of ukiyo-e woodblock prints. These brightly colored scenes were very different from Chinese block prints, he noted.

But what is distinctive about ukiyo-e lies not just in the scenes but in its depiction of the customs and practices of the urban world; this is what we look for. . . . The figures are predominantly women (apart from a few portraits of professional actors), and the women are more often than not prostitutes; so when one speaks of ukiyo-e, it is Yoshiwara pleasure quarters that come to mind, and in fact they are closely related. The pictures are richly beautiful and gorgeously colored, but they are always cast under a shadow; so we could say the colors are East Asian. When one looks at Chinese art or reads Chinese literature, one has the same feeling. But in these pictures it is naturally more apparent.[142]

Having plunged this far into his preoccupation with Tokyo's urban culture, Zhou was to become aware of another way of constructing locality that drew on Frazer and Lang and yet seemed immediate and contemporary.

In June 1910, Yanagita Kunio (1875–1962) published his *Tōno monogatari* (Legends of Tōno) in a limited first edition of 350 copies. Zhou bought copy 292. He wrote later that the book made a "profound impression" on him. "Apart from its literary qualities, it showed me the rich interest and flavor of folklore studies."[143] Written in a refined, restrained manner in the newly introduced "essay" style, the book was Yanagita's rendering of stories he had heard from a storyteller in the mountainous and isolated Tōno district.[144] In them ghosts, wild mountainmen, and goblins flitted in and out of the narration of the villagers' lives, which were frequently disrupted by murder, fraud, family quarrels, and attacks by wild animals. Yet the sense of the harshness of their lives is softened by the impression of unity with their surroundings. Yanagita, unlike the Victorian anthropologists but like Chinese writers of *biji* (jottings), includes plentiful details of physical settings and seasons, flora and fauna.[145] The book begins with a lyrical description of the countryside as seen by Yanagita from horseback and closes with a local song describing places and things. In his preface, Yanagita admitted, "I think a book like [this] goes against present day literary fashions." But, he added, "Quite contrary to the case of . . . tales [that] existed in the past and are now old, the legends of Tōno reveal facts which exist before our eyes."[146] In Zhou's opinion, Yanagita's publication of *Tōno monogatari* together with his *Ishi-gami mondō* (Discussions of stone-carved deities), which had appeared one month earlier, marked the real foundation of Japanese folklore studies, because "he did not just engage in comparisons and conjectures, but started from the real life among the people, so that there was a fresh, new vigor."[147]

What Yanagita had done, we may extrapolate, was to represent the remote locality as the place where "the real facts" of culture, in the Lang and Frazerian sense of survivals, could be found.[148] Reading Yanagita in 1910, Zhou may well have recalled Lang's insistence that the "cruder and wilder sacrifices" in Greek civilization were native and could not be blamed on borrowings from lesser peoples. The reason for believing this was that "the more strange and savage features meet us in *local* tales and practices, often in remote upland temples and chapels. There they had survived from the society of the village status, before the villages had been gathered into cities."[149] And yet Yanagita had turned inside out the Frazerian pathos of the notion of inexorable evolutionary progress measured against "survivals" by giving the "survivals" a sense of solidity and depth. "The legends of Tōno are present-day facts. This alone is their raison d'etre."[150] Added to the idea of locality as the site of history, we thus have the locality as site of the culture's unconscious desires expressed in custom and ritual and then given literary expression. Perhaps this is what Zhou most immediately appreciated about *Tōno monogatari*. Like Zhang Binglin's history, Yanagita's locality-centered researches bring the past into the present: significantly, in the 1930s he saw his work as forming a "new *kokugaku*" tradition, extending *kokugaku* scholarship with research into the oral and folk traditions as well as incorporating insights and methodologies from foreign folklorists.[151]

Zhou was to collect many of the books and journals published by Yanagita and his associates over the years. He admired Yanagita's scholarship for its "unadorned simplicity" and his writing for the charm of its "exquisite beauty."[152] But Zhou threw an interesting light on his appreciation of Yanagita by quoting British anthropologist A. C. Haddon's (1855–1940) view that he and his colleagues were men of letters by disposition and thus tended to lack scientific rigor.[153] There was nothing that could be done about this, Zhou said, and in any case, Yanagita's pioneering contribution to Japanese "local studies" was great and admirable. Perhaps Zhou's citation of a view that undercut the authority of anthropology reflected his impulse to protect that sphere of knowledge and intellectual inquiry from the claims of ideologies.

According to Ronald Morse, Yanagita had been in contact with Zhou and visited Peking in 1917, although it is not clear whether they met on this occasion.[154] There were similarities and affinities between the two men, although their careers followed different patterns. Most pertinent perhaps is Morse's comment: "Fearing the simple solutions of the left as much as the repressive nationalism and elitism of the right, [Yanagita] often found himself in dangerously exposed positions."[155] The worldviews of the left and right are usually congruent on their outer edges with the drive to rationalize human activities and aspirations and overwhelmingly articulate them in terms of the interests of the nation-state. Those who want to see the past flowing into the present are necessarily at odds with this vision.

One of the most interesting (and problematical) concepts developed by Yanagita was that of the *jōmin*, or "abiding and ordinary folk," which he coined in order to avoid politically loaded terms like "the people," "the masses," and "the populace."[156] The popular tradition belonged to the *jōmin*, and here the expression was used in opposition to intellectuals, who were held to have a logical and progressive mode of thought. But, on the other hand, "in civilized society there is no one, no matter how traditional, who has not come into contact with new cultural forms." Likewise, "no matter how educated a person is, he cannot live completely cut off from tradition." There was no implication of cultural inferiority in the term *jōmin*, and it could even be applied to the Imperial Household. Morse concludes, "Basically, Yanagita's concept of culture designates the interaction of various life-styles. The inner and the outer, the old and the new—all of this coexisted at any one point in time. The term *jōmin* was a linguistic strategy designed to pull together what he meant by Japanese culture."[157] The lives of the *jōmin* were "regulated by intersubjective relationships inscribed in customs and things," which had the result of undercutting class identities with ones based on native place.[158] Although Zhou never produced an analytical construct like *jōmin*, his concern with the customs and artifacts of a locality also had the result of undercutting nationwide class identities and the distinction between old and new. How should we understand the parallels in the thinking of Zhou and Yanagita? Although a hypothetical argument could be made for some kind of influence between them, I believe it is essentially meaningless to argue in these terms. Rather, their separate encounters with the various discourses of nation-building and the perceived need on both men's part to get around these discourses seem a more compelling explanation for the similarities in their views.

Yanagita found folk religion to be at the heart of the Japanese personality and culture, and this enabled Zhou to make some fruitful comparisons with China. Discussing Yanagita's work, Zhou commented on the differences between China and Japan:

I often think that the Chinese people's emotions and thinking are centred on ghosts (*gui*), whereas those of the Japanese are centered on spirits (*kami*). Therefore to understand China, one must study manners and customs (*lisu*); to understand Japan, one must research religion. Mr. Yanagita has been a prolific writer, although he has not written much specifically about religion. However, I have profited greatly from his book on Japanese festivals and his other books also.[159]

This distinction is a very interesting one. *Kami* ultimately became for Yanagita the basis of a concept of social cohesion based on place and independent of blood relationships; thus, it could be extended to the whole of Japan.[160] But for Zhou during the 1920s, when he was most preoccupied with folklore and myth, we could say that the problem of the nation could be explained in terms of the hold ghosts had over the lives of men. The structures of oppression existed at the level of the unconscious.

Thus, for example, in 1925 he endorsed the hope that increased knowledge about "our culture, past and present," would increase individual and national awareness and "nourish the national spirit so that a new national Han culture will freely arise." This "arbitrary dream" was the reason he supported the advocacy of a national literature. But he admitted to being "very oppressed by the theory of heredity," which led him to distrust the dream. As Gustave Le Bon had said, the affairs of men are controlled by ghosts:

It is almost enough to make one believe that the King of the Underworld has got the Chinese entered in his register as slaves. This is why I cannot help being lukewarm about all the various proposals. Since my insignificant aspiration is now just to be able to understand a tenth more, rather than to succeed by a hundredth part, there is no harm in it.[161]

As a heuristic device, we might imagine two hierarchies along which Zhou ordered Chinese society in terms of its beneficial and harmful aspects. As cultural area > locality > individual, it was open-ended and creative; in its harmful aspect, it was dominated by the family and emperor in their dark, shadowy forms of ghosts and "false Confucian" traditions of loyalty. For this reason, it is fair to assume, Zhou would have been suspicious of social initiatives based on the *xiangyue* type of community pact that developed in Ming China to reinforce hierarchy and ritual at the village level.[162] This would differentiate him from a conservative reformer like Liang Shuming (1893–1986), who sought to reorganize society by reviving such institutions.[163]

Although Zhou found it hard to subscribe to the idea of a "national literature" while the ghostly realm dominated life in the 1920s, he later encouraged Shen Congwen to explore the mythic dimensions of Chinese culture.[164] In his own writing, he never attempted to produce the same kinds of synthesizing discussions of folklore and culture found in Frazer. He probably felt more affinity for Apollodorus (fl. 140 B.C.E.), the supposed author of the Greek summary of myths and legends titled *Bibliotheca* and translated by Frazer in 1921. Apollodorus, according to sources quoted by Zhou, wrote in a "commonplace, natural style" and collated his material from existing texts "without embellishing" them. Being "neither a philosopher nor a literary stylist," he wrote without seeking to change the material to fit his purposes. In fact he was just "an ordinary man" receiving the legends of his country and recording them.[165] This is close to Zhou's own self-representation as an ordinary man with no special expertise, sifting through the writings of the past. Zhou showed his fondness for Apollodorus by translating the *Bibliotheca* from the Greek, but the book was never published.[166]

Victorian anthropology, mythology, Zhou's interest in Tokyo and Edo popular culture, Yanagita's writing, all of them first encountered in Japan, contributed in various ways to give depth and texture to the ideas of locality and culture in Zhou's work. But the heart of his thinking and writing was his aesthetics. Japan played a part here too, for his preferences in Japanese literature enriched and supported some of the aesthetic choices he made in his own writing.

## The Presence of the Past

Although Zhou apparently ignored contemporary Japanese literature when he began his reading program, he was certainly not ignorant of it, since all along he had read the literary magazines and newspaper serializations Lu Xun bought. Natsume Sōseki's *I Am a Cat, Kusamakura, Sanshirō, Botchan*, and *Mon* all pleased him. He liked Mori Ōgai's short pieces and had great admiration for the essays of Tanizaki Jun'ichirō (1886–1965) and Shimazaki Tōson (1872–1943). He translated Suzuki Miekichi's (1882–1939) "Goldfish" and praised the humorous, critical essays of Togawa Shūkotsu (1870–1939) and Uchida Roan (1868–1929).[167] One of his favorite authors, certainly one he quoted most frequently, was Nagai Kafū (1879–1939). Zhou did not care for fiction, saying that he did not understand it. As a result, he said,

When I read stories, I read them as if they were nonfiction, so fiction that is un-story-like or like an essay (suibi) gives me great pleasure. . . . As Fei Ming [Feng Wenbing] once said in a private letter: "I used to write fiction, but now I no longer like it, because on the one hand fiction has to be realistic—and that means intimate. But on the other hand it has to have a structure, and a structure is almost like a de-ception. You have to spend a lot of effort on it to the detriment of intimacy."[168]

It has been said that the works of writers such as Sōseki, Ōgai, Kafū, and Tanizaki, while deeply influenced by Western works and modern concerns, remain rooted in a specifically Japanese, historically grounded, relationship with the past. For them, the literary past never served as a monolithic tradition but as "a precious thread of continuity and sophisti-cation in a world that all too often seemed full of upheaval and continu-ous, ominous change. The Japanese literary tradition, and the psycho-logical and stylistic attitudes it fostered, retained a kind of dialectical energy that has provided vitality for almost a thousand years."[169] The dominant aesthetic concept involved here is that of mono no aware, as elaborated by the kokugaku scholar Motoori Norinaga (1730–1801). Basing himself on philological analysis of early Japanese poetry, Norinaga dem-onstrated that aware was once an exclamation, like ah!, expressing any deep emotion, "whether happy, amused, joyous, sad, or yearning" in re-sponse to things or events. Thus it could be translated as the "ah!ness of things," but the exclamation had come to be particularly identified with the relatively strong emotion of sadness. Sensitivity to the "heart" of the object or event was inseparable from the response to it.[170] Mono no aware might thus refer to the artist's ability to find deep significance in ordinary things and incidents and to convey the same intuitive but cultured re-sponse to life to readers. What gave Norinaga's work its enormous sub-sequent power was his nativist insistence that mono no aware was the original Japanese character of heart that had existed before (and had sur-vived) the world-ordering reach of Confucianism and Buddhism. He placed its locus classicus in the eleventh-century novel Genji monogatari, which had long been castigated as immoral by Buddhist and Confucian moralists alike. Norinaga's reading of *Genji* and his construction of *mono no aware* have shaped all later discussion of Japanese literary tradition, not to mention wider issues of values and cultural identity.

In terms of this discussion of Zhou Zuoren, Norinaga's aesthetics of *mono no aware* has two important corollaries. First, the purpose of literature becomes purely expressivist. "The essence of poetry is not to aid government, nor even to cultivate oneself. It is simply to express what one feels in one's heart. Some poems may be helpful to government or to moral instruction, but some can have a harmful effect on a country or on private life. It depends on the poem; each is composed according to the author's heart."[171] Part of this is extremely congenial to Zhou's way of thinking—though not all, because he brought the idea of self-cultivation into his own aesthetics.

Second, Norinaga constructed the sensibility of the "true heart" open to *mono no aware* as essentially feminine. "To be manly, resolute, and wise is a mere superficial appearance. As far as the depth of man's real nature is concerned, the wisest men do not differ from a woman or a child."[172] Such a concept of human nature has affinities with the "childlike heart" of Li Zhi and the Ming counter-tradition. If *mono no aware* is the dominant aesthetic concept of the Japanese literary tradition, then we already have some basis for imagining ways in which it became a resource for Zhou Zuoren. Norinaga's nativist project—constituting Japaneseness out of this aesthetic—need not have been an obstacle, because he worked within an intellectual and literary context that was in large measure constituted by Confucian and Buddhist systems and practices. It thus confronted the same didactic and patriarchal practices to which Zhou was opposed.

In fact Okakura's construction of Asia deploys a subject with a feminine sensibility, able to grasp with "tenderness and friendship" the "joys and sorrows" of a place fleetingly visited. It could be argued that this extension of the Japanese nativist aesthetic to the whole of Asia reflects either the cynicism of the logic of (Japanese) imperialism or the inevitable, lamentable self-inscription of Japanese-led pan-Asianists in the construction of a "feminine Asia" that falls into the discursive trap set by imperialism. To do so would be to miss another possibility. One of the charges against the ideology of imperialism is that it valorizes exaggerated versions of masculinity and rationality. In this case, to valorize feminine attributes is to bring to the fore that which is being suppressed. But, of course, this position can only succeed in not falling into the logic of imperialist ideology if both masculine and feminine are seen as relative, not absolute polarities.

With the drastic changes ushered in by the Meiji Restoration, for the modern writers who were heir to the Japanese literary tradition, perishability seemed to mark not only human life and nature but also the entire civilization. This was brought home especially to those writers who had traveled abroad at the beginning of this century. Kafū, for instance, had lived in America and France, where he had been able to grasp the "wholeness and beauty" of French culture. But his return to Japan showed him that "although Japan too had possessed such a wholeness, it was vanishing under the impetus of a mindless desire for change."[173] His writing has been described as "a series of critical reactions to the instant Westernization of Tokyo life." Although Sōseki and Ōgai made similar criticisms, they "acknowledged that [Westernization] was inevitable"; Kafū refused to do so and "made his life in the Tokyo backstreets where Edo culture still lingered."[174]

Zhou's favorite collection of essays was Kafū's *Hiyorigeta*, a series of vignettes of forgotten, decaying corners of Tokyo seen on foot. The title refers to the traditional wooden clogs made for braving uncertain weather that the essayist found indispensable to his forays.[175] Kafū equates the treacherous climate with the country's politics, and his clogs may symbolize both his distrust of the modernizing nation-state and his scorn of new-fangled commodities.

Zhou illustrates Kafū's attitude toward Japanese politics and culture with a quotation from another work to the effect that although Japan claimed to have entered a new epoch, there had been no change in the autocratic spirit of the past that had wearied and terrified the people's hearts.[176] That was the reason for the continued appeal of the muted colors of Japanese *ukiyo-e* woodblock prints, which were produced by cowering artisans in sunless courtyards. Japan, never having had a god like Apollo, could not be expected to produce anything of the same caliber as the Greeks. This was a constant theme that Zhou found in Kafū, always based on a comparison between vibrant European art and plaintive Japanese art. It was made at greater length in another quotation that Zhou made famous by reproducing it seven times.[177] It began, "I ask myself, what am I? I am not a Belgian like the painter Verhaeren, but a Japanese, born into a different fate and surroundings."[178] Despite Kafū's apparent loathing for the harshness of Japanese culture, he ended by proclaiming the deep emotional meaning the world represented in *ukiyo-e* has for him. He is brought to tears, delighted, intoxicated by the pathos of the lives of geishas and the beauty of the setting—rainy moonlit nights, falling petals, the sound of a temple bell. "Everything in this dreamlike world, transitory, lonely, productive of sighs, is near me, and takes me back to the past."[179]

Kafū's meditations on *ukiyo-e* prints bring Zhou to an important conclusion: Japan and China share so many similarities of background that, when expressed in art, they lead one to feel, "You and I are brothers." Currently China and Japan may be enemies, but in the long term they are both East Asian, "born into a different fate and surroundings from that of the West."[180] But this is not all. The section Zhou chose to translate in its entirety from *Hiyorigeta* is on customs relating to the countless *inshi* (shrines to evil deities) still found in Tokyo and patronized by the humblest members of the population. Visibly, then, a variant of the shamanistic Northeast Asian culture Yanagita found in Tōno has been discovered and given artistic form by Kafū in the center of the metropolis. One can begin to understand Zhou's fondness for Kafū. Both men apparently share the convictions that the dark sides of their cultures remain unchanged and that those who insist otherwise are ignorant and self-serving. Both also find beauty, interest, and meaning in cultural practices and relate them to specificity of place.

However, Zhou could not have found Kafū attractive just because he provided literary support for ideas found in Yanagita. To think so is to miss Kafū's importance as a literary referent. What Zhou must have appreciated most about Kafū was his aesthetic sensibility to the world as "lonely, transitory, and dreamlike"—terms that suggest the quality of *mono no aware*. Significantly, the section of *Hiyorigeta* on shrines translated by Zhou ends with the comment that the "naïve, ugly practices of ignorant people" give the author the same "boundless comfort" as *ukiyo-e*. This is because, however preposterous they may be, "when I think about them carefully, I keenly feel a profound, inexpressible sentiment akin to sorrow." Zhou's word "sorrow" (*bei'ai*) is his translation of the term *mono no aware* in Kafū's text.[181]

Having found *mono no aware* in Zhou's text, we need to ask what place it plays in his thinking. How did he understand it, and how does he appropriate it? How did he approach Japanese aesthetics? Zhou was clearly alive to contemporary discussions of aesthetics during his stay in Japan. He explored the poetic forms of *haikai* and *haiku*, despite his feeling, as he later said, that these were twice removed from him by virtue of being poetry, which he did not understand, and foreign.[182] But his interest in them prompted him to buy journals and secondhand books on the subject. Zhou held that *haikai* and its related forms had changed and developed so as to include within themselves "the abstruse, tranquil, Zen flavor of Matsuo Bashō (1644–94) [and] the brilliance and exquisiteness of Yosa Buson's (1716–1783) depictions." The term that I have translated "abstruse" is, in Zhou's text, *youxuan*, or in Japanese *yūgen*. This is another centrally important Japanese aesthetic term, sometimes defined as "mystery and depth" and often associated with the Nō drama. The poet Shōtetsu (1381–1459) described it as "feelings that cannot be put into words, for example, the effect of the moon veiled by a wisp of cloud or of scarlet mountain foliage enshrouded in autumn haze."[183] It differs from *aware* by going beyond emotional response and, even in some sense, beyond language. Zhou listed as a third attribute of *haikai* and *haiku* the "naturalness" of Masaoka Shiki (1867–1902). What Zhou found most interesting about Shiki was that although influenced by (European) naturalism, "he had never left the sphere of *haikai*, but continued to use 'mildness and plain language' (*pingdan su hua*) to express himself . . . while opposing the banality and vulgarity then prevalent in *haikai*."

But the aspect of Japanese aesthetic practice that had the most interest for Zhou was probably *mono no aware*. This is because *yūgen*'s similarity to the Chinese aesthetic category of *qu* rendered it superfluous, and injunctions to simplicity of language should be understood within the context of prevailing practice in any literary tradition. However, the acceptance of life as a blend of sorrow and joy that is the hallmark of *aware* has no apparent immediate counterpart in Chinese writing. This, indeed, is a point Zhou made in his essay "Old Age."[184]

This piece begins with an excerpt from an essay of Bashō's intertwining the themes of desire and old age. Bashō likened desire to the fragrance that suddenly surrounds a man lying on a mountain who is unaware of nearby plum trees. Thus although it brings dangers and suffering, one can pardon those who give way to desire much more easily than those who renounce love in order to ensure a moneyed old age for themselves. But by the time one reaches old age, the fullness of youth is but a dream. Now that he had reached fifty, Bashō found it preferable to retire and live in solitude, only opening the door to see the morning glories.

Bashō had been a warrior and then a monk, but "he was always a poet, and so his attitude was very gentle. He respected the purity of old age and also forgave the mistakes of love," Zhou said. This "rare understanding and wisdom" recalled the monk Yoshida Kenkō (1332–92), who had likened desire to "the fragrance of clothes fumigated with incense." One knows the cause, but one's heart moves in response to it. Zhou praised Bashō and Kenkō for being able to speak of desire without salaciousness yet recognizing its loveliness.

Zhou found Kenkō's most interesting observation to be on old age. The passage he quoted has been described as summing up the entire tradition of *mono no aware*:[185]

Were we to live on forever—were the dews of Adashino never to vanish, the smoke on Toribeyama never to fade away—then indeed men would not feel the pity of things [*mono no aware*].

Truly the beauty of life is its uncertainty. Of all living things, none lives so long as man. . . . Even a year of life lived peacefully seems long and happy beyond compare, but for such as never weary of this world and are loath to die, a thousand years passes away like the dream of a single night. What shall it avail a man to drag out . . . a life which some day needs must end? Long life brings many shames. At most before his fortieth year is full, it is seemly for a man to die.[186]

Zhou comments that Kenkō's somewhat pessimistic attitude could perhaps be attributed to the fact he lived in tumultuous times, whereas Bashō, who lived at the height of the Tokugawa period, produced writing that was meditative and serene. This led Zhou to the heart of the matter:

Their writing shares a fundamental tone that comes from the similarity of the flavor, which is a flowing together of the Confucian and the Buddhist, with perhaps the addition of some Zhuangzi and Laozi. It is very difficult to find such people among Chinese men of letters. Yan Zhitui [531–ca. 590] of the Six Dynasties is one of course . . . but for the moment I cannot put my hands on a like example of his. When we come down to the Ming-Qing transitional period, then there is Fu Qing-zhu [Fu Shan, 1607–84].[187]

In other words, the sensibility characterized by *mono no aware*, though rare among Chinese, cannot be said to be foreign to them. It was at home with, even had its origins in, those neglected strands of the culture from which Zhou constructed his alternative to what he construed as the dominant discourse of Cheng-Zhu Neo-Confucianism. Zhou's purpose was not so much to appropriate *mono no aware* and make it Chinese as to point to the common cultural heritage of East Asians. Among his contemporaries, it was Kafū who made Zhou feel that "you and I are brothers."

In this regard, the way Zhou presented his own relation to Kafū's text is instructive. He begins his essay with a long digression on how happy he is to have obtained a first edition of *Hiyorigeta*, although he had naturally read the book long ago and owned copies of later printings. There is nothing attractive about this edition, and yet, it has great emotional value for him. Newer editions, although easier to read, lack intimacy. Zhou's relation to the physical book echoes Kafū's to Tokyo, but in a subtle, indirect fashion. Zhou is careful to state that he became interested in Kafū after reading his *Shitaya sōwa* (Tales of Shitaya). This book relates the activities and friendships of a group of Edo poets who wrote in Chinese, including Kafū's maternal grandfather. Kafū's quotation of a quatrain by Ōnuma Chinzan (1818–91), a cousin of the grandfather, had prompted Zhou to buy one of Chinzan's poetry collections.[188] The Japanese world of Kafū thus contains "Chinese" literary culture. Zhou ends the essay by using Kafū's mention of foods offered to the deities as a springboard from which to discuss various textual references to the eating and cooking of *konnyaku* in China. Kafū's text is thus "naturalized" by being embedded in Zhou's literary and *zaxue* interests, while the commonalities of material culture underscore the shared artistic heritage. But here again Zhou avoids a heavy-handed flattening of everything into one big East Asian cultural unit. *Konnyaku* is known in China, but it is very rare. It is a typically Japanese product, and at the few markets where it can be bought in Peking, the Japanese method of preparation and name are used, he concludes. The "flowing together of Confucian and Buddhist" that Zhou found in Kenkō and Bashō was a variant of the pattern at the center of Zhou's own aesthetics and philosophy.

## Culture and Collaboration

One further issue needs to be addressed in this discussion of Zhou's many intellectual affinities with Japanese thinkers. Zhou's collaboration with Japan, an aggressive, imperialist adversary of China, which has made the separation of the man and his works (qi ren qi wen) almost impossible in China, needs to be acknowledged. My focus here is not the history of Zhou's collaboration nor the charges against him. It has been recently argued, in fact, that Zhou's case cannot be explained in categories, such as collaboration, passivity, or resistance, which are "only relevant in the intellectual context dominated by nationalism."[189] This is a view I share, although the reasons will become clear only later in this book.

The year 1934 was an important one for Zhou Zuoren. It began with his fiftieth birthday, and to celebrate the occasion he wrote a poem in which he described himself as half-Confucian, half-Buddhist, peacefully drinking tea and unconcerned about the outside.[190] Coming at a time of rising national sentiment against Japan, this poem gave rise to much public indignation. Lu Xun, commenting on the furor aroused by the publication of the poem, suggested that Zhou was gradually becoming a target of the masses and possibly getting closer to the Japanese.[191] The grounds for Lu Xun's assessment are not known to me, but it is no doubt related to the fact that by this time the brothers were ideological, and literary, adversaries. The main reason 1934 was special for Zhou is that he made his first visit to Japan since 1919 that year.

In a speech following the Japanese invasion of Manchuria in 1931, Zhou had noted soberly that although Japanese wrongdoing was clear to the world, the Chinese side had to bear some responsibility for failing to prepare for it.[192] China had had no national draft system since the Qing, because military power was in the hands of political parties and groups who preferred to be at one another's throats rather than unite. Despite its topicality, the speech was more a criticism of the hypocrisy of Chinese political life than a proposal Zhou believed anyone would take seriously.

Writing in December 1934, after his return from Japan, Zhou expressed great pessimism about China's chances in a war with Japan and stressed the need to avoid one.[193]

Six months later he published the first of a series of articles in which he tried to address the disparity between the qualities he had admired in Japanese life, such as a love of beauty and cleanliness, and the ugly realities of Japanese conduct toward China.[194] The articles presented Japan through cultural categories rather than an analysis of its economic and political forces and veered in tone from fond recollection to aggrieved sarcasm. But in June 1937, just one week before the Marco Polo Bridge incident, Zhou concluded his fourth article on Japan with the assertion that his previous statements about the country had all been wrong. He had based himself on his particular experience of Japan and had failed to understand those parts of Japanese culture, such as its indigenous religious heritage, which were not shared with China. Now, however, he suspected indigenous Japanese religious beliefs had made an important contribution to its present policies, Zhou added.[195]

It was in the first three of the articles that Zhou elaborated on the chilly winters and salty foods of Shaoxing and Tokyo. Consequently, it becomes crucial to reconsider them in the context of his subsequent collaboration. When he was writing them, Zhou must have been aware that he was converging to some extent with Japanese thinkers such as Watsuji Tetsurō (1886–1960) in his formulation of the link between climate and temperament. Watsuji, with whose writing Zhou was familiar, was the author of Fūdo (Chinese: fengtu), a study designed to clarify the relationship between climate and life.[196] According to notations at the end of each chapter, the study was drafted for the most part in 1928 and 1929 and revised in 1935. Zhou met Watsuji twice while on his trip to Japan in 1934.[197]

A philosopher admired particularly for his early grasp of Nietzsche, Watsuji has long been regarded as emblematic of the propensity of Japanese intellectuals for a "national narcissism" that eventually cloaked Japanese fascism.[198] Inevitably, we are doubly alerted to the possibility that Zhou's acceptance of certain Japanese intellectual trends may have nudged him toward collaboration with Japan. In Fūdo, prompted by a reading of Heidegger, Watsuji seeks to remedy the lack in Western philosophy of a spatial basis for man's self-objectification, in addition to time.[199] This spatial basis is climate, *fūdo*, the sum total of the "environment." Climate, which is always historical, not only shapes man's existence as a tool-using, social creature but also provides the basis for his self-comprehension. Since man apprehends climate in common with other men, this means his self-understanding must include himself as constituted in social relationships. Watsuji contrasts this view with one in which time alone (i.e., seen from the standpoint of the individual's personal history) is the basis for self-objectification; the result of this view is that the individual is abstracted from society.[200]

Having established this as the philosophical basis of his enterprise, Watsuji then proceeds to divide human cultural types into three climatically governed categories: monsoon, desert, and meadow. Japan and China fall into the monsoon category, in which unrelenting humidity, at once terrifying and life-giving, induces a passive, resigned attitude. Desert dwellers are "aggressive" (in order to wrest a living from their surroundings) and "submissive" (to the group). The gentler European environment—the meadow—was perceived by the Greeks as both docile and regular, thus enabling the development of reason, which remained the hallmark of Europe. Luckily for the Japanese, their cold winters have had a bracing effect on their monsoon character, enabling them to escape from Asian passivity. This type of thinking, with its orientalist overtones and exceptionalist view of Japan, is why Watsuji has been taken as a founding father of *Nihonjinron*, the notorious ideology of Japaneseness.[201]

There is no echo of such comments in Zhou's writing, nor of Watsuji's engagement with philosophy. Whereas Watsuji deployed *fūdo* on the global level, Zhou used the term *fengtu* in relation to locality. Zhou's 1923 "Place and Literature" begins:

> Everybody knows that there is an intimate link between *fengtu* and the inhabitants [of a place]: just as each country's literature has its own special character, within a country differences of style occur between the various regions. The works of literary men from Provence in the south of France are not the same as those from the north, so still more will this be the case in an enormous country like China.[202]

In essays he wrote after his visit to Japan, Zhou often turned to the trope of *mingyun* (fate/destiny) as environment in his reflections on China's situation. But although this concept superficially resembles Watsuji's notions, this was not a new idea for Zhou. In "National Essence and Europeanization," written February 1922, Zhou had described the development of parallelism and regulated verse as part of the fate/destiny of the Chinese language.[203]

In "About Destiny/Fate," an essay written in 1935, Zhou stated that he "believed in *mingyun*."[204] *Ming* he defined as "the nature a person is born with, that is heredity" and *yun* as "later influences, that is to say, environment." The relationship between the two terms was like that between two terms in a mathematical equation. To find their values, one needed a table of logarithms—and that was history. It was essential to read Ming history, because "the situation today is very like that of the Ming." Rather than continue with this train of thought, Zhou then quoted the passage from Kafū he made famous. In this passage, quoted above, Kafū recognizes that he is an Asian, "born into a different fate (*yunming*) and surroundings" from that of the West.

To judge from the thrust of "About Destiny/Fate," Zhou's focus was on Kafū's criticism of Japan. Kafū expressed outrage at the way the powerful could ride roughshod over the rest of society, adding that despite surface changes, the innate Asian spirit of autocracy had not changed in hundreds of years. This was even truer of Japan in the 1930s than when Kafū had written in 1913, Zhou said, whereas China's resemblance to the late Ming could be seen in its *bagu* and its political factions.[205] Zhou's anger at the politicized literature he saw sweeping across China is evident here. He had heard of an essay attacking those who read *Zhuangzi* and the sixth-century anthology, the *Wenxuan*, he says. This kind of thinking is an addiction, the persistence of which constitutes China's fate/destiny. The only cure would be to confront it fearlessly and refuse to be entangled in it, and "only then will one obtain wisdom."[206] In other words, implicated in the fate/destiny of the Chinese is a political environment which resembled that of the late Ming for its chicanery and harsh, literalist demands for ideological orthodoxy.

What this means becomes clearer when we see Zhou, elsewhere, describing the Buddhist ideas of karma (*ye*) and affinity (*yuan*) as "similar" to, but more poetic than, the concepts of heredity and environment.[207] In terms of the Buddhist idealist position that the mind is what creates karma, and that the environments in which beings live arise from their collective karma—that is, their perceptions, mental activities, and the re-sultant actions—Zhou's metaphor blames the contemporary situation of the nation on the way people think and their collective affinity for inher-ited patterns of behavior. By further implication, the remedy for the situation can only be envisaged at the level of the individual, since achievement of clarity of mind can only ever be an individual project.

An underlying focus on modes of thought and feeling explicated in terms of environment is thus common to Zhou and Watsuji, the differ-ence being Watsuji's smugness and normativity and Zhou's anger and gloom. But Watsuji's conclusion contains an interesting twist: now that humanity has acquired knowledge of these climatic zones, it can tran-scend its climatic limitations, in the sense that cultural zones can learn from each other. But, significantly, climatic distinctions will not disap-pear because of this new awareness:

In one sense, a meadow land may well be heaven on earth, but we cannot turn our own land, whatever it may be, into land of the meadow type. We can, however, ac-quire the meadow character and with this our own typhoon character assumes fresh and broader aspects. For when we discover this Greek clarity in ourselves and begin to nourish reason the significance of our own distinctive "perception" or "temper" becomes all the more vital.[208]

Contact with Christianity and European science had created yearnings among the Japanese, but they had failed to realize that "Japan's climate cannot become either meadow or desert," and this lack of discernment remained a problem today, Watsuji concluded.

Although this reasoning can obviously serve arguments for Japanese exclusivity, as it does in contemporary *Nihonjinron* arguments, it could conceivably be used to criticize an unthinking embrace of "reason" in the form of, say, the blind pursuit of industrial rationalization, which spurred Japan's imperialist drive in the first place. In prewar Japan, be-coming completely European was synonymous with becoming the world's leading imperialist power.[209]

William LaFleur has argued that although Watsuji did write things that "meshed with the needs of 'ideological production'" as Japanese im-perialism developed, he also tried to work out "a third option as alterna-tive to what he deemed a suspect Euro-universalism, on the one hand, and a narrow nationalism, on the other."[210] LaFleur's careful argument shows how a decade before he wrote *Fūdo* Watsuji came to equate the anti-Buddhist iconoclasm in Meiji Japan with the destruction of the classical Greek heritage during the European Dark Ages. Inspired by none other than the art historian Okakura Tenshin, Watsuji reacted against the Japanese nativist rejection of Buddhism and saw through the Meiji rhetoric of enlightenment. Buddhism and Greece thus came to hold symbolic value for Taishō intellectuals like Watsuji: Buddhism as a philosophy, a source of Asian cohesiveness, and proof of Japanese cosmopolitanism; Greece as a symbol of reason.

Zhou deployed Buddhism and Greece in his own arguments to make similar points. But the similarity of their projects, I would suggest, owes little to each other and much to the need to question dominant assumptions about culture and the nation at the time. Watsuji's ruminations on the effect of climate (or *fūdo*) on art lead to the conclusion that "in spite of their . . . faithful transplanting of modern European civilization, in the matter of their clothes, their food and their houses the Japanese have been unable to achieve any real Europeanization." [211]

This was what enabled Watsuji to plead that the Japanese should "remain conscious of, and love, our destiny, the destiny to have been born into such a climate," and not see themselves as a "chosen people" but as a people who had their own contribution to make to the world. [212] Whatever stimulus contact with Watsuji in 1934 may have had on Zhou's later formulations, it was certainly more in the form of confirmation of the structures of his mental world, in which environment as *fengtu* already held an important place.

Why did Zhou insist that China and Japan shared the same destiny, even as tension was mounting with Japan? To what extent was he choosing to come to terms with Japanese expansionism? Although Zhou's promotion of the idea of a common East Asian environment could, in the abstract, have "meshed with the needs of [Japanese] ideological production"—to borrow LaFleur's phrase—Zhou opposed Japanese expansionism. "A country's glory is in its culture—its scholarship and art. It is certainly not in its dependent territories or financial or military power," he chided in 1927 and repeated in 1935. He lamented that it was hard to reconcile the culture in his heart with the facts before his eyes; this forced him to admit that "high culture" had probably influenced only a minority in the past and had no influence on the majority at present.[213]

In sum, there was nothing in Zhou's construction of the nation and the individual that can be seen as prompting him to collaborate with Japan. It may be the case that his anti-exceptionalism, the view that there was no real difference between past and present, prevented him from seeing fascism as a qualitatively new formation. What I see as an outgrowth of second-order modernity, he saw as a resurgence of traditional Bakufu autocracy.[214] In this he may have been influenced by the apparently widespread (and misguided) trend among Japanese intellectuals to regard the upsurge of fascism as an embarrassment rather than a threat.[215]

It has been suggested that Zhou's collaboration represented a "cultural choice" between China and Japan, facilitated by his weakened sense of national identity and conviction that China could not win the war.[216] A better argument could be made, I think, based on Zhou's attitude to the issue of loyalty to the state as an ultimate good. Insisting on starving oneself to death after the country had fallen did not benefit the country and was not to be encouraged as part of an ethics of "beneficent ruler and loyal official."[217] Undoubtedly Zhou saw the demands on men for loyalty (qijie) as synonymous with demands for female chastity (zhenjie), which he abhorred. In fact, in the essay that announced his break with the May Fourth movement, Zhou described "forcing people to sacrifice their individuality in the service of an obtuse society" as "quite as unreasonable as enforcing loyalty to a ruler in the name of the Confucian prescribed relationships, or forcing people to go to war in the name of the nation."[218] He recalled with pity the dilemmas of late Ming figures who had to choose between upholding a dynasty that disgusted them and serving the invaders.[219] However, these attitudes, together with Zhou's rejection of popular notions of patriotism, such as those centered on the Song dynasty general Yue Fei (1103–41), are not adequate to explain why he collaborated.[220]

The full explanation probably rests in personal biography and in historical circumstance. Zhou's stated reason for refusing to heed the many public appeals that he leave Peking in 1937 was that he had too many dependents.[221] He finally accepted a position from the puppet authorities after an assassination attempt on him on New Year's Day, 1939, becoming education minister for the North China regime in 1941.[222] Zhou never attempted to explain why he had collaborated. He wrote an essay in 1940 on the futility of providing explanations for one's conduct and quoted it in full in his memoirs, but still without elucidating the reasons for his action.[223]

"His own justification and others' arguments aside," writes Yan, "what becomes truly extraordinary was his courage to raise a voice of protest against Japan's New Order in East Asia."[224] Edward Gunn has demonstrated that during the war Zhou tried to construct a version of Confucianism as Chinese that could not be assimilated to Japanese propaganda. He reiterated his belief in the oneness of humanity and argued that compared with that oneness the differences among peoples were trivial, but he held that Confucianism was the Chinese expression of that humanity.[225] Based as it was on the simple ordering of human relationships that had developed among the Chinese, Confucian thought wavered if the conditions in which the Chinese lived were imperiled, and then there was a danger of chaos.[226] He knew what he was talking about, Zhou said, from having observed "ordinary people" and discerned from their actions what their world outlook was.

Although in the 1920s Zhou had expressed misgivings about the use of mythology in the creation of a national literature, he now suggested that the figures of Yu the floodtamer and Ji the discoverer of cereals represented the Chinese people's outlook on life: to meet life as it came without going to the extremes of seeking eternal life or seeking death. Such a viewpoint was consonant with biology.[227] In 1939, Zhou claimed a personal interest in Yu, whose legend was connected to his own area of Zhejiang and whose temple Zhou had visited. "The Chinese sages and worthies delight in speaking of Yao and Shun, and what they say is profound and wonderful, but they are not the match of Great Yu, whose deeds were more concrete." Yu was a great statesman, a Confucian who was close to the Mohists. Moreover, he added, the peasants in the area could be counted as the descendents of Yu, and it was impossible not to respect them.[228] This shows a definite change in tone from the pessimism about the peasants found in prewar articles. However, if Zhou took Yu as a symbol of the Chinese, nothing in that symbol represented a great departure from his thinking. Yu merely reinforced the prewar themes of his work by illustrating one face of a universal human nature that followed the principles of biology and was intrinsically moral. He brought Yu and Ji into several of his later essays, suggesting that the ideal of service and bodhisattva-like commitment to others, which they exemplified, had been obscured in the discourse of Confucian orthodoxy.[229]

Despite this thematic shift in Zhou's writing, he remained resolutely open to the rest of the world, symbolized by Greece. Writing in 1944, Zhou called for the spirit of Greece to be brought into China to purge it of the "hideousness and the horror" that long years of autocracy and the imperial examination system had left in people's "weary hearts." To this end, he announced that he was translating W. H. D. Rouse's (1863–1950) *Gods, Heroes and Men of Ancient Greece*.[230] He continued to advocate diversity and individuality in writing. At the end of an essay on the Japanese *haibun* form, which combined humor, refinement, and varied levels of diction into a harmonious whole, Zhou commented that *haibun* could not be narrowly defined, for such essays had been written by Bashō, Montaigne, Lamb, and Milne among others. "In my opinion, these all constitute one genre, without regard for whether they are ancient, modern, Chinese, or foreign. The chief characteristic of this genre is that it expresses an individual viewpoint and does not carry messages for any political or religious viewpoint."[231]

Zhou's individualism was supported by his aesthetics, and it is to these that we must now turn.

# THREE

◈

# The Aesthetics of Place and Self

Zhou Zuoren's central contribution to modern Chinese literature—and the foundation of his reputation—was first spelled out in March 1922 by Hu Shi, as he was taking stock of the success of the new literature in the vernacular. Hu distinguished two types of vernacular essay (*baihua sanwen*), of which the long, argumentative essay (*yilunwen*) was one. The success of this form was obvious, Hu said, and he then proceeded to discuss what we may call the essay proper (*sanwen*):

In recent years, the most noticeable development as far as the essay (*sanwen*) is concerned has been the short essay (*xiaopin sanwen*) promoted by Zhou Zuoren and others. This type of short essay uses a mild conversational tone (*pingdan tanhua*) to harbor profound meaning. At times it appears quite awkward (*benzhuo*), but in fact it is quite clever (*huaji*). The success of this kind of literary work thoroughly dispels the superstition that "the vernacular cannot be used for belles lettres."[1]

A more recent assessment by Yang Mu is that Zhou created a literary form and language that "combined the grace and restraint of *wenyan* and the novelty of foreign languages."[2]

The mildness (*pingdan*) noted by Hu Shi, like the grace and restraint of the literary language noted by Yang Mu, point to Zhou's use of traditional Chinese aesthetics. In the 1970s, David Pollard compared Zhou's invocation of concepts such as *quwei, bense,* and *pingdan ziran* (mildness and naturalness) with references to them in traditional literary sources.[3] The framework for Pollard's approach was Zhou's 1932 lecture series on the origins of the New Literature, which rejected the standard May Fourth account of steady linear progress toward vernacular fiction. Instead, Zhou posited an oscillation between the principles of *shi yan zhi* (literature to express the aim or intention) and *wen yi zai dao* (literature to convey the Way). In my reading, Zhou's usage of *quwei* and *bense* is crucial to his attempt to distance literature from politics, which meant, in effect, from the domain of the nation-state, either as primordial imagined community or as political imperative. But in his references to these concepts, he was drawing on and continuing a debate over the relationship of the artist to the tradition that dates back at least as far as the Song dynasty and that continued into the Qing.[4] As we shall see, the notion of the tradition to which the artist might relate was always complicated by efforts to define an orthodox tradition.

In his lectures, Zhou gave a political reading to the *wen yi zai dao / shi yan zhi* dichotomy, asserting that the former principle had held sway during times of strong government and the latter during periods of disorder, which nonetheless favored creativity.[5] Zhou did not need to point out to his audience that both principles had first been enunciated within a Confucian moral philosophical framework, albeit fifteen hundred years apart, and may be interpreted exclusively within that framework. However, Chinese aesthetics draws on a natural philosophy shared by Confucian and Daoist traditions alike, and many of the assumptions of the *Zhuangzi* and *Laozi* have been particularly influential for theories of literature and the arts from Han times on. Zhou, who, as we have seen, was no Confucian sectarian, ridiculed "followers of Confucius" who regarded Daoism as inferior and maintained that China's Daoist and Confucian traditions were transformations of the same basic substance (*qi*).[6]

Underlying the two approaches to creative activity represented by *shi yan zhi* and *wen yi zai dao* in Zhou Zuoren's usage are the divergent answers given in the Confucian and Zhuangzian traditions to what A. C. Graham calls the basic question in Chinese philosophy: "Where is the Way?" to order state and social life.[7] For Confucius, for whom ritual and ceremony were of fundamental importance, nothing was superior to music for "changing ways and transforming customs."[8] For Zhuangzi, music provided a bridge for "mystical rather than intelligible communication with nature," nature being indistinguishable from Heaven or the Way, of which man was an integral part.[9] Thus were established two positions that provided later aestheticians with a fruitful "abiding tension between two parallel inclinations" to see art as both "a means of personal expression and communication of the ineffable" and as an instrument of education in normative values.[10]

Even in Confucius's day, the music associated with the collection of early Zhou songs, dances, and hymns he favored, the Odes (*Shijing*), was falling out of use, leaving only the text behind to assume a central place in the Confucian tradition as its oldest classic.[11] Thus while certain types of music could be labeled good or bad ("lewd," "harsh and conducive to arrogance"), the text was described as unimpeachable.[12] The study of the *Shijing* was governed by the notion that "the Odes articulate aims"—*shi yan zhi*. Steven Van Zoeren explicates the concept of *zhi* in terms of the elements, "heart" (*xin*) and "go" (*zhi*), that make up the character. "The *zhi* is where the heart goes: it is the heart in motion toward an as yet unrealized goal."[13] From its early meaning of "aim" or "ambition," *zhi* came to stand for "the whole thrust of a person's being," whether committed to moral or secular goals.[14]

By the Han, the vocabulary and concerns of the Confucian musical tradition, in which the emotions (*qing*) paralleled the *zhi*, had been incorporated into the discourse on the *Shijing*. The *locus classicus* is the *Preface* to the Odes of the Mao school: "Emotion (*qing*) moves within and takes shape in words. Words are not enough, and so one sighs it. Sighing it is not enough, and so one draws it out in song. Drawing it out in song is not enough, and so all unawares one's hands dance it and one's feet tap it out."[15] The result of this was to make the expression of the *zhi* appear to be a spontaneous overflowing of emotion, unmediated by artistry or calculation.[16] The moral significance of the Odes was seen to lie in their inscription and presentation of the paradigmatically normative aims (*zhi*) of their authors. Moreover, it was held, the study of the Odes would result in transforming the student's personality to conform to the demands of Confucian morality.[17] The assumption that *zhi* could be revealed to those astute enough to see it was then generalized to apply to the *shi* lyric and by extension the entire field of "lyric" writing, including certain types of essay.[18] However, with the *shi* lyric developed an aesthetic that was informed by Zhuangzi's conception of the Way and man's place in, and apprehension of, it.[19] For Zhuangzi, "intentions" (*yi*)—a word sometimes used interchangeably with *zhi*—were of value because they were concerned with something inexpressible, and it was this inexpressible something, not the words that pointed to it, that was to be prized.[20] Human emotions, for Zhuangzi, seem to emerge from the flow of existence (the Way) just as natural phenomena do.[21]

By being aware of these two positions and of the "abiding tension" between them of which Kenneth DeWoskin speaks, as well as of the tensions brought to the Confucian tradition by the split between music and text, or to put it another way, between *qing* and a normative *zhi*,[22] we can avoid the trap of falling into the orthodox Neo-Confucian view of denying the Zhuangzian position and downplaying *qing*. When Song Neo-Confucianism surfaced as part of a complex process of institutional and ideological change, the transformative function ascribed to the classics was reiterated as a duty for all literary endeavor. This was expressed as *wen yi zai dao* by Zhou Dunyi (1017–73), the man Zhu Xi credited with recovering the Dao that had not been transmitted since Mencius.[23]

Zhou Zuoren's appropriation of the *shi yan zhi* formulation to express the true goal of literature draws on what we could call the Confucian textual and musical positions and the Zhuangzian ineffable. That is to say, he made the idea of *zhi* as "the thrust of a person's being" central to his literary practice—a point demonstrated below in the discussion of *bense*. Having elevated the importance of literature by linking it (through his use of the expression *shi yan zhi*) so crucially to the writer's being, Zhou nonetheless refused to accept that one's deepest aims (and their literary expression) were bound by a normative social or political context. Therefore he cited the Confucian musical idea ("the emotions move within and take form in words") to describe the function of literature.

My view is no different from this. Literature only has emotions (*ganqing*) and not aims. If we had to say literature had a goal, that goal would be simply to "speak out." Just as when we talk about the weather in winter, we often say, "Today's really cold!" The intention behind this is certainly not to borrow money from the other person to have some clothes made, but just to very plainly and artlessly speak out this feeling (*ganjue*) and that's all.[24]

It seems puzzling at first that Zhou's example of the expression of such emotions is a banal exclamation about the weather, but weather for him signifies the shaping force of environment. Thus there is a closer relationship between "the thrust of one's being" and mere "feelings" than is apparent at first glance. More to the point here, perhaps, one could say that "weather" is a perfect example of "nature" and hence "the Way" and that literature expresses nothing more than the alignment of the possessor of "emotions and feelings" with it. If *zhi* and *qing* are now closely assimilable, they are contextualized within the sphere of Zhuangzi's concern for the ineffable as the ground of existence. Zhou had foreshadowed this position as early as 1922 in an essay on the contemporary small poem (*xiao shi*):

> In form, the small poem seems somewhat novel. In fact it is the very ordinary kind of lyrical poem (*shu qing shi*) that has been in existence ever since ancient times. Poetry (*shi*) has always been something that "articulated aims" (*yan zhi*). Although it could also be used to narrate or reason, its essential quality was predominantly to tell of the emotions (*shu qing*). From the ardent, profound emotions such as the bitterness and sweetness of love, the grief and happiness of parting, reunion, life, and death, naturally one can compose all kinds of grand and sweeping works. But our daily life is full of emotions that are not so pressing but are just as real. They arise in a moment and disappear just as quickly. They cannot last long enough to form the quintessence of a work of art, but they are enough to express the moment by moment changes in our inner life. In one sense it is this that is actually our real life.[25]

In other words, we could say that for Zhou the transient phenomena of human life and the natural world, which are privileged as that which is "actually our real life," become the true subject of literature, the task of which remains the expression of *zhi*.

Zhou differed significantly in the meanings he ascribed to *shi yan zhi* from Zhu Ziqing (1898–1948), whose 1947 *Shi yan zhi bian* remains a primary scholarly text on the subject. In fact, Zhu referred, with implicit disapproval, to Zhou's reading of literary history in his preface:

> In the modern period some people have used "poetry to articulate aims" and "literature to convey the Way" as markers of the two main currents of Chinese literature, saying that the rise and fall of these two has shaped Chinese literary history. *The meaning of "poetry to articulate aims" was originally more or less the same as "literature to convey the Way"*[italics added]; the two were certainly not in conflict. But now "poetry to articulate aims" has been opposed to "literature to convey the Way."[26]

Since Zhu considers the two expressions virtually synonymous, it is not surprising that he restricts the scope of *shi yan zhi* to the domain of *zheng-jiao*—transformation through education for the sake of rulership.[27] This he contrasts with Lu Ji's (261–303) dictum that "the poem (*shi*) follows from the affections and is sensuously intricate" (*shi yuan qing er qimi*), which he sees as marking the beginning of a poetry "singing of things" (*yong wu*) divorced from politics.[28] Stephen Owen, whose translation I have used, notes that Lu Ji's line "is indeed grounded in the traditional etymological definition" of *shi*, but the substitution of *qing* for *zhi* "is significant, and has been the subject of much discussion as a watershed in the understanding of poetry." He adds that the traditional Mao school exegesis of *zhi*, being strictly limited to the political and ethical "would have been too narrow" for poetry (*shi*) as it was practiced in Lu Ji's time.[29]

It is clear that for Zhu Ziqing, poetry as conceived by Lu Ji, far from widening the purview of poetry, could be nothing more than a very minor field, albeit one that survived better than the *xuanyan shi* (poetry on the profound) on Daoist themes.[30] Although Zhu Ziqing shows that the terms *qing* and *zhi* were used interchangeably over a very long period of time (particularly during the innovative Six Dynasties period), he seems to consider this to have been for the most part an attempt to buttress the somewhat dubious values of *qing* with the prestige of the absolute norm of *zhi*.[31] Perhaps Zhu's interpretation was colored by the pejorative connotations of frivolity that came to be attached by Ming and Qing critics to the "sensuous intricacy" (*qimi*) Lu Ji deemed the primary quality of poetry. Yet, as Owen remarks, "The essential attribute of poetry here is not principle (*li*) or the individual's engagement in social reality (although that is by no means excluded) but rather capturing the 'quality' of inner life."[32] This, it seems to me, is very close to Zhou's view of lyricism above. In Zhu's opinion, *qing* remained overshadowed by *zhi* until the Qing dynasty, when Yuan Mei (1716–98) commented that "a laborer thinking about his wife can *yan zhi*" and equated *qing* with the relations between the sexes. In this way, Zhu added, the expression *shi yan zhi* acquired its modern association with *shu qing shi*, the Chinese term used to translate the Western category of lyric poetry.[33]

The problem with Zhu Ziqing's analysis, as I see it, lies in his insistence that *zhi* can exist only in relationship to the traditional political process. This leads him to detach *qing* from any other serious or existential concerns, such as the quality of inner life, until the modern period when *shu qing* (lyricism) exists only in the narrow framework of emotions associated with romantic love. Moreover, he ignores the Zhuangzian dimension to literary creation, namely, the effort to express the inexpressible. The inexpressible should not be understood in theological terms. The assertion of Daoist thinkers that the Way is not communicable in words may lead some to feel that their concerns are irrelevant to literature. But as A. C. Graham points out, Daoists are trying to communicate "a knack, an aptitude, a way of living. . . . [They] do not think in terms of discovering Truth or Reality. They merely have the good sense to remind us of the limitations of the language which they use to guide us towards that altered perspective on the world. . . . Far from having no need for words they require all available resources of literary art, which is why all the classics of philosophical Taoism have won important places in the literary history of China."[34] The result, as James Liu asserts, is that "the awareness of the paradoxical nature of language and of poetry led Chinese poets not to abandon poetry but to develop a poetics of paradox, which may be summarized as the principle of saying more by saying less. . . . In practice, this poetics manifested itself in the preference . . . for implicitness over explicitness, conciseness over verbosity, obliqueness over directness and suggestion over description."[35]

Zhu Ziqing's narrow interpretation of *qing* and his stress on *zhengjiao* led him to completely misread Zhou Zuoren's use of the term *shi yan zhi*, which he saw as derived from Yuan Mei and foreign ideas of lyricism.[36] Following Zhu, Pollard suggests that the parallel in the West for Zhou's use of *shi yan zhi* would be Wordsworth's premium on the "spontaneous overflow of powerful feelings."[37] This raises the question of why Zhou chose the expression *shi yan zhi* instead of *shi shu qing*; Pollard answers by suggesting that "Zhou was asserting his sense of continuity with the tradition."[38] This is moving in the right direction, but it is not enough, because it does not come to grips with the notion of tradition. And it does not do so because it does not focus on the Chinese tradition of literary thought as, again in Owen's terms, a perennially fruitful terrain within which problematic areas of human endeavor (writing) and subjectivity can be explored.[39]

For Zhu Ziqing (as indeed in the dominant interpretation of Chinese intellectual and literary history since the rise of Neo-Confucianism), the periods when the political conception of *zhi* held sway were "normal" and others such as the Six Dynasties aberrant. In contrast, Zhou Zuoren accepted these periods as culturally legitimate. Once we understand this and see their literature as a product of what DeWoskin calls the "abiding tension" in the aesthetic tradition, Zhuangzi becomes our point of entry into Zhou's aesthetics.

## Literature and the Ineffable

At the beginning of his lecture series, Zhou answered his own rhetorical question "What is literature?" by stating that since no one has even been able to answer it, no two definitions are alike. In fact it is an "intrinsically difficult" matter. Although some fields of knowledge, such as chemistry and biology (with the periodic table of the elements and the theory of evolution as examples), can state with certainty what is true and what is false, "philosophy and religion and so on cannot produce these kinds of absolute truth." There is no sure way of choosing among the innumerable schools of philosophy that had arisen since ancient Greek times or to determine which is right and which are wrong. This is equally true in matters of religion, a fact that gave rise to the agnostic position. Literature, too, must be one of these fields "in which ultimate knowledge is lacking"; consequently, "it is very hard to define."[40]

Literature thus shares the unfathomability and multiplicity of manifestations of religion and philosophy. All three are concerned with something to which it is impossible to apply the kind of analysis that produces absolute truths, and none can be circumscribed by one definition. Zhou makes the same suggestion in more fanciful language in explaining the reason for the title of his 1927 book *Tan long ji* (Talking about dragons):

We (strictly speaking, I ought to say I) like to talk about literature, but in fact this comes down to shooting one's mouth off for a while. Sometimes we still haven't clearly understood literature itself. It's just as if we were writing a dragon classic or doing an ink painting of a dragon. If it were asked what kind of creature a dragon was, none of us would have seen one. There is a story that once there was a Lord She who was so fond of dragons he had crammed his house with carved and painted dragons. But when a real dragon descended, he was scared out of his wits, and to this day he remains a laughingstock. I'm afraid that I am just as ludicrous. However, I do understand one thing: I know at least that what I am talking about is a false dragon, but I persist in wanting to talk about them, without asking them to produce rain or give me some dragon ambergris. For those who want to know about real dragons, please go and look for Mr. Tame Dragon. I have got nothing of the sort here. So I can just talk empty talk, and now I am talking about illusory dragons, so that the emptiness of my empty talk will be even more easy to grasp.[41]

Like a dragon, then, literature is ungraspable; when it can be grasped and made "real" and able to serve some utilitarian purpose, it becomes a contradiction in terms, a tame dragon. It can be talked about, as long as we remember that whatever can be said is not real but false. The ideas of ungraspability and inexpressibility (all talk is empty) recall the Daoist paradox of the uncommunicability of the Way and its corollary that the philosopher must use every verbal art at his disposal to point to it. Zhou's earlier idea that no one can chose what is wrong or right among the multitude of philosophical schools brings to mind Zhuangzi's parable of the wind, which makes different sounds as it blows through different hollows but is all the same wind.[42]

This analogy presupposes a basic agreement among philosophers about the object of their inquiry. For Zhou, the philosophical/religious and the aesthetic are points on a continuum, rather than opposites. Thus he held the Chan Buddhist notion of the uselessness of words

most correct. We can almost say it is the most ideal kind of art, but in fact art has aspired to but cannot realize this ideal; perhaps only music has a little of this quality. Literature, which is caught up in the entanglement of words and language, grasps at symbols to fight its way out, but it can never quite make it.[43]

In the light of Zhou's frequent comments that he had no religious beliefs (although he distinguished this from being "anti-religious"), the suggestion that there was a transcendent or ungraspable reality, which could be pointed at, even if it always lay just beyond literature's grasp, may seem surprising.[44] However, Zhou was able to bring "the ineffable" into his literary theory and practice by drawing on the late Ming Neo-Confucian counter-tradition, which posited that the Way could be grasped as, and may constitute, the ordinary and the everyday and, by extension, be desacralized. In fact, Zhou's innovation lies precisely in the uncertain gap between religious concerns and literary ones. In his lectures, Zhou placed the origin of literature in religion. Religion he equated with politics—both came into existence originally as ways of helping men to live. Citing examples from ancient China and Greece, Zhou suggested that literature began with ritual, designed to placate gods or natural forces:

> For instance, ancient China had a rite to welcome spring. Its earliest aim was to make sure spring was welcomed in order to help the growth of the five grains and livestock. At that time it was thought that without this kind of rite, winter would stay forever without leaving and spring never return. . . . In Greece it was also like this.[45]

In Zhou's Greek example, once people realized that spring would arrive without fail, they still participated in the ceremonies but as spectators enjoying the fun. Gradually the form of the ceremonies changed and transformed into the Greek dramatic form of the tragedy. Thus literature broke away from religion and came into its true function as it came to express feelings, with no ameliorative hopes or propagandistic intent.[46]

This explanation for the origin of literature may have come from Jane Harrison, but Zhou made brilliant use of it: By equating politics and religion and disconnecting both from an (implicit) ineffable, Zhou was able to deflect the overarching force of the May Fourth nation-building project from what remained. This was not only the individual but also the ordinary and the everyday, which were, in a sense, resacralized. The process I refer to as resacralization is most clearly understood and realized in relation to the aesthetic category of flavor (quwei), to be discussed below.

However, the qualities of mildness and naturalness noted by Hu Shi in Zhou's work also sprang from the same cleared space, for with the removal of the weight of politics and religion from literature, the deployment of alternative perspectives becomes a possibility. Shortly after the establishment of the League of Left-wing Writers in 1930, Zhou confronted the threat of ideological control with a series of essays grouped together under the title "Grass, Trees, Insects, and Fishes."

In his "Preface to Grass, Trees, Insects, and Fishes"—the essay in which he spoke approvingly of the Chan idea of the uselessness of words—Zhou wrote of the many difficulties surrounding writing, political as well as literary.

> When I write, I often feel two difficulties: the first: what to say, the second, how to say it. According to Mr. Hu Shi, this is very easy to resolve, because you just have to "say what you want to say," and "let it just come out as you say it" and everything's fine. But for me, it's a very big problem. Of course, there are some things I do not want to say, but there are also some that I do, and at present there is no way to say

them. This doesn't just refer to major political issues. Even if I were to talk occasionally about children or women, there's no guarantee someone won't be able to find traces of reaction there, proof that I've fallen behind, and so come upon what the ancients called "calamity which comes by the pen" (biwo).[47]

The problem of content was troublesome enough, but expression was an even thornier problem. Here, Zhou expressed doubts about whether it was possible ever to express "emotions" (qing) completely in words (yan). Sighing, moving one's hands and feet, might convey emotions of affection (qing-yi), but they would need many changes and distance before they had become art fit to show anyone. By that time what remained would be very insignificant. "The sorrow of death, the joy of love, the deepest griefs, happinesses, the sweetness and bitterness of human life, can simply not be described in speech, let alone writing," he said, at least not by "ordinary people like myself."[48] The only kind of the affective emotions that could be expressed in words was that which, "while not too superficial, is also not very profound (shenqie). In other words, it is really something that is optional, not crucial, that is expressed just to comfort and divert oneself." From the context it is clear that Zhou is using the word profound in its sense of heartfelt and referring to the acuteness with which these emotions are experienced, rather than their place in a scale of value or authenticity.

Next Zhou discussed the "uselessness" of literature, compared with the power of words, such as those used in threats, death warrants, or ritual invocations that comforted those who made them. If, as he believed, sincerity (cheng) and intelligibility (da) were the prerequisites of literature, yet both were so hard to achieve, what was left?

To tell the truth, I am incapable of producing Chan literature, and I do not want to produce a literature of imprecations, and since ordinary literature cannot conquer the entanglement of words . . . isn't this the same thing as that "there is nothing that can be said?" Yet, despite this, it is still possible to write, to want to write. The crucial point is right here: having realized that there is nothing in the world that can be said, and that there is no possibility of my producing true literature, I then knew that there was no reason why I shouldn't just choose any topic and earnestly set myself to write, and perhaps at that time, perhaps it would be possible simply to say that there was nothing in the world that could not be said.[49]

Zhou did not see this as a simple matter. "This is also going to be very difficult and will need a lot of trial and error; it is not something that can be reached in one step." He concluded his preface by explaining why he had chosen to write on plants, trees, insects, and fish.[50]

First, they are things I am fond of. Second, they are also living creatures, very much connected to us, but in the end they belong to different species, so there is something for us to talk about. Just suppose there comes a time when it is not acceptable to talk about them, all is still not lost, we'll be able to talk about the weather.[51]

The last sentence links up neatly with Zhou's opening reflections on the political constraints on writing and adds a sense of urgency to what he has just said. As a literary topic, the weather seems to be the minimum demand, below even fish and trees in potential subversiveness. Yet as we have seen, when he gave his lectures on literary history in 1932, two years after composing the preface, the example Zhou gave of the kinds of feeling that literature expresses was precisely that—the weather. Although this could be seen as a political jibe, Zhou answers the central question of what it was possible to write about by mentioning first philosophical and literary concerns and only second political issues. Out of the tension between the political and the literary, Zhou sought answers to a number of questions: How was one to judge what was important about life, how did one hierarchize the emotions, how did one draw boundaries between the trivial and casual and the serious and noteworthy? And what result did this ordering and demarcation—or its rejection—have on the boundaries of the literary self?

The seven essays grouped with the "Small Preface to Grasses, Trees, Insects, and Fishes" in the *Gazing at Clouds* collection can be seen as an effort to explore these questions in practice, an effort that succeeds in illustrating the illusory nature of these boundaries. At first glance, the topics—goldfish, lice, trees, bats, the stalk of the amaranth plant—seem unlikely to thrill the reader. Zhou's texts succeed in holding the reader's attention because they are vehicles not just for the initial "emotions" of authorial liking or disliking but for his erudition, memories, and trains of thought, intellectual as well as emotional. The essays were written over a period of a year and a half, and all but two first appeared in print elsewhere.[52] The months separating the writing of the first essay and the last no doubt accounts for their varied tone; it is unlikely Zhou would have achieved such diversity had he written them in order to prove how restricted the intellectual climate had become. "Scarecrows" and "Lice" are humorous; "Denizens of the Water," written in a particularly intimate conversational style, explores with great affection beliefs about water spirits held in Zhejiang and Japan. Intellectual freedom and curiosity are the hallmarks of these essays, which means that they do reflect on political and social matters. Indeed the first essay in the set, "Goldfish," contains veiled suggestions that Zhou was re-acting to events in the literary world. In my view he is responding to the February 1930 establishment of the League of Left-wing Writers by chal-lenging himself to come up with something better.[53]

I think there are just two kinds of essays in the world, one kind has a title and one does not. Normally, in writing essays one has an idea, but not a definite title. It is only after the ideas have been written down and the whole thing summarized that the title is added. It seems easy to shine within [the scope of] this kind of essay, because one can express oneself comparatively freely, although it is a difficult matter to write the title afterwards. However, sometimes one's thinking is chaotic and lacking in concen-tration and one just has no idea what to write about. In this case settling on the title first and then writing has its advantages, despite the slight possibility it may approach expository writing ( *fude* ) and the danger of turning out an examination poem on a set theme ( *shi tie shi* ).[54]

A. A. Milne, in desperation at having to come up with an essay for his publishers, had once leafed through the dictionary in search of a topic and come up with goldfish, Zhou continued.

I thought this was very interesting, and so I am going to try my hand at writing on goldfish. In any case, since I do not have any great correct way that I absolutely have to voice or give first priority to publishing, there is no reason why I should not choose to write an expository "poem on things" ( *yongwu shi* ), although in my case I am not being badgered [by my publishers].

He then begins his ruminations on goldfish, beginning with his dislike of the bulging eyes of the artificially bred creature, which made it as repulsive and comical as the lapdog with its turned-up nose. The clumsy movements and bright colors of the goldfish reminded him of a traditional bride, clothed in red and tottering about on bound feet. Perhaps the Chinese liking for goldfish was in the same category as the liking for bound feet? He cared for neither and preferred ordinary fish, found in natural habitats and barely discernable among the weeds.

The essay ends with an important statement:

I have not done any writing for a few months, and the national situation ( *tianxia de xingshi* ) seems to have undergone a great change; consequently those who are of the intent to write new literature find it very hard to be noticed unless they sing one particular tune. Since I have never been a literary person, these changes in fashion have nothing to do with me in any case. But from the position of an observer [of literature], I feel they can be approved. Why is that? There are eternally two trends in literature, the speaking of intention (*yan zhi*) and the conveying of the Way (*zai dao*). Of these two, to convey the Way is easy, and to speak of intention difficult. This expository essay on goldfish began with a title and so is somewhat like an examination essay (*tiekuo*). Perhaps it may even be that it is a little short on *yan zhi* and long on *zai dao*? Although I have not dared to [count myself] as part of the new literature, I still think [this essay of mine] has fresh, new implications. That is why I have noted this here, with the intention of effecting a change in current styles.[55]

The three concluding sentences are written in *wenyan*. We can agree with Zhou that this essay, with its criticism of the national character, is perhaps a little heavier on *zai dao* than one would expect. What is surprising is his response to the recent upsurge of didacticism. Rather than directly express angry or sorrowful disapproval at the dominance of just one tune, he approves of its existence. This is an astute move to naturalize the *zai dao* trend into something that has always been there, against which his own efforts at *yongwu shi* represent something new and fresh. At the same time, this stance itself accounts for the quality of imperturbability (*pingdan*) found in the text. Taken as a whole, the essays bear out the claim in the "Small Preface" that there is an intrinsic value in writing about plants, insects, trees, and fishes, that they are "living creatures, very much connected to us."

The claim of intrinsic value for these living creatures, or indeed for anything appertaining to the "ordinary and the everyday," was best rendered in literary terms through the aesthetics of *quwei*. This was the category through which Zhou was able to detach the quotidian from dominant orthodoxies such as politics and religion. But the very recognition of their implicit value functions to resacralize them.

The many implications of resacralization can usefully be approached in terms of the debate on the relation of the artist to the tradition, which informed and shaped the aesthetic concepts Zhou chose to use. Consequently, a good starting place for this enquiry is a work that has been described as providing the "mainstream of critical impulse and theoretical direction" for Chinese poetry from Song to Qing. This is the *Canglang shihua* (Canglang's notes on poetry), written by Yan Yu (1187?–1264?).[56] This work encapsulates what we can loosely call the Zhuangzian ineffable and the evolving normative Neo-Confucian positions on literary creation, which is perhaps why it has been so seminal.[57] In particular, I am concerned with the nature of *qu*, implicitness, which is found in the binome *quwei*. Even as the *Canglang shihua* strongly influenced the fifteenth- and sixteenth-century literary critics known as the Former Seven and Later Seven Masters (*qianhou qizi*) in establishing an orthodox canon centered on the Tang poet Du Fu (721–70), the Zhuangzian position it enunciated allowed for other approaches. By the early Ming the normative Neo-Confucian position had become dominant, only to be challenged in the late Ming by radical Neo-Confucian thinkers. The question of how literary excellence relates to language was a perennial subject in the Chinese literary tradition, as is evident from the importance of the Zhuangzian paradox. As we will see, the *Canglang shihua* also touches on this. Qing writers went further into the question of the connections between language and literary excellence. This issue, which cannot be separated from that of the writer's relation to tradition, came to have a pressing urgency in the modern period.

The first chapter of the *Canglang shihua* makes three main assertions. The first is that poetry written in the Han, Wei, and Jin dynasties and in the time span known in Chinese literary periodization as the High Tang comprise the orthodox tradition. This corpus must be mastered so that it "ferments within one's breast," after which one will "spontaneously apprehend ultimate reality" (*ziran wuru*).[58] It was this proposition that, taken on its own, seemed to make the individual writer completely dependent on tradition, for without it, there could be no apprehension of ultimate reality. The question is whether orthodoxy was a starting point or an end in itself. Second, the pinnacle of attainment in poetry is "entering the spirit" (*ru shen*), which only Li Bai and Du Fu have achieved. The third proposition is the most notorious one: poetry can be discussed in the same terms as the Chan Buddhist tradition (*lun shi ru lun chan*). It can be divided into schools and sects, whose adherents are capable of attaining various degrees of enlightenment.[59] Thus, just as enlightenment in the Chan tradition can be reached through the methods of sudden enlightenment (*dun wu*) or gradual cultivation (*jian xiu*), so enlightenment for the practitioner of poetry can be reached through "poetry as meditation" (*can shi*) and "established models" (*ding fa*).[60] Moreover, the parallel between Chan and poetry is not just limited to similarities of approach, for, in fact, the "marvelous enlightenment" at which both aim is the same. According to the text, "In general, the way of Chan lies only in marvelous enlightenment, and the way of poetry also lies in marvelous enlightenment."[61] The analogy between Chan and poetry has been controversial—needlessly so, if we see enlightenment not in sectarian terms but in terms of the Zhuangzian idea of "communicating the ineffable" and the broader formulations of *shi yan zhi* such as that of Lu Ji. The real problem is the relationship between mastering the orthodox tradition and achieving, or conveying, the quality of enlightenment. Yan Yu notes that although Meng Haoran (689–740) had far less learning than Han Yu, his poems stood out far above Han Yu's since they are pervaded with marvelous enlightenment. "Only [the quality of] enlightenment constitutes 'plying one's proper trade' (*danghang*) and "showing one's real colors" (*bense*) [of poetry].[62]

Following Gong Pengcheng, I interpret *bense* and *danghang* as referring here to the established literary conventions and standards expected of *shi* poetry.[63] In other words, what made a *shi* poem a *shi* poem was its ability to convey the quality of "marvelous enlightenment," and this was not dependent on the poet's erudition. Having established enlightenment as the hallmark of a *shi* poem, Yan Yu developed the idea:

Poetry is concerned with a particular kind of material (*bie cai*) that is not related to books; poetry involves a particular kind of implicit meaning (*bie qu*) that is not related to principles (*li*).[64] Nonetheless, if one does not exert oneself in reading books and probing principles to the utmost, one will not be able to reach the ultimate of poetry. That which has been called "not stepping on the road of principles, not falling into the fishtrap of words" is superior. Poetry is what sings of one's emotions and nature (*yinyong qingxing*).

This last sentence has proved contentious. My translation for it follows James Liu, who gives equal weight to the two halves of the binome: *qing* (emotions, affections) and *xing*, which Stephen Owen usefully renders as "individuating nature."[65]

The *locus classicus* for the expression *yinyong qingxing* is the Preface to the Mao text of the *Shijing*. "The historians of the states understood clearly the marks of success and failure; they were pained by the abandonment of proper human relations and lamented the severity of punishments and governance. They sang their feeling (*yinyong xingqing*) to criticize those above."[66] Although in its original context the semantic weight of the terms falls most heavily on emotions and there is no need to reiterate the poet's inborn nature that serves as their ground, Liu's translation is sensitive to the full range of meanings—feelings and nature—in the binome. But the problematical nature of the expression in the context of Yan Yu's text can be seen from the fact that Richard Lynn omits it and Zhang Jian considers it out of place.[67]

The reason it has posed so many difficulties is that its interpretation touches directly on the question of the proper scope of poetry. Owen judges Yan Yu's use of the hoary phrase to be "an evasion, a hiding of his tracks" because he feels that Yan Yu's seeking after "an ineffable presence of truth" is in direct opposition "to the traditional concept of poetry 'singing what is in the heart,' which is inseparable from the individuality of the poet and the particularity of the poet's circumstances."[68] But whether seeking the ineffable presence of truth does in fact compromise individuality and particularity, whether the two are mutually exclusive, is a moot point. I shall argue that the "ineffable," when posited *against* imitation, actually became the ground from which it was possible to assert individuality. Owen's position draws on the animus against the Zhuangzian ineffable strand in Chinese literary tradition (particularly when expressed in Buddhist terms), which no doubt accounts for his pervasive scorn of Yan Yu.[69]

The *Canglang* continues:

For the High Tang poets, the main thing in their work was inspired implicit meaning (*xingqu*), like the antelope that hangs by its horns, leaving no traces to be found. So the marvelousness of their poetry lies in a crystalline transparency that cannot be seized; like sound in the air, color in appearances, the moon in water, the image in a mirror, the words have limits, but the meaning cannot be exhausted.[70]

My translation of *xingqu* as "inspired implicit meaning" (in which *qu* "implicit meaning" is the same character as found in *quwei*—flavor) is based on the readings of Zhang Jian and Gong Pengcheng. Zhang considers *xingqu* to be that which the poem conveys of the poet's experience of enlightenment. Since enlightenment is specifically independent of words, *xingqu* is the necessarily indirect and implicit echo or lingering flavor the work leaves with the reader.[71] Gong says that "that which Yan Yu calls '*xingqu*'" is "a nonobjective apprehension without a definite basis in objective knowledge," which gives the poem its beauty and special quality.[72] Thus *xingqu*, rather than being a quality of the poet, as James Liu seems to suggest, is a quality of the poem.[73] The text next reinforces its delineation of the ortho-dox tradition by listing the problems with the poetry of "recent times": it was discursive, intent on displaying the writer's talent and erudition, lack-ing in musicality. Disregarding "inspired intent" (*xing zhi*), the worst poets indulged in anger and abusive language.

There is, however, a problem, for if the orthodox tradition can be de-fined in terms of the inspired implicit meaning of enlightenment plus for-mal attributes such as euphony, what of the statement that the ultimate attainment of poetry is "entering the spirit" (*rushen*) and only Du Fu and Li Bai did this?[74] We can flesh out the meaning of *rushen* by turning to the passage that precedes the reference to Li Bai and Du Fu.

The properties of poetry are nine: nobility (*gao*), classicalness (*gu*), profundity (*shen*), distance or import (*yuan*), majesty (*chang*), heroic abandon (*xiong hun*), untrammeled-ness (*piao yi*), tragic valor (*bei zhuang*), and grieving submissiveness (*qiwan*). The three artistic aspects that have to be relied on are opening and closure, lines and structure, and diction. Poetry has two general polarities: carefree and uncompelled, and fortitude in grief. The ultimate in poetry is called "entering the spirit."[75]

This list recalls the celebrated *Twenty-Four Properties of Poetry* of Sikong Tu (837–908), whose poetics, according to some scholars, greatly influenced Yan Yu.[76] Maureen Robertson has suggested that in the mode of impres-sionistic criticism in which Sikong was writing, the critic seeks to provide a record of his own aesthetic response rather than to reveal features of a par-ticular artwork. She comments, "such a practice supposes that there are *categories* of appeal," encompassing natural and artistic phenomena, "that there is . . . a certain type of aesthetic appeal which [for example] leaping monkeys and vigorous angular brushstrokes share, an aesthetic message they both convey."[77]

The possibility that Yan Yu's list referred to categories of appeal rather than types of poetic style to which each poet could be assigned is an inter-esting track. As Robertson notes in passing, "from earliest times, Chinese philosophy had portrayed a world which was explainable in terms of corre-spondences which included both observable phenomena and abstrac-tions."[78] What this meant for poetry was that, to a remarkable degree, im-ages from the natural world became contexts for emotional or intellectual themes and vice versa. "Realizing this lends greater significance to [Si-kong's] phrase of 'mergence of thought with setting,'" which was "an extremely important notion in post-Tang criticism," Robertson says, and was "explored further by Yen Yu in the notion of 'rushen.'"[79]

Pauline Yu has demonstrated the central place of imagery in Chinese poetry and the way in which Chinese concepts of *bi* and *xing* (comparison and stimulus) differ from Western ideas of metaphor. Whereas metaphor is ideally plucked out of thin air and prized for its fictive artifice and novelty, the Chinese comparison/stimulus is based on an evocative image from a pre-established shared cultural code.[80] This principle was established in the earliest Chinese poetry. As the tradition developed, the idea of a conventional one-to-one relationship between images and ideas was challenged. Tang poetry [saw] the "'identification of the world of things and the world of ideas,' uniting the goals of 'expressing one's intent' by allowing sensuous imagery to embody meaning without discursive formulation."[81] The identity between the real world and the world of ideas, and eventually the integration of the self and the scene, came to constitute the heart of the Tang poetic achievement. Indeed, the image (or series of images) that served as the stimulus (*xing*) no longer functioned to introduce a topic that pointed to the "real" subject matter of a work but became the very center of the poem.[82] Owen's explication of *xing* as an "affective image" presented in words and able to "stir" a response or evoke a mood, unmediated by rational understanding but appealing to the affections, is also very suggestive.[83]

If excellence at manipulating imagery and perceiving and suggesting correspondences indirectly is what constitutes *rushen*, it becomes clearer why Du Fu and Li Bai would come to exemplify it.[84] In their work, the images document personal experience in unprecedented ways, yet the impression is always that the poet actually saw the images, and that "whatever intellectual or affective meaning they convey is something they embody or illustrate of themselves, embodied—not contrived—by the poet."[85] The process by which the poet came to find the image has been described as follows:

As important as conscious effort and laborious study may be to the writing of a poem, equally or more valuable is the poet's ability to adopt a more passive attitude and allow himself to be affected by and reflect spontaneously the world around him. This view can be traced back, of course, to some of the earliest Taoist, and then Buddhist, notions of ideal modes of behavior and cognition, ideas which were basic to critical texts before and after the Tang.[86]

*Rushen*, then, both is and is not related to enlightenment, for if enlightenment is a prerequisite for perceiving the images, it is also necessary to have a command of the existing poetic stock of images and a sensitivity to the possibilities within the language expressing them. This is something that both Li Bai and Du Fu had, in part thanks to the High Tang "rediscovery" of the poetic past in which both participated, albeit in very different ways.[87] For Yan Yu, Du Fu was more easily emulated than Li Bai, because he was the supreme synthesizer. "The poetry of Shaoling [Du Fu] finds its rules and regulations in the Han and Wei and obtains its materials in the Six Dynasties. As for the marvelousness which he himself achieves, this is what earlier generations have called the synthesis of the great achievements."[88]

## Archaism and the Late Ming Counter-tradition

It is precisely because Li Bai and Du Fu could be seen as ideal perceivers of images, both in the real world and in the poetic tradition, that there is a doubleness to the quality of *rushen*, an ambiguity about what should be contemplated. Thus, it was quite possible in a certain intellectual climate for the passive attitude before the world to be transferred to the world of books, in the end to the exclusion of the real world and one's own real experience. Such a trend was encouraged by the archaist literary movement of the Former and Later Seven Masters of the fifteenth and sixteenth centuries.[89] Although the ostensible concern of poetry remained enlightenment, the archaist movement came to serve the didactic purposes of providing a set of texts to study, which reinforced notions of cultural and political orthodoxy. As the notion of enlightenment lost its connotations of being grounded in individual experience and was considered accessible solely through book learning, poetry came to be seen as a form of self-molding—the ideal poet became an ideal cultural type.[90] The result was plagiarism and mediocrity, although the archaists differed considerably among themselves on the role of individual personality and the harmfulness of plagiarism.[91] The archaists were strongly oriented toward the Cheng-Zhu school, sharing its commitment to large-scale book learning.[92] If the principle of the investigation of things (*gewu*) could be extended to books as well as plants and insects, it could be extended to individual poems or authors.[93]

However, although Ming thought has been characterized as a continuation of Cheng-Zhu orthodoxy, as well as a protest against this orthodoxy, given expression in the school of Wang Yangming (1472–1529), it differed significantly from the Song in that "the Ming Confucians are more inner-oriented, almost always starting with the questions of mind and human nature and moving from these to an understanding of the wider world; whereas Sung thinkers, from Chou Tun-yi to Ch'eng Yi and Chu Hsi, take as their starting point the external universe, especially questions of cosmology, before moving to the personal universe of mind and nature."[94]

Despite the prominence of the archaists and, not surprisingly, given the reductionist use of cultural resources that archaism represented, a counter-tradition stressing the role of the writer's personal nature also existed during the Ming. Following Guo Shaoyu (1893–1984), Lynn traces its beginnings to the writing of the Yuan-Ming transitional figure Yang Weizhen (1296–1370), whom he sees as anticipating the late Ming Gongan school (named for Gongan in Hubei, home of the three Yuan brothers who were its core figures).[95] Yang identified poetry with the "personal nature" (xing-qing) of the poet, did not insist upon any set of perfect models, and said that no distinction could be made between the personal and spiritual qualities of the men of antiquity and those of the present.[96] The Japanese scholar Yoshikawa Kōjirō saw Yang Weizhen as the first in a line of "independent" writers and artists and as marking "the beginning of the Ming and Qing poetic world."[97]

What Zhou may have thought of Yang Weizhen is impossible for me to say, since I know of no reference to Yang in Zhou's work. However, he is unlikely to have agreed with either Guo Shaoyu or Yoshikawa, since in his view the late Ming Gongan and Jingling literary schools marked a real break with the archaists and the beginning of truly modern writing.[98] He would certainly have concurred that there was a Ming counter-tradition but would have dated it toward the end rather than the beginning of the dynasty. Zhou described the late Ming as a "period of the liberation of thought and writing. Most likely the change started after Wang Yangming opened up the Confucian sect and brought in the flavor of Chan (ba Rumen dakai, fangjin Chan wei lai)," a trend furthered by Li Zhi, he wrote.[99]

The philosophic concern with interiority and subjectivity in Wang Yangming's thinking eventually led to a split among his followers over which was more important—moral cultivation or intuitive enlighten-ment.[100] The Taizhou school, which favored the second approach and so was censured for falling into Chan Buddhism and outside "the boundaries of Confucian moral philosophy,"[101] exerted considerable influence on the literary counter-tradition. Li Zhi and Jiao Hong, two of the best-known Taizhou school figures, strongly influenced the Gongan school. Li Zhi equated propriety with following one's own innate capacity for moral judgment, and Jiao Hong saw man's nature as self-sufficient and self-illuminating.[102] Moreover, Li Zhi reiterated Yan Yu's idea that the "mar-velous enlightenments" of which poetry and Chan spoke were one and the same thing.[103] The Yuan brothers placed the writer's innate sensibility (*xingling*) at the center of poetry and considered originality more important than formal attributes.[104]

For Zhou, the late Ming became the site of entry into modern literary history. "What [the Gongan school] advocated was very simple; we could say it was more or less the same as Mr. Hu Shizhi [Hu Shi]. The differ-ence is that Matteo Ricci (1552–1610) had not yet arrived in China, and so Western thought was missing."[105] Zhou is mistaken here, for Ricci had ar-rived in Nanjing in 1599 and came to count among his friends Li Zhi and Jiao Hong.[106] However, the point Zhou is trying to make is that if we re-move Western science and philosophy from Hu's thinking, what remains is something very close to the most famous maxim of the Gongan school, "Uniquely express [one's] personality and innate sensibility without being restrained by convention or form" (*du shu xingling, buju getao*).[107]

Zhou described the influence of the Gongan school as continuing un-broken into the Kangxi reign period (1662–1723), and Zhang Dai (1599–1684?) as combining the achievements of the Gongan and Jingling schools. The two hundred years between 1700 and 1900 Zhou saw as a period of reaction against the expressivist counter-tradition. (This was no exaggera-tion. The Yuan brothers' writings were banned by the Qing court, and critics held them responsible for the deterioration of "moral education through poetry" [*shijiao*]. Throughout the Qing, Yuan Hongdao's poetry was said to have presaged the ruin of the Ming.)[108] "However," Zhou agreed, "the literary movement since the beginning of the Republic is itself a reaction stirred up by this reactionary force. So we can put it this way:

late Ming literature is the origin (laiyuan) of the present literary movement, and Qing literature is the reason for it (yuanyin)."[109]

Despite the Gongan school's historical importance, its literary output did not always live up to the promise of its theories.[110] Zhou Zuoren criticized Yuan Hongdao for using poetic forms that had already been exhausted but judged his essays much better. In one essay he suggested that Yuan's greatest achievement lay in his ideas rather than his practice.

Chonglang [Yuan Hongdao] opposed orthodox "imitative" literature, and it is for this people praise him. We cherish his achievements, and when we reread his writings to reappraise him, it is just like when we read Zola's novels. We want to see how close or distant he is from the theory of naturalism. That way we can understand the ideals and reality of the literary movement, we can understand the writer and his times. Isn't this more reliable than just depending on literary histories to discuss gains and losses or making irresponsible remarks without reading the texts?[111]

More concretely, in his lecture series on the history of Chinese literature, Zhou praised the writings of the Gongan school for their "freshness and flowing beauty" (qingxin liuli), but added: "Their decline also stemmed from these qualities. Their essays were too empty and light, clear without being deep. A pool of water should not be turbid, but if it is so clear that you can see straight to the bottom and take in all the plants and fishes at one glance, it has no interest."[112] This comment shows that Zhou did not see the debate between the archaists and the expressionists solely as "rote book learning versus self-expression," or even didacticism versus self-expression. As we saw above, perception of the ineffable, apprehended beyond the domain of zhengjiao by the writing subject, is integral to the shi yan zhi tradition. It is articulated by the use of xing, the stimulus or affective image that evokes a response in the reader. Interestingly, Owen, in discussing the work of Liu Xie (465–522), identifies xing with latency and concealment, meaning it operates in a pre-logical mode that appeals directly to the affections (qing).[113] Zhou's image for the lack of depth in the Yuan brothers' writing, the lack of anything concealed or latent, is indicative of a failure of xing. This leads me to suggest that for Zhou, given the extent to which poetic lyricism informed expressive writing in China, one could abandon traditional prosody and metrics but not the structuring of expressive language by "categories of appeal."[114]

That Zhou subscribed to a poetics of *xing* emerges quite clearly from his preface to a collection of poems by Liu Bannong, whom he praised for his ability to "control" the vernacular and not be controlled by it.[115]

I am not a believer in "traditionalism" [English in original], but I believe that the strength of tradition should not be underestimated. There are plenty of bad traditional ways of thinking that we should discard, but the traditions that transcend good and bad and that cannot be discarded are not necessarily few in number. If they correspond to the many rhetorical devices (*xiuci fangfa*) derived from Chinese characters, then when we write in Chinese, we will not be able to get rid of them.

Could not the "rhetorical devices derived from Chinese characters" refer to the freight of associations of all sorts with the images evoked by words? In the next sentence Zhou mentions "moderation" and "sumptuousness," and he seems to be referring to something similar to the "categories of appeal" mentioned earlier. Thus he is pleased that modern Chinese poetry, which began by imitating Western poetry, is now gradually moving towards "originality" (*duchuang*).

In the midst of freedom there is freely arrived at moderation (*jiezhi*), in the midst of sumptuousness (*haohua*), purity and astringency (*qing se*). Thus the beauty of the special characteristics of Chinese literature increases in response to foreign influences; it is not just a matter of throwing on a foreign overcoat.

Admitting that he is "very old-fashioned" and still deeply attached to "many Chinese artistic and intellectual traditions," Zhou then comes to the heart of the matter of poetic expression:

I do not admire simple, straightforward writing in the new poetry, and I do not like long descriptions or, worse, explanations. I admit only lyricism as the basic element of poetry and in terms of writing the "stimulus" (*xing*) form is the most interesting. In present-day parlance, perhaps we would call it a "symbol." If I might be permitted a trite observation, the symbol is poetry's newest technique, but also its oldest. In China it has always existed. We can look up to the "Airs" [the Guo Feng section of the *Shijing*] or down to popular lullabies, and we will realize that most Chinese poems use the *xing* form more commonly and to better effect than either exposition (*fu*) or comparison (*bi*).

Take, for example, the poem "The Tender Bright Peach" ("Tao zhi yao yao"). It is not necessarily comparing the bride with the peach, nor is it referring to the time of peach blossom or the fact that there is a girl to be married in a peach-tree owner's family.[116] In fact, it is only because the rich and gaudy peach blossoms and marriage share something of the same character that it is used as a stimulus. This use as a *xing* is not intended as a foil for anything but is to express real meaning. It is just done through a different locution, that's all.

Elsewhere Zhou had criticized Hu Shi's overly thorough exegesis of poems from the Airs section. Hu not only saw them as courtship poems but found a sociological explanation for each image. "Why do we need to understand everything when we read a poem, and why are we so unwilling to loosen our grip on the *Shijing*? Could it be that we are still poisoned by tradition?" he asked sarcastically.[117]

To return to Zhou's preface, he next complains that since the Chinese literary revolution was imbued with classicism (but not imitation of the past), contemporary writing was "like a glass ball, too transparent and without any indistinctness (*menglong*), so that it lacks any lingering fragrance (*yuxiang*) or aftertaste (*huiwei*)."[118] This, as we have seen, was the same complaint he made about Gongan school writing. For Zhou, the genius of the Chinese language lay in its capacity for allusive richness. It suffered almost as much from attempts to make everything crystal clear as from attempts to imbue an image with didactic meaning. The biggest challenge to the writer is to work out the relationship between his or her intent and emotions and their expression using a language whose literary development reflected the conviction that there was a web of correspondences between the physical and interior worlds. The relationship had to be disclosed anew by each writer, in a testing of the writer's ability to allow "sensuous imagery to embody meaning, without discursive explanation" or overdirectness. In the final analysis, the importance of *xing* for a nondidactic poetics is shown by the fact that the minute an image slips from being interpreted as a *xing* into becoming a *bi* comparison, it becomes a value judgment. Bai Juyi's (772–846) transformation of *bi* and *xing* into a single undifferentiated term referring to the political content and function of poems is one of the clearest examples. Zhu Xi (with obvious didactic intent) went through the *Shijing* relabeling every clear image previously annotated as a stimulus as a comparison.[119]

Evidently, although Zhou held the division between *wen yi zai dao* and *shi yan zhi* to be the motive force driving Chinese literary history, opposition to didacticism alone could not guarantee literary excellence. Thus, the question of the relationship of the writer to the tradition becomes refocused on language and linguistic practice. The writer's relationship to language was governed by his philosophic orientation to the world, but this was a precondition for the aesthetic and moral excellence first suggested in the Zhuangzian strand of the tradition, not a guarantee that it would be attained.

## 'Quwei' as a Poetics of Locality and Material Culture

Zhou's qualified approval of the Yuan brothers should not distract us from the fact that his interest in the late Ming writers lay in the philosophic grounding of the expressionist counter-tradition as a whole, which became the source of his oppositional aesthetics. This comes across clearly in an article marking the publication of Ming works in the Rare Books in Chinese Literature series (Zhongguo wenxue zhenben congshu) edited by Shi Zhecun (1905– ). Although he strongly supported the listing of late Ming titles, 90 percent of which had been banned in the Qing, Zhou saw defects in the series. He felt that not all the titles were well chosen, and the cheap production values of the series, which was aimed at a popular market, meant that the quality was not good enough for research purposes:

Perhaps not everyone will fully approve of reprinting this kind of books, feeling that they do not possess much intellectual or artistic value and that there is no benefit in reading them. There is a little truth to this, but it is not completely right. Ming literature and thinking did not undergo much development. In the intellectual sphere only the Wang Yangming school appeared, and literature took the road of fiction and had some creative achievements. But this was all outside the orthodox pale, and as a result it was very natural for the orthodox school, which adhered in learning to Cheng-Zhu and in literature to Tang and Song, to see it as utterly worthless. However, if we decide there is no need to be quite so orthodox and look more carefully at the two elements of intellectual and artistic heterodoxy, we see they combined together to become the atmosphere [breathed by] the late Ming literary world. Although from Li Zhi down to Jin Shengtan [1608–61] and those objects of censure by the Tongcheng school, the "former officials" [yilao—who refused service under the Qing] of the Wu Yue area, seem dissimilar, in reality they were all walking the same road. Consequently these late Ming works are all very important literary contributions, heterodox to be sure . . . but my prejudice is that heterodoxy in thinking or art is always more interesting than orthodoxy, because it has more daring and life in it.[120]

Perhaps Zhou initially came to his appreciation of "late Ming heterodoxy" when he found a copy of a book by Zhang Dai in Hangzhou in 1897, while on a visit to his jailed grandfather.[121] Be that as it may, we must now try to discover how his involvement with this civilizational strand shaped his ideas. The best way to begin is the article "Difang yu wenyi" (Place and literature), which shows him to be drawing on the late Ming countertradition as he was breaking with the May Fourth literary world.[122] It is in this context that we see him developing a specific meaning for *quwei*.

After asserting that "there is always a close relationship between the social customs and the natural conditions (*fengtu*) of a place and its inhabitants, as everybody knows," and that it is not surprising if these are reflected as differences within a national literature, Zhou goes on to discuss the new literature:

We often say good literature ought to be universal, but this universality refers to the largest possible range, just like the largest common denominator in arithmetic. Within this range, the utmost should be done to allow the greatest possible number of variations. It is absolutely unlike the unalterability of a single, indivisible number. In the past few years, China's newly arisen literature has gradually developed, and each kind of literary creation has seen a certain success, but we feel this is still insufficient. Why? Just because it is too abstract, upholds a universal demand, and works to a prescribed concept, so that it is unable to truly and forcefully express its own individuality: naturally the result is monotony. Our hope is to escape these self-imposed shackles and freely express the individuality that has come from the soil.[123]

This could be illustrated with the example of Zhejiang province, for although there were not necessarily any great differences between Zhejiang's social and geographical conditions (*fengtu*) and learning and arts and those of the adjoining provinces, yet in Zhejiang

a special character can be found to exist. In the literature of the past three hundred years, there are two trends that may be found elsewhere but are clearest in Zhejiang which we can call the naturally graceful (*piaoyi*) and the profound (*shenke*). The first is like the conversations of literary men outside the bureaucracy, mixing sobriety and humor, sometimes clear and elegant, sometimes abstruse, sometimes bold and unrestrained, not necessarily encompassing subtle principles but expressing the predilections of the speaker. The other is like a magistrate sending someone to jail, pungent in expression, characterized not by flowery language but by specific and clear understanding and incisive diction.[124]

This had been particularly clear in the late Ming. Although, Zhou continued, in the eyes of *guwen* specialists, literary style was just at its most torpid then, we believe that this was a very important period in terms of literary evolution, because those writers for the most part were unintentionally moving toward modern language. It's unfortunate that they were displaced by the dominant scholarly trends in the Qing.

Zhou did not intend the "naturally graceful" and the "profound" to be competing or ranked categories. As examples of the first type, he cited the writings of Xu Wenchang (Xu Wei; 1521–93), Wang Jizhong (Wang Siren; 1575–1646), and Zhang Zongzi (Zhang Dai), "who could have laid the basis of the modern essay," whereas the critic Mao Xihe (Mao Qiling; 1623–1716) represented the second. Similarly, Zhou contrasted the poet and essayist Yuan Mei with the moralizing philosopher and historian Zhang Xuecheng (1738–1801). Closer to his own time, Zhou saw the scholar official Li Ciming (1830–94) and the bibliophile Zhao Zhiqian (1829–84) as representative of the graceful and the profound, respectively. The fiery Zhang Binglin also provided an instructive contrast with his teacher, Yu Yue (1821–1906). These men were distinguished in Zhou's eyes by the extent to which they had preserved their individuality and remained relatively free of the "modes of thinking and writing" laid down by schools of orthodox Neo-Confucian (*daoxue*) or classical prose scholarship.[125]

   It is the inclusivity of the *piaoyi* and *shenke* categories that is striking—they recall Yan Yu's "two general polarities" of poetry, the "carefree and uncompelled" and "fortitude in grief." Zhejiang, then, provides a microcosm of the spectrum of Chinese literary endeavor, not a separate tradition that contributes to the larger one in the way a patch contributes to the overall design of a patchwork quilt. This means that the variations that make a work specifically Zhejiangese must occur at a subtler level, one that is not dependent on following a particular pattern. The trouble with the *daoxue* and classical prose scholars, Zhou continues, was that although they had been able to produce a universal mode of thinking and writing, "within this universal mode there were no changes, and so there was no artistic value." There was a lesson to be learned from this, Zhou said, because at present literature and thought were also bound by a universal restraint consisting of "a fixed, new view and literary form, which, if we follow only [them], will become a new *daoxue* and a new school of classical prose." This will result in artistic and intellectual stagnation.[126]

The artistic value he hoped to see depended on the individual's being able to "sing out the emotions" and write whatever he or she pleased in whatever mode.

No matter how solemn other peoples' writing, how optimistic their thought, or how much they stress love of country and repayment of one's debt of gratitude to it (*ai guo bao en*), if I want to write something unconventional, light, and marvelous, or something satirical and condemnatory, then that is my freedom. And no matter whether it [what I write] is reclusive or defiant, just as long as it is my own heartbeat formed by the fusion of inheritance and environment, just as long as it is not created according to preconceived, doctrinaire, inflexible notions, it has value and the right to be expressed. This type of work is naturally possessed of the national, local, and individual characteristics that are its life.

How did these three function together? Zhou emphasized that "when we speak of locality, we are not speaking about provincial affiliation, we are just talking about the influence of social customs and natural conditions (*fengtu*) and showing high esteem to the force of the soil (*tu zhi li*), which nourishes creativity." The use of the word "soil" (*tu*) here reflects back on the complex of meanings in *fengtu*. Zhou makes the point that what he means parallels Nietzsche's exhortation in *Zarathustra*, "Be faithful to the earth" (*zhong yu di*). This influence exists because "no matter how we put it, people are always 'sons of the soil' (*di zhi zi*). They cannot live without the soil, and this is the normal path of human life."

Although references to "sons of the soil" can be aligned with some of the worst excesses of twentieth-century nationalism, Zhou is using the expression here in opposition to nationalism.

Men today are too fond of living in the air, of living on beautiful and empty theories, just as in the past they lived on the classical prose of orthodox Confucianism. This is extremely regrettable. It is necessary to jump back down to earth and let the smell of the earth and the scent of growing things course through one's veins and be expressed in one's writing—this is real thinking and real art.

By this, Zhou made clear, he was not limiting himself to the "nativist art" (*xiangtu yishu*) that described local life: all literature needed to be grounded in the soil.

Perhaps some may suspect that what I am talking about is traditionalism or that subject so dear to Chinese, the national essence (*guocuizhuyi*). I reply, absolutely not. I believe the so-called national essence can be divided into two parts. The living part is in our blood and veins, it is the inheritance of "flavor" (*quwei*), and we are powerless to discard it or keep it. Naturally it is expressed in all our speech and actions, not needing to be protected or preserved. The dead part is the morality and customs of the past, which are unsuitable for the present, which there is no point in preserving, and which cannot be preserved.[127]

The translation of *quwei* as "flavor" is most inadequate and is only used here provisionally. As we will see shortly, Chinese aesthetics draws on a host of related words carrying the associations of taste (*qu*) and flavor (*wei*). These are words with a large and overlapping semantic range that includes the senses of interest, piquancy, delight, and delectation. The essential thing to note here is the suggestion that blood and veins are meant to carry both the "living part" of the national essence, which is the heritage of *quwei* and "smell of the earth (*tuqi*) and the scent (*wei*) of growing things," which are dependent on *fengtu*. In other words, the living, intangible "flavor" which is that part of the national essence that cannot be discarded is located in the locality.

This is the crux of the matter. With "Place and Literature," the locality becomes what mediates the writer and nation and serves to connect them in a meaningful way. It is only by writing as "sons of the soil," not by relying on the empty, doctrinaire dreams centered on the concept of the nation, that genuine literature can be produced. The many ramifications of this for the issue of national identity are explored in subsequent chapters; in this chapter, our focus is the aesthetics of this idea.

The idea that genuine literature relies on the *quwei* of *fengtu* is spelled out even more clearly in an essay Zhou wrote for the publication of the modern poetry collection *Old Dreams* (*Jiu meng*) by the Shaoxing poet Liu Dabai (1880–1932).[128] Zhou frames his comments by noting that he and Liu were from the same area, and so he knew of him, although they had never met. He still recalled the old-style poetry Liu had submitted to the local *Yucheng xinwen* (Yucheng news) newspaper in the early years of the Republic, and he knew that Liu had changed to writing new-style poetry. However, Zhou's disappointment is palpable: he disagrees with Liu's claim that although he writes in the new form, his poetry still has a strong traditional flavor (here the term used is *qiwei*).

I feel this is not at all the case. In my view, at least in the section titled "Old Dreams," he has forcefully moved away from the emotional taste (*qing qu*) of old *shi* and *ci* poetry, too far, if I might say so, inevitably diluting its poetic flavor (*shi wei*), although this could be because philosophic theory has entered the poems.

Zhou's chief complaint was that Liu's poetry showed no evidence of the *fengtu* of his hometown and thus lacked flavor. As his argument unfolds, he links this lack of local flavor to a lack of individuality:

In all other matters I dislike localism (*difangzhuyi*); it is just that with regard to art, I feel differently. Mr. Dabai is a person from Pingshui in Kuaiji, and this fact meant something to me [literally: "is a cause of heightened interest (*xing qu*) for me"]. When in 1912 *Yucheng News* published supplements carrying *Zhangshizhai wenji* [Collected literary works of Zhang Xuecheng] and *Li Yueman riji chao* [Diary of Li Yueman (Li Ciming)] and similar works, I was an avid reader, and I started collecting the writings of Qing literati from Yuezhong [i.e., central eastern Zhejiang]. Of course, this does not mean that now I have to criticize from a nativist point of view, but I feel that the force of *fengtu* is extremely important in art, and so in the end I keep coming back to it. When I was a child I went to Pingshui, but I can no longer remember it in detail. I just have an indistinct impression of the big stream at the back of my mind. When I recall the landscapes at Lanting, Jianhu, Shedi, Pingshui, Mupeng, and those places, I feel as though they are all hazily joined together, like a doubly exposed photograph in which one can still make out the forms. Our materials need not necessarily contain definite, clear local color, but as long as we do not place ourselves within the palisade of any school and just let [the work] naturally develop, then it will reach just the right level and have individuality.[129]

Zhou regretted the tendency to reject local flavor (*xiangtu de qiwei*) in the name of the cosmopolitanism that had developed in reaction to narrow nationalism. But this meant writers should be even more sensitive to their local qualifications because "cosmopolitanism and local flavor are mutually related in just the same way that, because we are individuals, we are part of humanity." What should Liu have done? "I wish he could have written more about his real dreams, old and new, that he could have written more clearly about the mountains at Pingshui, of the color of the water on Baima Lake, and of the sounds of the markets."

The connection between the locality and the qualities of *qu* and *wei* in writing is unambiguous. At the same time, Liu's failure to produce "flavorful" poetry in this collection stemmed from his unwillingness to draw on his experience of writing old-style poetry.

The new poets of today all like to turn their hands to old forms to show their versatility, which could be called excess curiosity. Mr. Dabai is rich in the implicitness of old *shi* and *ci* poetry. However, he does not make full use of it, which is a pity. I do not really care for the new poetry written to *yuefu* or *ciqu* models, but those practiced phrases are really necessary in new poetry, provided they are used appropriately, because poetry does not focus only on meaning (*yiyi*) and the vernacular is still Chinese (*Hanyu*)."[130]

The idea that poetry is not concerned only with meaning recalls Zhou's arguments about the centrality of the device of *xing*. Zhou intended poetry to use imagery to convey not just meaning but poetic meaning, and this poetic meaning, the flavor or taste of *shi*, arose from within the world, concrete and emotional, of the locality. It is quite unlike the explicit meanings of philosophic or other discourse.

This is not too far removed from the meaning of *qu* as implicit meaning in the *Canglang shihua*. Although Zhou naturally does not discuss *qu* as a fruit of enlightenment, he hints at it by suggesting its difficulty of attainment. Just after the list of suggested poetic topics for Liu Dabai ("the Pingshui mountains, the color of the water") comes an apologetic throwaway sentence: "Of course, this is only my individual request and does not count for anything—moreover, who among us could manage to get that far [in poetry]?"[131]

The question of how the poet should access enlightenment was answered by the archaists in ways that reduced the importance of the real concrete image and personal emotion in favor of the assimilation of a stock of images and emotions inscribed in texts. The Ming counter-tradition, with its recovery of personal intent and emotions, vastly expanded the explicit terrain of *qu*. The best-known discussion of *qu* from the period is probably that of Yuan Hongdao in a preface written for a work by Chen Zhengfu (Suoxue; *jinshi* 1583).

Yuan's opening definition is structured similarly to that of the *Canglang shihua*, "What people find hard to attain is *qu*. *Qu* is like the color on mountains, taste in water, the brightness of flowers, posture in women. Even someone who is good at talking cannot put it into words, only the intuitive know what it is."[132] With this list of similes for the indescribable, Yuan reveals that his version of *qu* refers to that which lies beyond immediately apprehended reality, although his images are less rarified than those (sound in the air, moon in water) in the *Canglang shihua*. But those who "admire the idea of *qu* and seek its likeness" by indulging their connoisseurship of calligraphy, painting, and antiques or by trying to "flee the world of dust and become 'aloof'" are on the wrong track. "This is just the skin and feathers of *qu*, it has nothing to do with its real vitality." Children, on the other hand, and the unlettered and down-and-outs are close to *qu*. "Whether in eating and drinking or in singing, they follow their inclinations, without inhibitions." The disparagement of those who attempt to flee the mundane as well as those whose interest in *qu* seems dictated by convention leads us to share Jonathan Chaves's conclusion: "*Qu* is the *ineffable essence at the heart of things*, and even partakes of a spiritual quality" (italics added).[133]

Chaves's definition is very fruitful, pointing as it does to the whole orientation toward seeing the Way in terms of the daily life of the individual that emerged in the heterodox Ming counter-tradition associated with Wang Yangming's followers in the radical Taizhou school. Thus Jiao Hong was, to quote Edward Ch'ien:

unequivocal in his affirmation of a norm which he enunciated in terms of the "daily uses of the people" (*pai-hsing jih-yung*):

> Whatever corresponds to the daily uses of the people is common virtue. Whatever is different from the daily uses of the people is heresy. Scholars should try to think about what the daily uses of the people are. They need not be too anxious about attacking heresy.[134]

Ch'ien notes that the *locus classicus* for the expression *baixing riyong* is the Xici section of the *Yijing*, where it is said of the Way that "The people use it day by day (*baixing riyong*) and are not aware of it."[135] Expanding on this, Wang Gen (1483–1541), the co-founder, with Wang Ji (1498–1583), of the Taizhou school, "had tried to make the Way 'answer to the everyday uses of the people.'"[136] In its very substance the Way was "all of the things which are productive and sustain life in the world, everything which is loved and practiced in common by the people and what they know and say in common." We also find Li Zhi saying, "To wear clothing and to eat food—these are the principles of human relations."[137]

The following of one's own inclinations is a corollary of following one's childlike heart, which Yuan (although he makes it clear by context without using the word *tongxin*) also sees as "the highest attainment of *qu*." Both the idea of the childlike heart and that of the "daily uses of the people" have the effect of bringing the ineffable into everyday life, so that human society and material culture thus become capable of triggering insight or enlightenment. The effect of this cluster of concerns is visible in Yuan's essays, particularly in his travel essays, which combined detailed descriptions with introspective, subjective remarks. At times the geographical place functioned as a peg on which to hang a variety of random digressions. At other times his descriptions ignored the scenery in favor of discussions of local products such as tea and vegetables.[138]

In many of Zhou's essays (including some of the most anthologized), local customs and material culture are vividly evoked and highly valued. As he commented once, it is far better to be remembered for a pastry recipe than for a book.[139] Why these things should be so important he explained most clearly in an essay on the seasonal customs of the Wu area, such as storing rainwater for tea or weighing women at the end of summer to see how much thinner they had become during the hot weather.

Why are we so interested in these seasonal changes and customs? The answer is very simple, it is because they make up the tiny changes in our ordinary lives. The history of peoples is just the succession of daily human activities (*riyong renshi*) and the movement of the stars, geography, and the cyclical movements of the natural world all influence human affairs and cause all sorts of variations [in them], mainly of a practical sort. But people's response to the seasons is the same. In Chinese poetry and painting these things are given a big place. A common refrain in literature is "petals in the wind and the moon on the snow," but although we object to "petals in the wind and the moon on the snow" because it is so hackneyed, there is nothing else wrong with it. By the pond new grasses sprout, courtyard willows thronged with birds—the feelings these arouse in us, just as much as the thought "ground's thawed, time to sow"—all are responses to changes in the natural world. We cannot call one refined and the other vulgar, but since the practical one is limited to practical considerations, its emotional effect is slight, whereas the ornate or subjective one arouses a more generally heightened interest (*xingqu*), and there seems to be more poetic import. If we add to this local considerations, things become more complex, varied and interesting (*duo qu*). To see the customs of a place, whether they are the same as our own or different, is always meaningful. If they are different, we can make comparisons; if they are the same, there is an added sense of intimacy.[140]

It is possible to understand *riyong renshi* here as synonymous with *baixing riyong*. The resonance of the phrase is heightened by the references immediately following it to the movement of the stars (*tian wen*), which as David Pollard points out, is a phrase from chapter 22 of the *Yijing*.[141]

The "tiny changes in our lives" are thus fitted into a context of cosmic dimensions, which means that the artifacts and customs of living are ascribed a meaning and significance that go beyond their materiality or any potentially utilitarian ideological value. Between "our ordinary lives" and the cosmos, however, we have "the history of peoples," but not of nations. In other words, a moral order is immanent in life itself. This is why so many of Zhou's essays are celebrations of what was truly valuable in "the history of peoples"—the culture of everyday life—but celebrations that resisted being co-opted by forces of whatever stripe in national life.

Although *qu* has been located in the material world, it is still implicit in the concept that the writer should have a certain attitude to the world in order to perceive it. Chaves makes an illuminating assertion: "It is also a quality in the mind or soul of one who perceives *ch'ü* in the outer world, in keeping with the dual function of many Chinese critical terms, i.e. their applicability to some quality in the world and to the same quality in the mind of the perceiver."[142] Zhou discusses *qu* from this perspective in an essay comparing Li Yu (1611–80) and Yuan Mei.[143] Li Yu, known principally as a dramatist, survived poverty and the disruption of the Ming Qing transition by traveling from patron to patron with his troupe of singing girls. Yuan Mei, whose skills as a poet made him wealthy enough to decline the life of an official, scandalized his contemporaries by accepting women as students.[144] Both were condemned for their allegedly libertine, hedonistic ways by orthodox literati of the nineteenth century, as could be expected, Zhou noted. What influenced Zhou's judgments of them was their attitude toward the "daily uses of human life" (*rensheng riyong*). He much preferred Li Yu. Writing about food and drink, for instance, Li Yu was like an "old rustic digging up bamboo shoots and choosing vegetables," whereas Yuan Mei was "like a cook in a dirty, greasy apron."[145] Li Yu, we can surmise, had some appreciation for things in themselves, whereas Yuan Mei stewed them to death.

The crystallization of all that Zhou found wrong with Yuan Mei was to be found in two lines from one of his poems: "Seal carved on three sides / inkstick rubbed at both ends." This showed his vulgarity (*su*), or lack of *quwei* (*mei quwei*), which is not to be equated with being without *quwei* (*wu quwei*) in the sense of having no personality or personal likes and dislikes.[146] At first glance, it would seem that the most appropriate translation here for *quwei* would be "taste," in the sociological sense of taste as a marker of refinement, but as we will see shortly, Zhou's use of the word is more complicated.

Generally speaking, there are several attitudes a person can take toward seals and ink. (1) Not to use them, and simply not be bothered with them. (2) Use the seal for recording one's name and the ink for writing with, and not demand anything else of them. (3) Love them. Apart from practical use, they are chosen for their superior fineness and agreeableness, cherished, valued, and used with pleasure. Maybe I have stated the case a little extravagantly, but actually it is not excessive. The woodworker cares for his ax and chisel, the farmer cares for his hoe and plow, everyone is the same, and it is not just an attitude restricted to the brush, ink, paper, and inkstone of scholars.

Zhou quotes an account of an incident in which an angry Taiping rebel leader used his teeth to tear at a piece of paper. This was also an example of recklessly wasting the gifts of Heaven (*baotian tianwu*) and was as much the action of a bad workman as ruining a magnificent tree trunk would be.

Although using an inkstick at both ends is not quite as bad, it is also extremely savage. A person not only uses an inkstick to write with, but also takes pleasure in the beauty of its shape. When it gets shorter, it is still loved, although this does no more good than loving a person can make them get younger. But to grind an inkstick at both ends shows more than lack of feelings, it shows callousness.

As for the seal, Zhou said, by carving it on three of its six sides Yuan Mei had been trying to get his money's worth from it, just as one might buy a penknife for the number of bottle openers and other gadgets attached. And, once fallen into the trap of instrumentalism, Yuan had even failed to think that the seal would not only look ugly but would be difficult to use into the bargain.

Yuan Mei, then, in Zhou's view, was painfully deficient in the ability to perceive the *quwei* of things and thus was condemned for his palpable coarseness in lacking *quwei* himself. If we accept that Zhou used the concept of *qu* to refer to both the quality of the ineffable manifest in the daily uses of the people and the same quality in the perceiver, then we are led to an important conclusion: in his literary practice, at least, Zhou retained an idea of man compatible with (if not assimilable to) the Neo-Confucian conception of "man's nature as identical with the . . . Principle of Heaven."[147] By this I mean that the unstated schema of man's relation to the rest of the existent order in Zhou's thinking is still compatible with a moral order that accorded reverence to man and the natural and the cultural worlds as all embodying the divine.[148]

In other words, Zhou saw the writer as worthy of respect to the extent that he or she apprehends and manifests the intrinsic value of human life and its "daily uses." This is underscored by his reference to human artifacts such as inksticks and paper as "gifts of heaven." To the extent that the writer fails, this is a moral failure, described in aesthetic terms as vulgarity. The apposition of "vulgarity" to "flavor" immediately brings to mind the related meaning of *quwei* as "taste," but Zhou's usage cannot be reduced to this pair. In the essay on Li Yu and Yuan Mei, Zhou attempts a definition of *quwei* as it applies to persons.

I have to confess that I prize *quwei* very highly. I believe that it is beautiful and good and that to be without it is calamitous. It includes many things, such as dignity (*ya* [usually rendered "elegance"]), lack of artifice (*zhuo*), honesty (*pu*), lack of glibness (*se* ["tartness"]), steadfastness (*zhonghou*), clarity (*qinglang*), depth of understanding about human affairs (*tongda*), moderation (*zhongyong*), discrimination (*you bieze*). What is contrary to these lacks *quwei* (*mei quwei*).[149]

It is clear from what follows that Zhou wants to differentiate his usage from the common twentieth-century usage of *quwei* as "taste":

There is the common expression "low taste" (*diji quwei*), which, although it appears to be an import from Japan and is in my opinion a faulty usage of language, can nevertheless *be borrowed* to explain what I mean, *since it seems a little easier to understand* [italics added] than "lacking *quwei*." To lack (*mei*) *quwei* is not the same as being without (*wu*) *quwei*. Unless a person so much wants to be dead that his only fear is being alive, ordinarily there is no one who does not hold a particular attitude to life. One person may be so calm and placid as to be almost unnoticeable; another has to make a choice about everything no matter how trivial. Although they tend in different directions, yet each has his own kind of *quwei*.[150]

Zhou's admission that Yuan Mei was guilty of something a little like (easier to understand as) bad taste raises an intriguing problem. The work of Pierre Bourdieu makes the claim that "taste" is a socially produced category that buttresses the claims of elites to their status. When it becomes possible for non-elites to acquire money, "taste" is the mechanism by which the older elites continue to assert their cultural superiority over the parvenus. To what extent, then, is Zhou drawing on an elitist discourse that conceals its stake in social power by making taste a moral attribute? Craig Clunas's study of conspicuous consumption in the Ming provides some fascinating insights. In his conclusion he states:

Perhaps one of the most striking recurrences of a broad cultural pattern in both Ming China and early modern Europe is what might be called "the invention of taste." For if the unequal distribution of cultural resources is necessary to the stratification of society, as Bourdieu has argued, and if those cultural resources are all full commodities, available to all who possess the relevant economic resources, what is to prevent the cultural and economic hierarchies collapsing into one another . . . ? Here, taste comes into play as an essential legitimator of consumption. . . . In China, this happens contemporary with, or even prior to, its establishment in Europe. There can be little doubt that from the late seventeenth century in England the concept of taste was a crucial development in promoting an acceptance of the fact that a difference existed between mere possessors of luxury and connoisseurs, whose judgment was based on a set of morally grounded aesthetic principles.[151]

However, in his discussion of the terms used to denote taste in the handbooks for connoisseurs that circulated in late Ming China, Clunas dubs *qu* "the word that isn't there," noting that although it was "a key value in the discussion of painting, of poetry and of personal conduct . . . [it] seems not to have spilled over into the world of things, and in many ways what is significant is that it is rather rarely seen in those connoisseurship texts which address themselves to a precise definition and categorization of objects."[152] One of the few places where it does appear in a connoisseur context is in a book on vases by Yuan Hongdao, Clunas tells us, adding that "it was almost 'his' word." Approving Chaves's elucidation of *qu* as "the ineffable essence at the heart of things" and Yuan Hongdao's attacks on those who equated it with connoisseurship, Clunas suggests that Yuan was probably most opposed to the values of the elite arbiters of taste.[153]

This puts *qu* at a certain remove from the discourses on taste with which Clunas is concerned, although no doubt they intersected. Zhou's emphasis on the moral qualities of *quwei* as found in persons seems to correlate with the Gongan school's usage distinguishing it from mere good taste, socially sanctioned. Perhaps it would be more accurate to say that it subsumed good taste, but included much more.

Earlier in the essay, Zhou explained that he has never liked Yuan Mei's personality. The word he uses for personality is *qiwei*, which in addition to its primary meaning of flavor or smell refers to the inclinations and temper of a person. "I feel that he is a little thin (*bo*) and light (*qing*). Naturally this is quite different from the common meaning of frivolous for the binome *qingbo*."[154] One has to intuit what qualities are conveyed by "thinness" and "lightness," but this is made easier by reading them against the positive constituents of *quwei* listed by Zhou. If "discrimination" and "dignity/elegance" are recognizable as markers of taste, other qualities such as steadfastness and depth of understanding of human affairs go beyond it.

Finally, we should not forget Zhou's remark that *quwei* is "beautiful and good, and that to be without it is calamitous." From this, it appears that aesthetics has its source in morality, and this was, indeed, one of the underlying assumptions of the Gongan school. It follows that if success at apprehending the intrinsic value of the world is a mark of morality, then the moral life hinges on perception. But if man, the world, and the divine are ultimately the same, then a failure of perception is a failure to heed one's own nature, which shares in the divine.

The view of literary creation as dependent on the exercise of independent moral perception was the fruit of the late Ming counter-tradition. The concept of the "childlike heart" had enabled the Gongan school to posit the primacy of "innate sensibility" (*xingling*)[155] and Yan Yu's assertion that "poetry is to tell of one's personal inborn nature" was given its due again. The broadening of the locus of *qu* into the "daily uses of the people" took it away from the texts in which the archaists had centered it. It is worth noting here parenthetically that Clunas finds Zhou's literary hero Zhang Dai "groping towards a recognition of the very relative, culturally defined nature of the 'menial crafts' [such as bamboo carving]."[156] Perhaps the differences in attitude between Yuan Hongdao and late Ming arbiters of taste that Clunas identified through their use or non-use of the aesthetic category of *qu* indicates a faultline in perception of social relations among late Ming elites.

The answer to the question of the relationship of the artist to the tradition was at root philosophic and encompassed a redefinition both of the artist and of the world. But, in terms of literary production, the question had not been answered satisfactorily. As far as Zhou was concerned, the Gongan school's major contribution had been to literary theory, not to literature. Yuan Hongdao's poetry was valuable only for having opposed the archaists' "fake antiques," and he had merely replaced Li Bai and Du Fu with Su Dongpo and Bai Juyi, even though he did not copy them. All he could do was to block the older tradition in favor of the relatively new.[157] Moreover, as we have seen, Zhou was not impressed with the transparency of the Gongan style. Zhou praised the Jingling school for correcting this fault by using archaic, abstruse diction.[158] However, neither school was long-lived, and Zhou contended that it was only in the early Qing that writers such as Zhang Dai fused the two to produce writing that was both mellifluous and meaningful.

## 'Bense': Individual Integrity and the Relation to the Tradition

This alerts us to look at the problem of the relationship of the writer to the tradition in another way, by returning to the question of language. On what basis can a writer appropriate language and control it so that he or she is driving it and not the other way around? How can she or he achieve the illusion of effortlessness in writing? One of the critical concepts that addresses this problem is that of *bense*. In an essay devoted to that topic,[159] Zhou made the important suggestion that *bense* is based on individual awareness and grounded in self-education. Pollard translates the term as "native hue" or "true colors," which suggests that it is an intrinsic quality of the writer that shows up in his work. Basing himself on the exposition of *bense* by the Ming figure Tang Shunzhi (1507–60), which he translates in part, Pollard concludes that *bense* is "a very important piece in the jigsaw puzzle in the theory of individualism in traditional China" and that Zhou's essay shows that he "understood *pen-se* in the same way as his predecessors."[160] How these predecessors may have understood it is therefore a key question.

By now, it should come as little surprise to learn that Tang Shunzhi's formulation of the concept of *bense* was influenced by the Taizhou school of Wang Yangming Neo-Confucianism.[161] His ideas have been described as anticipating many of the ideas later developed by the Gongan and Jingling schools.[162] As a young man, Tang had moved away from the injunction of the archaists to imitate Qin and Han prose and, by producing an anthology of the writings of the so-called Eight Prose Masters of the Tang and Song, expanded the available range of models for writers. Moreover, Tang rejected the archaists' attempt to attain the personal style of past writers by copying their phraseology, preferring to emphasize the study of the formal features of a work to ascertain the "method" (*fa*) of writing. However, Tang did not focus on the question of the writer's self-expression until he came into contact with Wang Ji, a founder of the Taizhou school. Wang Ji's theory that if the mind was understood to be essentially empty in its original nature, then it would be possible to allow all "individual ideas, volitions, and things" to display their own being, provided the basis for Tang's theory of *bense*.[163]

As could be expected from this, Tang's discussion of *bense* is prefaced by the demand that the would-be writer first exercise perception. In a letter to Mao Kun (1512–1601), Tang wrote:

Although a prose writer will naturally have a teacher and methods to follow on matters such as the arrangement of his composition and what is correct and incorrect, when it comes down to what is internal, the spirit, lifeblood, and marrow, he will never be adequate to these unless he cleanses his heart, stands independent of external appearances, and is possessed of insight that can see the past and the present.[164]

Tang goes on to contrast two types of writer. One has a "transcending mind," and his "insight can penetrate past and present" (*qian gu zhi yan*) so that whatever he dashes off, providing it expresses his feelings, will be excellent. The other has mastered all the rules, but, however artistically correct and polished, his work contains no "true spirit and ineradicable viewpoint" (*qian gu bu ke momie zhi jian*). In this fashion, says Tang, one can speak of the "native hue" of a work of literature.

Tang's conception of *bense* bears some resemblance to that in the *Canglang shihua*; in both cases a special kind of perception is a prerequisite for the achievement of excellence, which is not guaranteed by artistry. Tang's "person with the transcending mind" correlates with Yan's example of Meng Haoran, whose work was superior to Han Yu although he was less learned. But in Tang's theory, as we shall see, *bense* is important as a property more of the writer than of the work, whereas in the *Canglang shihua*, *bense* refers to a generic requirement of *shi* poetry, namely, the conveyance of meaning that is beyond words. Tang Shunzhi's concern, on the other hand, is with specific meaning (ineradicable viewpoint), which is expressed in words. The difference reflects the divergent demands of *shi* poetry and expository prose.

Developing his argument that excellence is based on the individual writer's voice, Tang asserts that pre-Han writing can be considered better than what followed because the Confucians (Ru), Daoists (Lao and Zhuang), Mohists, and other contending schools (*jia*) all stuck to their own views, spoke in their own voices, and did not plagiarize the views of others. As a result, all of them had their own *bense*. Since the Tang and the Song, however,

there is none who has not talked about nature and destiny and about ordering the ways of the world, filling up paper with dazzling exaggerations and in everything entrusting themselves to Confucianism. But this was not something that came from themselves through their own painstaking moral cultivation, and they did not really have any ineradicable viewpoint of their own. Instead they echoed others and stole their ideas, concealing their appropriation of others' words, just like a poor man borrowing the garment of a rich man.[165]

The fact that Tang praised the entire field of pre-Han writings, and not just the Confucian classics, as having *bense* suggests that he was interested in seeing them opened up as a field of intellectual endeavor and inquiry for his contemporaries. Although the central part of Tang's argument is concerned with the need for an independent viewpoint, which has priority over merely artistic excellence, he was not pitting independence *against* craft. As Tang made clear at the beginning of his letter to Mao Kun, the fact that he no longer urged writers to polish their language did not mean that he opposed artistry.

The development of the concept of *bense* as "one's own voice" in the Ming has been linked to debates in drama. In these debates, the importance of "words of true feeling" (*zhen qing hua*) was raised in contrast to the ornate diction being infused into drama by literati playwrights.[166] Together with the stress on content over form, this probably accounts in part for the association of simplicity with *bense*. Reading Zhou's article closely, however, it is clear that more is involved than the affirmation that a writer must let his own individuality show in his writing or use simple language. But just what is involved needs some unraveling.

In characteristic fashion, Zhou's opening device is to quote from another text. In this case, he cites the notes made on the topic of *bense* by the Qing scholar Hao Yixing (1757–1825), praising Hao's language and ideas as "superb."[167] Since Hao's notes are the peg on which the article hangs, we would be justified in understanding Zhou's title to mean "My thoughts in response to Hao's thoughts on the subject of *bense*." In fact Hao provides our entry into early Qing poetic theory. Hao, Zhou tells us,

often quotes from Wang Yuyang [Wang Shizhen; 1632–1711] and You Xitang [You Tong; 1618–1704]. . . . Recently I have been reading early Qing *biji*, and I feel many of them are excellent. Wang Yuyang and Song Muzhong [Song Lao; 1634–1713], You Xitang and Feng Dunyin [Feng Ban; 1614–71], Liu Jizhuang [Liu Xianting; 1648–95] and Fu Qingzhu [Fu Shan; 1607–84], all of them are [excellent].

These men, who flourished about a century before Hao, were engaged in a discourse that drew its sustenance from late Ming counter-traditional demands for self-expression (*xingling*) but took further the question of what and how a writer should study. The two seminal figures are Qian Qianyi (1582–1664) and Wang Shizhen.

Qian laid the groundwork, rejecting the still hugely popular archaists and enlarging the attack to include Yan Yu, whom he condemned for classifying poetry according to styles and period.[168] In this he represents a movement on the part of many late Ming and Qing critics to "ridicule the obsession with High Tang models . . . or reject the canonization process altogether on the grounds that dynastic eras bear no necessary relationship to the quality of poetry."[169] Instead of approaching poetry through Yan Yu's concept of *bense*, Qian focused on the operation of *bi* and *xing*.[170] That is to say, he rejected both Yan's formal prosodic models and the equation of poetry and enlightenment and sought instead to identify in earlier poems the concrete circumstances of the poet.[171] According to Gong Pengcheng, this was an inevitable development, for the Ming archaists with their stress on the analysis of formal features had lost sight of Yan Yu's solution to the problem of the relation between knowledge and emotions.[172]

Yet Qian seems similar to Yan in that he also sought in poetry a poetic quality that could exist outside the poem (*shi wai you shi*).[173] Poetic value he judged according to the poem's conveyance of the poet's *zhiyi* (intent and meaning), and it was the force of feeling that gave a poem its "fragrance" (*xiang*), fragrance being more prized than "color" (*se*) or diction.[174] If the poet's intent and inborn talent account for the nature of the poem, it is brought into being through the external factors of learning (*xue*), situation (*jing*), and that which is encountered (*yu*) in the poet's experience.[175] Fragrance in Qian's usage could thus perhaps be regarded as a secularized reinscription—secularized because it rejected Yan Yu's idea of enlightenment—of the poetics of *quwei*.

Qian's ideas, together with the example he set with his own anthologizing and scholarship on Ming poetry,[176] had a profound influence on early Qing poetics, freeing it from canonical restrictions. This is perhaps the most important point to be grasped here, because scholars were thus encouraged to explore any part of the literary tradition they liked. Consequently, for example, the Feng brothers, Feng Ban and Feng Shu (1593–?), who were close enough to Qian to be considered members of his Yushan school, differed with each other and with him both in the importance they accorded to the study of form and sound and the poetry they chose to study. Qian harshly ridiculed the Jingling school, notwithstanding its ardent advocacy of self-expression (*xingling*), for lacking in learning.

Jingling poetics were based on very subjective readings of pre-Tang and Tang poetry and focused on archaic words as the conduit of poetic meaning. Tan Yuanchun (1586–1631), for example, considered individual words in poems to be as powerful as a pair of eyes staring from a page. Consequently, writers in this school often sacrificed semantic coherence to abstruse diction.[177] Qian ascribed their faults to a refusal to study, which, he said, resulted in their choosing poetry like tea, going after the bad and throwing out the good. In this they were as laughable as someone staring into a butcher's shop while starving himself.[178] Writers needed to read books to nourish the will and the spirit, Qian said.[179] The combination of self-expression, learning, and rejection of classification was part of the broader intellectual trend to judge facts and texts according to their own truth or falseness. Thus Huang Zongxi (1610–95) and Gu Yanwu shared many attitudes with Qian.[180]

Wang Shizhen greatly complicated matters by accepting the arguments for self-expression while grounding his poetics in Yan Yu's and Sikong Tu's ideas of communicating the uncommunicable.[181] To this, he added the requirement that emotion be conveyed obliquely through imagery that produced an effect of purity, distance, and mildness (*qing yuan pingdan*), analogous to that produced by the landscape paintings of the Wang Wei school.[182] Wang reiterated the idea that poetry and Chan were the same, but instead of defining the acme of poetry as "marvelous enlightenment" he called it *shenyun*, a virtually untranslatable binome that refers to the expression of personal character and emotion.[183]

This points to a very different conception of the poetic self from that held by Gao Bing (Yanli; fourteenth century) and the archaists, in which the poet was to emulate not only the diction but also the emotions of canonical poets. If we accept Edward Ch'ien's account of intellectual history, we can attribute Wang's new reading of enlightenment poetics to the monistic idea of the universe in late Ming Neo-Confucianism.[184] In this view, since everything partakes of the same nature, the expression of the self is not seen as conflicting with the expression of the ineffable. By the same token, the self does not have to be expressed directly but can be conveyed with restraint and distance, to heightened aesthetic effect. The influence of these ideas of Wang Shizhen's was probably what enabled writers to turn away from the excessive clarity and lightness of the Gongan school.

Wang likened literature to a "mystical dragon" (*shen long*), which could never be observed in its entirety, whereas arts like painting and sculpture could attempt to present things completely. These ideas were attacked by Zhao Zhixin (1662–1744) in his *Tan long lu* (1709).[185] This controversy points to an area of tension within poetics, generated by the impetus from evidential studies to understand poetry as a text to be made clear and stripped of ambiguity. Thus Yuan Mei opined that "writing poetry is like writing history"[186]—a view, in the scheme of things, entirely consonant with Zhou's judgment about his vulgarity. The title of Zhou Zuoren's book *Tan long ji* is very likely a reference to this dispute, judging from the preface (quoted earlier in this chapter), in which Zhou ridiculed the idea he imputes to Mr. Tame Dragon that literature can be fully understood. Finally, we should note that Hao Yixing was himself concerned with linguistic accuracy: a keen observer of the natural world, he annotated the *Er-ya*, checking textual accounts with his own observations in the field.[187]

Now that we have a context, we can consider Zhou's text in depth, beginning with the opening anecdote from Hao Yixing:

Behind a monastery in the Western Capital was a flourishing bamboo grove. Gentlemen often met there to enjoy their leisure. Wen Lugong [Yanbo; 1006–97] also visited there and was very fond of it. The monks had an uninscribed board, and they begged him to think up a name [for the grove]. He happily assented, but many months passed and nothing happened. The monks repeatedly went and asked him, and he said, "I still haven't thought of a good name, please wait a little longer." Over half a year later, he returned the board, on which was written "Soaring Bamboo Canopy." How marvelous! The topic and the name fit perfectly. If others had been asked to do this, they would have come up with "Verdant Bamboos Brush the Azure Firmament"; therefore he was greatly esteemed.[188]

Hao's comment on this anecdote (which he has taken from You Tong's *Genzhai xushuo* [More words from the First Hexagram Studio]) is as follows:

I say that during the time [Wen] Lugong had not yet come up with the best name, stored up in his breast were just words like verdant bamboo, azure, and so on. So he weighed up his thoughts for half a year and then he obtained the name most apposite to the reality (*zhen quan*) [of the bamboos]. This is the outlook shared by the authors of imperishable writings.[189]

*Quan* has the meaning of expounding, explaining, the principles or characteristics of something. From this, it would seem that the quality in Wen Lugong that enabled him to arrive at his happy choice of name was related to his ability to perceive something of the truth of a matter. However, as the tale makes clear, this perception was not instantaneous but required arduous development. In fact, a double operation was required: the writer had to perceive the true nature of the bamboos and recognize that the words that first came to mind (or that filled his breast) were inadequate. Therefore he had to seek exactly the right word or phrase to make this perception linguistically available to others. This means that he had to apply his perception carefully to the language at his disposal—that is, the language available to him both as a speaker and as a literatus.

Zhou Zuoren shared the concern for simplicity, although he cites a different authority:

There is only one formula for writing, and that is stated in just one word: simplicity. As is stated in every English composition textbook, the first thing the student has to learn is simplicity, that is the key. But this is not something very easy. What a three-year-old can achieve in his speech an eighty-year-old man finds hard to attain.[190]

He then quotes Feng Ban to the effect that there is no hard and fast divide between the written language and ordinary talk. But, Zhou suggests, this cuts both ways:

Actually, ordinary talk is also not easy, for the very reason that it contains literary words. On the whole, for ordinary speech to be elegant may be somewhat easy, because you just have to use a little time on powder and paint, and that's enough, just the same as for writing. But to produce *bense* is difficult. Why? Because in the first place, in order to be sure of *bense*, it's necessary for the original character and features (*benlai de zhidi xingse*) to come into their own. Second, it's a human feeling (*ren qing*) to lack self-confidence and want to rely on ornamentation, but you have to wash away this previously applied makeup before the *bense* can show through, and that is what is difficult. The writer in the anecdote thought for six months before he discarded words like "green shoots brushing the azure firmament" and came up with a plain, honest "soaring bamboo." This was an extremely important experience for a literary figure and an extremely good lesson for posterity.[191]

In this passage it is not clear whether Zhou regards *bense* as a quality of the individual's expression, either as text or speech, or of the speaker/writer. The "original character and features" (i.e., disposition) surely belong to the writer, but the "ornamentation" is found in language, which recalls Chaves's insight about the dual function of Chinese critical terms. But this points to the fact, I think, that Zhou cannot conceive of expression apart from the person expressing it; hence, the process of "washing away makeup" applies simultaneously to the perceiving mind and to the language used. In this way, striving for *bense* in writing can be seen as somehow synonymous with a process of moral and intellectual self-cultivation aimed at removing the obscurities that hinder the ability to perceive.

Although the expression might be seen as inseparable from the expressing self, however, this does not mean that the individual is *constituted* by language. Otherwise one might wonder how the writer could ever know when to stop "washing away makeup." Might he not wash away his face? The problem does not arise, however, since there seems to be a gap, or an asymmetry, between language and the expressing self in which the "original character can show through." This suggests that it is in the power of this original character "to know" that which is normally hidden by the "powder and paint" of language. But because of "lack of self-confidence," one abandons what one knows. Here we should recall Zhou's reference to lack of self-confidence as "a human feeling." In my reading this resonates closely with Jiao Hong's insight that the mind which has for some reason lost its self-awareness loses its self-confidence.[192]

The centrality of this conception of the self to Zhou's notion of *bense* will become clear shortly, as we continue to follow his essay:

Many years ago I came across an anecdote in the literary jottings of the Song writer Tang Zixi [Geng; 1070–1120] that pleased me no end. It read: "Guan Zidong [Zhu; twelfth century] was staying in the Bi Yong [palace outside Kaifeng, where nominees for office were trained]. The north wind was blowing very hard, and inspired him with the lines: "The long night: when will dawn arrive? / The bitter cold: keeps sleep away." He went to his teacher and asked, "Although long night parallels bitter cold in that the caesura is in the same place, the whole thing does not seem stable." The teacher said, "Keep it just as it is, just as you would keep the essence (*cun xing*) in a medicine."[193]

Regardless of the rights and wrongs of the question of the caesura, Zhou tells us, this story had so enchanted him that he had taken the name "Medicine Decocting Studio."

I really don't know too much about decocting medicine, probably it's similar to warming wine and curing tea; the heating time is most important. You have to just reach the point of getting rid of the unwanted elements and still not lose what is essential (*benxing*). If this method is acquired, it really can be applied to the business of writing. Retaining the essence (*cun xing*) and retaining *bense* (*cun bense*) are not necessarily the same thing, but I think both are very good ways of putting it, very helpful to those of us who want to write. That is why I have quoted these two anecdotes together.[194]

We have to take seriously Zhou's comment that retaining the essence and retaining *bense* are not necessarily the same thing, but the ambiguity and overlap between them is lost in translation, for the word *xing* carries the weight of "personal character" or "nature" and once again we confront the inextricability of the expression from the person.

We see that Guan Zhu's experience was in a direction opposite to that of Wen Lugong. Rather than arduously strip through layers of superfluous words, he had to know when to stop, to realize that the words he had found were the right ones. Perhaps this was because Wen's task hinged more on "conveying the characteristics" of the bamboos, whereas Guan's was to express the immediacy of his experience of a cold sleepless night. The metaphor of decocting medicine is even more apposite to the idea that language is something external to one than that of face-washing, since it suggests that control of language is something of a skill that depends on experience. In both cases, excellence depended on recognizing the fit between the language and the reality and on conveying something individual in the manner of doing so.

In the rest of the essay, basing himself selectively on comments by Feng Ban, Zhou developed the idea that the budding writer must write "cautiously and simply" before moving on to the "complex and unrestrained" and voiced his opposition to "theorizing." But the reader is not allowed to get away with the idea that simple diction and self-expression equate with *bense*, for the essay concludes:

The injunction to be careful is well worth the attention of language teachers in primary schools. It is not the same as the formulation for literati about preserving the essence, in that its application is naturally much wider and consequently the benefit from it is greater. I've been writing for thirty years and have recently begun to understand what it is to be careful. Even if I have not derived other benefits from it, I have been able to avoid highflown theorizing. But as for *bense*, that is like gazing at a distant road and not being able to see it.[195]

It is this last sentence that makes me feel justified in arguing that Zhou intends *bense* to stand unequivocally for the fruit of the writer's moral and intellectual self-cultivation. To put it another way, the concern is with how the writing self constructs him- or herself through (self-)education. It is the stress on intellection and education that differentiates it from the more diffuse *quwei*.

Some clues about how this process was conceived as operating emerge if we return to the way dramatists used *bense*. As mentioned above, the idea of voice was linked to the concept of *bense* in drama. We must now expand this a little, recalling that dramatists such as Tang Xianzu (1550–1616) and Xu Wei were both involved importantly in the Ming counter-tradition.

Drawing on the writing of the dramatist Wang Jide (d. 1623), Gong Pengcheng shows how during the Yuan dynasty the *bense* of the *qu* drama was felt to reside in the flavor of "garlic and fermented milk," which denoted its northern, unaristocratic origins. However, as educated writers from non-theatrical families started to write plays, the concept of what constituted the *bense* of drama changed. The original northern style was still considered acceptable for minor plays (*xiao qu*), but major plays required the infusion of ornate diction and an altered structure to qualify generically. Thus the *bense* of *qu* drama eventually changed to incorporate both requirements.[196]

What is noteworthy about Wang Jide's discussion of *bense*, Gong points out, is the analogy he makes with the concept of the *jia*, or family, the implication being that just as a mature man of ability can set up his own independent *jia*, so when a work or style is mature enough to be distinguishable from others, it can be seen as belonging to a particular "family." *Jia*, based on the same analogy, also means school, and we recall Tang Shunzhi's argument that the Confucians, Daoists, and so on were all schools with their own voices and *bense*.

Recalling the broader intellectual currents in which poetics and drama developed, Edward Ch'ien has referred to the way in which the existence of different and contending philosophical schools led to a preoccupation with "intellectual genealogies," such as Huang Zongxi's *Records of the Ming Scholars*, large numbers of which were produced in the late Ming and early Qing.[197] All these genealogies "tried to individualize a school or thinker either historically in terms of transmission and development or logically in terms of relatedness in the formation of concepts, or both."[198] Thomas Wilson describes the Confucian tradition that emerges in Huang Zongxi's writings as "a multiplicity of contending schools and doctrines, none of which could claim to stand for the entire tradition or occupy a privileged status," which was a conception "based on an understanding of mind as infinitely variegated."[199] Late Qing thinkers were impelled by a desire to "map the variations within Confucianism" in genealogical terms. Just like a family lineage, "the [guiding purpose] of a school is likely to differentiate into a variety of persuasions which bear a certain family resemblance, but which are distinguishable in terms of partiality and universality . . . and profundity and shallowness because they embody differences in individual self-attainment or perception (*chien* or *shih*)."[200] The idea of differences in attainment is crucial, because it encompasses the inevitability—and desirability—of diversity of thought. The basis for this in the restructured Neo-Confucianism with which Ch'ien is concerned is the conviction that the Way is unitary in structure but pluralistic in articulation, and that it is the individuality of each "attainment" that is to be valued. Here we will have to bracket the metaphysics involved in the notion of the Way and regard it as signifying existential "reality." What is important for our purposes is the notion of attainment.[201]

Lest it be charged that this is straying too far afield from literature, the definition of *bense* given by a modern scholar in a manual of literary terms takes almost the same starting point. Zhou Zhenfu returns to Tang Shunzhi's discussion of *bense* to ask where the "true spirit" and "ineradicable viewpoint" come from. In answer, he quotes Huang Zongxi: "From ancient times to the present, it has not been necessary for a writer to begin by excelling. Each of the nine classes of literature and the hundred schools of thought (*jiuliu baijia*) had its own clarity of understanding about things, and when this gushed out, it constituted excellence."[202] No one, it seems, could hope for perfect knowledge; thus even when Du Fu wrote a poem about a dance, he obviously did not understand as much about the dance as the dancer, but his poem expressed his understanding, Huang continued. "That which is literature can be nothing other than the writing down of what has been understood in one's mind. If the mind is not clear, laboring to produce elegant sentences is nothing other than twigs and leaves without their own life."[203] Clearly, the idea of *bense* is inextricable from the concept of attainment, arrived at through clarity of mind. This helps solve the dilemma of whether *bense* belongs to the author or the text, because attainment was manifested in the texts thinkers produced, and this was what gave impetus to the concern with linguistic precision as a way of ensuring that the thinker's attainment was really understood.

As we have seen, Edward Ch'ien equates attainment with perception, which is his gloss for *jian* or *shi* taken separately. Zhou Zuoren uses both together in the compound *jianshi*, which he names as a requisite of the ideal essay.[204] The translations in Chinese-English dictionaries of *jianshi* as some combination of knowledge and experience do not convey the embeddedness of the term in the context we have just been discussing. But the *Zhongwen da cidian* takes its primary definition from the *Complete Writings of the Cheng Brothers* (*Er Cheng quan shu*): "The views and observations derived from the study of affairs and things." The next gloss is "synonym for wisdom." Thus, the basis of *jianshi* is study that encompasses moral and intellectual concerns and that results in self-attained perceptions of a maturity and consistency sufficient to enable one to constitute one's own school of thought or be recognized as contributing to an already established one.

This interpretation of *bense* as a concomitant of *jianshi* as just defined explains the high moral tone of Zhou's statement that although he had been writing for thirty years, *bense* was still like gazing at a distant road.[205] However, there is an important difference: Zhou rejected the idea of schools and fixed theories, as he makes clear in the same essay on *bense*, and he did this in the name of his primary desideratum for writing, simplicity. But simplicity, it seems, is something that has to be taught or, at least, that must be fostered at the beginning of one's education. Zhou quotes from Feng Ban's criticisms of Xie Fangde (1226–89) for suggesting that beginning students produce "unrestrained talk and highflown theories" (*fang yan gao lun*) before practicing restraint and caution. This was nonsense and could only "ruin" (*jiaohuai*) the students. Zhou agreed with this and went on to quote from Feng's injunctions to his descendants forbidding them to theorize. Feng's words were "the roar of a great master," Zhou said; the harm done by theorizing was "incalculable," and nowadays the damage had spread to literature.[206]

Zhou sees *jianshi* as independent of schools when he describes *jianshi* and *quwei* as the two most important qualities to be found in writing. In an essay about Yu Yue's literary style, Zhou suggests that it is difficult to discuss prose because "there are many differences in literary standards." Consequently,

those who like to discuss principles (*yili*) [i.e. in the style of the Tongcheng school] advocate not only that writing should have substance and be convincing but also that the substance must be the orthodox views of a certain school; so if what is written is not a choleric defense of traditional ethics, it is a denunciation of heterodoxy. Then there are those who prize metrics and euphony and want every piece of prose to declaim well, just as men of old used to declaim Han Yu's Valediction to Dong Shaonan, first absorbing its *qi* and then putting it into voice, everyone clamoring together like so many clashing symbols and gongs and quite rousing to listen to. But beyond these viewpoints there is another one, which is not to turn writing into either curses or Peking opera, but to treat writing as speech written down, containing something interesting in sentences able to communicate. These are the requisites of ordinary speech and can be used in discussing writing. I subscribe to this view. A lot of famous prose handed down through the ages is, in my mind, just hackneyed or merely fashionable, while much of what has been qualified as pedestrian or shallow really has something [worthwhile] in it. This is because the writer has got his own ideas and can say them. Just as I said once before, the knowledge born of experience (*jianshi*) and *quwei*, these alone constitute the ideal essay.[207]

Yu Yue's miscellaneous writings perfectly illustrated both his scholarly attainments (*jianshi*) and the separate, personal quality of perception that enabled him to appreciate and communicate it (*quwei*). These embodied his opinions on "the substance of things and the human feelings involved" (*wuli renqing*) expressed in an honest, direct (*chengyi*), and perfectly deft and intelligent (*fengqu*) manner.[208]

Since Zhou considered Hao's comments on *bense* to be "eminently suitable for perusal by writers," it is worth looking at those he did not quote, to gain a deeper appreciation of what was at stake. Here is the first:

"In riding, one chooses a superior horse, among oxen one chooses those of the middle grade, and one makes use of people of lower grade." This is an excellent saying. A horse is required to go long distances, an ox to carry burdens, and the person one uses is required to stay within bounds. If a smart slave or a violent servant is cleverer than his master, it is not impossible he could take advantage of him. In the past, Sima Wengong [Sima Guang, 1019–86] had an old servant who had been with him over thirty years, and who addressed him as Bachelor Junshi [i.e., by his personal name and his first degree]. Zizhan [Su Shi] saw this and instructed him to call his master "Prime Minister." Sima Guang was startled, and when he found out the reason, he sighed and said, "What a pity, the old servant's been ruined by Su Dongpo." But these days the number of masters who are ruined by their servants is greater and even more deplorable. (Excerpted from [You Tong's] *Genzhai xushuo*, 8.)

Note: Yuyang [Wang Shizhen] once visited Wang Tiaowen [Wan; 1624–91], whose servant boy announced him [familiarly, using his courtesy name]: "Wang Yishang's here!" Yuyang laughed and said, "He is not inferior to the household servant of Xiao Yingshi [717–68]" [who remained loyal despite ill-usage because he admired his master's talent]. (Excerpted from [Wang Shizhen's] *Xiang zu biji*, 8.)

I say: Wang Tiaowen's servant seems to have had an air of polish; thus, he does not measure up to Sima Guang's servant. Some will say that the fact Su Dongpo managed to ruin him shows he was not totally "uncarved." I say, "not so." If the [legendary] people of Wuhuai and Getian had been born in the Zhou, Qin, Chu, or Han, they would also have been ruined by education.[209]

The first anecdote is "framed" by a piece of received wisdom on choosing horses, oxen, and servants that functions as a metaphor for language which serves discursive thinking. If allowed to get out of hand, language can overwhelm the perceiving mind that is using it, but, on the other hand, life is inconceivable without it. The unstated assumption is that in the relationship between perception and language, something is always lost. The function of language is seen as naming. The variable is education, which if accepted uncritically, as Sima Guang's servant did (although the implication is he could not help but do so), leads to "ruination." But, as Hao points out in his comment, education is unavoidable once culture exists. Yet Hao still holds that the "polish" of the pert servant made him less admirable than Sima Guang's servant. What then, are we to think of education?

This impasse shows that this mode of interpretation, pursued to the bitter end, is too mechanistic. Given that independently arrived-at perceptions, even when partial and imperfect, are what permit *bense* to emerge, we may consider the anecdotes to be a record of the attainment of all those involved, each showing something of the truth of a situation and the individuality that enabled each actor to attain part of the truth. In this case, Sima Guang's servant can be valued both for his ability to retain his perception of his master as a young man and for his unworldliness, and Wang Tiaowen's for his worldly (even potentially subversive) ability to assess his master. Moreover, we may feel we understand a little more about Sima Guang, Su Dongpo, and Wang Shizhen from their comments. But the acceptance of this plurality of views does not mean that all judgment is suspended: Hao makes his own judgments, both in his comments and, prior to that, in the act of anthologizing the anecdotes. Moreover, we, as readers, may make our own. The last section of Hao's comments explores this point further, but with more attention to language:

My late father succeeded in the annual examinations and therefore was given a door poster on which was written just the two words *ming jing* [meaning both "familiar with the classics" and "senior graduate"]. Mou Moren [Ting; 1759–1832] approved it as being simple and to the point. My father replied, "How would I dare say *ming jing?*" In this he seemed to dislike officiousness.

Gu Jingyang [Xiancheng; 1550–1612] visited Li Sancai [d. 1623]. The first time he saw him, he was served coarse rice, soup, and vegetables. The next day he was served a fine meal. Gu was surprised; so Li explained, "Yesterday it so happened I had nothing, and today it so happens I have something, that's all." Gu deeply appreciated this, but felt Li was trying to deceive people into thinking he was a free spirit, although there was nothing wrong with what he said. Pei Jingong [Du; 765–839] said: "Chicken, fish, onions, or chives, when you have them to eat, you eat them; birth, old age, sickness, death, when the time comes, that's the same thing." (Both anecdotes excerpted from the *Genzhai xushuo*, 4.) [Hao's comment]: I say: Pei Jingong's words are true *bense*.

Depth of insight becomes inseparable from its mode of expression in this last section. Thus the door poster, though simple and to the point, is superficial, going no deeper than a pun on a title. Similarly, Mou Moren's comment added nothing of intrinsic interest to the situation. Both could be faulted for "officiousness," because their language failed, for lack of imagination, to go beyond the obvious external success of the graduate. The tale about Li Sancai is a little puzzling, since we seem to have to rely on the author's judgment that although his words appeared to convey some profundity, they were intended to deceive. The basis of his judgment becomes clearer with the next anecdote. Pei made almost exactly the same point as Li, but much more directly. Also, the concrete images of the foods not only individualize the insight, they give it something of a poetic flavor. In fact, it is the poetic element that both anchors and unsettles the speaker's reference to birth, age, sickness, and death. This enables us, other things being equal, to descry the comment's *bense* and possibly judge it superior to that of Li.

Zhou Zuoren's notion of *bense* is based on individual awareness. But what differentiates the manifestation of this awareness from *quwei* is that its attainment is based on the relationship of the writer to language. This relationship depends on education. Education need not be understood necessarily as anything more formal than reading. Edward Ch'ien has noted that in the restructured Neo-Confucian discourse reading was understood "not [as] a passive performance of reception but [as] entail[ing] the active exercise of critical judgment."[210] Qian Qianyi's slogan that one should have many teachers makes sense in this context.[211] Hao Yixing's notes on *bense* provide the would-be writer with several exercises in critical judgment about language and the way it works, and this was Zhou's reason for recommending it.

It is because *bense* is inseparable from notions of attainment and critical judgment that it is so important in arming the writer against the hegemony of the nation-building project. The practice of simplicity and clarity of language in both reading and writing becomes a method of maintaining one's integrity and intellectual alertness. As the word *practice* suggests, the effort of self-education must be a continuous one. Thus, Zhou laments in an early essay that he can feel his own "true features" (*zhen xiang*) in his heart but cannot convey them in his writing because he is "not cultivated enough."[212] The idea that language could belong to a particular social class—an idea Zhou denied, just as he denied any sharp demarcation between the vernacular and literary languages—is, of course, alien to this view.[213]

Zhou's own reading practice served to demonstrate the self-education on which the concept of *bense* was based. His reading and his appreciation of the insights of others were never trammeled by loyalty to any particular school or thinker. This, then, was the modern answer to the vexing question of how the writer should relate to the tradition. But it is evident that a prerequisite for the free deployment of *bense* was freedom of literary and intellectual life—something Zhou considered sadly lacking in his society.

# FOUR

## ∼

# Zhou Zuoren's Humanism, the Self,

# and the Essay Form

### The Debate over the Essay

Zhou Zuoren's aesthetics of *quwei* and *bense* were grounded in a concept of the self traceable to the radical Neo-Confucianism of the late Ming. Zhou's innovation was to capitalize on its respect for the self as an autonomous moral agent but to secularize these aesthetics by disconnecting them from any religious or political dogma, while leaving them open-ended so that they could reflect the ineffable in the hands of those writers who wished them to do so.

Feng Wenbing, a close associate of Zhou and a practitioner of Chan meditation, is a good example. Zhou's preface to Feng's *The Tale of Mr. Never Existed (Moxuyou xiansheng zhuan)* likens it to Zhuangzi's discourse on the wind in the *Qiwulun* chapter, which was also a perfect description of good writing.[1] Some months later, he wrote to Feng that he had reread the book and had "suddenly came to the realization" that the book was a record of Feng's spiritual journey (lit. the "recorded utterances of a worthy" [*xianzhe yulu*]). "Perhaps it is a little easier to understand than [the writings of] a Chan monk, but because both are traveling the same route, although there may be differences in degree, they are not very different from each other."[2] His preface had neglected that aspect by focusing on the book's language, Zhou said, adding: "Perhaps the language of a recorded utterance can be obtained and criticized, but [as for] the frame of mind (xinjing)—Chan—from which the utterance came, how could that be [obtained and criticized]?"

From the early 1920s and into the 1930s, aesthetics, particularly the aesthetics of quwei, became inseparable from questions about the origins and nature of the modern essay in China. As we have seen, Zhou was acknowledged by Hu Shi as early as 1922 as the leading figure in establishing the short essay (xiaopin sanwen) in the vernacular as a genre, particularly for the mild, calm (pingdan) conversational manner of expression he brought to it. Five years later, Zhu Guangqian (1897–1986), although incredulous Zhou could admire poetry about a fly washing its hands and feet, described Zhou's essays on foods, people, and places as a "big release" from "pretentious new poetry" and fiction "piled high with adjectives." The reader felt as if he or she were sitting with Zhou, savoring green tea and watching frogs in the courtyard, far away from the hectic life of publishing and lecturing.[3]

Literary critics and authors on the May Fourth scene like Hu Shi might find Zhou's writing disconcerting, but they prized its "traditional" flavor. With it Zhou had effected a double victory: his writing spoke for baihua and thus the project of New Culture, and it was also a victory against the National Essence group who claimed tradition as their own. Zhou thus reassured those who may have doubted the capacity of the new, national literature to be truly and fittingly literary; he also provided a model of literary style. The trouble was that most people wanted this indigenization of what was conceived of as the fourth Western literary form after fiction, poetry, and drama to exist within the context of the literary history that was being produced simultaneously with literature as part of the process of nation-building. In terms of what I have been calling the dominant May Fourth nation-building discourse, the use of the vernacular symbolized a break with a feudal past. Since this past was defined in terms of undesirable attitudes and subject matter, the new literature also entailed efforts to keep these out of writing.

Zhou had never accepted the idea that the vernacular was opposed to

"dead" *guwen* or the class-based formula of Chen Duxiu that distinguished the "old aristocratic literature" and the new "literature of the
people." What this would mean for the essay can be glimpsed from the
way he first suggested in 1921 that the creation of a modern essay form
might proceed:

In foreign literature there is something called the essay, which can be divided into
two kinds. One is critical and scholarly, and the other is narrational and artistic and
is also known as "belles lettres." This second type can also be divided into the factual
narration of events and the lyrical, although many contain both aspects. This type
of essay seems to be most developed among the English-speaking peoples. Writers
already well known in China such as Addison, Lamb, Owen, and Hawthorne all
wrote very good belles lettres, and more recently Galsworthy, Gissing, and Ches-
terton have shown themselves to be particularly skilled at belles lettres. Reading a
good essay is like reading a prose-poem (*sanwen shi*), because it really is a bridge between poetry and prose. In China, the prefaces, jottings, and anecdotes (*shuo*) written in *guwen* can also be called a kind of belles lettres. But in contemporary literature
in the national language (*guoyu wenxue*), we have not yet seen this kind of essay.
Why don't those creating the new literature try their hand at it?[4]

By including the "prefaces, jottings, and anecdotes in *guwen*" in the same
category as belles lettres, Zhou was leaving the door open to the expression of a traditional sensibility. He subtly paved the way for this in the
preceding sentence by suggesting that the essay bridged poetry and prose,
for, in China, lyricism has been of overwhelming concern in genres other
than poetry, including the personal essay.[5] At the same time, with his
reference to prose-poems at a time when Turgenev (1818–83), Baudelaire
(1821–67), and Tagore were all the rage, Zhou could emphasize the modern credentials of lyrical prose expression. Pollard has thrown doubt on
Zhou's familiarity with the English-language essayists he mentions.[6] His
familiarity with the essays of writers such as Havelock Ellis and Andrew
Lang is not questioned, but he did not present them as literary models.[7]

In advocating the creation of a new essay form, Zhou was turning
away from the May Fourth preoccupation with fiction and poetry:

I believe that in a piece of writing outward form and content really are related.
There are many thoughts that cannot be turned into fiction and are not easy to turn
into poetry (I only mean this in regard to form; in terms of character, belles lettres
are also fictional, and fiction is also poetry—Kuprin's "The Evening Guest" . . . is
an example). Consequently, these thoughts can be expressed in essays.[8]

Finally, Zhou stipulated, writers should write with genuineness and clarity. One could set oneself to write after having read foreign models but only by using one's own words and ideas, not by copying others.

During the 1920s, as writers eagerly developed the essay as a vehicle for personal expression, they also tried to define and shape it as a category of the new literature and to lay down stylistic criteria. Given the radically innovative nature of the period, there could be no firm consensus on how the genre should develop. There were two areas in which Zhou came into conflict with others: one was over the function of *quwei*; the other was the function of the essayist as critic. In practice, the second concern was an extension of the first, for both concerned the scope and acceptability of a certain type of individual response. Reading Zhou's essays and articles of the 1920s, we see often see him spinning round to meet an attack or trimming his rhetorical sails before the winds of one event or another in an attempt to maintain intact the moral independence of the writer.

Here his positions are often remarkably close to those of Li Zhi, who most forcefully developed the implications of moral and intellectual independence found in the late Ming notion of self-attainment. In one of his most important statements, Li held the "childlike heart" to be the "true mind of man" (*tongxin zhe, zhen xin ye*); its loss resulted in the loss of the "true person" (*zhen ren*).[9] Li Zhi called this state of mind the "childlike heart" not to suggest a babbling infant but to make an analogy with human growth. Just as a man starts off as a child, the childlike heart is the starting point for the growth of the mind (*tongzi zhe, ren zhi chu ye; tongxin zhe, xin zhi chu ye*). The childlike heart is that which exists at the beginning of mind and is lost when overlaid with received opinion (*wenjian*) and principles (*daoli*).[10] Underpinning this was Li Zhi's insistence that no person should take any sage, past or present, as infallible, not even Confucius. To depend on Confucius for attainment was tantamount to admitting that there were no fulfilled human beings before Confucius. Moreover, Confucius had never required men to imitate him.[11] Similarly, one should not follow the Buddha slavishly but retain one's freedom to take what one wanted from each or any Buddhist school as one pleased.[12]

Most famously, Li Zhi declared that no book could remain valid throughout the ages and that the Six Classics, the *Mencius*, and the *Analects* were merely a collection of words of praise written by historians, containing much that did not come from the mouths of the sages. But even the true utterances of Confucius or Mencius would not hold good in all cases. In his own time, Li Zhi continued, "The *Mencius* and the *Analects* have become the false reasoning of orthodox Neo-Confucianists and the staging posts of false men."[13] As we saw in the previous chapter, for Li Zhi, speaking of Buddha and speaking of poetry were identical pursuits in that both aimed at transcendence. Thus Li Zhi's "On the Childlike Heart" ends with the words, "Where can I find a true sage, one who has not lost his childlike heart, so that I can speak to him of literature!"[14]

Zuo Dongling argues that the significance of Li Zhi for late Ming literary thought is that he provided a philosophical basis for linking the naturalness and spontaneity of human nature with complete freedom of creativity. Literature then became part of man's enjoyment of life, which came with release from the fetters of received opinions, mundane concerns (*shisu*), and conventional relationships (*lijiao*).[15] Reading became an activity valued for its intrinsic joy, since it enabled the mind to expand and roam and, occasionally, to find a kindred spirit.[16]

Zhou's desire to retain the type of subjectivity found in the "prefaces, jottings, and anecdotes" written in *guwen* became more explicit as literary critics endeavored to define the May Fourth literary field. Writing in February 1923, he commented that "literary and artistic criticism ought of itself to be a literary work, expressing in writing the author's impressions and appreciation. It is definitely not a one-sidedly intellectual judgment."[17] China's contemporary deficiency in literary criticism started here, he added. "First, critics think the word 'criticism' means faultfinding . . . and that for this reason censure and disdain are obligatory in their essays; otherwise they will not count as criticism. Second, those who do criticism think it is a matter of issuing legal judgments: once the judgment has been passed, the work's fate is sealed."[18] This state of affairs had occurred in the past thanks to -isms and factions supported by worthies such as Dr. Johnson and Belinsky but would not work nowadays.

The defect of these two types of criticism lies in believing that there is one transcendent, objective truth that is an adequate criterion for all generations and that they just happen to understand and possess this truth as a result of which they are endowed with the authority to pass judgment for generations to come. It is not only the proponents of "literature to convey the way" or those who believe they ought to write for the laborers and peasants who are likely to slip up this way. This flaw is also unavoidable in those who defend a particular school of thought.[19]

Literature did not need the imposition of supposedly scientific methods such as the reduction of the structure of a piece of prose to a mathematical equation—science was necessary but was not enough on its own.

There is a need for analysis in research, but synthesis is necessary for appreciation. Literary principles are like a craftsman's tools. Mencius said, "The master-worker gives a man a square and compass, he cannot give him artistry."[20] We can use scientific principles to understand a work's surface, but we cannot use a square and compass to determine its artistry.[21]

Zhou distinguished between academic literary research concerned with theory, dating, and so on and "literary criticism that has a literary quality." This division corresponds exactly with the one drawn by Kang-i Sun Chang between "lyric criticism . . . closely related to aesthetic experience" and "commentary . . . the study of objective information." This mode of criticism first developed in the Six Dynasties, which Zhou invokes by citing the Six Dynasties poet Tao Qian (Yuanming; 365–427):

Tao Yuanming spoke in a poem of "Enjoying novel writings together/[and] analyzing uncertain meanings with each other" (*qi wen gong xinshang/yi yi xiang yu xi*). Literary criticism consists precisely in "enjoying novel writings together"; it is a matter of synthesizing its flavor. And "analysing uncertain meanings with each other" is part of the work of intellectual analysis. Real literary criticism ought to be a literary work. Rather than to say that it expresses the true face of its object of criticism, it would be better to say it is a reflection of the critic.[22]

Zhou quoted extensively from Anatole France's (1844–1924) famous comments in defense of subjective criticism: "Criticism, like philosophy and history, is, in my view, a kind of novel destined for intelligent and curious souls . . . and every novel is an autobiography." In reading criticism, one learned of the responses of the critic to his subject, and this was an unavoidable result of the fact that "we are all locked into our personalities, as though locked in prison." Yet France's metaphor of imprisonment, with its suggestion of separation from the rest of the world, did not fit exactly with Zhou's description of the exercise of the critical func-

tion, which stressed reliance on "our shared human feelings." These enabled us to

> understand all works of art, but the varying tastes we go on to develop give rise to
> the differences among us and then to the appearance of love and hate. We ought
> to admit that this is an unalterable fact, but at the same time we ought to remem-
> ber that it is just our subjective likes and dislikes, and they cannot affect the objec-
> tive value of the work, because we have no way of fathoming its absolute true
> value.[23]

Tastes (*quwei*) were not to be absolutized, because they belonged only to
a specific time and place. When frozen into an absolute stipulation for all
works of art, they became as cold and oppressive as a beautiful woman
turned to stone. Moreover, although the writer-critic must strive to give
expression to his or her impressions, it is even more important that the
critic understand that personal opinions were a random aggregation of
tastes and flavors and could not constitute an authority over others.

A month later, in a preface written for *In My Own Garden*, Zhou again
spelled out his idea of criticism as "subjective appreciation" rather than
"objective examination," as "lyrical essay" rather than "arrogant faultfinding," adding that he had found these alternatives because he lacked
enough confidence for the first option and had too much self-respect for
the second.[24] This preface is interesting for the account Zhou gives of his
shift from a concern with literature as a project of national regeneration
to literature as an individual project.

> Three summers ago [1921], when I was convalescing in the Western Hills, I wrote a
> "random thoughts" (*zagan*) piece called "Overcoming Karma" ("Sheng ye") in which
> I said that because "other people's thinking is always better than ours, and other
> people's writing is always more marvelous," we ought to write less of our own and
> translate more. This is what I meant by overcoming karma. Three years have
> passed, and I still have failed to cultivate myself in the overcoming of this karma. In-
> stead I have written several dozen pointless essays. Mentioning this has the inevita-
> ble effect of making me a little shameful, and yet perhaps this is not necessary. We
> are too demanding in our desire for imperishable works, wanting to be of benefit to
> society, and we have smothered ourselves too much. Actually, imperishability is ab-
> solutely not the aim of writing, and a writer does not have the duty to be of benefit to
> society. It is just because he thinks in a particular way that he wants to say it in that
> way—this is the basis of all literature.[25]

The goal of this self-expression was not the realization of the solitary ego but the understanding of others. "I am someone who loves literature, and I want to understand other people's hearts through literature and to find in literature the happiness of being understood by others," Zhou said, adding in conclusion, "Because I am lonely, I seek comfort in literature . . . perhaps in China there will be those who have similar feelings to mine."[26]

Zhou's idea of the writer-critic came under attack a few months later from Guo Moruo and Cheng Fangwu (1897–1984), both members of the Creation Society.[27] Guo argued that the duty of the critic included pointing out shortcomings and rejecting ugliness, and Cheng criticized Zhou for not giving adequate weight to reason as one element of taste.[28] Cheng's efforts at creating a "constructive criticism" represented a deepening of the May Fourth ideal that literature and art should serve society. Literature was the political world expressed in writing, according to Cheng, with criticism paralleling in the literary field the place of the legal system in the nation.[29]

A year later, in February 1924, Zhou said that had he been able to find a "pure belief" or an entrenched prejudice or an -ism of his own, he would naturally have been happy. But instead,

the only progress I have made this year is to know that I know nothing. I used to think that I did have some knowledge and that if I found a teacher among the sages of past and present I could take [his teachings] as a standard and create my own views, judge everything, and that would have been a simple enough method. But I gradually came to feel that this kind of teacher was a little hard to find, and I began to find myself in a bad way, like a blind man who has lost his stick. Since I was unwilling to believe other peoples' preformulated sayings and could also not come up with any opinions of my own, in the end all I could do was to confess [these failings] honestly. Repeating Montaigne's phrase "What do I know?" I read the newspapers everyday, which really leaves me confused. As for all the struggles in politics and international relations, I can never grasp who is right and who is wrong, because I always feel that what both sides say sounds convincing, but there is something unreliable about both.[30]

The lightness of tone so far is a prelude to something more serious.

I often voice doubts to myself: could it be that I am without innate knowledge (liangzhi)? I feel that I am forced to answer, "So it would appear," although this answer will greatly displease those friends of mine who promote the study of [the philosophy of] Wang [Yangming]. It is true, my heart is really empty, like that throne in the old palace—but this is in effect a matter of great relief to me . . . probably my being without knowledge is not something that has just begun today, it is just that previously I thought I knew. Now I have suddenly come to the realization that this is a truly good thing, because I no longer have to search for a means to remedy this state of affairs since I have understood what the game is. Knowing that I know nothing is in fact my first real knowledge.[31]

The reference to innate knowledge should almost certainly be seen in the context of the debate over science and religion sparked in February 1923 by Zhang Junmai (1886–1969), a German-trained philosopher and constitutionalist politician who worked closely with Liang Qichao.[32] Zhang wrote an article entitled "Philosophy of Life" opposing a metaphysical view of the world to positivistic science, in which he explicitly identified *liangzhi* with the inner experiential knowledge he opposed to science.[33] This article immediately drew the ire of May Fourth intellectuals, who saw it as an attack on science.

Yet, in a different context, Zhou might have found some of Zhang's metaphysical views congenial. In a speech published in May 1921, Zhou had made the link between literature and religion that he was to repeat over a decade later: What religion, broadly speaking, understood as the unity of human beings and the divine was also the concern of literature, he said. Schopenhauer's vitalism was just another name for the concepts of "the divine" (*shen*), "the one/oneness" (*yi*), and "the boundless" (*wuxian*) found in Christianity, Indian Brahmanism, and Sufi. Such noumenal thought (*benti sixiang*) was also the province of literature, which had its origin in religion and which still shared much common ground with it.[34] But there was the rub. Zhou's prime concern was to make literature independent of ideology or activism. He certainly did not find congenial the close links Zhang and his associates were making between the Confucian worldview and Zhang's political activities. "As a good disciple of Wang Yangming's unity of thought and action, Zhang tried to implement his ideas for national salvation," writes Zhang's biographer.[35]

From the structure as well as the title of Zhou's essay, we see him moving toward a position analogous to the "childlike heart." The slow movement of doubt, from having wished for a teacher and thinking that he did have knowledge to questioning whether he did or did not have any innate knowledge, leads to the absolute stripping away of sources of authority within his own thinking. Finally, when he finds himself "with an empty heart like a vacant throne," he knows he has come to his "first real knowledge." Zhou concluded his essay by reiterating (no doubt for the benefit of the Creationists) his position that criticism was something he could not and would not do, but that he was very happy to read other peoples' writing so as to "broaden [my] knowledge and experience (*jianshi*)."

The Creationists were not the only leftist critics on the Chinese literary scene, which had witnessed an upsurge of criticism from about 1923. For instance, grouped around the journal *Chinese Youth* (*Zhongguo qingnian*) were the future labor organizers Deng Zhongxia (1897–1933), Yun Daiying (1895–1931), and Xiao Chunu (1894–1927) whose articles called for works that would not only be inspired by revolutionary sentiments but also be grounded in revolutionary practice.[36] Deng dismissed the poets of the Literary Association (including Zhou) as "lazy and superficial" and called for works that, instead of seeking self-expression, would "bring out 'the great spirit of the nation.'"[37] Jiang Guangci (1901–31), returning from the Soviet Union in 1924, saw revolution as the mainspring of creativity and his mission as the promotion of proletarian literature. His arrogant claims for his own ideas put him in conflict with those most likely to share his views, such as the Creationists, whom he joined in 1925 but then left in 1927 to found the Sun Society.[38] Jiang's colleague and intellectual successor was Qian Xingcun (1900–1977), better known by his pseudonym A Ying.

The Creationists were to become increasingly dogmatic in their views of literature and convinced of their right to attack anyone who thought differently. They turned on the journal *Yusi*, set up in Peking in November 1924 by, among others, Zhou, Qian Xuantong, Liu Bannong, Lu Xun, and Li Xiaofeng (1897–1971), with Sun Fuyuan as editor.[39] Zhou wrote the editorial statement, which appeared in the first issue. It began: "The few of us who have gotten together to produce this journal have done so with no ambitions or extravagant hopes. We just feel unhappy that life in China at present is too dull and dry, the intellectual world too dreary."[40] The journal was to be a place where "those who want to say a few words" would find the freedom to publish, but no -isms or propaganda would be carried, nor did the journal have any interest in economics or politics. However, the founders did have an aim: "All we want to do is to break down the turbid and stagnant atmosphere in Chinese life and thought. . . . What we advocate is the promotion of free thought, independent judgment, and beauty in life."[41]

The journal was able to live up to these ideals (at least to the extent permitted by external circumstances) and attracted a wide range of contributors including Lin Yutang (1895–1976), Li Jinfa (1900–1976) the Symbolist poet, Gu Jiegang the historian, and the folklorist Jiang Shaoyuan (1898–1983). Many of Zhou's most biting essays of social criticism and the prose-poems Lu Xun later published as *Wild Grass* appeared in the first three years of the journal. However, the political situation grew increasingly tense after March 1926, and the journal was forced to stop appearing in Peking in October 1927 after the warlord Zhang Zuolin closed the Beixin Bookshop, which published it, and Zhou's ties with it slackened. Starting with number 153, *Yusi* was issued from Shanghai, where Lu Xun edited it for a few months, but the journal finally was forced to close in 1930.

By attacking *Yusi*, the Creationists were able to challenge two of the most prestigious figures on the literary scene, whom they accused of pursuing *quwei*—their own interests and tastes. The pursuit of *quwei* was possible only for those with "leisure" and, by extension, the class background and money to be able to support them. Lu Xun, of whom it has been said that his link with *Yusi* "remains one of the many paradoxes of his personality,"[42] responded to his critics in his own biting fashion, often in the pages of *Yusi*. However, the desire to meet the leftist critics on their own ground was one of the reasons Lu Xun started reading and translating Plekhanov and Lunacharsky from 1928.[43] Lu Xun's increasingly serious engagement with Marxist literary theory was to have an important outcome. By March 1930, with the sinking of differences among writers in Shanghai that made possible the setting up of the League of Left-wing Writers, a major ideological and organizational battle had been won. The League, with Lu Xun an important source of its prestige, came to exert considerable influence in the intellectual world of China.[44] However admiring readers such as Zhu Guangqian may have been mid-decade of Zhou's ability to transport them to an oasis of serenity, there was less and less room, it seemed, for an aesthetics of *quwei*.

Zhou's *Water Plantain Collection* (*Zexie ji*), published in September 1927, can be seen as a model of what such an aesthetics meant in practice. In the preface Zhou explained that he had grouped together what he felt to be the best of his recently produced "short essays of response and reflection" (*ganxiang xiao pian*). "If they can express a part of myself, then I will be more than content," he said, explaining why he had published them:

It is definitely not to "convey the Way" or "transmit the Dharma." When friends asked me which were the best of these casually written essays of mine, I was covered with confusion and unable to respond. But then looking at it from another position, although it cannot be said that they are good, I am rather fond of them since I feel they can express a little of the mood and flavor of the times. There are also a few others that I have added to the collection to become a book from the Bitter Rain Studio.[45]

To explain the differences among the essays, Zhou borrowed Isaac Goldberg's description of Havelock Ellis as combining "rebel and recluse" and applied it to himself. The "rebel" essays, including "Ways of Dying" ("Sifa"), "Eating Martyrs" ("Chi lieshi"), and "Meeting with Harm" (Pengshang), referred with indirect but unmistakable irony to the bloodlettings of the previous two years. "Meeting with Harm," dated June 1926, begins by mentioning his childhood fantasies about armor, folk beliefs about venomous snakes, and Tang dynasty tales of magic swordsmen and then proceeds to recent newspaper reports of passengers drowning when their pleasure craft was hit by naval vessels.

From this, we can tell that getting into harm's way is a frequent occurrence in China. As for the complete responsibility, of course it belongs with those harmed. For instance, if I were wearing armor covered in spikes, or if I were a poisonous snake or a magic swordsman and someone came up . . . to look, or offended me, and got hurt, who could say it was my fault?[46]

The reason people had died recently, Zhou concludes, obviously referring to the March massacre, was that they had been petitioning, when they ought to have realized that that was a measure used only with reluctance in present-day constitutional nations and not in other places.

For instance, in Russia in nineteen hundred and something, because [people had not realized this], troops once opened fire in front of the Winter Palace, and the toll was even higher, but from that time on they ceased petitioning. . . . I hope petitioning will come to an end in China from now on. Let's all work for it. [47]

The "reclusive" category included Zhou's reflections on tea drinking ("Chi cha"), instructions about boat travel in Shaoxing ("Wu peng chuan") and "Bitter Rain" ("Ku yu"). Written as a letter to Sun Fuyuan, who was traveling, this last essay began,

> In recent days Beiping has had a lot of rain. I don't know if you will have had any on the way to Chang'an, but I think it will definitely add to the special piquancy (*jia qu*) of your journey. It is not always very pleasant to travel in the rain. It often used to rain when I was on the Hangzhou–Shanghai train, which was always very troublesome; so I have no particular sense of heightened pleasure (*xingwei*) from train travel in bad weather. But to lie in a black-topped boat, quietly listening to the sound of rain beating on the awning, the slow, regular sound of the oars, and the calls of the sailors, does indeed form a type of poetic scene (*shi jing*). [48]

As we have seen, such a poetic scene, with a real existence in the external world, functions to convey to readers the flavor the writer has perceived in it and something of the writer. Zhou's essay did not dwell in memories of Shaoxing for long, though, and most of it was given to describing the chaos just caused by the heavy rain in Peking, which was not accustomed to such storms. The details all ring true—the unfamiliar noises of crashing wind and rain, the damaged brickwork, the smell of rooms from which floodwater has now receded, the delight of children allowed to paddle in the courtyard, even the sudden influx of striped frogs. Zhou's ability to infuse these elements with warmth and interest and thus to give them intrinsic significance is what gave readers like Zhu Guangqian their sense of "release." The essay ends:

> I fear this great storm will have brought considerable misfortune to the poor living in the countryside, but I have not seen it with my own eyes, and reliance on imagination alone is not useful. So I shall not replace [my own experience] with hypocritical tragic sighs. If someone says what is recorded here is only the affairs of an individual and of no benefit to human life, I admit it. All I wanted to do was to talk about individual matters, nothing else. [49]

Although this refusal to lament the plight of peasants he could not see attracted the wrath of critics, it is instructive to see what Zhou wrote about the suffering of those he did see, such as the refugees who flocked to Peking in unprecedented numbers in summer 1926.

I do not know what their homes were like, because I've never seen them and cannot imagine them, but to see these lives turned into beggars by human actions is sorrowful enough, and what particularly distresses me is the women's feet. Of course, their feet have always been like that, it is not that they were bound after calamity struck, or that they became particularly tiny through fleeing. But they are really horrifyingly small. When in the past I saw some of these mysterious tiny feet . . . each time it would make me feel I belonged to a barbaric people and sigh with regret something to the effect that "I most love natural feet." Now, seeing these feet on the bodies of refugees, I feel despair.[50]

By seizing on the image of bound feet, Zhou at once underscores the physical vulnerability of the refugees, the brutality of their lives before warfare overtook them, and the distance between their cultural world and that of the urban middle class. The reader is also left in no doubt as to the owner of this particular voice, particularly with the reference to "natural feet," the title of a famous early essay of his.[51] The *quwei* of the author and his vision were quite distinct. Although not uncompassionate, Zhou's observations seem intended to provoke the reader more to sober reflection than to an activist indignation on behalf of the refugees. This was not welcome to critics who wished writing to serve revolutionary politics. In fact, Zhou's essay went on to make ironic references to destiny—a stance even more unacceptable to critics.

For many critics, Zhou's construction of himself as "rebel and recluse" was evidence that he was aware that he had a choice between *shi yan zhi* and *wen yi zao dao*, but, as the last sentence of "Bitter Rain" made crystal clear, he was unashamed of his self-indulgent leanings and therefore lost the battle between his good and bad selves.[52] For Zhou this constructed bipolar self may have resembled an ideological battleground, but it was actually something much more positive. A year earlier he had written "Two Demons" ("Liangge gui"), his translation for the Greek *daimon*, which followed the same logic, albeit in a much more playful vein. The primary meaning of *gui* is ghost rather than demon, and Zhou begins his essay by explaining how he arrived at the title:

In our minds there live *du daimone*, which we could say are two—demons (*gui*). I hesitate to use the word *gui* because they are not the ghosts into which people turn after death, and they are not the devils of religion, such as [when we speak of] good and evil spirits, good angels and fallen angels. Perhaps we should say they are a kind of spirit, but this sounds too dignified; so the best thing is to put them out a little by calling them demons.[53]

This has still not made clear what these two demons are, but the best way to understand what Zhou means is to go straight to the meaning of *daimon*, which the Oxford English Dictionary gives as "an attendant or indwelling spirit, one's genius."

According to the friends who believe in Wang [Yangming's] teachings, man possesses something called innate knowledge. Priests talk of the soul, some scholars take the notion of conscience to be self-evident, but I, it seems to me, have none of these. What I have is these two demons, directing all my actions. . . . Sometimes the hooligan is in the ascendant, and I wander around with him, finding out all the secrets, getting drunk, getting into fights. . . . But then just before I start behaving really badly, the gentry comes out and commands: "Stop it immediately!" Funnily enough, when he hears this . . . the hooligan complies."[54]

This state of affairs was not burdensome to Zhou, for rather than act in accordance with Ibsen's dictum "all or nothing," he was attached to both the hooligan and the gentry. "I have learned a lot both from the marginalia of the gentry contemplating his navel and the coarse, abusive language of the hooligan," he concluded. If we interpret the essay in the light of the meaning of *daimon* as "one's genius," then the two facets of his literary persona represented by the gentry and the hooligan become equally valid, as does his refusal to adopt either a "conservative" or "revolutionary" tone in his writing. The respect Zhou shows to both these sides recalls his earlier decision while convalescing in 1921 not to try and unify his thinking.[55]

In 1934, Zhou published two pieces of doggerel verse (*dayou shi*), written around the time of his fiftieth birthday (in *sui*), in which he spoke of himself as a half-Confucian, half-Buddhist, weary of the world but unable to wear a monk's robe. This newest twist to his dual self-characterization (gentry/hooligan, rebel/recluse) reinforced the persona of the recluse and called forth much condemnation.[56] The incident demonstrated the size of the gap between Zhou and his friends and many of the younger generation,[57] for many of whom, no doubt, Zhou's literary history with its theory of Ming origins seemed equally irrelevant. By all accounts, Zhou was annoyed and upset by the criticism.

The persona of the recluse is complex. Most commonly, the image of the recluse can symbolize the man of integrity who refuses to serve a corrupt government or, depending on point of view, the selfish coward who refuses to risk his neck for what is right. With hindsight, this second version of recluse symbolism seemed both to foreshadow and to mock Zhou's subsequent collaboration. An alternative would be to accept that eremetism also served as a mode of individualism in which introspection underscored autonomy.[58] In this case, one could suggest that by invoking and playing with the persona of the recluse, Zhou was seeking yet another way of carving a space for himself outside established discourses while expressing his discontent with a government that invoked Confucius. However, locating Zhou's eremetism purely in a politics of contingency ignores the fact, noted in Chapter 1, that the charge of reclusive individualism was first made against Zhou in his Shirakaba days by Hu Shi.

After *Yusi* closed down, Zhou found one outlet for his work in the journal *Camel Grass* (*Luotuo cao*), which was set up by his protégé Feng Wenbing in May 1930, but over which he exerted the decisive influence.[59] "We have no new flag to wave, but we still have some leisure for relaxation," the editors announced. "National affairs" would not be featured in the journal; however, "whether the subject is literature and art, ideas, even idle conversation and antiques, [it will be treated] in a quite unexpected manner. You may laugh or scold as you please, but we ourselves, the authors, will know if we have written something good, and if it is bad, we will recognize it. That is just the way it is."[60] Published in the first issue of *Camel Grass* was Zhou's essay "Denizens of the Water," mentioned in the preceding chapter.

Zhou wrote fewer of his "rebel" essays after 1928, and his collections focused more on Ming and Qing literati writings. As a result, some critics judge that although Zhou's earlier collections, *In My Own Garden*, *Talking About Dragons*, *Talking of Tigers*, and *Water Plantain*, were innovative and laid the groundwork for the modern essay, his later works such as *Talks in Wind and Rain*, *Melons and Beans Collection*, and *Notes from Night Reading* were in the nature of *biji* writings and personal comments on books read and hence less valuable as literature.[61] This judgment proceeds from an idea of the literary as individual creation and a rejection of the assumption, on which Zhou worked, of criticism as lyrical appreciation. Zhou defended himself against this argument by commenting rather bitterly:

It is said that the best way to understand somebody is to see his study, and the one who shows his study to other people is most exposed to the danger of having people see his real features. When, in the light of this, most of the books thus randomly mentioned have not been read by the contemporary sages, of course that amounts to a confession of one's own decline.[62]

As the literary scene polarized in the late 1920s and early 1930s, Zhou's conception of the essay was attacked head on, and not only by leftists. Criticism focused on his claim for its origins. We have already seen that in March 1923 in "Literature and Place," Zhou named the Ming figures Xu Wei, Wang Siren, and Zhang Dai as writers who "could have laid the basis for the modern essay" (*jinti sanwen*). In May 1926 Zhou wrote to his former student Yu Pingbo about the possibility of editing a collection of essays that could serve as materials on the origins of the modern essay. "I often say that the essay and *xiaopin* of today are by no means a new product of the May Fourth; in effect 'it has always been there' and has merely undergone a renewed development."[63]

A few months later, in the preface to a reprint of Zhang Dai's essays edited by Yu, Zhou could say that of all the modern genres, *sanwen* had been the one least subject to foreign influences. Indeed, "rather than calling it a product of the literary revolution, it would be better to see it as the result of a literary renaissance." Arguing that in terms of literary development, "both renaissance and revolution identically stand for progress," Zhou asserted that in their emotional temper and their opposition to Confucian ritual norms, the essays of Ming and Qing writers such as Zhang Dai contained a strong flavor of the modern (*xiandai de qixi*).[64] Two years later Zhou praised Yu's *Table of Nuts and Fruit* collection for achieving lyricism even when the essays concerned textual analysis:

Pingbo has used the idea of a table of nuts and fruit for his title possibly because they are a mixture. Of the thirty-two essays in the book, something like one-fifth have the nature of textual scholarship. But just as melon seeds and fruit paste candies are all snacks to go with tea, these essays, as much as the other lyrical ones, are all literary works. Whatever Pingbo writes has its own special style (*fengzhi*). Oh, I know that in this day and age when everybody is hunting out counterrevolution, mentioning subjects like style or *quwei* is somewhat tabooed, because they are all close to "being leisurely." . . . I would even like to add, this style belongs to Chinese literature, it is both as old and as new.

Tang and Song writers had also produced essays that revealed their individual nature and spirit (*xingling liu lu de sanwen*) but only as a diversion, and it was not until the Gongan school in the Ming that writers seriously produced essays which genuinely expressed individuality. Apart from the few comrades who were intent on "conveying the Way," modern-day essayists were quite like their Ming counterparts, notwithstanding the European influence on language and the obvious changes in thinking over four hundred years. Nonetheless, Zhou concluded forcefully, "The modern essay is like a river that has been buried in the sand and has after many years been unearthed. It is an ancient river, but it is also new."[65] A few months later, in a preface to another of Yu Pingbo's essay collections, Zhou described the contemporary Chinese essay (*sanwen*) as "a synthesis of Gongan school and English *xiaopin wen*."[66] Yu's essays were first and foremost *literary* in character (*zui you wenxue yiwei de*) and merited the appellation *xiaopin wen* because "they not only enunciate principles or narrate facts but are predominantly lyrical." What made them literary was that unlike the essays of "outpouring" (*xuyu sanwen*—promoted by Hu Menghua [fl. 1930s] and Wu Shuzhen [fl. 1930s]),[67] they also possessed the flavor of astringency and simplicity. They achieved their prized refinement—meaning naturalness, not rural gentry style—through the sparing admixture of Europeanized language, *guwen*, dialect, and other elements to the spoken language, the whole ruled by knowledge and *quwei*. It was this quality of literary refinement that brought Yu Pingbo's essays close to those of the Ming.

   Zhu Ziqing challenged the significance of the Ming for the modern *sanwen*. Although he accepted Zhou's view that "unconventional literati" (*mingshi pai*) writings from the Ming period were closest to the modern essay, he rebuked Zhou for not admitting that the "direct influence" on the modern *sanwen* was foreign.

Even if we look at the essays in Mr. Zhou's own books, such as his *Water Plantain Collection*, for example, where, in either style or thinking do we find anything derived from the *mingshi pai*? At the very most, one could say that there are some similarities in sentiment. I would prefer to say that there is more "foreign influence" in his work than Chinese. As for other writers, such as Mr. Lu Xun or Mr. Xu Zhimo, there is sometimes even more foreign influence in their work.[68]

The very fact that the essay was flourishing was a bad sign, Zhu said, showing that "the force of history is too strong." As a result, the new fiction, poetry, and drama, which had dominated the scene at the beginning of the literary revolution, had slackened off, permitting the essay to regain its old pre-eminence.

From this point on, the debate on the origins of the essay deepened, leading to three distinct positions. Against Zhou's stance, there was the belief, voiced by Lu Xun, that the essay was a product of the May Fourth and New Literature movements. Third, there was the ingenious Marxist view on the historical mission of the essay. This was first suggested by Feng Sanwei (dates unknown) in 1928 and expressed more fully by Fang Fei (dates unknown) in late 1933: that the needs of readers for solace, of writers to express their frustrations, and publishers for economically viable short pieces had combined in the era of mature capitalism to favor the development of the *sanwen*.[69] A major impetus to the debate must have come from the "instant success" of Lin Yutang's magazines *Lunyu* (Analects), launched in 1932 to promote humor and satire, and *Renjian shi* (This human world) and *Yuzhou feng* (Cosmic wind), launched in 1934 and 1935, respectively, and devoted to *xiaopin sanwen*.[70] Lin, who had been a contributor to *Yusi*, wrote that the magazines were designed to carry on the *Yusi* tradition spearheaded by Zhou Zuoren.[71] He complimented Zhou by hailing the *xiaopin* as the only success of modern Chinese literature and defined the genre as "placing the self at the center, adopting a tone of leisure and ease," but able to cover any topic under the sun.[72] The magazines, according to C. T. Hsia, served the needs for "mental relaxation" of writers (and presumably readers) tired of "Nationalist and Communist cant." But they proved so popular that the League launched its own personal magazine, *Taibai*, in competition with Lin Yutang's magazines.[73]

Although, being human, Zhou must have appreciated the adulation he received as foremost representative of the modern *xiaopin wen*, Lin Yutang's success may well have had the drawback of reinforcing the artificial (to Zhou's eyes) divide critics made between his *biji*-type writings and his more obviously lyrical writings. After agreeing to edit one of the volumes of collected essays in the *Great Compendium of Modern Chinese Literature*, Zhou commented that he would select essays of any length, adding, "I do not necessarily always like the so-called small essay [i.e., *xiaopin wen*.] And I also very much disapprove of the name *xiaopin wen*. I believe writing [*wen*] is just writing, there are no divisions into "big" and "small."[74]

Lu Xun argued that in the course of Chinese history the *xiaopin wen* had emerged at times of political turmoil but had disappeared as the succeeding regime became entrenched. The late Ming essay, with its capacity for voicing discontent, had disappeared under the Qianlong emperor's (r. 1735–95) literary suppression and been replaced by insipid and ornamental literary knickknacks. It was to combat these that the May Fourth *sanwen* and *xiaopin wen* had successfully drawn on the humor and poise of the English essay. Thus, the essay had sprouted from the revolutions in literature and thought, and its future was to continue the struggle. But now, he wrote in 1933, as *Lunyu* celebrated its success, "the tendency is to promote especially those points of resemblance with old writings, such as gracefulness, beauty, and meticulous craft, so that the essay becomes a mere knickknack, something for elegant people to caress."[75] Although there was a flourishing Shanghai market for *xiaopin wen*, Lu Xun added, the essay was like a prostitute, driven out of the alleys where she used to operate and forced to put on makeup and loiter on city streetcorners. It was at a crisis point and faced the choice of extinction or life—and life would be won only if the *xiaopin wen* became a dagger or a spear, able to carve out the bloody route to the future together with the reader. This is a characteristically ambivalent position: Lu Xun implies that the late Ming essay was "progressive" in its time, and there is the suggestion that the present time of turmoil might resemble the late Ming. But this train of thought is dropped: what the present needs is dagger-and-spear type literature, a conclusion that says more about Lu Xun's tragic view of his own age and his own need to struggle than any intrinsic belief in the efficacy of literature to effect change.[76]

A representative of the dagger-and-spear position with none of Lu Xun's ambivalence was A Ying, whose "On the *Xiaopin wen*" ("Xiaopin wen tan") appeared the same year.[77] A Ying distanced himself from previous assessments, which he considered formalistic and lacking due regard for the real nature of the essay. Implicitly rejecting the idea that Zhou had had a shaping influence on the essay, he saw its origins in pointed *suigan lu* ("random thoughts") such as Lu Xun's *Hot Winds* (*Re feng*) collection or in the less acerbic but nonetheless progressive writing exemplified by "A Short Letter to Mr. G. C. Willany" by Liu Fu (Liu Bannong). The real *xiaopin wen*, concerned with meticulous craftsmanship and beauty, first emerged with Bing Xin's (1900–1999) "Smile." However, the first piece to be noticed and classified by readers as belles lettres (*meiwen*) was Zhou's "Flies," from which "all progressive significance had been more and more lost."[78]

In using the term *meiwen*, which Zhou had coined and used as the title of his 1920 article, A Ying intended to attack Zhou's whole concept of the essay, a point to which we will return. A Ying argued that after the first excitement of the democracy movement had died down, the intellectual establishment in China found itself split between those who wanted to carry on struggling and those who "could only halt in their tracks or become despondent, talk about the wind and the moon and their own personal trifling affairs. 'Flies' was the first representative of this tendency."

After the May Thirtieth incident (1925), A Ying noted, many essayists realized that the main fight was now against imperialism and eschewed individualism. But, he continued in a direct attack on Zhou,

although the backward, "flowers in the wind and moon on the snow" (*feng hua yue xue*) writers occasionally still voiced some complaints against the current state of society, for the most part they carried on as before, wasting their time in the leisurely pursuit of *quwei*. Probably the more blood was spilt in the pursuit of social progress, the more they intensified their flight to the pinnacle of *quwei*-ism. So not long after the New Literature movement began, . . . Hu Shi gradually lost his progressive spirit, and Zhou Zuoren and the others started writing about snacks to accompany tea, wine, birdsong . . . *baguwen* and so on, tirelessly spending all their energy on it.[79]

Zhou's success had nothing to do with the literary style Hu Shi had praised for its mildness, A Ying charged. Rather, Zhou represented that current of thought which hoped for change but could not face the bloody combat necessary to bring it about.

No doubt it was attacks such as this that made Zhou describe himself in the preface of *Talks in Wind and Rain* (1936) as ever more isolated and lonely. After explaining that the title was intended to suggest the rising storm outside over which it was hard to make oneself heard, he noted that he could have called it *Feng yue tan* (talking about wind and moon, i.e., romance) had he wanted to:

The wind and the moon are perfectly permissible topics for conversation, and to tell the truth, I think I know something about them. I understand a good deal more about them than those upright fellows who lash out wildly at wind and moon and those elegant gentlemen with their jokes. But I'm not going to talk about them now.[80]

Interesting though it might be to pursue this debate, I do not intend to do so here. It is more important to consider the significance of these fights over the origins and direction of the essay, for they go beyond the immediate questions of the essay's contemporary political or ideological role. A debate over origins is a means of defining the legitimate sources of a literature or a genre in order to shape its present and future. But this debate meant more. It was also, in effect, a conflict about what were legitimate sources, not only for the literarily constructed self presented to readers but also for the actual self of the writer and, by extension, the selves tolerated within the discourse of the modernizing nation-state.

By claiming that late Ming writers had exerted the most influence on the modern essay, Zhou was violating the basic tenet of the literary revolution that only "living" vernacular fiction qualified as a respectable ancestor for the new literature. In Chatterjee's terms, Zhou's claim must have suggested to his contemporaries that a "failure" had occurred in the enlightenment project.[81] For the late Ming to receive the lion's share of credit for the modern essay was a contradiction in terms, since "modern" by definition meant "post-[European] Enlightenment." Because writing was one means of constructing the new national identity, the late Ming essay constituted an inadmissible resource.

My argument may seem unnecessarily bound to the terms of May Fourth discourse and its historiography and/or as replicating a problematic binarism in Chatterjee. Thus, it may seem to ignore the actual practice of writers in the 1930s, who were as able to make use of the resources of the past as they were those of the present in creating a Chinese modernity: Shi Zhecun's reworking of the supernatural tradition in Chinese fiction together with his Freudian insights into the workings of the subconscious might be taken as a case in point.[82] How also are we to account for the popularity of Lin Yutang's magazines and the facts that reprints of late Ming *xiaopin wen* found a ready market, and Yuan Hongdao became a literary hero of the early 1930s?[83]

However, the point is that if readers and writers of the 1930s were much more confident about drawing on the full range of their literary and linguistic heritage than those of the May Fourth, this represented a deepening of the process by which the modern national identity was being constructed. It did not challenge the process. Even as *xiaopin wen* modeled on the late Ming were enjoying a vogue, some on the literary left were also seeking ways to create an indigenized national language and literature and rejecting the *ouhua* (Europeanized Chinese) of the May Fourth period. Both sets of writers and readers were involved in finding a place for what was Chinese in the literary construction of a national imaginary that proceeded from the acceptance of modernity as an ethic. It is therefore important to distinguish between the significance of the popularity of the *xiaopin wen* and the significance of Zhou's claim for the origins of the modern essay.

There is in fact some tension between Zhou's explanation for the importance of the late Ming and the way it was invoked by others. Lin Yutang, for instance, saw the hallmark of *xiaopin wen* to be a "literary tone" (*bidiao*) characterized by appositeness, forthrightness, and flair. These qualities gave a work its "individual tone," which could be rendered in English as "familiar style," which Lin translated as "leisurely tone" (*xianshi bidiao*) or "leisurely conversation form" (*xian tan ti*) or "engaging form" (*wei yu ti*).[84] Subject matter could range from "the immensity of the cosmos to the insignificance of a fly."[85] But it followed that since the genre was defined in terms of tone or style, the question of "origins" was to be approached in another way.

In the first place, Lin considered that most good *sanwen* from premodern China were to be found in the narrative passages or, less frequently, in the disquisitions of the protagonists in vernacular novels.[86] After the literary revolution, it became natural for writers to insert a familiar conversational tone into their expository writing (*xian tan shuo li bidiao*). However, Lin felt that there ought to be a Chinese ancestor for *xiaopin wen* because only this would enable the genre to put down roots. This is a typical "nation-building" appropriation of figures from the past as a means to a particular end. Lin decided that in addition to the established canonical figures of the traditional *xiaopin* such as Liu Zongyuan (773–819), the standard for determining which premodern Chinese writings could play the role of ancestor was "purely a familiar and easy writing style" that held the reader's attention just as an engrossing conversation would. His example was the *Mingliao zi jiyou* by the late Ming Daoist Tu Long (1542–1605), whose style he found akin to that of Laurence Sterne (1713–68).

Despite having opened up a canon that was broader than Zhou's, Lin was unwilling to make any serious claims for it. At the end of his essay, he dealt with the question posed by Zhou Zuoren's claims for the Gong-an and Jingling schools in his *Origins of New Chinese Literature* by saying that this was Zhou's individual opinion. Zhou held it because, being adept at Ming writing, his own style had become virtually indistinguishable from that of the Yuan brothers. Thus, he implies, Zhou's claim reflects and reinforces his own status as the leading essayist of the day. It is because the Zhou Zuoren style is a Gongan/Jingling style and because Zhou has many followers that the modern Chinese essay can be given this filiation. In Lin's argument, what is at stake is a question of style—something that is constituted by the foregrounding of certain widely distributed linguistic or rhetorical traits. There is none of Zhou Zuoren's preoccupation with aesthetic categories here.

When we recall the extent to which aesthetics was grounded in philosophy, the reason for the general refusal to engage with Zhou's arguments even by those who seemed close to him generically becomes clear. Zhou's aesthetics of *quwei* and *bense* derived from a vision of a moral order, and his originality consisted in being able to maintain a view of the self as a moral agent that was not predicated on the disowning of the entire cultural heritage. Equally important, it was not predicated on an essentialized "Chinese" way. While acknowledging and responding to the impetus to change propelled by the influence of Western civilization, Zhou was able also to find indigenous sources for his construction of the moral self.

For the philosopher Charles Taylor, at the heart of the complex of "higher goods" underpinning modernity is the "affirmation of ordinary life," a term designating "those aspects of human life concerned with production and reproduction, that is, labour, the making of the things needed for life and our life as sexual beings, including marriage and the family."[87] Taylor argues, quite rightly, that "the affirmation of ordinary life," derived from the Judeo-Christian idea that "God created the world and saw that it was good," can be seen as underlying the Western respect for the individual as a laboring and sexual being. We have seen how congenial Zhou found the expression of these values in the Shirakaba group's New Village project and Ellis's ideas about sex.

But the crucial ingredient of the affirmation of ordinary life was also available to Zhou in the Neo-Confucian concept of the "daily uses of the people" discussed in the preceding chapter. (This, incidentally, also suggests how Taylor's sense of Western exclusiveness constitutes a blindspot that threatens his project to retrieve moral sources.) Zhou's ability to tap an indigenous source for a basic insight of the modern condition made it unnecessary for him to insist that modern writing (and by extension modern attitudes) could have had their genesis *only* in Western sources. The manner in which he exercised this ability is extremely important: he did not arrive at the "daily uses of the people" polemically from a reactive position ("Our ways are just as good as theirs"); rather, he found them in a literary practice that ignores the construction of nationality. This goes a long way toward explaining the confidence with which Zhou held his ground against both the die-hard traditionalists and the despairing modernizers.

In appealing to the late Ming, Zhou was quite sensitive to shifts in philosophic and hence literary discourse. In his view, the centrality of "innate sensibility" in late Ming literature did reflect a change in the structure of the writing self. For although some Tang and Song figures had occasionally produced essays that reflected their own sensibilities, it was only in Ming times that members of

the Gongan school could ignore the *guwen* orthodoxy and write all their essays in a lyrical vein. Although later critics condemned them as shallow and empty, they really expressed their own individuality. . . . Formerly writers had had a dualistic attitude to their work, but they took an integrated (*yiyuande*) attitude. In this they are just like modern writers.[88]

Zhou spelled out the resources available to modern and premodern writers in the preface he wrote for the volume he edited in the *Compendium of Modern Chinese Literature*, which came out in 1935–36. This was in many ways his summation of his side in the debate on the origins of the modern essay. He quotes extensively from his previous statements, asserting near the conclusion:

I believe there are two factors in the successful development of the modern essay: one is external help and the other is internal response. The external help is the influence of the new thinking in Western science, philosophy, and literature, and the internal response is the renaissance of the expressivist (*yan zhi pai*) literary movement. Without this historical basis, this success would not have been so easy, but without the addition of outside thinking, even if it had succeeded, it would not have had new vitality and would have toppled.[89]

However, modern writers would not consider the Gongan school the founding fathers of the New Literature, nor would modern writers copy them. Why?

The reason is very simple. Although the fundamental tenor in the new essay is still Confucian and Daoist, it has been transformed by and immersed in Western modern thought, and so it naturally has a new coloring and flavor. Consequently it is not the same as what went before, even if from the outside there are similarities. I do not hesitate to say that the fundamental tenor of Chinese thought is Confucian and Daoist because that is a fact; it is not something that can be changed by fiat. Moreover, I am not opposed to it, because I think this basis is by no means inferior to Western religious thought, since it more easily admits general knowledge of the material world and thoroughgoing renewal.[90]

Here Zhou has cleverly turned the tables on those such as Zhu Ziqing who insisted that the only resemblance between the old and the modern essay was one of emotional flavor. The outward similarities are now upstaged by the fact that the "fundamental tenor" remains Confucian and Daoist. Confucianism, Daoism, and Legalism, Zhou continued, were really three aspects of the same thing. When the Confucian ideal and practice were united, the result was the Mean, but practice without the ideal led to Legalism, and the ideal without the practical side to Daoism. Confucianism had gradually departed from the wisdom of its founders and had been close to being lost, although some like Tao Yuanming and Yan Zhitui had managed to stay vigorous.

Then foreign thinking had poured in, in the form of Buddhism. Buddhism, Zhou asserted, was originally a great, admirable system of thought, but it, too, had deviated. The result for letters had been either a religious literature or one concerned with almost Daoistic emptiness.

This more or less described the Gongan school, but now a new stage had been entered, because

now the foreign influence is materialistic scientific thought, which can cause China's innate Confucian-Daoism to undergo a thorough refining. . . . If we successfully synthesize a view of life based on scientific general knowledge with the addition of clear, pure feelings and limpid intellect then "With this as intent, the expression of feeling must be excellent; with this as the way, what could hinder its conveyance?"[91]

Although logically speaking, Chinese literature should have effected that kind of synthesis of old and new, in fact this had not taken place—all that was being produced was "new Chinese *bagu* or old proselytizing foreign talk." And this was scarcely to be wondered at, because (in an echo of Zhu Ziqing but with opposite ends) the past was too strong and the present too weak, Zhou concluded.

This is one of Zhou's clearest statements in the context of the debate on the essay that the moral "sources" of the Chinese writing self were to be found within the Chinese tradition as well as in modern scientific knowledge. Zhou had in the past voiced his own personal commitment to Confucian values, which he deemed to have avoided the slide into either Legalism or Daoism. Nonetheless, it was always possible to read this as his own perversely chosen idiosyncrasy. In this preface, however, a Confucian-Daoist sensibility constitutes the ground from which everyone begins. The "past" that was too strong refers to the past dominated by Cheng-Zhu conservative orthodoxy.

A particularly pertinent example of Zhou's expression of his own beliefs is the following, written in 1944:

I have been affected in all sorts of ways by ancient and modern, Chinese and foreign influences. . . . In terms of knowledge (*zhi*) and emotion (*qing*), the biggest influences have come from the West and Japan, respectively. But in terms of intention (*yi*) [the influence] has been purely Chinese. Not only have I not been persuaded by foreign ideas to change, but I also have this standard to evaluate the foreign things I have taken in. What I have always called the Confucian spirit, although this is a broad term, is clearly different from the Confucian teachings [as they developed] after the Han, and especially after the Song. But it is quite permissible to use this term to refer to the Chinese philosophy of life, which is based on the affirmation of life.[92]

The interesting tripartite division of intention, knowledge, and emotion raises some questions. Looked at from the "stance of disengaged reason,"

knowledge is the basis for judgment, but here intention is a more fundamental category, by which knowledge and emotions are evaluated.
Ching-mao Cheng, in his discussion of Zhou's comment and the meaning of *yi* (which could also be translated as "thinking" or "meaning"), refers to a passage in the Mencius on the proper interpretation of an Ode.[93]
Mencius says that, in interpretation, one may not overemphasize one
term or one sentence and so "violate the scope" (i.e., the *zhi* "intent or
aim" of the writer). Instead one must "try with [one's] thoughts (*yi*) to
meet that scope and then [one] shall apprehend it."[94] Van Zoeren considers that in this instance *yi*, which he translates "intention," is synonymous with *zhi*.[95] He also notes the tendency in discussions of the Zhou
and early Han dynasties to assert that "language was inadequate to express" intention. Thus Zhuangzi's parable about the fishtrap and the
fish, "Words exist because of intentions (*yi*); once you've gotten the intentions, you can forget the words. Where can I find a man who has forgotten words, so I can have a word with him?"[96]

There are more restricted usages of *yi*, in which it refers to the aim behind a given speech act or utterance,[97] but from the context it is clear that
Zhou is using *yi* in a way more nearly synonymous with *zhi* as the thrust
of one's being. If this is correct, Zhou's view of the self has at its center an
evaluative moral consciousness. This view of the self is quite consistent
with the one that emerged in the discussion of Zhou's aesthetics, in
which the self was seen as ontologically identical with the Way and
therefore could bring the Way into existence by fidelity to its (the self's)
own being. Since the Way is expressed in human life, the evaluative
moral consciousness serves as a common constituent of selfhood that
transcends cultural and historical boundaries. Thus, the inclusive formula *gu jin zhong wai*—ancient or modern, Chinese or foreign—which
denoted both the universality of the truth about human existence and the
diversity of expressions of that truth.

## Zhou's Anti-Exceptionalism

It may be objected that although Zhou said he had always evaluated
things by a "Confucian spirit" that he chose to define on his own terms,
in fact this Confucian spirit was a reinvention by which modern, univer-

salistic truths about human dignity and so forth could be reclothed in nativist garb—a suspicion reinforced by the fact one has to go back before the Han to find the Confucian spirit. In addition, given that the date of the essay just quoted is July 1944, the invocation of the Confucian spirit could have been intended to rebut Japanese propaganda claims about the unity of East Asian cultural perceptions—or, more cynically, could have been Zhou's preparation against the day when he would be called to account for collaborating.[98]

However, the idea that one must return to antiquity to find both a true understanding of human nature and a true spirit of open-minded inquiry that did not distinguish between Chinese and foreign was not invented by Zhou but was integral to the restructured Neo-Confucianism of the late Ming. This was the point made by Jiao Hong in his rejection of arguments that it was improper to use Buddhist insights to clarify the Confucian teachings because the Buddha had been a barbarian prince.[99] For Jiao Hong, "a genuine spirit of open-mindedness had prevailed in ancient China until the late Chou when Mencius launched an overly zealous crusade against Mo Ti and Yang Chu. . . . Taking their cue from Mencius, later Confucians had attacked Buddhism and Taoism without knowing what they were about."[100]

The view that we have anything to learn from past ages either philosophically or methodologically is intrinsically opposed to another characteristic stance of modernity. This is the sense of moral and historical exceptionalism that Taylor sees developing particularly in the Anglo-Saxon Christian world in the nineteenth century. It arose from the recognition that "the imperatives of universal justice and benevolence" could be addressed by mobilizing citizens for political change.

This recognition is of great importance, because it appears that the new moral consciousness has become inseparable from a certain sense of our place in history. . . . The imperative of benevolence carries with it the sense that this age has brought about something unprecedented in history, precisely in its recognition of this imperative. We feel that our civilization has made a qualitative leap, and all previous ages seem to us somewhat shocking, even barbarous in their apparently unruffled acceptance of inflicted or easily avoidable suffering and death.[101]

This sense of historical exceptionalism, filtered through Darwinism and scientism,[102] was intrinsic to the Enlightenment mode of history, which brought the experience of the new moral consciousness to China along with a distinct sense of anxiety about "our place in history." So even where May Fourth intellectuals invoked the values of the past, as, for example, Cheng Fangwu with his idea of righteousness (*yi*), their aim remained the transcendence of all the norms of the past and the creation of new norms on a new base.[103] But the anti-exceptionalist strain evidenced by Zhou's appeal to the place of pre-Han Confucianism in his self-construction is not something he developed after his break with May Fourth activism; rather, it is evident even in his programmatic "A Literature of Man." As Ching-mao Cheng has shown, this article was written when Zhou was at the height of his ideological involvement with the Shirakaba group and dealt more with the utopian vision of life the new literature was intended to promote than with literature.[104]

Quite obviously, contemporary Shirakaba discussions did provide a framework for Zhou's thinking, yet we also find him resisting the idea that the new discovery of man was an evolutionary imperative. After appealing for a *new* literature of man, Zhou promptly qualified his terminology:

Actually, "new" and "old" are rather inappropriate terms; according to the principle that "there is nothing new under the sun," we can only talk of right and wrong, not of new and old. We use the term "new" here only in the sense of "newly discovered," not "newly invented."[105]

This was the case with the Americas and electricity, which had existed for all time but had only become known within the past few hundred years. It would be a great error to equate their newness with that of a fresh fruit or a new style of dress. Similarly, "When, for example, we speak now of 'A Literature of Man,' doesn't this phrase sound like something new and fashionable? But to think so is to ignore that as soon as men were born in the world, humaneness [lit., "the human way"—*ren dao*] was also born." However, because of ignorance, we had shut our eyes to the real way of being human and had dashed about blindly, losing the path and unaware of the sunlight illuminating the world.

Although Zhou affirms that the truth about man was discovered for the first time in Europe in the fifteenth century and about women and children in the nineteenth, and that in China "the problem of man has never been solved, let alone of women and children," he does find some laudable beliefs among ancient Chinese. Thus he invokes Mozi to explain the moral reasons why one should promote humanitarianism:

The individual loves humanity because he is a part of it, and this is its relationship to him. Mozi said, "To love men is not apart from loving oneself, because one is part of what one loves," which is most presciently put. It is exactly the same as what was said above about benefiting oneself to benefit others and benefiting others through benefiting oneself.[106]

Still later, on the question of love between parents and children, Zhou finds that "according to the ancients, 'the love between parents and children has its source in natural disposition.'"

Although "A Literature of Man" calls urgently for the promotion of a humane literature, Zhou ended his essay with a warning against behaving like the Qianlong emperor and attacking and abusing those old and modern writers who did not have the same viewpoint as oneself. The only viewpoint to be taken was "the viewpoint of our age," which meant that "criticism and proposals [for the betterment of literature and thus society] are two distinct things. When we criticize the writings of the ancients, we have to recognize the age they lived in and evaluate them correctly and give them their rightful position."

On the question of Chinese and foreign, "geographically and historically there are many differences, but communications have improved and the circulation [of ideas] has quickened, so that mankind can hope to move gradually closer together, as the people of the same age." Thus one's anxieties should be for the whole of humanity, with no difference between Chinese and foreign, although "when we produce our own creative works, we naturally tend toward Chinese things, which we understand better."[107]

Clearly, even at his most utopian, Zhou was not a convinced exceptionalist. Later he explained his turn away from utopianism as motivated by the realization that idealistic activism may satisfy one's own feelings and interests but not be very effective in awakening the world.[108] He reiterated the point, quoting Havelock Ellis: there was no point in either trying to suppress or promote books as moral or immoral, since they had no impact on the way the vast majority of people led their lives.[109] In his memoirs, Zhou said that this essay marked his awakening from any hope of religion as a force in our lives.[110] Since religion in Zhou's vocabulary shared the functions of politics, this attitude is far from the conviction that the moral improvement of society can and must be attained by the intellectual mobilization of the citizenry, which Taylor sees as foreshadowing the exceptionalist position.

For many observers, Zhou's decisive turn away from activism has been inexplicable except in terms of personal foible. Even Pollard speaks of his "extreme socially negative position," which he attributes partly to rivalry with Lu Xun, although he later qualifies this considerably.[111] The disjuncture between Zhou's professed concern for humanity during his May Fourth period and his subsequent quietism or eremitism provoked comment from his contemporaries.[112]

However, there is a basis on which to reconcile the two—Zhou's conviction that human integrity and human rights were profoundly threatened by attempts to impose a particular viewpoint in the name of whatever good. He came to it through his personal experience in the course of the 1922 anti-religion movement.[113] Zhou's opposition to the movement is recorded by Ernst Wolff among others and is suggested by articles included in his early collections.[114] But the full extent of his involvement, which pitted him publicly against Chen Duxiu, has been documented only in the post-Mao era by Shu Wu.[115]

The movement began after plans for a conference of the World Student Christian Federation to be held in Peking in April 1922 were given wide publicity. On March 9, a group of Shanghai students announced the setting up of the Anti-Christian Student Federation. Their manifesto denounced Christianity and the Christian church as "devils" aiding tyrants in the current struggle between capitalist oppressors and the proletarian oppressed. Modern Christianity and the Christian church were the vanguards of the current economic invasion of China by desperate capitalists, they charged.

In just over a week, on March 21, the anti-Christian movement was broadened to include all religion with the formation of the Great Federation of Anti-Religionists (Fei zongjiao da menghui). Its manifesto began,

We swear to sweep away the poison and harm of religion on behalf of human society. We profoundly deplore the fact that in human society religion has spread poison which is . . . ten thousand times worse than floods or fierce animals. If there is to be religion, mankind may just as well not exist; if there is to be a human race, religion must not subsist. Religion and humanity cannot both exist.[116]

This manifesto was followed by telegrams and meetings calling for the banning of the April meeting. No less a figure than Cai Yuanpei joined Chen Duxiu, Li Dazhao, the biologist and future Guomindang leader Li Shizeng (1881–1973), and a host of other intellectuals in these activities.[117]

Disturbed by the intemperate language of the two manifestos, which seemed too threatening and redolent of the past,[118] Zhou and four colleagues at Beida, Qian Xuantong, Shen Jianshi (1885–1947), Shen Shiyuan (1880–19?), and Ma Yuzao (1880–1945), published a statement in *Chenbao* on March 31, advocating freedom of religious belief. It read:

We are not followers of any religion, neither do we support any religion, but neither do we approve belligerent attacks on any religion. We believe that people should have complete religious freedom, within the limits of the law, without being subject to interference from anyone. Freedom of belief is written into the constitution, and members of the intellectual class should be the first to defend it, or at least not be the first to destroy it. For this reason, we announce our opposition to the activities of the anti-Christian and anti-religious movements.[119]

This led to a spate of counterattacks from those who felt that an illustrious May Fourth leader like Zhou should have known better.[120] To these, Zhou responded, "If we lose the guarantee of freedom of speech, even if we are fortunate enough not to be eliminated this time, who can say it won't fall on our heads next time?"[121] In a follow-up article, he argued that he did not want to protect just religious freedom but "individual freedom of thought."

I believe that even if this interference with religious belief has taken place only on paper, in days to come thought will be banned—this is only the first step toward interfering with thinking outside the sphere of religion. . . . Many of the few freedoms written into the constitution have already been despoiled by our rulers. Although this freedom of belief was sometimes infringed in the Yuan Shikai period, it has nonetheless survived intact until the present. I do not want to see this freedom, which was spared by the emperor and the military, being destroyed at the hands of the intellectual class.[122]

Finally on April 11, *Chenbao* carried an "Open Letter" from Chen Duxiu and Zhou's reply under the headline "The Debate on Religious Freedom."[123] Chen upbraided the five for ignoring the right of the weak and oppressed to oppose religion, accusing them of "taking gifts such as freedom and humanitarianism to fawn on the powerful" and being the "dogs" and "slaves" of militarists and capitalists.

In the light of subsequent history, Zhou's response was prophetic. He reiterated that Chen's rhetoric undeniably signaled the beginning of oppression of individual freedom of thought, adding, "Oppression of freedom of thought does not necessarily need to use the force of government. To use the strength of a majority to interfere with a minority of dissenters also constitutes oppression."[124]

It might be argued that it is not altogether fair to read Zhou's comments only in the light of the series of attacks on "freedom of thought," which culminated in the Cultural Revolution: it is our situatedness after this event that gives Zhou's words such poignancy—a poignancy redoubled by knowledge of Shu Wu's own history as victim and pawn in the literary purges of the 1940s and 1950s.[125] Moreover, the scientific, rationalistic arguments being presented against religion at the time have been characterized as "almost a repetition of those going on in the West in the last three or four hundred years."[126] But this makes Zhou's ability to identify the stuff-matter of intolerance across the ideological spectrum all the more unusual. I believe this ability was closely related to his anti-exceptionalism, manifested in his repeated warnings and complaints that there was no difference between contemporary dogmatism, inflexibility, and stupidity and those of Song Neo-Confucians.[127]

## "Confucian Intentionality and Western Knowledge"

We may recall Zhou's hope that modern Western thought based on materialism would exert an influence on China's Confucian-Daoist heritage analogous to that of Buddhism. But what precisely was the content of that thought? How was Western thought to be appropriated? What was to be its relation to the Confucian-Daoist heritage?

Zhou's confident reference to a Confucian-Daoist heritage in 1935 reflects both the maturing of his ideas and changes in the political context. Nine years earlier, as his fears of domestic reaction and Japanese imperialism mounted, he had all but denied that there was any such thing.

When, during a visit to China, former Japanese premier Kiyoura Keigo (1850–1942) claimed a special understanding of China because he had since childhood "respected the Confucian teachings that formed the ethical and moral basis of Chinese civilization," Zhou responded that all the Chinese people possessed was Daoist religious shamanism and that the Confucian ritual (*lijiao*) claimed by warlords was grounded in superstition and cruelty.[128] "Old China hands" (*Zhina tong*) in Japan who thought they could understand the country by reading Confucius and Mencius were completely wrong. Confucians of the past had merely idealized superstition and sought to become officials. But Zhou distinguished between Confucians (*Rujia*) and the "materialist tendency" in Confucian teachings (*Rujiao*), which most had abandoned. This tendency "is a great merit of the Chinese people, and if we exaggerate slightly, we could say it is akin to [similar tendencies in] ancient Greece." Although there were now no true Confucians in China, "the present reform movement is really only the renaissance of materialist thinking." From this position, Zhou was able to argue against essentialized notions of East and West.

I do not know where any absolute differences between so-called Eastern and Western civilization reside, I just feel that the essence of Greek culture, which forms the basis for Western civilization, and China's present-day thinking have some resonances between them. Therefore China's current absorption of the new world civilization is preparing its own "rebirth."[129]

Zhou's vehemence is understandable, for Kiyoura belonged to a generation of politicians still influential in Japan whose intellectual orientation centered on "defense of the *kokutai* (national essence), with a concomitant hostility towards democracy, pacifism, socialism and the labor movement" and who scorned the Chinese New Culture movement as "the misdirected ardor of youth."[130] Yet Zhou's argument that the New Culture movement represented the "renaissance" of Chinese materialist thinking paralleled the arguments he made much more confidently about literature and the late Ming.

In an article written in 1928, Zhou claimed scientific learning did not belong to any one people or part of the world. Consequently, to argue in terms of "Chinese and Western medicine" was wrong, and he preferred to speak of "new and old medicine." In this case, although he had no reason to be partial to either "Chinese" or "Western" medicine, he hoped that "new" would develop quickly, particularly since the forces of reaction were trying to smother the new on all fronts and insisting that a local version of pre-scientific medicine should be revered as "Chinese."[131] The butt of this article was the powerful journalist and educator Zhang Shizhao (1881–1973), whose belief that China should develop institutions suited to an agrarian economy instead of Western forms of parliamentary government earned him the fear and scorn of New Culturists.[132] Zhou's insistence on keeping the binaries of old/pre-scientific and new/scientific apart from the potent Western/Chinese one makes sense in this context, especially when, as he said, "everything new in the political and moral sphere gets labeled left or Red" and was opposed by an essentializing archaist insistence on tradition.

But to see this as just a defensive tactical move in a struggle between two competing elite discourses on the shape of the nation—authoritarian nativist versus liberal democratic—is perhaps to miss the significance of Zhou's construction of human subjectivity as sharing a fundamental, universal similarity. This construction differed in significant ways from the universalism of the ideology of modernity. Underlying it was a view of "humanness" that did not make it a product of a Cartesian philosophical leap. "As soon as men were born in the world, humaneness was also born in the world."

During the May Fourth movement, Zhou proclaimed, as had Li Zhi, that he did not believe there was any classic or sacred book in the world that would remain a valid teaching for hundreds of thousands of years. Only biology, which recorded the life of living creatures, could do that. He sketched out a biological view of man (and woman) with ramifications for the entire institution of the family. Biology showed that in nature parents existed to care for their offspring, thus contradicting traditional views that children were procreated to offer sacrifices to their ancestors. This freed men and women from concubinage to procure sons, but enjoined on them the evolutionary duty to make sure that their children were better than they were. But Zhou did not leave parent-child relationships in the realm of duty: "It is, in the final analysis, an organic relationship, with a natural disposition to love mutually binding [them], from which arises a lifelong warmth and concord."[133]

From the beginning, Zhou seems to have found support in biology for a view of life that recognized affective and social life, rather than ignoring or thwarting it. He praised the French entomologist Jean-Henri Fabre (1823–1915) for his account of insect life, which left the reader feeling grateful, "as if we had heard of the lives of distant relatives."[134] In later years, Zhou altered his earlier dictum to say that to the extent that classics and sacred books "conformed to the facts of the natural order of things and human sentiments," they were able to teach us. One could even go so far, he suggested humorously, as to reverse the passage in the *Analects* about the value of reading the Odes: Knowing more about birds, beasts, and plants serves to stimulate the mind, to lead one to observe, to teach sociability, to regulate resentment. From them one learns the immediate duty of serving one's father and the remoter one of serving one's prince.[135] This had a new significance and conformed to reason, Zhou said.

What is interesting here is the interpenetration of society and culture with the rest of the animate natural world. If insects feel like distant relatives and the natural world teaches us sociability, then the dichotomies of culture/nature, mind/body, and reason/feelings are not exclusive binaries. Zhou's famous essay "Flies," which, as we saw above, was cited as proof of his denial of progressive thinking, is an astonishing attempt to recapture, through literature, the kind of sensibility banished by the germ theory of medicine, yet without denying science. As a child, Zhou writes, he and his brothers played with flies, and such childish games (which he recounts in detail) were also known to the ancient Greeks.

We have now been baptized by science and know that flies can transmit germs, and so we have a strong dislike for them. Three years ago, when I was sick in hospital, I wrote a poem which concluded,

> all you flies, large and small,
> the destroyers of beauty and life;
> flies, you friends of the Chinese people:
> I bring down on you a curse, wishing your total destruction,
> apart from human strength I invoke
> the blackest of black magic.

And yet, in reality, they have another habit which is even worse, which is that they like to fly onto people's faces and hands and feet and lick them. Although the ancients gave this the fine-sounding name of "drinking in beauty," it is not very pleasant for the one being drunk from.[136]

Here Zhou has turned away from the theme of flies as carriers of disease to flies as nuisances, but nuisances whose right to live is accommodated by having their interaction with people described in the poetic, if ironic, phrase "drinking in beauty." In the rest of the essay, Zhou introduces a range of literary references to flies. He tells the Greek myth of Muia, the importunate lover of Endymion who bothered him so much with her songs and chatter that he turned her into a fly, and Homer's likening the bravery of soldiers to that of flies. The *Shijing* also speaks of flies, and the Japanese poet Kobayshi Issa (1763–1827) wrote over twenty *haiku* on flies, including one that read, "Don't hit it! A fly washing his hands, washing his feet!" Whenever he read this, Zhou confessed, "I always think of my own poem and feel ashamed, but my own state of mind cannot reach this level, and so there is nothing for it."[137] The essay ends on an inconclusive note: whereas the Greeks used the name Muia for people, the Chinese, who shared their dining tables with flies, only used "fly" as a nickname, and then only in a few instances.

Why should the essay have aroused such ire? Perhaps because even while acknowledging science, it did not allow science to set the ethical parameters of the writer's sensibility. Zhou's poem refers to flies as destroyers of life and beauty, but while wishing them extinction, the poet wants to achieve this by magic as well as by human strength. When he deliberately turns away from pursuing their identification with dirt and decay, he is failing to fulfill the potential of their symbolic value. Even the references to Chinese sharing their dining tables with flies, which echo the discourse on national character, are left undeveloped. Perhaps the essay was also a way of reaffirming Zhou's refusal to unify his thinking. As an alert reader might have remembered, he had written about flies in one of his "Miscellaneous Letters from the Mountains." Plagued with swarms of flies in the temple where he was convalescing, Zhou marveled at the ingenious kindness of the Buddhist Issa, who had placed a louse on a piece of pomegranate because its smell was similar to that of human skin. Much as he admired Issa for this, Zhou said, he was burdened by conflicting responses: on the one hand, flies were "sentient beings the same as I am," but at the same time he knew they carried germs on their feet, they made him itch, and he wanted to kill them. "There is really no way to attenuate this clash between feeling and knowledge (*qing yu zhi*), because

I believe in what 'Mr. Science' has to say. Yet I do not want to take up his scalpel and destroy the beautiful world of the poet."[138] Zhou does not resolve the conflict between "science" and the "beautiful world of the poet" here, but he brings that beautiful world to life.

Yet there was an area of "biology" where Zhou had the highest hopes for reconciling science and the affections: subsumed under biology was a concern with sexuality, which is why of all the Western thinkers to whom Zhou was exposed, Havelock Ellis was probably the most important. Zhou had equated his reading of Ellis's *Studies in the Psychology of Sex* in Tokyo with the experience of enlightenment, by which he had gained "an understanding of man and society."[139] At the basis of Zhou's appreciation of Ellis, then, was Ellis's seven-volume work, which spoke to the Victorian discourse of sexuality but radically reversed its premises. In place of the Victorian focus on sex as pathology, Ellis's project was to foster acceptance of as inclusive a range of sexual behaviors as possible, by depicting them as essentially innocent, unremarkable, and endowed by nature.[140] Underlying Ellis's discussion of sex was the notion of "a unified human energy system, in which the different emanations of that energy could be converted from one form into another."[141] Ellis also argued that with the advance of civilization, sexual instincts became more intense and more refined. The centerpiece of his work was an exploration of heterosexual intercourse explicated in terms of female response, thereby putting women's sexual rights firmly on the agenda.[142]

The heart of Ellis's legacy for Zhou, that which constituted "science," was this encyclopedic discussion of human sexuality, which, by making acceptance of sex a mark of civilization, complemented the Lang/Frazerian insights correlating savagery with ignorance and fear about sexuality. We see Zhou drawing on this when he defended Yu Dafu's (1896–1945) "Sinking" against the charge of pornography. Ellis's rejection of norms of false modesty as destructive to women, physically and morally, struck a deep chord in Zhou and was part of the May Fourth ethos.[143] Ellis's view of humankind apprehended through its varied forms of sexuality had for its basis a holistic view of the world that resonated quite strongly with Zhou's. Wolff points out that Ellis sought to place sex in the wider general scheme of a "humane way of life" and quotes from Ellis's introductory statement, "Sex lies at the root of life and we can never learn to reverence life unless we know how to understand sex."[144] His work on sex should be seen in the context of the ethical revolt by a number of humanistic and socialistic thinkers against late Victorian capitalism and its culture.[145]

Apart from his books on sex, Ellis published over two dozen others in which he developed a personal philosophy affirming that man's task was to realize his own essential goodness and that of life, or as he termed it, "the vision of the world as Beauty." This vision could not be arrived at *directly* by struggle, for as Henri Bergson (1859–1941) had suggested, "No intellectual striving will bring us to the heart of things, we can only lay ourselves open to the influences of the world, and the living intuition will be born in its own due time."[146] Moreover, at the heart of Beauty there was Truth and then finally Love. It is perhaps not fortuitous that Love is at the center of the universe, because for Ellis it was also at the center of sexual relations between humans, providing the partners with emotional and intellectual fulfillment.[147]

The desire for "sustained erotic companionship" at the center of the love relationship was best fulfilled by monogamy, in Ellis's view, but he strongly criticized the concept of marriage as a legal contract. It was an utterly private matter between two individuals. The state had the right to be concerned about the children produced by sexual partners, and so could require their parents to register their relationship, but it could not withhold divorce from either party. Despite his affirmation of female sexuality, Ellis saw woman as the biologically passive, modest creature that had to be courted to be brought to arousal, whereas the male was dominant and active. In addition both sexes craved variety as well as monogamy. The love relationship therefore was inherently tension-filled, both physically and psychologically, and required the "art of living" to keep it in balance.[148]

The idea that living is an art that consists in balancing the instinct for asceticism and that for license was one of Ellis's most congenial insights as far as Zhou was concerned.[149] By making asceticism an instinct, instead of an externally imposed constraint on natural desires, Ellis had found another way of arguing for the autonomy of the self-regulating individual subject. Ellis led Zhou to the reflection that behind the mask of traditional Confucian ethics, life in China was dominated by the two extremes of asceticism and license. In the absence of either freedom or restraint, there was only oppression and debauchery. China had once known the true meaning of *li* (rites) when the rites had functioned as "the art of living," but after the advent of Cheng-Zhu Neo-Confucianism asceticism had taken over, and the rites had degenerated.[150] This was the view that informed his attack on the "Shanghai-style" literature he found prurient and filled with loathing for women. "Moderation and restraint" were what Zhou espoused as a "follower of the Mean" and what he equated with the Greek ideal of *sophrosune*.[151]

It is apparent that Ellis's construction of man/woman privileges the individual over society. That is to say, the human subject is seen as constituted by biology and a self-won spirituality with which society does not have the right to interfere. One obvious criticism of Ellis's work from a contemporary perspective, however, is that it tends to reify as male and female qualities such as sexual dominance and passivity that are socially constructed rather than biologically endowed.[152] It is undoubtedly true that Ellis reads too much back into biology, but it is equally true that a much more dynamic and subtle view of the interaction between the social/cultural and the biological is needed than is found in arguments about gender that deny biology.[153] In the context of Zhou's desire to evaluate Western knowledge by Confucian concepts of intention or idea, we find that Ellis's construction of human sexuality was congruent with Li Zhi's ascription of moral primacy to the husband-wife relationship. Li Zhi's contention that the genesis of all life depends on procreation and the irreducibility of the principles of *yin* and *yang* enabled him to dispute the importance given to patriarchal father-son or ruler-minister relationships. Moreover, it enabled him to deny the Cheng-Zhu Neo-Confucian monism of principle (*li*), which sustained these relationships.[154]

Although there was some ambiguity in his position, Ellis saw the individual as being in an asymmetrical relationship to civilization. Civilization, he noted, was a garment to which each individual could contribute a patch, a button, or some embroidery. "But the individual himself, with his own personal organic passions, never becomes part of the garment, he only wears it." The garment itself was "infinitely less precious than the humanity it clothes, still not without its beauty and its use."[155] The source of Ellis's ambiguity about the relation of the individual to civilization can be understood through his reference to the "*organic* passions" of the individual, which indirectly reveals his links with the discourse of eugenics, which links civilization to race. Ellis believed that before having children, a couple ought to consider whether they would thereby be improving "the quality of the race," although he seemed to recognize that this conflicted with his romantic conception of marriage.[156] In his feeling that it was cruel to bring into the world an "inferior" child, Ellis was more closely the intellectual forerunner of prenatal testing and genetic counseling than of the Nazis (although critics of the contemporary Human Genome project warn that the two streams could come together). Zhou introduced Ellis as "a eugenicist and scholar of psychology" in an early article on obscenity, equating lack of prudishness with "health" on both the individual and the wider cultural levels.[157] Despite the May Fourth enthusiasm for eugenics—to which, incidentally, the third of the Zhou brothers, Zhou Jianren, was an important contributor[158]—the subject does not feature much in Zhou's writing. This is surely because the promotion of eugenics requires the kind of governmental and educational intervention that was anathema to him.

Ellis's systematic concern to assert the primacy of the individual must have encouraged Zhou in his determination to do the same thing. Ellis's individual was diametrically opposite to that constructed by Freud, and it is instructive that Ellis's genuine admiration of Freud as a sexual liberator coexisted with a deep-seated hostility to Freud's project.[159] It was unfortunate, Ellis commented, that Freud should have regarded hate as a primary motive and love as a secondary one.[160] This cluster of values must have helped to buffer Zhou against the Nietzschean pessimism about the human subject that, through Lu Xun, became part of the May Fourth ethos.[161] After the collapse of Shirakaba idealism in Zhou's world, Ellis, whose quest for the love at the center of the universe was similar, remained. It was not energy (drives) alone that made civilization, but "sincerity, intelligence, sympathy, grace and all those subtle amenities which go to make what we call . . . humanity," Ellis said.[162]

Although Ellis was Zhou's primary source in the "discovery of the female sex" with which Shu Wu credits him, his reading of women writers such as the feminist and pacifist Olive Schreiner (1855–1920), the founder of modern birth control Marie Stopes (1880–1950), and the poet Yosano Akiko (1878–1942) must surely also have contributed.[163] He was also very concerned that children should be allowed to have their own games, books, and fantasies.[164] Here perhaps Western "knowledge" shades into Japanese "feelings," for Zhou was deeply affected by Kobayashi Issa's "A Year of My Life" and its account of Issa's love for his daughter.[165] He was also impressed by the fondness shown for children by Japanese writers through the ages.[166]

We could place a complex of beliefs about sexuality and the equality of women and, derivatively, of children, at the heart of the Western ideas that Zhou hoped would leaven Chinese thinking in the same way that Buddhism had. The importance of these ideas was aptly symbolized by Zhou's statement that his "winning method" by which to judge the level of attainment of any Chinese man of letters was to look at his attitudes toward Buddhism and women.[167] This suggests that what Zhou saw as crucially important about science was not the accumulation of scientific knowledge but the wisdom about human life scientific knowledge could promote. He praised Yu Lichu (Yu Zhengxie; 1775–1840) and Jiao Litang (Jiao Xun; 1763–1820) for recognizing that women and men were equal as persons and endowed by nature to enjoy sex.[168] Elsewhere he described Ellis, Li Zhi, and Yu as all arriving at the same truths about "human feelings and the natural order of things" (renqing wuli) with the difference that Li and Yu had come to them through intuition and Ellis through science, which had Greek civilization as its basis. The results were about the same, although wisdom based on knowledge was probably somewhat more reliable, he added.[169]

When someone who understands human feelings and the natural order of things says something, it doesn't matter whether the form of expression is outmoded or novel, the content is equally valid. It is like gold, which does not fear the fire, it is completely impervious to attack, and because it is impartial, it can be equable.[170]

Thus Zhou wrote, applying the epithets of "impartial and equable" (gongzheng heping) to Li Zhi.

The fact that wisdom is supposed to grow out of knowledge gives Zhou's idea of science an interesting twist. It could perhaps be defined as "that basis of knowledge which enabled the Greeks to arrive at sophrosune," visible in Ellis as restraint and equivalent to the Confucian Mean. This equivalence becomes the basis for thinking that scientific knowledge and human emotions are common to all categories in the formula gu jin *zhong wai* (ancient, modern, Chinese, foreign). The wisdom that grows from their proper understanding thus resembles the "innate knowledge" of Wang Yangming or the "childlike heart" (*tongxin*) of Li Zhi in that they are common to all of us.

Given Zhou's admiration for Li Zhi, we might take the notion of the childlike heart as a concept that linked Zhou's interests in anthropology and his literary aesthetics. Victorian anthropologists held that the unified psychic structure shared by humanity manifested itself in myth, which Zhou defended for expressing emotion and intuition. Mythmakers were poets, and literature reflected "basic human nature." Zhou's interest in children and their games and stories parallels on one level the quest for the true childlike nature with which humans are born before it becomes overlaid with prejudices. The Gongan school, following Li Zhi, located *quwei* among children and the dispossessed. Similarly, Ellis's attempt to naturalize sex speaks to the conviction of a unified psychic structure and valorizes a version of the feminine denied in the masculinist Victorian discourse on sex, paralleling Li Zhi's desire to give *yin* parity with *yang*. It should be stressed that Zhou did not make these connections explicit in his own writing; the idea of *tongxin* as a unifying concept should be taken as suggestive rather than programmatic.

My aim in linking Zhou's humanism to the Confucian notion of "idea" or "intention" rather than the Western "knowledge," which is often taken as its starting point in discussions, has not been to set up a sterile East/West or traditional/modern antithesis, but to suggest that, in terms of the construction of self my reading permits me to find in Zhou, such oppositions are irrelevant. Once this perspective is admitted, it becomes unnecessary to go through Zhou's work weighing the importance of "influences." This is because his objective was not synthesis, the search for a hierarchically ordered combination of elements that would contribute to universal progress, but a search for truths about human existence compatible with his own faculty of moral discrimination. It is Zhou's stance of being at once a solitary yet particularly constituted individual, the fact that his ideas are presented as a function of his own *bense*, that distinguishes this humanism from one that relies on a constant "essence" defined in corporate and hence exclusivist terms, or in universalist and necessarily abstract terms.

"Originally the thinking of humankind was common to all, it was impossible to distinguish far or near, light or heavy, but the influence of heredity and environment are also facts; amid this great unity (*datong*), it was inevitable that there were some small differences, and this is what gives the literature of a particular time or people its special color," Zhou said in a lecture in 1920.[171] The idea of the underlying unity of humanity was a guiding thread in Zhou's writing. If we are to take his self-attribution of Confucian "idea" seriously, as I have done, then it makes sense to investigate further the model of selfhood that could give rise to such a conception. Song Neo-Confucianists gave a metaphysical dimension to the Mencian idea of humaneness (*ren*), which epitomized man's mind (*xin*). Mind became the unifying moral center of human consciousness, but at the same time cultivation of the mind to realize its oneness with the unifying principle (*li*) and to recognize human interrelatedness required immense efforts of willpower and study.[172]

In the restructured Neo-Confucianism of the late Ming, the unifying principle came to be seen as identical with mind; consequently to pour one's efforts into trying to study it as something outside oneself was misguided. Striving to follow received opinion and reifying socially prescribed norms led people to lose this original mind. The ontological oneness of heaven, earth, and the myriad beings, including human beings, provided the ground for both existence and knowing. True understanding of existence could only be achieved experientially, through learning that conformed with one's own particular endowment. It followed that particularity of circumstances and endowment would lead to different accounts of reality, but there was no epistemological gap between the knower and the object of knowledge. Thus the knowing of right and wrong was common to all.[173]

This idea is at odds with the Cartesian notion of the modern subject as uniquely placed in a self-conscious objective relationship to reality. The split between subject and object is mirrored in the dichotomies between past and present, traditional and modern, sacred and secular, that sustain modernity. Postmodernist critiques of the ideology of modernity that dissolve the subject into a series of positional alterities nonetheless place themselves on the modernist side of the divide, and so reinforce the Cartesian articulation of reality. In neither case does there seem any possibility of giving the model of selfhood I attribute to Zhou and read through his aesthetics any more than sentimental consideration.

Here Anthony Cascardi's contribution to the debate about modernity proves enormously helpful in finding a way out of this morass. Cascardi sees the subject as the ground of modernity, but finds inadequate the two most common views put forward to explain it: either that it is the emergence of the philosophical concept of the subject itself that marks a radical break in historical time, or that subjectivity *qua* self-consciousness gradually emerges over the *longue durée* of the Renaissance.[174] Instead, he argues that the understanding of selfhood as subjectivity was an invention by which European thinkers made sense of changes in relationships between individuals that had their basis in a series of destabilizing socioeconomic events starting in the sixteenth century. The concomitant shift in values could be grasped or articulated only by transforming a social lack into a sense of historical loss and positing the individual as a subject able to grasp and act on the world. In this way, the subject becomes the ground of modernity. The Cartesian philosophic discourse

may be regarded as a practice, but it is not just one practice among many. Rather the case to be made about Descartes as the "inventor" of subjectivity is closer to the one that Alasdair MacIntyre has made for Luther, viz., that he is able to grasp the moral experience of his public and in so doing leads to the acceptance of a discourse in which their experience may be comprehended in stock "Lutheran" terms.[175]

The recognition that the subject is an abstraction, conceived within European philosophic discourse to make sense of specific historical circumstances, frees us from the enormous normative burden it carries even in its deconstructed postmodernist form. If this is the case, then civilizations must have equal parity. What happened in sixteenth- and seventeenth-century Ming China in response to a parallel series of dislocations, including a rise in population, increased social differentiation, and social unrest, is equally valid as a civilizational response, a way of making sense of shifts in values.[176] However, these shifts are articulated in another set of terms: instead of seeking Cartesian subjecthood, the self is oriented toward the goal of self-attainment. Thanks to the restructured understanding of the nature of reality, attainment is now seen as inherent within the personhood of each individual, which in turn supports the notion of the fundamental equality of persons. "As heaven, earth, and I have the same roots, who [among men] is superior to me? And as myriad things are one with me, who is inferior to me?" asked Li Zhi.[177] This self is thus underpinned by a Buddhistic awareness of the "emptiness" of the self, which involves the refusal either to reify socially assigned roles or reject them in favor of something else, but sees both self and non-self as two sides of the same reality. What is important here is the articulation of self-attainment as a universal possibility, not whether individuals do or do not feel inclined to attempt it. Moreover, whereas the Cartesian subject is inscribed in philosophy, the subject that emerges in the late Ming takes literature as the primary sphere for self-inscription.

Unfortunately, a set of social relations and practices reflecting this new articulation of individuality was never firmly established. Instead, the conservative Qing gentry reaction, which emerged in a cluster of contingent, historical circumstances and not solely because of some inherent cultural imperative, deployed a discourse on ritual, bolstered by evidential scholarship, as a way of counteracting the new individualism.[178] This helps to explain the fact that the basis for Zhou's claim that the Gongan school writers were "moderns" is their "integrated" attitude to writing. Grasping modernity as a framework within which to inscribe what appears desirable in the construction of reality, Zhou posits an individuality that is free of the compartmentalized roles sanctioned by ritual and thus able to see itself as whole. It is important to realize that the claim is that the Ming writers were "holistic" in their *attitude* to writing, which Zhou opposed to demands that writers be unified in terms of their literary *practice*. Thus we see him refusing to choose between his two demons, the rebel and recluse, and refusing to support any one school of thought.

Zhou broke with the May Fourth discourse when he realized that the project of modernity necessitated the creation of subjects in whom selfhood oriented toward self-attainment constituted an *obstacle* rather than a desirable goal. Zhou's claims for the origins and the functions of the essay were his way of combating the limitations of the Cartesian subject, particularly the subject's inability to account for value, and this inevitably brought him into conflict with the discourse of nation-building.

My claim here is not that the subjectivity produced in the late Ming was necessarily better than the Cartesian one; rather, under the conditions of early modernity (my first-order modernity), there were parallel if necessarily different developments within the two civilizational spaces. However, as the distinctive features of second-order modernity, including the synergies between nation-building and imperialism, came together globally, the idea of the Cartesian subject was mobilized to become a crucial part of it. In Taylor's terms, the stance of disengaged reason solidified into the foreclosing of all other options, including value.

What would have happened had there been a slightly different concatenation of events in China (less gentry reaction, a different mix of policies at the Qing court) is anybody's guess. The contingency of events has been demonstrated by James Polachek, who showed that the Tongcheng school's narrow-minded support of Cheng-Zhu Neo-Confucianism accorded with the ambitions of a Peking-based group of literati, many of them linked to Tongcheng, in the 1830s.[179] This group, partly through a series of contingent events, promoted a xenophobic and populist response to the political problem of British incursions into south China. It also forged a heroic mode of literati self-image.

Second-order modernity, which had its origins in European socioeconomic history, has achieved such dominance throughout the world that it is often hard to imagine alternatives. But given that institutions and structures congruent with the globalization of economies emerged outside Europe before the onslaught of second-order modernity, why should we assume that the economic integration of the world could proceed only according to the dynamics of second-order modernity? In the words of a question framed by Arif Dirlik, what alternative modernities are being erased by this view?[180]

Speaking from the present, we can say one reason is that the success of global capitalism has made it easy to view it ahistorically as a *deus ex machina*: in a sense it has taken over from the point at which History left off. This is why it is now possible to be theoretically sanguine about the alleged supersession of nation-states by global capital. The fact that societies being drawn into the era of global capital seem compelled to go through bloody reconfigurations of national identities, or the mobilization of fundamentalist ethnic or religious identities on the model of national identity, indicates that such a view is far too simplistic.

The nation-state or its surrogate fundamentalisms remain the most potent focuses for self-identity, and they demand a particular instrumentalist subjectivity that, even when paying lip service to "tradition" (such as "Asian values") asserts itself against alternative visions of selfhood. The "Asian values" invoked by authoritarian governments in East Asia would no doubt be seen by Zhou as in a direct line of descent from Song Neo-Confucianism and the Tongcheng school. It is here that we can notice the ideological way in which the subject functions as the ground of modernity: even those who deplore these developments nonetheless find these alternative visions to be incomplete when held against the norm of (Cartesian) subjectivity. In doing so, they are tacitly perpetuating the colonialist dismissal of the native civilizations that stood on the sites of modern nation-states while approving of the use of authoritarian traditions that fit the needs of modernity (and capital).

It is crucial to my notion of second-order modernity that imperialism/colonialism and nation-building be seen as linked together in a dynamic whole. Zhou was a dissenter against this modernity, and inevitably his construction of the self as a self-sufficient moral agent found itself at odds with the ideological demands of those busy imagining the nation-state.

# FIVE

⁓

# The Construction of the Nation

## The Rhetoric of Nationalism

The mistrust of didacticism that runs through Zhou's writing can be read as a commentary on the ideological construction of the modern nation-state. Zhou's attack on Han Yu and the *daotong* system takes us to the heart of his criticism, for Han Yu was a pivotal figure in the attempt to construct a single foundation for sociopolitical action and individual cultural production in the wake of the An Lushan (d. 757) rebellion.[1] Han Yu's radical innovations in *guwen* as a literary form redefined learning in terms of the Confucian "way of the sage," and he particularly attacked Daoist and Buddhist traditions, which he claimed ignored the proper ordering of human institutions.[2] Although Han Yu himself never ceded to the requests of his friends to actively propagate his ideas, his "conception of sagehood as spiritual wisdom expressed through political action was to form the intellectual basis for the spiritual and political world of Neo-Confucianism."[3] Han Yu invented the lineage, or *daotong*, by which the appropriate teachings for this program (what later came to be known as the Four Books) were transmitted from Yao and Shun via

Mencius to himself. Zhou's criticism of Han Yu thus goes far beyond the issue of didacticism.

It is also a criticism of the notion that there is a homogeneous definition of what it is to be Chinese and a rejection of the demand that self-cultivation must benefit the state. Such notions are precisely the kind of civilizational elements that modern nation-building projects draw on and aggrandize in order to gain legitimacy. Zhou's criticism was thus quite different from that of Yan Fu, who charged that in attributing the origins of human culture to the teaching of the sages, Han Yu had misunderstood the potential for creativity of the people. Consequently, Yan Fu charged, the sages and the rulers had had no inclination to develop the physical, moral, and intellectual resources of commoners.[4] Zhou was explicit that his criticisms of Han Yu were also directed at the present-day "defenders of the Way."[5] In the context of the early 1930s, this is a criticism of the Guomindang, which since 1928 had enjoined its officers to study the Four Books and with its New Life movement was attempting to Confucianize China's modern national identity. But Zhou is not limiting his attack to one version of Chinese nationalism. His assertion that the Tongcheng school and Zeng Guofan (then the idol of the Guomindang) were ancestors of the May Fourth movement inculpates all the competing versions of nationalism. As we saw in the previous chapter, in arguing for the Ming origins of the essay, Zhou's project was clearly to suggest the (historically grounded) existence of an alternative to the dominant discourse. Zhou's opposition to nation-building discourses, however, did not translate into a lack of concern for the society in which he lived or obliviousness to the problems faced by other peoples.[6] His twin moves of aestheticizing and depoliticizing were made within specific historical contexts dominated by politics, and at times they mediated or enunciated political positions, as we will see in this chapter.

Every upsurge of nationalist rhetoric filled Zhou with the dread he voiced during the anti-religion movement: that eventually thought would be suppressed. Just after his public debate with Chen Duxiu, he predicted that the intellectual sphere would soon witness a flourishing growth in movements to promote national essence (guocuizhuyi) that would manifest themselves as attempts at restoration (*fugu*) or outbreaks of anti-foreignism (*paiwai*).[7] This was not a new concern. Zhou had long been keenly sensitive to the many ways in which nationalist feelings were inculcated. Responding in 1921 to a newspaper report of discord over the way to commemorate the French war dead, he mused skeptically on the difficulties involved in weighing "national honor and national humiliation." There was also a lesson for China here:

China is currently proposing education on national humiliation. As a father of primary school children, I formally register my opposition to this. We expect from educators that they will impart the fundamentals of knowledge to children and develop their ability to act, but that insofar as political isms are concerned, they will let the children choose for themselves when their intelligence is fully mature. We hope that educators can train fully formed individuals who are also good members of world society. We do not want them to act on behalf of pigs and turn our children into loyal officials of Napoleon to be buried under the Arc de Triomphe![8]

He concluded by likening nationalist (*guojiazhuyi*) educators who took advantage of the pliability of children's minds to manipulate them to pimps training child prostitutes. Two years later he complained that schools were trying to make pupils into obedient citizens and that the sight of children parading through the streets in a demonstration reminded him of the children's armies sent to fight in the Crusades.[9] The only kind of national humiliation that needed discussing was not "the loss of some national right or other but the shame of a country's citizens failing to qualify as upright people."[10]

Zhou also mocked appeals for citizens to prefer "national products" as a way of getting people to accept badly made, overpriced goods. These were like traditional appeals to suffer on behalf of the country and to accept the loss of life and property without complaint. From this perspective, a Chinese would count it as nothing to be executed by a fellow national. "In sum, anything which bears the word 'national' is good, and as for what kind of a mysterious thing this country is, perhaps we should say, 'it is a word for the sake of which we must suffer discomfort and loss.'"[11]

In 1924, Zhou's understanding of the mechanisms by which nationalist sentiments are constructed was deepened by the enthusiastic response given in some quarters to the American film *Birth of a Nation*, shown in

China under the title *Soul of Freedom*. Although he did not see the film, he read a special publication that went on sale to mark the release of the film. Deeply shocked by it, he declared the film "immoral." Conscious that he was seemingly negating his position that art should not be criticized from a moral viewpoint, Zhou continued:

Although I do not accept that when art touches on private emotions this is going to degrade public morals, I nonetheless believe that works that encourage violent acts are immoral. I do not consider anything that incites to be art. *Soul of Freedom* is a film that preaches the extermination of blacks . . . therefore I maintain it is immoral.[12]

Zhou admitted that he was not exempt from feeling that a barrier to intimacy existed between him and black people ("at least, I do not have the courage to love a black woman"), but this was based on racial differences, not on differences of kind. The message of the film, that Lincoln's freeing black slaves marked the beginning of national calamity but that the Ku Klux Klan's program of wiping out blacks marked the birth of the nation, was contrary to human justice. He could not approve of the film, "even though it is a masterpiece of the Americans, who are worshipped by the Chinese."

The film drove home to Zhou the need to exercise great care when describing foreigners in drama, particularly in comedies or films.

Everybody in the world has a little anti-foreignism in him- or herself, which can at any time be revealed, but in comic or popular works, it is easier to see, this exerts a more baleful influence and promotes loathing between peoples. There are special reasons for not including the Jews here,[13] [but] others like the Germans in Russian plays, Chinese in American plays, and Japanese in Chinese plays are all made to look very ugly, and this is wrong. This is not just calumniating foreigners; *it is unwittingly sowing the seeds of imperialism.* (italics added)[14]

Zhou's insights into the way nationalist and imperialist discourses implicate and mutually energize each other, feeding on ideologically instigated antagonisms, are astonishingly perceptive. Commenting on the fact that the publication described the film, said to be promoted by the U.S. government and welcomed by Americans based in China, as "particularly relevant to the Chinese situation," he warned:

If the Chinese fall under the spell of this kind of work and really start to emulate it, they will probably start to make a film about Tang Jiyao[15] setting up a . . . group to exterminate the Miao (the nearest analogues to the blacks in present Chinese society), which could lead to violence or "righteous taking up of arms" to uphold the Han and wipe out the Miao. This would really be a case of one calamity bringing on another.[16]

If he had misunderstood the film, Zhou said, the blame belonged to the author of the promotional literature, which was written in Lin Shu's style of *guwen* and was "full of aspirations for imperialism and hatred of peoples of different race or nationality." The postscript to this affair, as far as Zhou was concerned, came three months later when Shanghai police announced the discovery of a KKK cell, composed of two U.S. citizens and five Chinese. Zhou both pitied and ridiculed the five Chinese, who were oblivious to the ironies involved in their decision to help pursue the goal of "ridding the world of people of color."[17]

Shortly afterward Zhou noted a trend to raise the status of the xenophobic Yihetuan (Boxer) secret societies, whose rebellion had disrupted North China at the end of the nineteenth century, and to forget their cruelty. Given the realities of the contemporary world, if the Chinese people decided, out of a desire for self-defense, to advocate militarism and resist foreign powers, "although I would not encourage it, I could still approve of it, because this could still be considered one way of dealing with the situation," he wrote.[18] The methods of the Boxers, which amounted to superstition and slaughter, were nothing more than banditry, however. Although there was nothing to stop young people from training in the martial arts and the use of artillery, Zhou continued, he did not believe that the Chinese were going to raise a second Yihetuan army, as some imperialists claimed. More likely, however, was the emergence of a *spiritual* Yihetuan army, who, if they had no other outlets for their energies, would write resolutions to "kill the demons" and pour their energies into accusing anyone who thought differently from themselves of being "dogs and slaves of the foreigners." This would not cause much loss to the "barbarians" but would damage China greatly.

[No foreign-imposed] indemnities of whatever size could prevent the development of the normal desire for self-defense and resistance, but one stupid and cruel outbreak of violence would bring its own most painful retribution, which would cost future generations far more than the heaviest punishments from enemy countries.[19]

Zhou saw these developments and the increase in censorship as fulfillments of his earlier predictions about the suppression of thought and trend toward restoration.[20]

The last months of 1924 saw the war between the Zhili and Fengtian cliques come to an abrupt halt when the warlord Feng Yuxiang (1882–1948) accepted a huge Japanese bribe, which came in the form of a loan to Zhang Zuolin.[21] Arthur Waldron has recently argued that that war was qualitatively different from previous ones, bringing a host of social, economic, and political changes of which the most important was the rise of a nationalist and revolutionary movement.[22] Although I cannot engage with Waldron's provocative thesis here, it is intriguing that Zhou Zuoren began 1925 by writing an essay in which he announced that he had decided to take down his "writer's signboard" since his thoughts had returned to nationalism. He had believed he owned his "own garden," but in fact he had just "rented someone's land and produced a few skinny radishes and bitter vegetables." Now, he had come to see himself as an itinerant, mostly jobless, laborer, and although he might open up new land in two or three years, for the present he had to acknowledge himself to be "an ordinary person" (*suren*), not a literary figure.[23]

At the time of the Boxer Rebellion, Zhou said, he had supported the dynasty against the foreigners. Later, after reading revolutionary periodicals, he had become anti-Manchu and supported nationalism for about a decade, although his nationalism softened at the time of the 1911 Revolution. In the spring of 1924, he had reduced the scope of his May Fourth dreams of cosmopolitanism (*shijiezhuyi*) to Asianism (*Yazhouzhuyi*). This changed

after the Qing court had to move out of the Forbidden City, and Japanese and British imperialist adventurers started to stir up trouble. As their plots and machinations have still not ended, I have become aware that my ideas were not keeping up with events. I feel that since the foundations of the republic have not stabilized, I must start from the facts and that I have to use [a position of] nationalism (*minzuzhuyi*) as my starting point.[24]

But Zhou immediately hedged this nationalism with provisions:

I do not believe that one ought to love one's country, but from the viewpoint of [safeguarding] individual existence nationalism is appropriate and does not run counter to "higher" kinds of isms. Those who have not been through the baptism of national revolutionary thought and the oppression of terror during the period of [anti-Manchu struggle] and the restoration [of 1917] will probably not be able to understand this frame of mind. . . . I am just expressing the movement of my thoughts, and I do not mind whether people see it as too extreme or too obstinate, just as long as no one compliments me for being a cosmopolitan again.[25]

Zhou's decision to take down his signboard as a writer, if only for the next two or three years, and his decision to "start from the facts" must be seen together. Literature was the sphere in which he put his efforts to cultivate his own aesthetic responses to the world around him, and his cosmopolitan aspirations had provided his dominant political orientation. With this announcement, he seems to be serving notice that his aesthetic aspirations—and indeed his much-praised reputation for aesthetic mildness (pingdan)—were to be put on hold. In other words, to use the terminology that he devised a year later, he would allow his "hooligan" demon free reign (see Chapter 4). This was an indictment of the situation in China. As he commented, although he most admired mildness and naturalness in writing, it was really hard to expect that in present-day China anyone of his irritable temperament could calmly produce equable, mild writings.[26]

How did Zhou's reversion to nationalism affect his writing? It would seem from the essay quoted above that one of his main concerns was to distance himself from his reputation as a cosmopolitan or Asianist, and around the same time he produced a number of articles criticizing Japanese policies.[27] Over the next two or three years, he produced a stream of denunciations of Japanese imperialism—the attack on Kiyoura mentioned in the preceding chapter is one example—that were harsher in tone than earlier such essays.[28] His angriest attack came in response to Japanese comments after Li Dazhao's execution on the futility of his death.[29] Zhou also chafed at the symbols of British imperialism. Why should a newly minted copper coin need to be emblazoned in English with the words "The Republic of China," he asked in an article dated April 1925.[30] Did that mean that the republic was owned in part by the British?

However, although Zhou may have expressed himself more often and more forcefully on these issues, there was no qualitative shift away from his earlier suspicion of nationalist rhetoric, and he continued to warn against it.[31] In one article he took himself to task over an earlier piece and apologized unequivocally for suggesting that the Japanese did not think in the same way as other people.[32] A week after the 1925 May Thirtieth incident, he expressed outrage at the British action "because they have not treated the Chinese people like human beings."[33] The Chinese should respond most vigorously by breaking off economic relations, which was the only feasible method, and realize that the enemy was "brutal British bureaucrats," not individual Britons: "our aim is self-defense, not revenge." Outweighing the anger and intransigence in his articles on current events during this period is the fact that he did continue to perfect his aesthetics of mildness and to develop his theory of Chinese literary history.[34]

Zhou's fear that one day thought would be suppressed in China underpinned his sensitivity to the languages of xenophobia, self-aggrandizement, and "othering," which are such salient features in the construction of national identity. This remained a constant in his thinking, as did his opposition to ideology. He ridiculed Peking intellectuals for their "so-called nationalism," which manifested itself in a movement to "support the flag" and supposedly aid in "exterminating the Reds."[35] At the end of 1927, the terrible year in which Zhou had to deal with Li Dazhao's execution and the banning of *Yusi*, he wrote:

These past six years, almost every day I've been afraid of the arrival of reactionary movements and now they have finally come, . . . unfortunately, [my] prediction has come true. What is this reaction? It is not necessarily preserving the old and restoring the ancient, it is any cudgel-and-yelling-ism that seeks to unify thought. It goes without saying that the "suppression of Reds" in the north is one example of the type of reaction I fear, but so also is the "purging of the [Communist] Party" in the south, because what it is after is certainly not only crimes of conduct but crimes of thought. To kill people for their thoughts is what I find most terrifying. If China wishes to improve, it must immediately cease this dreadful business of killing people and let all the new schools of economics, politics, religion, and art have the freedom to think and discuss. The *Mencius* says, "Who can unify the kingdom? He who does not take pleasure in killing people can unite it."[36] This platitude is still just as useful today. But what is its use? Cudgel-and-yelling-ism is now sweeping over the whole of China. Eight or nine years ago I feared it, and [this fear] still has not changed. It's just that my hopes that reaction would diminish and reason gain the upper hand have changed. They are now on the wane—and that probably represents some kind of progress.[37]

For Zhou, the contest over who should rule China was entirely artificial against the reality of its existence as a civilizational sphere. When in October 1926 rumors spread that southern troops saw all northerners as the enemy, Zhou denied categorically that there was any foundation for this.

I believe the Chinese people are completely united. Geographically speaking there is north and south, but there is no north and south among the people. Historically, either because of invasion by different races or because of powerful groups and interests, the strange spectacle of the division of north and south has been acted out many times. But as soon as the opportunity presents itself, they come together again, and even though many years of disunion may have passed, no traces of the division remain. This is a historical fact, which proves the unity and solid strength of the Chinese people's national character.[38]

Although there were differences in diet and northerners and southerners had a variety of nicknames for each other, "these are just jokes."

To sum up, the chaos since the founding of the republic cannot be settled on the basis of geography or people but on the basis of thought, and it is not a war between the people of two different places but a war of thought. It would be better to call it a war between democratic thinking and thinking [governed by] one's elders and betters.[39]

Early in 1928, after *Yusi* had been forced to close down in Peking, Zhou described the situation in the capital as too dangerous for him to continue writing about national affairs and declared that he would try to turn into a hermit.[40] In November of that year, several months after the Guomindang consolidated its military gains and announced a period of political tutelage for "New China," Zhou announced his decision to "close his doors and devote himself to reading." This was the only option left for those who wanted to dissipate the sense of oppression generated by the Chinese present, he remarked with bleak sarcasm. Since materialism had dislodged the belief in souls and rebirth, no one could afford to casually throw his or her life away as a hero. Moreover, reading (or studying) had been recommended in previous years as a way of "saving the country." The question was What should one read? For his own part, he was going to turn his attention to the classics and the works in the history section of the *Siku quanshu*:

On the surface, what history teaches us is about the past, but the present and the future are also contained in it. The official histories are a little like the imposing portrait of an ancestor, but you can still see something of the grandchildren in them. The unofficial histories are more like snapshots taken on a trip to the park. . . . By reading the histories, one can also see [contemporary] ghosts; no matter what they call themselves . . . one can find their original form in ancient books. Those of shallow learning are reckless in their differentiation of events. [They hold that] either the twentieth century, or the Northern Expedition, or the rise of the Peasant Army represents a change in era. From this time forth, a new world has come into being, bringing enormous changes, that will be completely different from the past. It is as if the people of old had died in the blink of an eye, and new men had dropped from the heavens or sprung out of the ground . . . like two completely different animals.[41]

Zhou's stated intention of closing his doors and studying, or "playing it safe," led him to write fewer essays on contemporary events for a short period, but, as we saw in the preceding chapter, the setting up of the League of Left-wing Writers galvanized him into writing his "Plants, Trees, Insects, and Fish" series of essays. At the same time, his reading of Ming and Qing writers supplied him with more angles from which to criticize contemporary developments.

Midway through the "Nanking decade" as the Nationalist regime consolidated itself, Zhou wrote that "the new policies [brought by] Western learning have become transformed into the eight-legged essay of Neo-Confucian orthodoxy."[42] Engineers discussed education, philosophers discussed military affairs, militarists discussed morality—all without any independent views of their own. Meanwhile, facile calls were being made to sacrifice one's life for the nation, which Zhou deplored.

For people to give up their lives for a righteous cause is a difficult and hence extremely precious thing, this is indisputable. Consequently, it can certainly never be considered a bad thing to esteem integrity. However, a great many abuses also stem from this, the greatest of which is the use of death as a pardonable way to confront any problem, regardless of the wrong done to the country and harm to the people. To treat one's own life as precious and take the lives and deaths of thousands of people lightly is an enormous error.[43]

In 1934, the Chiang Kaishek regime launched the New Life movement, which sought to "militarize the lives of the citizens" to prepare them for "self-sacrifice," and to promote Confucian values.[44] As could be expected, this was accompanied by a heightened nationalism articulated in essentialist terms. Zhou identified three manifestations of this nationalist discourse, prevalent particularly among the young. First, there were calls to "bring into play China's intrinsic culture," which he likened to the eminent Qing official Zhang Zhidong's (1837–1909) slogan of "Chinese learning for the essence." Also in evidence was the desire to focus on the shortcomings of European culture in order to find equivalents of domestic evils such as opium-smoking and footbinding. "From my experience of the past thirty years," Zhou commented, "it seems as if Chinese thinking has been unable all along to escape from these two circles." He found most horrifying a proposal that Zhu Yuanzhang, the brutal founder of the Ming dynasty, should be glorified as a sage and genius.[45]

As this sampling of Zhou's writings from the 1920s to the mid-1930s has shown, he consistently opposed the rhetoric of nationalism and was well aware of its place in the nation-building process. I now turn to Zhou's treatment of the categories through which, since the late Qing, the modern discourse of the nation had been articulated and show how his aesthetics and his countervailing construction of the locality enabled him to de-reify them.

## People, Language, Class, Locality

Since the late Qing, the people had been the most important component of the nation, and language (more specifically, the use of the vernacular) was the instrument by which the people's commitment to the nation was to be mobilized. With the May Fourth radicalization of this discourse, the people had come increasingly to be seen as the laboring masses. This trend brought intellectuals on the left into a painful confrontation with their class origins. This was resolved to some extent by acceptance of the Communist Party's claim to represent the toilers, particularly in the face of the Nationalist Party's apparent unwillingness to disturb the rural status quo. However, the Nationalist Party claimed that it was exercising the sovereignty of the nation on behalf of the people.[46] Despite their surface differences, both the Communist and the Nationalist projects were founded on the will to create and control the "people."[47]

For Zhou, as we saw in Chapter 2, the relationship between the intellectual and the people was mediated by the locality. In this view, he was following Zhang Binglin in seeing intellectuals and the people as both equally contained by the locality. To explicate his understanding of the relationship between the people and the intellectual, Zhou used two images popularized by Kuriyagawa Hakuson (1880–1923): the ivory tower, symbolizing pure art, and the crossroads, symbolizing concern for society.[48] Other people had left their ivory towers and gone to the crossroads, but he had built his tower at the crossroads, he asserted. When Zhou described the crossroads and the pagoda nearest his Shaoxing home, the specificity of the locality reinforced his claims to real knowledge of society, which he said he had acquired as a youth through his fondness for street life. And yet he liked his privileged vantage point in the tower and had not slipped in among the crowd to become one of them. He disliked feeling jostled and afraid and could relax only in his tower. But, "in present-day China this is a most untenable attitude. The crowd sees the tower and says you are the intellectual class (which is a crime). The gentry and merchants see a tower and say you are setting up a political party (and should be suppressed)."[49] He concluded that it was, in any case, a mistake to think of the tower and the street as fundamentally separate. Differences in attitude between the tower and the crossroads were to be expected because every individual thought for himself.

There is evidence that, at the time of the 1911 Revolution, Zhou's political aspirations were centered on the locality. This should not be surprising, given that local self-government was widely considered to be integral to constitutional government.[50] Zhou wrote a short newspaper piece supporting local self-government (difang zizhi) as the surest way to consolidate the republic and stressing the role of primary education in making this a possibility.[51]

The publication date of "Place and Literature," March 1923, strongly suggests that Zhou wrote it in the aftermath of the failure of the Federalist movement of 1920–23. Prasenjit Duara has shown how the demand for a federal system of provincial self-government (liansheng zizhi) balanced two contradictory movements: on the one hand, provincial autonomy was seen by radicals, including May Fourth intellectuals, as a way of guaranteeing the democracy a centralized national government would not provide; on the other, militarists supported the movement to further their own ambitions.[52] As the extent of militarist manipulation became clear in 1922, support for the movement plummeted. By 1923, the circumstances that made federalism a possibility had passed, and it seemed "a completely unrealizable dream."[53] It is somewhat intriguing therefore to see Zhou publishing his article in the tenth-anniversary number of the Hangzhou-based *Zhijiang ribao* on March 23 (whether he chose to do so or was asked to write an article is not known). The facts of publication themselves evoke the recent provincial challenge to the ideology of state centralization. An awareness of the potential for the federalist movement to feed a series of mini-nationalisms, however, seems to have impelled Zhou to spell out the desirability of a literature that stressed evocation rather than representation.

In the opening sentence, Zhou addresses the ghost of federalist expectations hovering over his title and lays it to rest by placing localism (*difangzhuyi*) within the realm of intersubjective relationships:

It is a perfectly clear fact known to all that the Chinese usually harbor localism. A good example is the way, in the aftermath of the food-poisoning incident at the Zhejiang First Normal School, newspapers have carried the requests of the local-place associations (*tongxianghui*) to which the fatalities belonged for commemorative steles to be erected.

Having deflected any hopes that he would proceed to a stirring new definition of what "localism" could achieve, he continued, "Under the present circumstances, to advocate a localist literature would obviously be most small-minded and thoughtless, and this is not what I intend at all."[54]

It is left to the reader to decide what the implications are: that local identity as politics is just as dead and buried as the unfortunates at the Normal School and that it would be tactless to raise the issue? That it is just as poisonous as their food? The bulk of the essay, as we saw in Chapter 3, is an impassioned plea for a literary treatment of the locality grounded in an aesthetics of *quwei*. After commenting on the unoriginality of much of Zhejiang's contribution to the new literature, Zhou ended: "I hope from now on it will improve and escape from the prejudices of National Essence and local style (*xiangfeng*) and truly deploy its special characteristics, so as to create a part of the new national literature."[55]

Zhou rarely wrote about the county or the locality as a political or social entity. But there was one social initiative that impressed him, and that was the rural education program in Dingxian, south of Peking, which he visited in 1934 with Yu Pingbo. He expressed great respect for it. Unlike most politicians and educators, he opined, those involved clearly understood the program's aims and objective conditions. At the same time, the poverty in Dingxian shocked him. The answer, he said, quoting Mencius and Confucius, was for the government to develop the political will to genuinely care about the people's livelihood.[56] This was undoubtedly a dig at the Nationalist Party, which had reversed the Mencian principle that adequate food and clothing were a prerequisite of virtue and cynically insisted that only the virtuous would be strong enough to obtain the necessities of life.[57] But by making Confucius and Mencius the arbiters of the role of government, Zhou was displaying a quite unmodern lack of expectations about how a government should behave.

Zhou's refusal to accept the implications of a class-based identity (discussed further below) did not stop him from having a pessimistic view of the masses, whom he likened, during the May Fourth movement, to a raging river capable of sweeping all before it in the absence of good government.[58] His lack of faith in the folk as a source of moral virtue or national regeneration had several origins, now familiar to us. Primary among these was his conviction that enlightened ideas and behavior could truly occur only at the level of the individual and depended on independent thinking by, and respect for, the individual. But as his experience of the anti-religion movement in particular had brought home to him, most people were only too ready to be roused by slogans and to trample on the rights of the minority. He then related this to his understanding of the pattern of the Chinese past, which had fostered certain habits of behavior. This made Zhou at times an active contributor to the discourse of (bad) *national* character, shared evenly by all classes. But whereas his contemporaries increasingly saw nationalism as a panacea, he believed nationalism would only make it worse. In the letter he wrote to Mu Mutian on national literature (mentioned in Chapter 2) Zhou suggested a program of his own to combat the dangers:

> We must diagnose the paralysis of baseness and cowardice;
> Eliminate the running poison of lewdness and salaciousness;

> Cut open the scar of befuddled ignorance;
> Castrate the madness of national self-aggrandizement.[59]

Similarly, Zhou was unable to see class as the key to the transformation of society. He refused the popular May Fourth distinction between, on the one hand, literature that was bad, pre–twentieth century, aristocratic, and written in *guwen* and, on the other, literature that was good, twentieth century, popular, and written in the vernacular. He preferred to conceptualize the differences as informed by a concern with the worldly or the transcendent, both attitudes common to man, without regard for economic or social differences.[60] He repeated this position almost a decade later, stating his disagreement with a recent speech in which Hu Shi had described the national revolution as a result of the literary revolution.[61] Zhou said China was divided ideologically between two classes: bourgeois (he used the English term) and anti-bourgeois. But the working class shared the values of the bourgeoisie and aspired as fervently as any bourgeois for wealth, status, honor, glory, wives, concubines, and servants.[62] The ideologically anti-bourgeois position was akin to the premodern literature of the recluse and reflected discontent with social realities. But, Zhou concluded, true literature should escape all class entanglements. What we have here, then, is a restatement of the *wen yi zai dao* and *shi yan zhi* schema transposed into the language of class analysis. But this dichotomy was one that underlay all of Zhou's thinking.

He agreed with the view that if a work purporting to be proletarian literature revealed a decadent attitude toward women and love, this was reason enough to doubt its credentials, since the proletarian movement had to include the problems of women.[63] On the other hand, Zhou praised a social issues play titled *Infanticide* by the Japanese writer Yamamoto Yūzō (1887–1974). "I believe this capitalist society ought to be overthrown, but literature is not propaganda—it is not the means to an end, it is its own goal. But when anti-capitalist ideas penetrate into someone's mind and flare up and come into being again as words and language, then this can be good literature. It is art that moves people and not curses or orders."[64]

Zhou's opposition to capitalism as a system was consistent and, interestingly enough, seems to have been articulated most commonly in the context of the condition of women and children.[65] Whereas many of his May Fourth contemporaries attacked the urban-based, popular "Saturday school" of fiction as representing "old culture and old literature," Zhou saw it as a contemporary phenomenon produced by a combination of the capitalist economic system and old-style education.[66] For Zhou, the existence of classes and the class struggle were of the same order as evolution. They had always been there and had not been invented by Marx. Moreover, any reasonably educated person who was not a warlord, a bureaucrat, or a capitalist able to rely on force or wealth to maintain the status quo would approve of communism, he asserted. Like Christianity, Pure Land Buddhism, and utopianism, it promised paradise to believers. But he rejected the possibility of there being a theoretical or programmatic means to implement communism. As for how the struggle would work itself out, there was no sure way of knowing.[67]

The key to Zhou's stand on the language issue is found in his assumption, voiced in his discussion of Liu Bannong's poetry, that there existed a number of "traditions that transcend good and bad and that cannot be discarded." It is the ideological neutrality of these traditions that safeguards their continued existence in Zhou's scheme of things. This can be seen even in his harshly worded discussion of *baguwen*, which he proposed all university students of Chinese should be made to study. Although it was very close to the Tongcheng literary style, Zhou said, he was also anxious to show that *bagu* had deep cultural roots—like a monster in a children's story, you could cut it into pieces, and each piece would spring back to life.[68] Zhou described *bagu* as a crucial link between past and future in Chinese literature and literary history; by understanding it, one could plumb the depths of tradition and reveal the origins of the modern reaction against it.[69] He did not seek its origins in institutions, though, but in language itself. Although *baguwen* itself only went back as far as the Song, Zhou said, its principles were rooted in the visual aspects of Chinese characters and the musicality of the tone system. These were the same features of the language that were exploited in riddles, verbal games, and Chinese opera, in which sound counted for more than sense.[70] In effect, the examination essay tested the skills needed to solve riddles, rather than clear thinking, and its inherent musicality proved soothing.

These features were compounded by the fact "thousands of years of dictatorship" had nourished a stubborn propensity to obey and to imitate, which left people "unable to think or speak for themselves, unable to act without instructions from their superiors."[71] Zhou saw these same skills being used by his contemporaries, "who did their utmost to solve problems within a prescribed framework." *Bagu* could thus not be "laughed off as a rotten cultural relic of the Qing. Its spirit is still alive and well in the minds of people who have never seen *bagu*," Zhou warned. Characteristically, Zhou found the antidote in individual awareness and reflection. "The best way is to examine the school essays of our ancestors and compare them with our own work," he said, adding that, as he opposed "unified thought," this possibly painful process should be undergone voluntarily.[72] His suggestion that *bagu* should be studied at the university level using the tools of cultural anthropology and historical linguistics can also be seen as intended to contribute to clarity of thinking.[73]

That Zhou's attack on *baguwen* was intended as a criticism of thinking styles rather than the linguistic features of the language is shown by the fact he made the same complaints against the *ce lun* (questions and themes) format that had replaced *baguwen* in the examinations after 1898.[74] It required knowledge of a host of new subjects—economics, military science, water conservancy—about which no individual could know everything. Consequently, to perform successfully, Zhou implies, the candidates had to be able to spout theory. Contemporary rote invocations of theory—popularly known as foreign (*yang*) *bagu*—were in fact more closely related to *ce lun* than *bagu*:

Both [*ce lun* and *bagu*] are writing to order, but doing *baguwen* makes people mediocre and rotten and doing *ce lun* makes them reckless both in the way they slavishly copy and in the way they talk nonsense. If you do *bagu* alone, you learn to fill in the right words, to dance when someone claps, and there is no thought in what you say. But those who can both do *bagu* and talk nonsense rely on their ability to do *ce lun*.[75]

The problem with this "theorizing" was that it became public opinion, and the damage done to the country was enormous; calling it "*yang bagu*" was an injustice, because it was a good old Chinese product with its roots deep in the Chinese *xiucai* mentality.[76]

Notwithstanding its heavily ironic and satirical tone (Zhou acknowledged in his final sentence that the piece should not be taken entirely at face value), Zhou's essay on *baguwen* suggests that the Chinese language, at its most basic level, served as a shared resource within Chinese society.[77] It was the basis of the highest level of elite literary attainment (poetry), folk productions (operas, riddles), and an institutional form that led to cultural disaster (*baguwen*). It is true that these usages can be assigned to class categories, but, I would suggest, this is different from showing that the linguistic features themselves had a class nature. Although he did not say, as he did in his essay on Liu Bannong, that these features were inherently neither good nor bad, Zhou still represented language as transcending any social or political framework. The use made of language—now that the Qing dynasty was gone—depended on the individual. This contrasts with Lu Xun's view, as late as 1934, that Chinese characters were "an instrument of a policy to keep the population ignorant . . . a tumor on the body of the broad masses of the laboring people, full of bacteria. If we do not cut it off, we will die."[78]

On the question of the reform of the written language, which was widely debated in the 1910s and 1920s, Zhou had taken a moderate stance.[79] He favored replacing the phonetic transcription system (sometimes known by its first four syllables as *bo po mo fo*) with a Latin one, but suggested that conversion to an alphabetic system was so distant as to be meaningless to contemplate.[80] What he advocated for the present was to reduce the number of strokes in characters, not merely as a measure to help the undereducated but as a means of saving the time and energy of everybody, including schoolchildren. Responding to charges from the proponents of national essence, Zhou stated:

We certainly do not fear others saying that it is because we cannot write complicated characters and want to make it easy on ourselves that we are advocating reform of the written characters, or even the use of foreign writing systems. . . . If we find a particular way of doing things very inconvenient or a cause of hardship, of course we can take measures to change or eliminate it. This holds true for all customs and morality, including Chinese characters. Chinese characters exist to serve us, not the other way round.[81]

Here Zhou was reiterating a principle that was crucial to him. However, Zhou patently did not want to discard Chinese characters and warned against ending up with a writing system like that of Vietnam.[82] Whatever the arguments in favor of adopting a world language like Esperanto as China's national language, Zhou wrote elsewhere, "the primary national language of China can only be the language that destiny has fixed, for good or ill, as the inheritance from our forebears. We can improve or augment it to the limits of possibility, but we fundamentally cannot go beyond that."[83]

This set the direction in which Zhou's thinking was to develop. In an important wartime essay on the future of Chinese literature, he referred to Chinese characters as the defining feature of the modern written Chinese vernacular. Something written in Latin script or the phonetic system would not be Chinese literature, because "writing written in Chinese characters is to a greater or lesser extent influenced by the Chinese literary tradition, and this is its special characteristic."[84]

## Time and the Aesthetics of Ear and Eye

Zhou Zuoren came to see language as one of the most vital constitutive elements of the Chinese civilizational entity to which localities and individuals belonged. In opposition to the constructors of a restrictive, artificial national identity, Zhou produced a version of "China" that sought to de-essentialize even as it was grounded in language and place. To do this, he drew on the language of the defenders of "national essence" in the journal Critical Review (Xueheng) but turned their categories inside out. Writing in February 1922, Zhou seized on the position expressed by Mei Guangdi (1890–1945) that although imitation was wrong, it was nonetheless slightly better to imitate the ancients than foreigners because "one could sometimes get more spiritual essence."[85]

The Critical Review group were mainly the U.S.-educated students of Irving Babbit (1865–1933), and this slip in logic reveals the price to be paid for situating themselves discursively within his conservative humanism. Lydia Liu has suggested that, following Babbit's calls for a humanistic internationalism, they hoped to help create a "new authentic world culture" that would be forged from the best of East and West.[86] Yet their weakness was that all their positions were authorized by Babbit, "who not only sought to appropriate ancient Greek civilization for modern Europe . . . but presumed to speak with authority on Confucianism as well."[87] Moreover, the national essence promoted by the Critical Review group was modeled on the West.

This is helpful in understanding the reason for Mei Guangdi's inconsistency. No matter how passionate a supporter of Chinese civilization at one level, at another Mei had already accepted the implication of this structural inequality—that any new vision of Chinese civilization had to be congruent with, and authorized by, a Western model. Mei's palliative for this painful inequality was to make "the ancients" the object of emotional and ritual attention—imitation—a contradictory move that provided emotional comfort while avoiding the conclusion that what was Chinese was no longer viable on its own. At the same time, imitation of the ancients, while reproducing the (albeit discredited) archaist (*fugu*) mode of apprehending essence, was a nationalist gesture, a claim of superiority. The "national" of National Essence highlights the dilemma of trying to reconcile a particular essence with the universalizing claims of modernity, in other words, the contradiction that lies at the base of the nation-state.

Zhou cut through the problem by recasting it in terms of imitation and influence and maintaining that "national essence" was inimitable and, therefore, impossible to reify.

My opinion is that imitation is slavery, but that influence is permissible. Since national essence is only the inheritance of *quwei*, there is no point in imitating it. Europeanization is a kind of external factor, we can permit and accept its influence to the fullest extent, but of course we will not imitate it.[88]

By making national essence the "inheritance of *quwei*," Zhou is trying to make it intangible and unobjectifiable.

If "national essence" does not just mean writing that anthologizes and studies the Tongcheng school and thinking based on the Confucian teachings of the three bonds and five virtues but includes everything with national characteristics, then what I have called "inheritance" means the same thing.[89]

The formula "everything with national characteristics" (*baokuo guominxing de quanbu*) seems to bring us perilously close to a reification of people/nation, but as Zhou makes clear in the next line, this "everything" depends on, and can only be articulated by, the individual: "We advocate respecting each person's individuality, and naturally we also respect the national character (*guominxing*), which is a composite of individualities, in the same way."

The demand for respect meant that any national literature which emerged as the artistic expression of this plurality of individualities must be allowed to develop naturally at its own speed, "like a seedling." This development was ultimately in the hands of the individual:

I believe every educated Chinese, provided only that he or she does not imitate, can use any freely chosen words[90] to write down any kind of thoughts, and the result will be a "Chinese" literary work. It will combine the author's own special individual characteristics and national characteristics, even though there may be many outside influences.[91]

National essence, thus defined, was "continually seeping through our brains and spirits, there is no need to take special measures to preserve it, since it will naturally always exist and cannot be obliterated." Its only enemy is imitation. No "phenomenon from a particular period" can be expected to endure in peoples' hearts forever, and those who try to imitate the ancients end up with "a handful of hair and feathers"—the same expression used by Yuan Hongdao in describing those who try to find *quwei* by acquiring its trappings.

Pinpointing the difference between his definition of national essence and that of Mei, Zhou wrote:

They have a prejudice that national essence is superior, and only on this condition are they willing to accept some reforms that do not harm the main principle. I, on the other hand, take these inherited national characteristics as a grounding (*su di*) for everything else; [the national character] should, to the fullest extent possible, submit to influences from every direction, fusing with and being permeated with them as one body and continually changing, so as to create a lasting yet ever new national character.

That was why "we welcome Europeanization as a breath of fresh air, not something to inject into our veins to replace our own circulation."[92] Applying these principles to the question of the national language, Zhou suggested that any innovations that respected the "natural proclivities" of Chinese as an uninflected, monosyllabic, language written in Chinese characters (*Hanzi*) should be welcome. Here we have returned to the linguistic traditions that "transcend good and bad."

This discussion of "national essence" is very similar to the one in his essay "Place and Literature," written a year later and discussed in Chapter 3.

Locality and the Chinese language are both identically described as "an inheritance of *quwei*" that flows in the veins. Clearly, these two are the main constituent elements of "Chineseness" for Zhou, but he is unwilling to impose a limiting framework on them. The early dates of "Place and Literature" (March 1923) and "National Essence and Europeanization" (February 1922), the two seminal essays in Zhou's attempt to de-reify the concept of the nation by drawing on the aesthetics of *quwei*, show that the most important elements of his thinking matured as he made his break with the May Fourth discourse. The mental habits that enabled Zhou to turn categories around and reverse or empty them of content, like his ability to identify intolerance across the ideological spectrum during the anti-religion movement, may well have come from Buddhism.[93] If so, he was not the first radical Chinese thinker to have used it as a resource.

The absence of time from this open-ended, aesthetically grounded vision of the nation requires comment, because of the importance of time for the modern conception of the nation as "a solid community moving steadily down (or up) history."[94] The ideological construction of the modern nation-state probably owes more to Herder (1744–1803) than to anyone else, and at this point it will be instructive to see how the Herderian vision was articulated in literary terms. Here we can very profitably turn to Mikhail Bakhtin's (1895–1975) discussion of Goethe (1749–1832).[95] Bakhtin sees Goethe as "intimately and fundamentally linked to a *feeling for time* that awakened in the eighteenth century and reached its culmination on German soil in Lessing, Winckelmann and Herder."[96]

What is the feeling for time in Zhou's thinking? We have seen that his model of literary history was not a narrative of "becoming" but an oscillation between two states that could be modified or intensified by events and personalities and that his aesthetics and his literary history are interdependent. We will see how the absence of temporal linearity and the aesthetics of *quwei*, realized in the locality, combine in Zhou's work to produce a radically different vision of the nation. Bakhtin in his discussion of time and space in Goethe's work begins with the suggestion that

the ability to *see time*, to *read time* in the spatial whole of the world . . . is the ability to read in everything *signs that show time in its course*, beginning with nature and ending with human customs and ideas (all the way to abstract concepts). Time reveals itself above all in nature: the movement of the sun and stars, the crowing of roosters, sensory and visual signs of the time of the year.[97]

There is in Zhou's writing a sense of time reflected in the progress of the seasons and human customs. Thus the passage from "Qing jia lu" (Qing jia records) cited earlier: "Why are we so interested in these seasonal changes and customs? . . . It is because they make up the tiny activities in our daily lives." But Bakhtin is concerned to show that in Goethe the observation of natural and human time is linked to the artistic visualization of historical time, whereas I suggest in my discussion of the "Qing jia lu" passage in Chapter 3 that Zhou was concerned with people and their activities, not specifically nations "moving up or down historical time." Goethe's literary projects foreshadow the attempt to condense and summarize real life and the real world in the novel. But this real world was to be made real by being shown to reside in a particular place whose events had a specific, purposeful historical background.

What I find interesting is Bakhtin's emphasis on the "exceptional significance" of visibility for Goethe's creativity:

All other external feelings, internal experiences, reflection and abstract concepts are joined together around the *seeing eye* as a center, as the first and last authority. Anything essential can and should be visible; anything invisible is inessential. . . . In his understanding of the *eye* and *visibility* he was as far from crude primitive sensualism as he was from narrow aestheticism. For him visibility was not only the first, but also the last authority, when the visible was already enriched and saturated with all the complexity of thought and cognition.[98]

The contrast with the aesthetics of *quwei*, where it is not the gaze that is privileged but intimation or evocation in all its olfactory guises—flavor, lingering fragrance (*yuxiang*), aftertaste (*huiwei*)—is striking. Of course the contrast is not absolute, because *quwei* is evoked by the representation of concrete images. But visibility cannot be the last authority, for *quwei* is intangible and cannot be spelled out. For Goethe "the word coincided with the clearest visibility."[99] This is diametrically opposed to Qian Qianyi's assertions that in appraising poetry, "the use of the eye is timebound and limited; it cannot attain to the fragrance or stink revealed by the sense of smell. I discard the eyes and use the nose."[100] In other words, the eye could only reveal words (the visible) and was inferior to evocation.[101]

Goethe's method revolved around the effort to assign everything he saw in a landscape to some temporal stage or "epoch of becoming." What he saw were "remnants or relics of various stages and formations of the past and as rudiments of stages in the more or less distant future."[102] It was essential for him to link everything up along a single temporal line, to be able to connect past and present to the future. Moreover, the past had to be creative in the sense that it must have an effect on the human history of the present. "Such a creatively effective past, determining the present, produces in conjunction with the present a particular direction for the future and to a certain degree, predetermines the future. Thus one achieves a *fullness of time* and it is a graphic, visible completeness."[103] This linear historical vision, Bakhtin continues, "always relied on a deep, painstaking concrete perception of the locality," because it was only in the locality that history became reality for people by being transformed into "a corner of the historical world."[104]

Each event in a locality was necessarily tied to time, to the past and the present, and to the wider world. Goethe proceeded from the concrete visualization of localities to want to embrace the whole of the world in his work, so that "the entire world and all of life are given in the cross section of the *integrity of the epoch*."[105] In other words, his literary projects were intended to make the world smaller, more real, more visible, and more concrete. One of the ways of doing this was to situate the fantastic in the concrete. Thus Goethe wrote a fairy tale but included in it spatial markers from a real place.[106]

The obverse practice was to discover the fantastic in a local place and incorporate it into the concrete, national world. Hence the discovery of folklore in the second half of the eighteenth century. As Bakhtin says:

This was primarily a matter of national and local (within the boundaries of the national) folklore. The folksong, the folktale, the heroic and historical legend, and the saga were above all a new and powerful way of humanizing and intensifying one's native space. With folklore, there burst into literature a new, powerful and extremely productive wave of *national-historical time* that exerted an immense influence on the development of the historical outlook.[107]

A typical example of the mechanism by which this process worked can be found in Pindar (fifth century B.C.E.):

Through a complex and skillful interweaving of local myths with general Hellenic ones, he incorporated each corner of Greece, retaining all its local wealth into the unity of the Greek world. . . . Using skillful associations, metaphoric correspondences and genealogical links, Pindar interspersed these local myths with general Hellenic myths and created a unified and closely woven fabric . . . [that] produced a kind of national poetic substitute for an inadequate political unity.[108]

Although, as we saw above, undoubtedly some hoped that China would be enabled by its folklore movement to follow the same route, Zhou felt such aspirations were unreliable dreams.

Quite apart from his misgivings, however, there was a structural difference in Zhou's conceptualization of the nation. For Zhou, the national essence constitutes the *su di*, the "plain background," against which the localities provide infinite variation and difference. This is exactly opposite to the Pindar/Goethe process of incorporating diverse local elements into a homogenized whole that somehow becomes able to determine its own destiny.

This basic structural difference explains why Zhou always insisted on being open to the outside world, which is why the Wei-Jin period (220–420), with its weak governments and the influx of Buddhism, was one of the high points in his literary history. A telling difference with Herder is that Herder saw foreign cultures as "cancers" and foreign languages as inimical to the free development of German intellection: "We speak the words of strangers and they wean us from our own thought."[109]

To sum up, we find in Zhou a construction of China that depends on the diversity of individuals and localities and is not threatened by outside influences but welcomes them. These are major differences with the dominant construction of the nation in Chinese literature for most of the twentieth century. The aesthetic grounding for this vision of the nation—which depends ultimately on a view of the self—accounts both for its importance and for its potential.

The potential I see here resides in the way in which Zhou's construction of locality illuminates the related concept of community. (At this point I am excluding for a moment the "imagined community" of the nation-state.) Locality and community are not equivalents, although they often overlap. Not all communities are spatially defined, and some localities are created for mere administrative convenience and do not exist as communities, whereas others are claimed as home by many communities. Zhou's construction of locality with its specific landscape, its customs and socially grounded material culture, and its particular types of intersubjective relationships parallels community in many ways. But, as has been noted by Partha Chatterjee, the relationship of the community to the modern nation-state has always been theoretically problematical. He suggests this is because of the suppression of narratives of community in post-Enlightenment discourse, which gave rise to two extremes, both of which lead to the erasure of community. Either a doctrine of the sovereignty of the individual is postulated, or there is taken to be only one political community, the nation-state.[110]

Chatterjee bases his argument on a reading of Hegel's attempt to reconcile two key ideas: the idea of (individual) rights and the idea of community. Hegel's solution was the concept of civil society. However, as Chatterjee shows, as civil society becomes the domain of the market economy and civil law, there is no place for the ethical and affective claims of any pre-contractual community. These can emerge in Hegel's narrative only in the family, but Hegel is unable to show where any objective separation between family and civil society, private and public, can occur. All he can do is to allow civil society to take up the role of the universal family, thereby "immediately open[ing] himself to appropriation by that powerful strand of thinking that claims that this role of the family can be played by the only legitimate community in modern society—the nation—a role that must then be enforced by the disciplinary mechanisms of the nation state."[111]

Chatterjee's project is to show that narratives of community were displaced by the march of capital, which had its own narrative and which produced "both the normalized individual and the modern regimes of disciplinary power. . . . If there is one great moment that turns the provincial thought of Europe to universal philosophy, the parochial history of Europe to universal history, it is the moment of capital—capital that is global in its territorial reach and universal in its conceptual domain."[112]

Chatterjee's arguments and insights are suggestive in explaining why in Japan, where capital accumulation was far enough advanced to support imperialism, thinkers found it so hard to isolate the concept of community from nation, allowing the two to be assimilated. But in China's case, where the spread of capitalism was much less certain, the nation-state also became the only ultimately acceptable political community and marker of identity. Consequently, rather than privilege capitalism as the main player, I would prefer to transpose Chatterjee's terms into my (admittedly looser) category of second-order modernity. It was capitalist society, writes Chatterjee, that was able to "reunite capital and labor ideologically at the level of the political community of the nation."[113] But it could also be said that socialist societies were able to reunite Leninist bureaucratic formations and labor, and fascist societies were able to unite elite and masses, all at the level of the political community of the nation. The whole discursive apparatus of nationalism, which emerged together with imperialism, takes on a life of its own and ought, in my view, to be given equal weight with capitalism and the epistemological systems underpinning nationalism and capitalism.

These lead to the rationalizing modernity (second-order modernity) that is best articulated and served by the form and function of a nation-state. Thus Chatterjee's location of the suppression of the narratives of community in the post-Enlightenment discourse of nationalism and modernity highlights what I see as the most important feature of Zhou's concept of locality: because it starts out from a completely different basis, it cannot be reduced to a surrogate or mini-nationalism. Chatterjee suggests that discussions of community might be more helpful to post–Cold War theorizing about the nation than is the popular topic of civil society. The challenge is to see community as a locus of belonging with which nation-states have to come to terms, rather than to search for an ideal sphere for abstract individuals. The conclusion to be drawn from this is not that the nation-state ought to be done away with but that it must become at once more fluid and more accommodating.

## Conclusion

Zhou's challenge to the dominant construction of the nation was articulated through his aesthetics. As we have seen, the aesthetic categories he deployed were not a new invention but drew on literary and philosophical traditions available within the civilization. Because these aesthetic categories and practices sustained certain modes of cognition and hence certain modes of relationship to the world, they have had the potential, at least, of opening the writer and the reader to the philosophical possibilities they represent. As noted in Chapter 1, Li Tuo has suggested that the structural use of imagery links the Jing pai writers of the 1930s (for many of whom Zhou was a mentor) with Wang Zengqi and the "searching for roots" writers of the 1980s. In other words, recourse to a traditional aesthetic practice is the hallmark of this posited linkage, and this aesthetics, as I have tried to show, cannot be divorced from a particular way of apprehending the world that is at odds with the realist literary project typical of nation-building. My claim here is not that Zhou Zuoren was the ideological father figure for all these writers, which certainly cannot be the case, but that having seen how these aesthetics functioned in his usage, we can ascribe some of the same significance to their use in the works of others.

The dominant literary figure in this context is Shen Congwen, whose "lyricism" is a byword and whose rejection of the short story in favor of something nearer the essay was explicit.[114] Shen held that

all forms of art enable writers to express a feeling of poetry (*shide shuqing*) and there is no exception for short stories. Because of his obeisance to the form of poetry, a fiction writer will develop a special sensitivity to language, thereby producing patience in handling diction. He will acquire just the same kind of sensitivity to the varieties of humanity, clever or foolish, altruistic or self-seeking. In this way a fiction writer can touch on "life" in ordinary circumstances of sadness and happiness. Above all, if a fiction writer can make a poet's pathos toward life his own impetus, he will assuredly increase the profundity of his works.[115]

The sensitivity to language and to life of which Shen speaks is surely the attitude that makes possible the qualities of *quwei* and *bense* in an author or a work, and in fact, Shen himself refers to seeking to bring to light "the divine" (*shenxing*) hidden in the world.[116] Similarly, David Wang, in a most illuminating analysis, finds that Shen's lyric discourse enables him to emphasize not only the creative force of language but also "the freedom of human perception."[117]

However, whereas Wang wants to save Shen Congwen from his reputation as a "lyrical stylist, vanguard regionalist and political conservative" and recuperate him for the May Fourth project by suggesting that "his works must be understood as a dialectical part of, rather than an exception to, post-May Fourth realism," I would prefer to see Shen as engaged in an altogether "alternative" discourse.[118] To be sure, in seeking to disassociate Shen from realism, I have in mind here the classical nineteenth-century European mode of realism that defers to the prior existence of a stable, knowable, external world. This classical realism, exemplified by the texts of writers such as Balzac and Tolstoy, does not make "freedom of human perception" its credo but seeks to represent external reality through a human perception focused on certain coordinates of the real. Through this effort of locating his or her text in social life, the writer aspires to reveal its hidden truths. This mode of realism provided the springboard for May Fourth theories of realism.

Damian Grant, in a masterly study, distinguishes between "conscientious realism," which sought to represent a pre-existing social reality, and "conscious realism," which appealed to a "higher" level of reality and brought back into writing what conscientious realism had sought to banish. The result was the "rehabilitation of dream, aspiration, intuition and other states and faculties beyond the control and the cognizance of science."[119] Objective reality, now dispersed among countless subjectivities as the "stuff of experience," gained its significance only by being produced through a responsive consciousness.[120] This "conscious realism" Grant finds in the works of Proust, Woolf, and Joyce. There would indeed be grounds for locating Shen in this expanded realism (which some might prefer to label "modernism"). However, my concern is to posit a break between Shen's literary practice and that predicated on the May Fourth discourse, because I think Shen's aesthetics provides grounds for distancing him from the particular discursive construction of the self underlying the May Fourth nation- and subjectivity-building project.

For Wang, it is the irony in Shen's work that links him to the realist tradition, and he comments that it is only through allowing Shen's lyricism and irony to illuminate each other that one can appreciate "that in a most subtle way, Shen Congwen's art expresses the humanism of the May Fourth movement."[121] But what is the content of May Fourth humanism? If anyone personifies May Fourth humanism, it is Zhou; yet although Wang sees Zhou Zuoren and Feng Wenbing as Shen's "immediate predecessors," Zhou is almost invisible in his account.[122] No doubt this is because Wang sees Lu Xun as setting the "discursive paradigm" of modern Chinese literature.[123] Lu Xun was indeed the paradigmatic May Fourth intellectual, but this need not mean that there were no alternatives to the dominant May Fourth discourse. In fact, it is only by suggesting the existence of an alternative discourse that Zhou becomes comprehensible. It is also in the context of this alternative discourse, with its aesthetic and philosophic basis, that humanism can be redefined as a concern for particular and local human selves, rather than abstractions.

Shen's allegiance to the humanistic ideals of the May Fourth movement is not in doubt. He took the name Congwen ("follower of literature") and left the West Hunan countryside, where he was a soldier in a warlord army, for Peking in the 1920s to pursue his ideal of studying. Unable even to punctuate, he was determined to learn the craft of a writer to help rehabilitate the emotions and reason of the Chinese people, who were suffering the depredations of the wealthy and powerful. Literature could also stimulate humanity's sense of concern and justice, as well as the love needed to repair the divisions among people.[124]

This earnest belief in literature's efficacy is something that Zhou disavowed early, but Shen never did. However, Shen steadfastly refused to have anything to do with politics. During the 1930s, he described politics and commercialism—which he saw as linked in a bizarre alliance in Shanghai—as the bane of literature.[125] In the essay just cited, Shen defended himself against charges that he did not understand "reality" and had fallen behind. The whole essay is an attempt to assert the independence of his view of reality. "Unfortunately the reality I understand is completely different from that of intellectuals who have been brought up in hothouses. It is also different from another type of person who, coming from a small town, supposes himself to belong to the worker-peasant elements," he began.[126] Whereas Zhou represented himself as "rebel and recluse" or "half-Confucian half-monk," Shen chose the persona of "the countryman"—*xiangxia ren*. Shen represents his journey through these various realities as an attempt to avoid moral corruption: as a soldier he had felt that the revenge of the dead was their silence, which said, "You killed my body; I will rot your soul." His practice of literature was part of his attempt to escape from this corruption, and he nurtured the aspiration to "progress in my own inner life of study, so as to prove the significance of life and the possibilities in life," ignoring friends who advised him to try something easier and more lucrative.[127] Unlike Zhou, who announced he was closing up his literature shop in the mid-1920s (although he did not keep this promise), for Shen, literature became the symbol of his faith and hope in life, and he refused to abandon it. Yet both were similar in that they saw politics (whether manifested as ideology or the factionalism of writers) as the biggest threat to literature and thus freedom. "Politicians should leave literature alone . . . and let it freely develop in the sun and the fresh air," Shen said in words that were an echo of Zhou's.[128]

Shen's "countryman" persona also suggested skepticism about the value of goal-oriented philosophies. His parable-like story "Knowledge" tells of a young man attracted to student life by the May Fourth movement. On leaving his landlord family in inland China, he felt he had succeeded in becoming a Nietzschean superman and proceeded to study the "philosophy of life." Ten years later, filled with knowledge, he decides to return home and instruct the peasants on how to live. Not far from his home he comes across an old man who is laboring away, while his dead son's body lies nearby under a tree. After a series of conversations, the returned student realizes that the country dwellers' understanding of life is far superior to his own, because they regard death as much as life to be an integral feature of the flow of existence.[129] If Shen did, in fact, share the Zhuangzian outlook of the story, we might expect him to find expression in an aesthetics that acknowledged or encouraged such values.

The strongest reasons for seeing Shen as operating within the aesthetic parameters opened by Zhou are to be found in the imagery and structure of his writings. To take one example, the story "Quiet" ("Jing") can be read in terms of *quwei*. The focus is not on the narration of a set of events, but on the depiction of a peaceful country setting through the eyes of a girl named Yuemin, one of a family of war refugees who have taken temporary shelter in a small town. The placid landscape with its human figures, such as the little nun washing clothes, seen from a rooftop, is the counterpoint to the conversations Yuemin has with her sick mother and other women folk indoors, in which they try to hide their anxieties from one another. The family is waiting for news of the girl's father, a military officer. The quietness of the story is the filter of Yuemin's perception, now disturbing, now consoling, depending on the state of her thoughts and mood. At the very end of the story, Yuemin hears voices next door, and her heart starts to pound as she imagines it is her father and brother come to find them. But then everything grows quiet again and she smiles faintly to herself. A shadow is cast in the shape of a flag, and we learn in the last sentence: "It was just the shape of the little paper flag planted in a place far away, a flag on the grave of the Papa for whom they were waiting."[130]

Shen's achievement is to practice the poetics of *quwei* through his fictional character Yuemin. It is her gaze that brings the scene to life and that transcribes it into subtle shifting flavors of joy and sorrow, tied to images such as the kites in the sky, the changing colors of the river, and the tired, old, gray ferry boat. Yet her subjective response does not devour the story, becoming its center, because the landscape itself and the figures within it also exist in their own right. Shen thus conveys to us the *quwei* of landscape and the *quwei* of Yuemin. When the reader glimpses the servant girl surreptitiously whitening her face with toothpowder, any initial feeling of superiority is deflated by Yuemin's own action, which is to leave the room so as not to embarrass her. Yet this is not the only level on which the text operates.

The narrative closure through which we suddenly become aware of the futility of all of Yuemin and her family's hopes and fears conveys its own particular *quwei*, evoking whatever emotional reactions the reader brings to it. Whatever these are, and however the reader conceives of the authorial persona, there is a level of restraint in the text that leaves the reader in charge of interpretation. The disjuncture between the closure of the text for the reader and the lack of effect it has at the level of the protagonists—we never know if or how the family learns of the father's death—serves to displace narrative as a center of meaning. Meaning resides not so much in language as in what language evokes—the meaning left when the words have gone. This is not the only way to look at this text, but by relating Shen to these aesthetics, we can, I would suggest, better understand the subversive potential of his desire to bring forth the "divine" in ordinary life.

Wang Zengqi, who started writing in the 1940s and was Shen's student in Kunming, also iterated a desire not to write story-like stories but essay-like ones and likened his style of writing to a Chinese ink-painting, which obtains its effects from different gradations of gray.[131] He also claimed "mildness" (*pingdan*) as a quality in his work, along with *qijue* (the unexpected). The essay-like quality of his writing is quite apparent in "Three Stories" ("Gushi sanpian"), a set of anecdotes published in his *Wanfanhua* collection, for which it is very hard to find any unifying theme.[132] Although Wang himself says that there is no unifying link among them and that he put them together because they were too slight to stand alone, they could be seen as exercises in interpretation.[133]

The first, "Praying for Rain," is set in Kunming. It is planting season, and the rains are late. A group of ragged children finally take it upon themselves to parade around the town to the temple. Very few of the children are even aware of gods such as the Dragon King, who sends rain, but they are aware of Heaven, which is fickle. Although this suggests the Daoist idea of Heaven as an impersonal force for which the joys and happiness of men mean nothing, the adults nonetheless tacitly approve, since they believe that children will have more success in moving Heaven to mercy. When it rains that night, ending the crisis, the little boy who led the procession wakes up convinced the rain is his doing. Despite its placid, undramatic style, "Praying for Rain" succeeds in conveying a sense of the underlying anxiety in the community. It does this with the startling image of a population whose eyes have all turned blue from staring into the sky. When the rain finally comes, the little boy notices that his mother's eyes are once more black and shining.

The first-person narrator of the second anecdote, "Lost," is a land reform cadre based in a village in Jiangxi, who despite his best efforts to act logically and rationally is totally unable to find his way back to the village at night. When he eventually returns, he discovers that his fellow land reform activists believed that he had been eaten by a man-eating tiger. Although the story of the man-eater was first heard among the villagers, the prosaic villagers seem to have a far better grip on reality, not to mention the terrain of their countryside, than the outsiders.

It is in the third story that the issue of interpretation comes to the fore. The first-person narrator is fond of taking walks near a famous fishing spot, and one day he starts talking to an old man selling earthworms as bait. Wang gives a vivid description of the old man, including the fact that when he shaves his head, the contrast between tanned and white skin makes him look like an unearthed bronze vessel scrubbed with hydrochloric acid. In the best traditions of the intellectual as amateur fieldworker, the narrator starts to question the earthworm seller about his life and habits and soon discovers the old man to be a mine of information on flora and fauna. Among the usual strollers at the poolside are two intellectuals who are fond of debating theory together. They stop the narrator to question him about the value of the old man's existence. One sees him as a useless relic of a dead way of life—"he even looks like a Han funerary object"—who can serve only as "filler" in the interstices of society in the atomic age. The other is more forgiving. He argues that although grindstones have not changed much since the Han dynasty, they can still grind soybeans into beancurd milk, which the other man enjoyed for breakfast. If these arguments are transposed into the sphere of culture, the two can be seen as debating the place of the traditional in a rapidly modernizing society. Tradition, suggests the second, can make the daily business of living more palatable but is by no means essential.

Asked to give his view, the narrator first sums up all the sociological information he has gleaned about the old man and then proceeds to explain that his interest in the man is aesthetic. He is a writer of fiction, he says, and "just like an old teacher of mine, what attracts me about this world are phenomena. I am not good at abstract thought. . . . I am a gourmet of life." As for the old man, "he is a decent, old-style laborer who lives by his own efforts, at least he is not a parasite," he concludes.[134] At this point a biologist intervenes. From the environmental point of view, the old man should not be allowed to dig up worms since they benefit agriculture. At this, the three are dumbfounded, and the anecdote ends. Despite their disagreements, all the arguing intellectuals have been enunciating their positions within a rationalist, instrumentalist discourse of utility. Even the narrator's aesthetic interest in the old man is not qualitatively different, and his defense of the man's existence tails off lamely, "At least he is not a parasite." However, the text does what the discussion fails to do. It makes the old man appear so vividly before us that it puts the claim for the value of his existence in altogether different terms, letting the images of his habits and knowledge speak for themselves against the grain of the discursive framework of the protagonists.

This anecdote, with its detailing of different points of view, could slip easily among those cited in Zhou Zuoren's essay on *bense*, the manifestation of a person's attainment or experience. Because the anecdote is presented by the first-person narrator who controls all the information presented, the reader is led to expect that the point of the story will be to show the narrator's superior understanding of the world. When it ends with the narrator dumbfounded and the question of value patently left unresolved, meaning has to emerge through an imagery focused on details. To return to the first two anecdotes, within this mode of interpretation, the "meanings" of "Praying for Rain" and "Lost" transcend whatever sociological or ideological conclusions a reader might find there. What remains are the images, drawn from material culture, which involve the reader in the specificity and irreducibility of existence.

Although it may be comparatively easy to suggest that Shen Congwen and Wang Zengqi are working within an aesthetic framework we recognize from Zhou, what about the heterogeneous group of young writers described in the 1980s as the Searching for Roots school? My claim here is not that a genealogical link exists between Zhou and all these writers.[135] However, I maintain, as I said in Chapter 1, that the use of imagery becomes the thin end of the wedge that prises open existing discourses and opens up the writer to a more stringent, thoughtful use of language and the reader to new ways of seeing. Two brief examples from the works of Ah Cheng (Zhong Acheng; 1949– ) and Han Shaogong (1953– ) can serve to illustrate this point.

Ah Cheng's novella "The Chess King" ("Qiwang") is particularly interesting in the context of my argument about Zhou, because it not only strives for purity of language but speaks to the issue of Chinese civilizational identity in a world of nation-states. Initially, critics hailed it above all for its coupling of restrained, understated prose with extremely precise images, which they proclaimed as something rare in literature since the May Fourth movement.[136] The view that the language of the story reversed the didacticism of the dominant May Fourth discourse (which culminated under Mao in the flowery, formulaic language of Cultural Revolution fiction) is undoubtedly correct.[137] But, paradoxically, the story itself soon became thoroughly implicated in the post-Mao reconfiguring of Chinese national identity.[138] The presence of Daoist, Buddhist, Confucian, and cosmological elements, which structure the text, convinced some critics that the work contained "China's entire traditional culture. According to them, reconstructing China's cultural identity by revitalizing its tradition [became] the precondition for its membership in the international community of arts and letters."[139] The question then becomes: To what extent does the text itself contribute to replacing a discredited, Mao-centered national imaginary with a cultural-essentialist one?[140]

Undeniably, the structure of Ah Cheng's narrative demonstrates that the story was a self-conscious and ambitious attempt to reverse what the author saw as the impoverishment of Chinese culture since the "rupture" imposed by May Fourth iconoclasm. Furthermore, for the Roots writers in general, a retrieval of traditional culture and aesthetics represented the only way in which China could join the mainstream of world culture. Yet, as Gang Yue's careful reading also suggests, Ah Cheng's effort to reimagine and redefine "a nation's local history" against the grand narrative of (universal) History need not immediately be written off as "bad nationalistic imagination."[141] Chess and eating are the central tropes in the story. The most important food episode is the snake banquet, in which the protagonists, who are urban youths rusticated to the countryside during the Cultural Revolution, share a meal improvised from the simple ingredients available to them. Although this can be seen as reversing the terms of Lu Xun's castigation of China as a "cannibal banquet," Yue suggests that the meaning of food put forward in the text is rooted in the materiality of food and the requirements of the body. Hunger (and food) thus become "nonpolitical" and need not just replicate the terms of a master narrative or its opposite.[142] Similarly, although chess is taken to stand for the Way or Chan Buddhism, their meanings are indeterminate, ambiguous, and unconstrained by concepts of time and space. Consequently although both Daoism and Buddhism were incorporated into the post-Mao ideology of nationalism, this cannot circumscribe them.[143]

Han Shaogong is regarded as a leading figure in the Searching for Roots school, in part because of his essay "The Roots of Literature," in which he suggested that by setting fictional works in rural settings away from the cities, writers could rejuvenate Chinese culture as a whole.[144]

Han's best-known work from the 1980s is "Da da da" (Ba ba ba), which takes as its allegorical protagonist a retarded boy.[145] His speech is limited to the syllables "ba ba ba," so that he appears to be calling every male he meets daddy, and an obscenity with which he addresses his mother. The story is apparently set in the time of the Cultural Revolution, and the village in which it is set shows no signs of having been touched by progress of any kind. It is impoverished and benighted, and after an incident of cannibalism, the story climaxes in a pitched battle with a neighboring village. Many of the villagers are slaughtered, but the retarded boy survives. It has been suggested that the retarded protagonist of "Ba ba ba" is a modern-day descendant of Lu Xun's Ah Q and so represents the national character.[146] Despite the overpowering allegorical intent, the language of the story has something of the precision and understatement of Ah Cheng's.

Although "Ba ba ba" is problematic if seen as an attempt to establish an alternative discourse to the May Fourth, the potential of the story's aesthetic stance should not be ignored. In an early article, Han showed a concern for clarity in language as a means of enhancing its expressivity; by drawing attention to the expressing self, clarity could eventually lead in the direction of an alternative construction of the self in relation to the nation.[147] Han's interest in archaic diction and dialect recalls the desire of the late Ming Jingling school writers to see the "souls" of the ancients in their abstruse diction. But at the same time, it also shares something of Zhou Zuoren's conviction that Chinese characters had their own unique rhetorical beauty and functioned best when used as *xing*.

In more general terms, the focus on locality could be seen as a major step toward the alternative discourse, for the locality is the locus of the "flavor" that this aesthetics seeks to apprehend. In the fiction produced by writers associated with the Roots school, the locality is artistically recreated in such a way as to speak against the homogenizing rhetoric of the People's Republic. Here again, Han Shaogong's early work fascinates with his wavering between the potential of his aesthetic stance and his involvement with the discourse of "the nation" as "the people." To me, Han's search for literary roots in an authentic Chu culture, which he identifies with the minority hill people of West Hunan, is suspect. His argument that the (Han) Chinese culture descended from the Yellow

River civilization is moribund and needs reviving with the seething, molten layer beneath its crust (the Chu in their present minority incarnation) recalls similar eugenicist and racist arguments made in the 1930s.[148] Both are ultimately anchored in the discourse of civilizational superiority/inferiority to which I referred in my discussion of Lu Xun, because they start from the fear of China as impotent if not dead.

However, Han has recently produced a far more interesting work, which combines fiction and reminiscence in indeterminate proportions and is structured like a lexicon.[149] *Maqiao Dictionary* is set in the area of Hunan province where Han spent six years as an educated youth during the Cultural Revolution. Instead of chapters, it is organized under headwords, which, just as they would be in a real dictionary, are listed by stroke order in the front of the book (although headwords do not appear in the book in the same order). Each entry discusses how the word is used in Maqiao or identifies local referents in myth, legend, or anecdote. With its ruminations on etymology and local custom, the book strongly resembles *biji* writing, or perhaps Yanagita Kunio's *Tōno monogatari*. No one narrative thread runs through the book, although sometimes a narrative will run through several headwords and protagonists will reappear. Han has evidently worked to distill his language into a supple, understated, yet humorous prose style. What is arresting about the book in the context of Zhou Zuoren is the extent to which so many of the categories into which Zhou organized his interests, together with his distrust of overarching narratives, are replicated here.

To do justice to the "Roots" writers and the issues involved, one would have to do a detailed study of the cultural criticism debates that raged in China during the 1980s, a task beyond the scope of this study.[150] But in summing up my argument about Zhou, I would like to refer to the figure of Li Zehou, the "mastermind" of contemporary Chinese cultural criticism.[151] Although it might be rash, not to say presumptuous, to do so, I believe there are instructive contrasts between their modes of reflecting on Chinese culture that illuminate what I have been trying to say here. Li's work can be broken down into three parts: an attempt to construct a new theory of the aesthetic based on a Kantian notion of human subjectivity and a Marxian notion of the humanization of nature; a rereading of modern Chinese history in the terms of enlightenment and national salvation; and the proposition of *xiti zhongyong*, that is, that Western learning should be taken as the essence and Chinese thinking applied in its application.[152] Only the last two parts will concern us.

In Li's account, the positive Enlightenment values of science and democracy with their potential for destroying a 2,000-year-old feudal culture have been negated by the struggle for national salvation, in other words, the Communist Party's leadership of national revolution. This occurred, Li holds, because the salvation struggle relied on the traditional voluntarist mentality of small peasants. In my reading, the Enlightenment project itself and the national salvation project were inextricably linked and had at their base the creation of a modern nation-state. Whereas Li blames Chinese tradition for turning Marxism into a monster, I see Marxism, an expression of the drive of second-order modernity to rationalize our relationship with the world, as endowed with its own potential for monsterhood.

The difficulty with Li's project, as Mu Ling reads it, lies mainly in the *xiti zhongyong* part, which is full of inconsistencies. Essentially *xiti zhongyong* is a modification of Chinese culture with what is useful in Western culture. Chinese culture has the moral function of monitoring, directing, and restricting Western learning.[153] Ling argues that this would be merely to repeat the tragedy of the swallowing of Enlightenment values by the drive for national salvation, which Li clearly saw in the case of Marxism.[154] Ling concludes that Li Zehou is at heart a conservative, and this is shown in his disagreement with the proposal of complete Westernization. For Li, tradition "has been sedimented into a cultural psychological structure" and is subsumed in "behavior, ways of thinking, and emotional attitude." A mixture of good and bad elements, it cannot be cast away like a coat. Instead, it is to be submitted to "creative transformation," a process of "understanding tradition" in which the good and bad elements are sorted out.[155]

Superficially, Li's view of tradition as sedimented into psychological structures appears similar to Zhou's. However, their premises are very different. Li's theory of sedimentation, developed in his commentary on Kant, is closely linked to his theory of subjectivity. Working from a Marxian perspective that makes changes in production the determining factor in social change, Li considered the subject of history to be not the individual but humankind or society, which is able to produce the means (tools, language) to transform nature.[156] However, Li rejected the doctrinaire Marxist notion that sees the mind as a "mirror" of its surroundings, so that knowledge is just the reflection of objective reality. In order to explain how the gradual increase in our ability to mold our environment results in a gradual transformation of human physiology and psychology, Li proposed, with Kant, that knowledge is a product of the synthesizing activity of our own minds. But whereas Kant held that the categories into which humans sort out knowledge exist *a priori* in everyone, Li deemed this to be an ahistorical view that neglected the role of the social activity of tool making.[157] The structures of the mind—the sedimented psychological structures—are shaped by the dominant mode of production in a society. In China's case, this was small-scale agriculture in a kinship context—which had produced its own characteristic cultural-psychological formation.

What was this formation? Since Chinese agriculture was predicated on living in harmony with nature rather than mastering it with tools, Li argues, the Chinese view of the world was moral and aesthetic rather than logical and mathematical. Instead of making objective reality the focus of their attentions, Chinese philosophers saw no real contradiction between nature and man and concentrated on ascribing vast transformative powers to the moral will of the superior man.[158] This subjectivist tendency, most developed by Wang Yangming, was responsible for Maoist voluntarism and the tragedies it brought. What China needs is a transformation of its psychological structures through a protracted historical process of producing and applying technology.[159] It is here that the difficulties with Li's *xiti zhongyong* emerge, because as Mu Ling shows, Li is unable to produce consistent definitions of what the Western essence is: is it just technology (understood as the mode of production) or is it Western ideologies and learning? And if it is the latter, how can they transform the sedimented psychological structures if these structures can be transformed only by changes in technology and the mode of production?[160]

This fundamental impasse in Li's philosophical system—how to reconcile Chinese and Western, modernity and tradition—was avoided by

Zhou Zuoren by taking as the starting point the construction of the individual and seeing respect for the individual as central to broader questions about the organization of human society. The individual is not
primarily marked by an essentialized national/cultural identity but
shares the same fundamental biological and social needs with the rest of
humanity. Although Zhou's individual, especially as it emerges from his
aesthetics, is conceived as a subjective moral being, this is a restrained and
prudent subjectivity, constantly watchful against making unwarranted assumptions and mindful of the inadequacies of its knowledge.

No doubt Zhou would recognize in the inflated voluntaristic Maoist
subjectivity that Li labels a direct descendant of Wang Yangming
activism the pernicious traits he saw fostered by Cheng-Zhu Neo-
Confucianism. Similarly, Zhou once commented that science had not
developed in China because the Chinese were bad at observing natural
phenomena and Confucianized or Daoisized what they saw.[161] By this he
was referring to an anthropomorphizing tendency to explain natural
phenomena in terms of human relationships or an (inaccurate) theory of
transformations of qi. Zhou might well share Li's perturbation on this
count, but he would not have extended this into a fundamental incom-
patibility between Chinese and Western thinking, since, for him, thinking depended on the individual and scientific knowledge and, once produced, was not culturally specific. Another crucial difference between
them is that whereas Li sorts elements of the Chinese tradition into good
and bad, Zhou holds that some parts of the tradition transcend good
and bad. What this does is remove the anxiety from the construction
of "Chinese tradition," an anxiety that is the direct result of acceptance
of the belief that before the modern West, all other civilizations are
inferior.

～

I have argued in this study that a belief in the inferiority of Chinese civilization was a central premise of the May Fourth movement and underlay
the entire discourse of the nation. As I have tried to show, drawing on
Chatterjee, Taylor, and others in Chapter 1, the ideological construction
of nation-states depends on making an ethic out of certain types of rationality associated with the rise of science in the West. But paradoxi-

cally, the celebration of disengaged reason as an ethic itself leads to silence about ethics outside private life, a sense of rupture with the past, and a suppression of alternative modes of organizing human society apart from the nation-state. Historically, the development of the world system of nation-states in the crucial period of late eighteenth and nineteenth centuries was accompanied by the development of essentialized views of cultures and civilizations, often justified by their place within a linear narrative of world history. The process of nation-building thus became the effort to eliminate anything that stood in the way of development along this trajectory and to foster whatever promoted it. The process also repeated the initial essentializing gestures. Li Zehou's anxiety over good and bad is a manifestation of the same essentializing thinking. Zhou's formula that some aspects of tradition transcend good and bad shifts the exercise of judgment about what is acceptable from pre-assigned categories of good/bad to concrete instances, thus valorizing the individual.

In terms of the view that premodern Chinese culture was feudal and thus inimical to the individual, this seems most paradoxical. However, I have argued that Zhou drew on a less-heeded strand of the civilization than the orthodox Cheng-Zhu Neo-Confucianism in order to make his own pungent criticisms of it. My argument reiterates Nandy's premise that all civilizations are capable of self-criticism and self-regeneration. This insight was denied by Chinese cultural criticism of the 1980s, which could not escape from the premise of Western superiority and Chinese inferiority and essentialized a civilization into a mode of production.[162] In the 1990s, the premise of inferiority in cultural criticism has been displaced by a neo-authoritarian nationalistic discourse, which has mobilized conservative Confucian values, and an equally nationalistic cultural nativism, which seeks to establish the notion of a Chinese rim.[163] The reasons for this change are extremely complex, and there are scholars who argue against the crude nationalism these trends represent.

Zhou's contribution to the discussion of Chinese identity makes him a seminal figure. His aesthetic stance served also as a resource for writers such as Shen Congwen and Wang Zengqi. Their work and the work of the Roots writers, however immature, had the effect of opening up a space in which new ways of seeing and being can develop, in which a nonjudgmental (aporetic) "lyric vision takes on a moral dimension, since it refuses to impose a new dogma on a Chinese society already overloaded with dogmas."[164] It was Zhou Zuoren, however, who showed that the same moral stance had been available to critics of the traditional Cheng-Zhu orthodoxy and thus demonstrated the capacity of his civilization to critique itself.

*Reference Matter*

# Notes

For complete author names, titles, and publication data on items cited here in short forms, see the Works Cited, pp. 313–33.

The following abbreviations and short forms of titles are used in the Notes:

| | |
|---|---|
| JWW | Zhou Zuoren, *Zhou Zuoren jiwai wen* |
| LXQJ | Lu Xun, *Lu Xun quanji* |
| *Nianpu* | Zhang Juxiang, *Zhou Zuoren nianpu* |
| SCWWJ | Shen Congwen, *Shen Congwen wenji* |
| *Ziliao* | Zhang Juxiang and Zhang Tierong, eds., *Zhou Zuoren yanjiu ziliao* |
| ZTHXL | Zhou Zuoren, *Zhitang huixiang lu* |
| ZTSH | Zhou Zuoren, *Zhitang shuhua* |
| ZZRQJ | Zhou Zuoren, *Zhou Zuoren quanji* |

## Chapter 1

1. The periodization of the movement is somewhat difficult. The movement takes its name from the date of student demonstrations in Peking on May 4, 1919, protesting the government's acceptance of humiliating Japanese demands. The demonstrations erupted against the background of intense ferment among students and professors at Peking University, who were calling for an intellectual revolution in order to modernize China socially, politically, and culturally. The demonstrations

marked its transformation into a nationwide patriotic social movement. The movement is often regarded as the birthplace of modern Chinese literature written in the vernacular, but it is more correct to say that it marked the emergence of a whole series of radical literary practices and experiments for which the ground had been prepared at least since the end of the nineteenth century. I choose to date the New Culture movement from 1917, when Chen Duxiu's radical publication *New Youth* (*Xin Qingnian*) was launched in Peking, until 1923 when in the words of Hu Shi, "the controversial period" was "almost over and the era of constructive and creative work" could begin. See McDougall, *Introduction of Western Literary Theories into Modern China*, p. 6. However, May Fourth literature can be applied loosely to "new literature" (*xin wenxue*) published between 1917 and 1937 (the outbreak of the Sino-Japanese War) or even up to 1942, when Mao Zedong's Talks at the Yan'an Forum on Literature and Art represented the culmination of ideas that had long been debated by writers. See Chow Tse-tsung, *The May Fourth Movement*; Schwarcz, *The Chinese Enlightenment*; Goldman, *Modern Chinese Literature in the May Fourth Era*; and Lydia Liu, *Translingual Practice*.

2. See Hockx, "The Literary Association."

3. Mao, "On New Democracy," 2: 372. See the discussion in Lee, *Voices from the Iron House*, pp. 133, 191.

4. Among the first to do so were Qian Liqun and Shu Wu.

5. The most detailed source of information on Zhou is the chronological biography (*nianpu*) compiled by Zhang Juxiang. See also Qian, *Fanren de bei'ai*; Woolf, *Chou Tso-jen*; and Huang Qiaosheng, *Dujin jiebo*, which is a biographical study of the three Zhou brothers.

6. For an account of the breakup and for various hypotheses, most of them weighted against Zhou's wife, see Qian, *Fanren de bei'ai*, pp. 42–51. Since Qian's account, other scholars have speculated that the quarrel was over Hata Nobuko, with whom Lu Xun had tried to initiate or resume a love affair. See Li Jie, "Zuowei Tang Jihede de Lu Xun, zuowei Hamulete de Zhou Zuoren."

7. See Yan Jiayan, *Zhongguo xiandai xiaoshuo liupai shi*, pp. 205–48. Qian (*Fanren de bei'ai*, p. 100) describes Feng and Yu as representative of Zhou's "inner circle" of associates and the Jing pai writers as his "outer circle."

8. Zhou's post-1949 essays have also been published as *Zhitang jiwai wen: sijiu nian yihou*, ed. Chen Zishan.

9. Dong Bingyue, "Zhou Zuoren de 'funi' yu wenhuaguan."

10. Shu Wu, "Zhou Zuoren gaiguan," pt. I, p. 89.

11. Schwarcz, *The Chinese Enlightenment*, p. 161.

12. This argument is made by Qian, *Fanren de bei'ai*, pp. 53–54.

13. Qian Liqun, *Zhou Zuoren lun*, p. 4.

14. See, e.g., ibid., pp. 119–46; Qian, *Fanren de bei'ai*, p. 2; and Shu Wu, "Nüxing de faxian."

15. Foucault, *The Archeology of Knowledge and the Discourse on Language*.

16. I reject the view that individuals are constituted by discourses (that they can think only what the discourse allows them to) because this does not explain why one discourse succeeds another. Nor does it take account of the variability in the positions of individuals vis-à-vis the institutions involved, i.e., in the possibility of dissent or distance from the discourse. See Hayden White, "Foucault Decoded." A more important reason for rejecting the reductionistic notion of discourse and discursive power is that it is based on a notion of language as fundamentally obstructive of our understanding of reality. The evidence against such a notion comes from studies of linguistics associated with Noam Chomsky. For an accessible discussion and development of Chomsky's thinking, see Pinker, *The Language Instinct*. Pinker (esp. pp. 55–82, 404–30) makes it quite clear that the shared human ability to conceptualize exists independently of the particular languages used to express thought.

17. See Patrick Tort, *La Pensée hiérarchique et l'évolution*, pp. 7–57, 524–46.

18. William Thomas, "Introduction," in Mill, *The History of British India*, pp. xviii–xxii. For an account of how Utilitarian philosophy and practice were brought to bear on India, see Stokes, *The English Utilitarians and India*.

19. Avineri, *Hegel's Theory of the Modern State*, p. 224.

20. Inden, *Imagining India*, p. 71.

21. Duara, *Rescuing History from the Nation*, p. 4.

22. W.-K. Cheng, "Vox populi," pp. 90–100. Cheng argues that Yan replaced China's sinocentric worldview, which was based on its declared cultural-moral superiority, with a conception of the world as defined by material achievements. This enabled Yan to speak of the pursuit of wealth and power as an end in itself. The classic study of Yan Fu remains Benjamin Schwartz's *In Search of Wealth and Power: Yen Fu and the West*.

23. The term "ethic" is taken from Partha Chatterjee, *Nationalist Thought and the Colonial World*, 14–16; see below for more discussion.

24. W.-K. Cheng, "Vox populi," p. 65.

25. Tang, *Global Space and the Nationalist Discourse of Modernity*, pp. 61–62.

26. Philip Huang, "Liang Ch'i-ch'ao," p. 87.

27. My quotation is from Duara, *Culture, Power and the State*, p. 2, but Duara sources the distinction to the historian Charles Tilly.

28. Hsia, "Yen Fu and Liang Ch'i-ch'ao as Advocates of New Fiction." Two important essays by Liang are included in Denton, *Modern Chinese Literary Thought*.

29. My thinking here is indebted to W.-K. Cheng's excellent thesis.

30. W.-K. Cheng, "Vox Populi," pp. 69–74.

31. Ibid., p. 87.

32. Ibid., p. 102.

33. Lee, "In Search of Modernity," pp. 110–15, 120–21.

34. See Schwarcz, *The Chinese Enlightenment*, pp. 6–8.

35. Marston Anderson, *The Limits of Realism*, 25.

36. Hung, *Going to the People*; Schneider, *Ku Chieh-kang and China's New History*.

37. The most useful introduction is still Link, *Mandarin Ducks and Butterflies*. See Rey Chow, *Woman and Chinese Modernity*, for a revisionist view. See also Lydia Liu, *Translingual Practice*.

38. David Wang, *Fin-de-siècle Splendor*.

39. Duara, *Rescuing History from the Nation*, p. 235.

40. See Christopher Lupke, "Nationalist Literary Policy, Cold War Ideology and the Development of the Culture Industry in Post-war Taiwan," unpublished paper cited in Michelle Yeh, "Introduction," *Anthology of Modern Chinese Poetry*, p. xxxviii.

41. Joseph W. Esherick makes this point in his stimulating "Ten Theses on the Chinese Revolution."

42. The notion of deployment of modernity, which is now widely invoked, was first put forward by Lydia Liu in the first issue of *positions*.

43. I am referring to Samuel P. Huntington's article "The Clash of Civilizations" published in 1993.

44. Bayly, *Imperial Meridian*.

45. Chaudhuri, *Asia Before Europe*.

46. Shiba, "The Formation of the East Asian Maritime Economy."

47. Goody, *The East in the West*.

48. Plaks, *The Four Masterworks of the Ming Novel*, pp. 3–54 and *passim*.

49. Brook, *The Confusions of Pleasure*.

50. The classic text here is Rudolph and Rudolph, *Modernity of Tradition*.

51. Berman, *All That Is Solid Melts into Air*, p. 232.

52. This is particularly so for those interested in the way the Russian literary heritage was appropriated by Chinese writers. Mau-sang Ng's *The Russian Hero in Modern Chinese Fiction* remains the key text here.

53. Bauman, *Modernity and the Holocaust*.

54. Bauman recapitulates his underlying argument in "Social Manipulation of Morality: Moralizing Actors, Adiaphorizing Action," published as an appendix to the 1991 edition of his book (pp. 208–221).

55. Bauman, *Modernity and the Holocaust*, 44.

56. Gellner, *Nations and Nationalism*.

57. Benedict Anderson, *Imagined Communities*.

58. Smith, "Opening Statement: Nations and Their Pasts," p. 360.

59. Gellner, *Nations and Nationalism*, p. 124.

60. Greenfeld, *Nationalism*. The rest of this paragraph draws on Greenfeld's Introduction, esp. pp. 1–21.

61. Gellner, *Nations and Nationalism*, pp. 96–97.

62. In any case, Lenin, writing in 1917, was trying to explain events since the beginning of the twentieth century, not the origin of the world system of nation-states. See Carrère d'Encausse and Schram, eds., *Marxism and Asia*, p. 24.

63. Lenin, "Imperialism, the Highest Stage of Capitalism"; Carrère d'Encausse and Schram, *Marxism and Asia*, pp. 15–25.

64. Giddens, *The Consequences of Modernity*, p. 57.

65. Here I am drawing on the definition of capitalism in ibid., pp. 55–58.

66. Pagden, *Lords of All the World*, p. 181.

67. Ibid., p. 186.

68. Ibid., p. 189.

69. Bayly, *Imperial Meridian*, p. 107.

70. Hevia, *Cherishing Men from Afar*.

71. Bayly, *Imperial Meridian*, pp. 147–55.

72. Greenfeld, *Nationalism*, p. 14.

73. In this sense, Greenfeld's narrative rather resembles Berman's account of the inexorable sweep of modernity. It is intriguing that the Russian example seems to provide the narrative climax to both these works.

74. Partha Chatterjee, *Nationalist Thought and the Colonial World*.

75. Partha Chatterjee develops this approach in *The Nation and Its Fragments*.

76. Partha Chatterjee, *Nationalist Thought and the Colonial World*, pp. 40–41.

77. Ibid., p. 10.

78. Taylor, *Sources of the Self*, pp. 53–90, 143–76, 338–47.

79. Here I am referring to the ideas in Ashis Nandy's *Intimate Enemy*.

80. Partha Chatterjee, *Nationalist Thought and the Colonial World*, p. 16.

81. Ibid., p. 17.

82. Ricoeur, "Civilizations and National Cultures," p. 278.

83. Ibid., p. 283.

84. Tort, *La Pensée hiérarchique et l'évolution*.

85. This argument is developed in great detail in ibid. Here, I am relying on the succinct account given in Tort's "Introduction à l'anthropologie darwinienne" pp. 125–27.

86. A fascinating and complicating factor, which it is impossible to discuss here, is the importance of science in the development of English national identity in the seventeenth century. See Greenfeld's discussion of England as "a land of experimental knowledge," in *Nationalism*, pp. 78–86.

87. Tort (*La Pensée hiérarchique et l'évolution*, pp. 36–38) does not suggest that the sciences function totally apart from dominant ideologies. Rather, he argues that sci-

entists can draw initially from a single "text" in which science and ideology are united. Thus Darwin's move to the idea of transformative evolution was paralleled by German linguists who had been moving to a transformational view of languages (i.e., toward inflection).

88. Ernst Renan, "What Is a Nation?" ("Qu'est-ce qu'une nation?"), lecture delivered at the Sorbonne, March 11, 1882, trans. Martin Thom in Bhabha, *Nation and Narration*, p. 11. Renan gives examples of what have come to be forgotten battles between different groups whose descendants are now all seen as French. But in the non-West, what is "forgotten" is the prior civilizational moral order.

89. Bauman, *Modernity and the Holocaust*, p. 95.

90. Ibid., pp. 95–96.

91. Greenfeld, *Nationalism*, pp. 371–87.

92. Ibid., p. 352.

93. Ibid., 389–94.

94. Bauman, *Modernity and the Holocaust*, 92.

95. Ibid.

96. Ibid., p. 93.

97. Nandy, *Traditions, Tyranny and Utopias*, pp. 20–55; idem, *The Intimate Enemy*, pp. 1–28.

98. Rabindranath Tagore, *Nationalism*, p. 12.

99. Ibid., p. 17.

100. Ibid., p. 21.

101. Hay, *Asian Ideas of East and West*, pp. 186–243.

102. Rabindranath Tagore, *Nationalism*, p. 19.

103. Ibid., p. 26.

104. Margaret Chatterjee (*Gandhi's Religious Thought*) argues convincingly that Gandhi's understanding of religious truth was neither derivative nor a construction intended to serve particular ends.

105. Duara, *Rescuing History from the Nation*, p. 221.

106. Devji, "Hindu/Muslim/Indian."

107. Duara, *Rescuing History from the Nation*, p. 48.

108. Nandy, *The Intimate Enemy*, pp. 1–29.

109. Ibid.

110. Hsia, "Obsession with China," pp. 533–54.

111. Huters, "Lives in Profile," p. 270.

112. The often-cited texts referred to here are the "Preface to *A Call to Arms*," "A Madman's Diary," and "The True Story of Ah Q." They can be found in English translation in Lu Xun, *Selected Works*, vol. 1.

113. Marston Anderson, *The Limits of Realism*, p. 76.

114. Li Jie, "Zuowei Tang Jihede de Lu Xun he zuowei Hamulete de Zhou Zuoren," pt. II, p. 12.

115. Xu Shoushang, *Wo suo renshi di Lu Xun*, pp. 8, 18; and idem, *Wangyou Lu Xun yinxiang ji*, p. 20; quoted in Yu-sheng Lin, *Crisis of Chinese Consciousness*, p. 108.

116. Lee, *Voices from the Iron House*, p. 14; Cheung, *Nicai yu Lu Xun sixiang fazhan*, p. 50.

117. Lu Xun, "Preface to *A Call to Arms*," in Lu Xun, *Selected Works*, 1: 37.

118. Lu Xun, "Mr. Fujino," in Lu Xun, *Dawn Blossoms Plucked at Dusk*, p. 85.

119. Ozaki, "Rōjin to Nihon," p. 29, cited in Larson, *Literary Authority and the Modern Chinese Writer*, p. 99.

120. Larson, *Literary Authority and the Modern Chinese Writer*, p. 99.

121. Lu Xun, "Wenhua pianzhi lun," in Fen, *LXQJ*, 1: 44–57. See the discussion of this and Lu Xun's Mara poets article in Lee, *Voices from the Iron House*, pp. 20–22.

122. Lu Xun, "Moluo shili shuo," in Fen, *LXQJ*, 1: 63–114; Nietzsche, *Thus Spake Zarathustra*, pp. 41–43.

123. Lu Xun, "Preface to *A Call to Arms*," p. 36.

124. Lee, *Voices from the Iron House*, p. 25.

125. Hu Shi, "Yibushengzhuyi" (Ibsenism), *Xin qingnian* 4. no. 6 (June 15, 1918); cited in Marston Anderson, *The Limits of Realism*, p. 32.

126. Lu Xun, "Suigan lu sanshiba" (Random thoughts, number 38), in *Re Feng*, *LXQJ*, 1: 311–14.

127. Yu-sheng Lin, *The Crisis of Chinese Consciousness*, p. 116n27. Lin's source is a letter from Zhou Zuoren. Lin notes that the Zhou brothers were living together when the article was written. It was published in *Xin qingnian* 5, no 5 (Nov. 15, 1918).

128. The Chinese title of Le Bon's work is given as *Minzu jinhua lun*, i.e., *Des lois psychologiques de l'évolution des peuples*, (1894).

129. Lu Xun, "Preface to *A Call to Arms*," in Lu Xun, *Selected Works*, p. 38.

130. See Marston Anderson, *The Limits of Realism*, pp. 180–202.

131. W.-K. Cheng, "*Vox populi*," pp. 234–36.

132. Lu Xun, "Yijian xiao shi" in *Nahan, LXQJ*, 1: 456.

133. Lee, *Voices from the Iron House*, 167.

134. Pollard, "Translation and Lu Xun," p. 10.

135. Lee, *Voices from the Iron House*, p. 189.

136. Ibid., p. 124.

137. Eagleton, *The Ideology of the Aesthetic*, pp. 252–55.

138. Foot, "Nietzsche's Immoralism," pp. 19–22.

139. See Pusey, *China and Charles Darwin*, pp. 444–56.

140. W.-K. Cheng, "*Vox Populi*," p. 98; Lee, *Voices from the Iron House*, pp. 195–96.

141. On Mao's praise of Lu Xun, see Lee, *Voices from the Iron House*, pp. 133, 191.

142. See, e.g., Schwarcz, *The Chinese Enlightenment*.

143. A major philosophical school based on the teachings of the brothers Cheng Hao (1032–85) and Cheng Yi (1033–1107) and Zhu Xi (1130–1200).

144. Wilson, "Genealogy and History in Neo-Confucian Sectarian Uses of the Confucian Past," p. 8.

145. Ibid.

146. Yu-sheng Lin, *The Crisis of Chinese Consciousness*, p. 55.

147. Ibid., p. 53. The work of these thinkers is usually seen exemplifying the most radical form of the development of Neo-Confucianism during the Ming dynasty, but it is not usually referred to as "counter-traditional." However, I believe it is justified to speak of a late Ming counter-tradition, because this is what it effectively became in its influence on literature. See as an introduction to the period the two conference volumes on seventeenth-century Chinese thought edited by de Bary, *Self and Society in Ming Thought* and *The Unfolding of Neo-Confucianism*.

148. Kai-wing Chow, *The Rise of Confucian Ritualism in Late Imperial China*.

149. Elman, *From Philosophy to Philology*, pp. 242–43.

150. Hiromu Momose, "Fang Tung-shu."

151. Chow Tse-tsung, *The May Fourth Movement*, pp. 48–53; Schwarcz, *The Chinese Enlightenment*, pp. 46–54.

152. Zhou, "Maozi hao de mingren" (The famous occupants of the Maozi Building), *ZTHXL*, 2: 351–60; Chow Tse-tsung, *The May Fourth Movement*, pp. 52–53.

153. Schwarcz, *The Chinese Enlightenment*, pp. 66–67; Zhou, "Maozi hao de ming ren," *ZTHXL*, pp. 354–57.

154. Hockx, *A Snowy Morning*, p. 47.

155. Qian, *Fanren de bei'ai*, pp. 8–9. The English translation members of the *Xin chao she* chose for the name of their group was the Renaissance Society. Luo Jialun, writing in the first issue of their journal, explained that the Renaissance was the tide that followed the Dark Ages in Europe and that the new world tide of the twentieth century would be the Russian October Revolution. See Chow Tse-tsung, *The May Fourth Movement*, pp. 55–61. Schwarcz, *The Chinese Enlightenment*, focuses on the New Tide Society.

156. Chow Tse-tsung, *The May Fourth Movement*, pp. 55–57.

157. Hung, *Going to the People*, pp. 41–46.

158. Chow Tse-tsung, *The May Fourth Movement*, p. 34.

159. Chen Duxiu, "Xiandai Ouzhou wenyi shi tan," *Xin qingnian* 1, no. 3; cited in ibid., 272.

160. Hu Shi, "Letter to the Editor," *Xin qingnian* 2 (Oct. 1, 1916); cited in Chow Tse-tsung, *The May Fourth Movement*, pp. 273–74. This and the other key documents are conveniently available in the volume subtitled *Constructive Theory* (*Jianshe lilun ji*) of the *Compendium of China's New Literature* (*Zhongguo xin wenxue daxi*),

edited by Zhao Jiabi (1908–). Lydia Liu, *Translingual Practice*, pp. 214–38, discusses the importance of the *Compendium* in legitimating the May Fourth intellectuals' claim to speak for Chinese literature.

161. Hu Shi, "Wenxue gailiang chuyi," *Xin qingnian* 11, no. 5, cited in Chow Tse-tsung, *The May Fourth Movement*, p. 274; in *Jianshe lilunji*, pp. 34–43; translated in Denton, *Modern Chinese Literary Thought*, pp. 123–39.

162. Chen Duxiu, "Wenxue geming lun" (On the literary revolution), *Xin qingnian*, 6 (Feb. 1917); cited in Chow Tse-tsung, *The May Fourth Movement*, p. 275; *Jianshe lilun ji*, pp. 44–47; translated in Denton, *Modern Chinese Literary Thought*, pp. 140–45.

163. Chow Tse-tsung, *The May Fourth Movement*, p. 276.

164. Zhou Zuoren, "Cai Jiemin: er" (Cai Jiemin [Yuanpei], pt. II), *ZTHXL*, 1: 333.

165. From this moment, according to one analysis, "all pretense of real strength in the central government was gone. . . . Democracy had vanished, and the era of 'warlordism' begun" (Spence, *The Search for Modern China*, p. 288).

166. Zhou Zuoren, "Fubi qianhou, yi" (Before and after the restoration, pt. I), *ZTHXL*, 1: 319.

167. Zhou Zuoren, "Cai Juemin, er," *ZTHXL*, 1: 333–335. The translation appeared in *Xin qingnian* 3, no, 2 (Feb. 15, 1918): 134–36.

168. Zhou, "Cai Juemin, er," *ZTHXL*, 1: 333–35.

169. Chen Duxiu, reply to Hu Shi, "Letters to the Editor," *Xin qingnian* 3, no. 3; cited in Chow Tse-tsung, *The May Fourth Movement*, p. 276; *Jianshe lilun ji*, p. 56. Zhou apparently did not use *Xin qingnian* as a source, but took the Chen quote from a piece by Li Jinxi (1890–1978) in the first issue of *National Language Weekly* (*Guoyu zhoukan*). See Zhou Zuoren, "Cai Jiemin, er," *ZTHXL*, 1: 333.

170. Zhou Zuoren, "Cai Juemin, er," *ZTHXL*, 1: 334.

171. See the illuminating exegesis of Hu Shi's "eight points" in W.-K. Cheng, "*Vox Populi*," pp. 180–86.

172. Chen Duxiu, "Jinggao qingnian" (Call to youth), *Xin qingnian* 1 (Sept. 15, 1915); cited in Yu-sheng Lin, *The Crisis of Chinese Consciousness*, p. 66.

173. Chow Tse-tsung, *The May Fourth Movement*, p. 46. Apart from being yet another example of the medical metaphor, Chen's appeal to youth represents what Nandy (*The Intimate Enemy*, p. 16) calls modernity's delegitimization of age.

174. Even so urbane a figure as the Cambridge-educated Xu Zhimo (1896–1931) asserted in 1922, "We have no art precisely because we have no life" (Lee, *The Romantic Generation of Modern Chinese Writers*, p. 156).

175. Zhou, "Cai Juemin, er," *ZTHXL*, 1: 334–35.

176. Yu-sheng Lin, *The Crisis of Chinese Consciousness*, p. 99.

177. Hu Shi, "An Autobiographical Account at Forty," pp. 80–90.

178. Zhou, "Sixiang geming" (The revolution in thought), in *Tan hu ji*, *ZZRQJ*, 1: 188–90. The article first appeared in *Meizhou pinglun*, no. 11, on March 2, 1919 and then in *Xin qingnian* 6, no. 4 on April 15. See *Nianpu*, p. 90.

179. Hu Shi, untitled in "Tongxin" (Letters to the editor), 4, *Xin qingnian* 3, no. 3; "Ji Chen Duxiu," *Jianshe lilun ji*, p. 53.

180. Hu Shi, "Jianshe de wenxue geming lun" (On a constructive literary revolution), in Zhang Ruoying, *Zhongguo xin wenxue yundong ziliao*, p. 80; Chow Tse-tsung, *The May Fourth Movement*, pp. 277–78. This article was written in the vernacular.

181. He Degong, *Zhongri qimeng wenxue lun*, pp. 127–29.

182. Zhou, "Riben de xin cun" (Japan's New Village), *Yishu yu shenghuo*, *ZZRQJ*, 3: 721–30. This article, carried in *Xin qingnian* 6, no. 3 (Mar. 15, 1919), consists mainly of passages translated from Mushakōji's book *Atarashiki mura no seikatsu* (Life in the New Village).

183. The articles are included in Zhou's *Yishu yu shenghuo* collection. For a discussion of the influence of Shirakaba theories on Zhou's May Fourth writing, see Ching-mao Cheng, "Zhou Zuoren de Riben jingyan," pp. 878–84.

184. Qian, *Fanren de bei'ai*, pp. 2–3; Hu Shi, preface to *Jianshe lilun ji*, p. 29.

185. Zhou Zuoren, "Xiaohe yu xincun (xia)," ("The Stream" and the New Village (movement), pt. III), *ZTHXL*, 2: 390–93.

186. Qian, *Fanren de bei'ai*, p. 22. Qian (ibid., p. 20) provides a list of Zhou's publications about the movement.

187. Lu Xun, letters to Qian Xuantong, dated Aug. 7 and 13, 1919, *LXQJ*, 11: 366. The second of these is quoted in Qian, *Fanren de bei'ai*, p. 22.

188. Qian, *Fanren de bei'ai*, p. 22. The story in question is Lu Xun's "A Story of Hair."

189. Qian, *Fanren de bei'ai*, p. 22. Hu Shi, "Fei gerenzhuyi de xin shenghuo" (The non-individualist new life), in Hu Shi, *Wencun, juan* 4, pp. 1043–59. It was originally published in *Shishi xinbao* (Current events news), Jan. 15, 1920. The quote is from *Mencius* (Legge tr.), book 7, pt. 1, 9.5.

190. Hu Shi, "Bu xiu" (Immortality), in Hu Shi, *Wencun, juan* 4, pp. 975–988. I have found Lydia Liu's (*Translingual Practice*, pp. 94–95) discussion of this helpful here.

191. Ching-mao Cheng, "Zhou Zuoren de Riben jingyan," p. 883.

192. Zhou Zuoren, "Xin wenxue de yaoqiu" (The demands of the new literature), in *Yishu yu shenghuo*, *ZZRQJ*, 3: 572–76.

193. Ibid., p. 576.

194. Zhou Zuoren, "Shan zhong za xin" (Miscellaneous letters from the mountains), in *Yu tian di shu*, *ZZRQJ*, 2: 348.

195. Qian, *Fanren de bei'ai*, p. 23.

196. Zhou Zuoren, "Ziji de yuandi" (In my own garden), in *Ziji de yuandi*, *ZZRQJ*, 2: 5.

197. The word *diding* is glossed in *Zhongwen da cidian* as an alternative for dandelion. Wolff (*Chou Tso-jen*, p. 144*n*22) provides evidence that Lu Xun used the word to mean violet and surmises that this is a dialectal usage. Since this second meaning seems more likely in the present context, I have followed Wolff.

198. Zhou Zuoren, "Ziji de yuandi," *ZZRQJ*, 2: 5–6.

199. Ibid., p. 6.

200. Zhou Zuoren, "Zixu" (Preface), in *Yishu yu shenghuo*, *ZZRQJ*, 3: 559.

201. See Lee, "On the Margins of the Chinese Discourse."

202. Li Tuo, "Yixiang de jiliu (tigang)."

203. The *locus classicus* is the "Shen si" chapter of the *Wen xin diao long* by Liu Xie (ca. 450–ca. 520). The most recent translation and discussion is in Stephen Owen, *Readings in Chinese Literary Thought*, p. 204. See also the earlier works by Vincent Yu-chung Shih, *The Literary Mind and the Carving of Dragons*; and Siu-Kit Wong, *Early Chinese Literary Criticism*.

204. See Brennan, "The National Longing for Form," p. 47, for the idea of nation as a trope of belonging.

## Chapter 2

1. Zhou, "Zui chu de yinxiang" (Earliest impressions), *ZTHXL*, 1: 175–76.

2. Ibid., 1: 176.

3. The full quotation from Ellis (*Affirmations*, pp. 235–36), which Zhou used many times, reads, "The Greeks considered the dislike of nakedness as a mark of Persian and other barbarians; the Japanese—the Greeks of another age and clime—had not conceived the reasons for avoiding nakedness until taught by the lustful and shamefaced eyes of western barbarians. Among ourselves [i.e., the English] it is 'disgusting' even to show the foot."

4. Zhou, "Zui chu de yinxiang," 177–78. Zhou's comments on footwear are quoted from his 1941 essay "Riben zhi zai renshi" (Getting to know Japan again), *Yaowen ji*, *ZZRQJ*, 4: 357–65.

5. Ching-mao Cheng, "The Impact of Japanese Literary Trends on Modern Chinese Writers," describes some of the predominant attitudes to Japan at the turn of the century.

6. Imamura Yoshio, "Rojin to Nihon bungaku ni tsuite no nōto" (Notes on Lu Xun and Japanese literature), in idem, *Rojin to dentō* (Lu Xun and tradition) (Tokyo: Keiso shobō, 1967), p. 246, cited in Ching-mao Cheng, "Zhou Zuoren de Riben jing-yan," p. 885.

7. Zhou, "Riben de yi shi zhu" (Japan: food, clothing, and housing), *Ku zhu za ji*, *ZZRQJ*, 3: 514. Also, "Riben de yi shi zhu (shang)," *ZTHXL*, 1: 179.

8. Zhou, "Riben de yi shi zhu," *ZZRQJ*, 3: 514.

9. Zhou, "Riben zhi zai renshi," *ZZRQJ*, 4: 358.

10. Zhou, "Huai Dongjing" (Recalling Tokyo), *Gua dou ji*, *ZZRQJ*, 4: 47–48.

11. Zhou, "Riben zhi zai renshi," *ZZRQJ*, 4: 358.

12. Zhou, "Huai Dongjing," *ZZRQJ*, 4: 48.

13. See James Liu, *Chinese Theories of Literature*, pp. 6, 63; Siu-Kit Wong, *Early Chinese Literary Criticism*, pp. 169, 21–23.

14. Zhou, "Zixu er" (Second preface), *Yu tian de shu*, *ZZRQJ*, 2: 266.

15. See Henderson, *The Development and Decline of Chinese Cosmology*, pp. 1–53.

16. Wang Bo, "Teng wang ge xu" (Preface to *Pavilion of the Prince of Teng*) is most readily available in the much reprinted prose anthology *Guwen guan zhi*. For a recent edition, see Wu Yixia et al., eds., *Guwen guan zhi*.

17. Zhou, "Choubei zazhi" (Preparing to set up a magazine), *ZTHXL*, 1: 198.

18. Taine, "Author's Introduction to This Translation," in idem, *A History of English Literature*, p. ix.

19. Taine, *A History of English Literature*, pp. 20–21; see Said, *Orientalism*, p. 232, for the deterministic bent of nineteenth-century racial and linguistic theories.

20. Zhou, "Choubei zazhi," *ZTHXL*, 1: 197.

21. Zhou, "Riben yu Zhongguo" (Japan and China), *Tan hu ji*, *ZZRQJ*, 1: 379; also cited in "Guanyu Riben yu" (About the Japanese language), *Ku zhu za ji*, *ZZRQJ*, 3: 522.

22. Zhou, "Riben de yi shi zhu (shang)," *ZTHXL*, 1: 179.

23. The Zhou brothers did not attend Zhang's public lectures; rather they were members of a special Sunday morning class in philology he gave for them and half a dozen other young men, among them Qian Xuantong. See Zhou, "*Min bao* she ting jiang" (Lectures at *Min bao*), *ZTHXL*, 1: 214–16. The brothers knew of Zhang Binglin's ideas long before these classes. Lu Xun had arrived in Tokyo one month before Zhang's abortive April 1902 rally there to mourn the execution, 242 years earlier, of the last Ming claimant to the throne, which symbolized the Manchu conquest. Although the rally was canceled, it "opened a Pandora's box of student nationalism" (Young-tsu Wong, *Search for Modern Nationalism*, p. 35; Zhang Taiyan, *Zhangshi congshu*, Wenlu 2, pp. 47b–49a). Lu Xun's political loyalties were not clearly defined at this time, and there is much scholarly debate about how close he may have been to the revolutionary position and opposed to the reformist one at that time, and whether in fact he joined Zhang's Guangfu Hui (Restoration society) in 1904 or 1908. See Lee, *Voices from the Iron House*, 14; see Young-tsu Wong, *Search for Modern Nationalism*, p. 184n1, for some additional sources on the issue. Zhou Zuoren reports having bought revolutionary publications in Shanghai in 1901; see his "Qing lian ge" (Green Lotus Tower), *ZTHXL*, 1: 79. He also notes that revolu-

tionary publications such as *Su bao* were eagerly read by students at the Jiangnan Naval Academy; see his "Fengchao" (Political unrest), *ZTHXL*, 1: 112.

24. On Zhang Binglin's scholarly training and background, see Young-tsu Wong, *Search for Modern Nationalism*, pp. 5–7; Shimada, *Pioneer of the Chinese Revolution*, pp. 3–15; and Furth, "The Sage as Rebel." On *guoxue* and *guocui*, see Wang Fansen, *Zhang Taiyan de sixiang*, pp. 77–78.

25. Young-tsu Wong, *Search for Modern Nationalism*, pp. 48–50.

26. Zhang Taiyan, "Dongjing liuxuesheng huanyinghui yanshuo ci" (Speech at welcome meeting held by Chinese students in Tokyo, July 15, 1906), in idem, *Zhang Taiyan zhenglun xuanji*, pp. 276–77. For commentary, see Shimada, *Pioneer of the Chinese Revolution*, pp. 36–37.

27. Najita, *Japan*.

28. Gluck, *Japan's Modern Myths*, pp. 111–15.

29. Zhang Taiyan, "Dongjing liu xuesheng huanying hui yanshuo ci," in idem, *Zhang Taiyan zhenglun xuanji*, p. 269.

30. Young-tsu Wong, *Search for Modern Nationalism*, pp. 24–30; Wang Fansen, *Zhang Taiyan de sixiang*, pp. 72–74; Furth, "The Sage as Rebel," p. 113.

31. Young-tsu Wong, *Search for Modern Nationalism*, p. 64.

32. Wang Fansen, *Zhang Taiyan de sixiang*, pp. 71–72.

33. Zhang Binglin, *Zhangshi congshu*, bielu 3, p. 43b; cited in Young-tsu Wong, *Search for Modern Nationalism*, p. 64.

34. See Hao Chang, *Chinese Intellectuals in Crisis*, pp. 119–41, for a thorough analysis of Zhang's Buddhism. For a different interpretation, see Young-tsu Wong, *Search for Modern Nationalism*, pp. 52–60. For Zhang's rejection of evolution and materialism the key text is his "Si huo lun" (Four delusions), in *Zhang Taiyan quanji*, 4: 442–56.

35. Hao Chang, *Chinese Intellectuals in Crisis*, p. 138.

36. Zhang Taiyan, "Dongjing liuxuesheng huanying hui yanshuo ci," in idem, *Zhang Taiyan zhenglun xuanji*, p. 276.

37. Ibid.; Zhang Binglin, "Guimao yuzhong ziji" (Note to myself in prison in 1903), in *Zhang Taiyan quanji*, wenlu juan yi, 4: 144.

38. Shimada, *Pioneer of the Chinese Revolution*, pp. 115–22.

39. Zhang Binglin, "Da Tie Zheng" (Reply to Tie Zheng), in *Zhang Taiyan quanji*, bielu juan er, 4: 371.

40. Cole, *Shaoxing*, p. 6; Zhou, "Sanbu xiangtu shi" (Three books of poetry from my native place), *Feng yu tan*, *ZZRQJ*, 3: 270.

41. Cole, *Shaoxing*, p. 8.

42. Ibid.

43. Zhou, "Tao Junchang lun Jingling pai" (Tao Junchang [1636–1725] on the Jingling school), *Feng yu tan*, *ZZRQJ*, 3: 315.

44. Young-tsu Wong (*Search for Modern Nationalism*, p. 81), provides the following list of subjects into which Zhang reclassified Chinese learning: dialogue (*minyan* [i.e., proverbs]), institutions (*zhidu*), thought (*xueshu liubie*), philosophy (*xuanxue*), literature and history (*wenshi*), geography (*dixing*), customs (*fengsu*), anecdotes (*gushi*), technology (*fangshu*), generality (*tonglun*), arts (*yiwen*), and poetry (*yunwen*). This reclassification had a great influence on modern academic scholarship.

45. Wen-hsin Yeh (*The Alienated Academy*, p. 25) describes Zhou and his colleague in the folklore movement Liu Fu (Liu Bannong) as members of the "inner coterie" of Zhang Binglin's disciples at Beida. Along with seven others (including Lu Xun), they were invited to Beida when Cai Yuanpei became the university president and "sought to tap the prestige of high classicism associated with Zhang Taiyan."

46. Zhou, "Shaoxingxian guan" (The Shaoxing county hostel), *ZTHXL*, 1: 304–5.

47. See the discussion of "My Old Home," "In the Tavern," and "The Misanthrope" in Lee, *Voices from the Iron House*, pp. 80–86.

48. Lu Xun, Letter to Cao Juren dated June 18, 1933, in *LXQJ*, 12: 185. See Shimada, *Pioneer of the Chinese Revolution*, pp. 26–28, on whose discussion I draw here.

49. Zhou, "Xie ben shi" (Taking leave of my teacher), *Yusi* 94 (Aug 28, 1926).

50. Zhou, "*Min bao she ting jiang*," *ZTHXL*, 1: 216.

51. Lee, "Tradition and Modernity in the Writings of Lu Xun," p. 27.

52. Qian Xuantong, "Duiyu Pan Gongzhan laixin 'duiyu xin wenxuede sanjian yaoshi' de dayu" (A reply to Pan Gongzhan's letter on three important points for the new literature), in *Xin qingnian* 6, no. 6; quoted in Shu, "Zhou Zuoren gaiguan," pt. I, p. 94.

53. Zhou, *Zhongguo xin wenxue de yuanliu*, *ZZRQJ*, 5: 313–71.

54. Zhou, "Di'er jiang: Zhongguo wenxue de bianqian" (Second lecture: changes in Chinese literature), in *Zhongguo xin wenxue de yuanliu*, *ZZRQJ*, 5: 327–30.

55. Ibid., p. 330. This translation of the term *daotong* is from Hartman, *Han Yu and the T'ang Search for Unity*, p. 159.

56. Zhou, "Disi jiang: Qingdai wenxue de fandong (xia)—Tongcheng pai" (Fourth lecture: the Qing literary reaction (pt. II)—the Tongcheng school), in *Zhongguo xin wenxue de yuanliu*, *ZZRQJ*, 5: 345.

57. Ying-shih Yu, "T'ung-ch'eng pai," in Nienhauser et al., *Indiana Companion*, s.v.

58. Ibid.

59. Zhou, "Disan jiang: Qingdai wenxue de fandong (shang)—baguwen," (Third lecture: the Qing literary reaction (pt. I)—baguwen), in *Zhongguo xin wenxue yuanliu*, *ZZRQJ*, 5: 339. *Baguwen*, the so-called eight-legged essay, was a prescribed form of exegetical composition for the civil service examinations during the Ming and Qing dynasties. The topic was usually a short quotation from the Confucian classics or the Four Books. Candidates were expected to demonstrate a complete grasp of the text and commentaries and their relevance to contemporary events while fol-

lowing prescribed metrical and rhetorical rules. The essay became a major literary form in its own right, the importance of which "cannot be overestimated" (Andrew Plaks, "Pa-ku wen," in Nienhauser et al., *Indiana Companion*, s.v.). The essay was dropped from the examination system in 1901 and replaced with a simpler form designed to accommodate Western learning (see Ichiko, "Political and Institutional Reform, 1901–11," in the *Cambridge History of China*, vol. 11, *The Late Ch'ing*, pt. II, p. 377).

60. Andrew Hsieh, "Tseng Kuo-fan," in Nienhauser et al., *Indiana Companion*, s.v.

61. Zhou, "Disi jiang," *ZZRQJ*, 5: 350.

62. In his 1922 article "Wode fugu jingyan" (My experience of archaism), *Yu tian de shu*, *ZZRQJ*, 2: 341, Zhou blamed his assiduity in using his newly acquired arcane diction for the fact that only twenty copies of *Yuwai xiaoshuo ji*—the volume of European short stories he and Lu Xun translated in Tokyo—were ever sold.

63. Lee, *Voices from the Iron House*, p. 40.

64. Lu Xun, "Guanyu Taiyan xiansheng er san shi" (Some things about Zhang Binglin), *Qiejieting zawen mobian*, *LXQJ*, 6: 545–47.

65. Lu Xun, "Wu chang hui" (The fair of the five fierce gods), *Zhao hua xi she*, *LXQJ*, 2: 261–66.

66. Lu Xun, "Suo ji" (Fragmentary recollections), *Zhao hua xi shi*, *LXQJ*, 2: 291–301.

67. Zhou, "Wode zaxue: san" (My miscellaneous learning: three), *Kukou gankou*, *ZZRQJ*, 5: 415.

68. The translation of Ji Yun's title is taken from W. Y. Ma, "Chi Yun" in Nienhauser et al., *Indiana Companion*, s.v.

69. Zhou, "Wode xin shu: yi" (My new books: one), *ZTHXL*, 1: 135–36.

70. Ibid. Edward Schafer ("Yuyang tsa-tsu," in Nienhauser et al., *Indiana Companion*, s.v.) notes that Duan Chengshi (800–863), the author of the *Youyang zazu*, collected data on every subject from travelers and foreigners and could be regarded as a "pioneering field linguist" who took care to cross check information and record his doubts.

71. Zhou, "Ziji de gongzuo: si" (My work: four), in idem, *Zhitang huixiang lu*, 1: 283. The article, entitled "Gu tonghua shiyi" (An elucidation of ancient children's stories), was eventually published in the monthly journal published by the Compilation Group of the Ministry of Education in Peking. It is included in Zhou's collection *Ertong wenxue xiaolun*, *ZZRQJ*, 5: 283.

72. John C. Y. Wang, "Lu Xun as a Scholar of Traditional Chinese Fiction."

73. See Lee, *Voices from the Iron House*, pp. 32–36.

74. Zhou, "Wode zaxue: er" (My miscellaneous learning: two), *Kukou gankou*, *ZZRQJ*, 5: 414.

75. Zhou, "Wode zaxue: shijiu" (My miscellaneous learning: nineteen), *Kukou gankou*, *ZZRQJ*, 5: 440.

76. Hung, *Going to the People*, pp. 83–93.

77. The process is similar to that described in Johnston, "The Whole Achievement in Virginia Woolf's *The Common Reader*."

78. Zhou, "*Feng yu tan houji*" (Postface to *Feng yu tan*), ZZRQJ, 3: 399.

79. Zhou, "Fulu erbian," (Appendix: two pieces), *Feng yu tan*, ZZRQJ, 3: 394–98.

80. Zhou, "Riben zhi guankui zhi san" (A personal view of Japan, pt. III), ZZRQJ, 3: 385–93.

81. Helmut Wilhelm, "Chang Er-ch'i" in Hummel, *Eminent Chinese of the Ch'ing Period*, s.v.

82. Lu Xun, "Wu chang hui," *LXQJ*, 2: 261.

83. Lu Xun, "Xiao yin" (Preface), *Zhao hua xi shi*, *LXQJ*, 2: 229–30.

84. Zhou, "Guxiang de huigu" (Memories of my native place), *ZTHXL*, 1: 291–92.

85. Zhou, "Mai tang," *Yaowei ji*, ZZRQJ, 4: 319–21.

86. I have used the translation in Wolff, *Chou Tso-jen*, pp. 92–95.

87. *Yueh yen* (*Yue yan*; Yue maxims) by Fan Yin (Fan Xiaofeng), first published in 1882 and republished with a colophon by Zhou in 1932, detailed customs of the Shaoxing area.

88. Hara Sen (Kōdō), compiler of *Sentetsu sōdan*, a biographical dictionary of Edo scholars published in 1805.

89. Zhu Zhiyu (Shunshui; 1600–1682).

90. Shunzo Sakamaki, "Chu Chih-yu," in Hummel, *Eminent Chinese of the Ch'ing Period*, s.v.

91. Kakasu Okakura, *Ideals of the East*, p. 1.

92. On Nivedita's important contributions to Okakura's book, see Hay, *Asian Ideas of East and West*, pp. 35–44. Nivedita's introduction, in fact, seeks to root a resurgent Hinduism in the idea of an Asian unity initially owed to India. I believe Hay's account has greatly overemphasized Nivedita's importance in formulating the idea of pan-Asianism, whatever her editorial role, since he discounts the domestic Japanese context. Irokawa (*The Culture of the Meiji Period*, pp. 212–15) places Okakura's book in the context of the dilemma felt by some Japanese intellectuals over Japan's wars with China (1894–95) and Russia (1904–5), as it became clear that the national quest for "civilization" and "modernity" required Japan to become an imperialist power. Concepts like Okakura's "principles of Asia" set out in *Ideals of the East* were among the "only possible alternatives," Irokawa (p.215) states, adding that "while grasping to find a non-Western type of modernity [Okakura] denied the idea of a 'yellow peril.'"

93. See Shimada, *Pioneer of the Chinese Revolution*, pp. 76–83.

94. Najita, *Japan*, pp. 116–17.

95. Fukuzawa was one of the members of the Meirokusha (Society of six Meiji men) that sought to bring enlightenment to Japan after the Meiji Restoration. They

"stood on common ground in their iconoclasm toward history and agreement on the need for cultural disengagement with the immediate past." In particular they posited the Enlightenment as "an antithetical universal" to the "metaphysical ethics of Neo-Confucianism" (Najita, *Japan*, pp. 88–89).

96. Karatani, *Origins of Modern Japanese Literature*, p. 43.

97. Okakura, *Ideals of the East*, pp. 237–38.

98. Zhu was one of the most prominent exemplars of these ties, but there were others. See Jansen, *China in the Tokugawa World*, pp. 54–64, on the flow of loyalist refugees, merchants, painters, and priests, many from the "centers of old bourgeois culture along the Yangtze" (p. 60) and their activities in Japan.

99. Zhou, "Riben de renqing mei" (Japanese sensibilities and their beauty), *Yu tian de shu*, ZZRQJ, 2: 339.

100. Zhou, "Pai Ri pingyi" (An assessment of the Expel Japan movement), *Tan hu ji*, ZZRQJ, 1: 389.

101. Ibid.

102. Hung, *Going to the People*, pp. 43–46.

103. See C. H. Wang, "Chou Tso-jen's Hellenism."

104. Hyman, "The Ritual View of Myth and the Mythic," p. 136.

105. Zhou, "Wode zaxue: ba" (My miscellaneous learning: eight), *Kukou gankou*, ZZRQJ, 5: 423.

106. Zhou, "Choubei zazhi," ZTHXL, 1: 197.

107. Tambiah, *Magic, Science, Religion and the Scope of Rationality*, pp. 42–45.

108. Ibid., p. 44.

109. Andrew Lang, *Myth, Ritual and Religion*, 1: 33.

110. Ibid., 1: 251, 258.

111. Ibid., 1: 340. In the revised version of his book (1899), Lang made these statements even more strongly, "thus injuring his thesis that the irrational elements could be explained as survivals" (Dorson, "The Eclipse of Solar Mythology," p. 39).

112. In general, five features distinguished this psychological state: (1) the belief that everything in nature was alive and aware; (2) belief in magic and incantations; (3) belief in ghosts and spirits; (4) curiosity; (5) credulity. There was a tension between these last two, for although the savage's curiosity represented the beginnings of scientific and/or religious thinking, it was too easily satisfied with stories. See Zhou, "Xisu yu shenhua" (Custom and myth), *Ye du chao*, ZZRQJ, 2: 475, quoting from the first chapter of Lang's book.

113. Ibid.; Zhou, "Wode zaxue: qi" (My miscellaneous learning: seven), *Kukou gankou*, ZZRQJ, 5: 422.

114. Zhou, "Wode zaxue: ba," 5: 423.

115. Vickery, *The Literary Impact of the Golden Bough*, p. 13.

116. Ibid., p. 67.

117. Zhou, "Huisang yu maishui" (Returning from funerals and buying water), *Ziji de yuandi*, ZZRQJ, 2: 119.

118. Torii, almost certainly Torii Ryūzō (1879–1953), was the author of a work entitled "Looking at the Earliest Culture of Our Country from an Anthropological Perspective." See Zhou, "Han yi gushiji shendai juan yinyan" (Preface to a translation of the chapter on the Age of the Gods in the *Kojiki*), *Tan long ji*, ZZRQJ, 1: 39.

119. Vickery, *The Literary Impact of the Golden Bough*, p. 22.

120. Zhou, "Shamande lijiao sixiang" (Shamanistic thinking about morality), *Tan hu ji*, ZZRQJ, 1: 313. See also Shu Wu, "Nüxing de faxian," p. 138.

121. Zhou, "Zuzhou" (Imprecations), *Tan hu ji*, ZZRQJ, 1: 295.

122. I owe this translation to Pollard, *A Chinese Look at Literature*, p. 125.

123. Zhou, "Xing de xinli" (The psychology of sex), *Ye du chao*, ZZRQJ, 2: 487.

124. Zhou, "Shenhua yu chuanshuo" (Myths and legends), *Ziji de yuandi*, ZZRQJ, 2: 23.

125. Zhou, "Wenyi shang de yiwu" (Supernatural beings in literature), *Ziji de yuandi*, ZZRQJ, 2: 20–23.

126. Zhou, "Shenhua de bianhu" (In defense of myth), *Yu tian de shu*, ZZRQJ, 2: 368. On the debate on children's reading matter see Hung, *Going to the People*, pp. 119–22.

127. Zhou, "Xu fa zhao xu" (Preface to *Whiskers, Hair and Nails* [by Jiang Shaoyuan, 1898–1983]), *Tan long ji*, ZZRQJ, 1: 27–29.

128. Zhou was fascinated by the "battle" between Lang and Max Muller (1823–1900), who used philology to explain the meaning of myth. Lang's victory in this issue may well have had the general effect of enhancing the anthropological view in Zhou's eyes. See, e.g., "Xu shenhua de bianhu" (More in defense of myth), *Yu tian de shu*, ZZRQJ, 2: 370–71.

129. See Vickery, *The Literary Impact of the Golden Bough*, pp. 88–93, on the pervasiveness of Frazer's influence on British classicists, including Jane Harrison (1850–1928).

130. Zhou, "Xila shenhua yinyan" (Foreword to *Greek Myths*), *Tan long ji*, ZZRQJ, 1: 41–46. This is a translation of the foreword to an abridged version of Jane Harrison's *Our Debt to Greece and Rome* (1924).

131. Zhou, "Shenhua de bianhu," ZZRQJ, 2: 370.

132. Zhou, "Wode zaxue: shisi" (My miscellaneous learning: fourteen), *Kukou gankou*, ZZRQJ, 5: 432.

133. Zhou, "Wode zaxue: shiba" (My miscellaneous learning: eighteen), *Kukou gankou*, ZZRQJ, 5: 438.

134. Zhou, "Xue Riben yu (xu)" (Studying Japanese, con't.), ZTHXL, 1: 233–37.

135. Zhou, "Wode zaxue: shiqi" (My miscellaneous learning: seventeen), *Kukou gankou*, ZZRQJ, 5: 436.

136. Zhou, "Xue Riben yu (xu)," *ZTHXL*, 1: 234.

137. Kato, *A History of Japanese Literature*, pp. 44–48.

138. Zhou, "Xue Riben yu (xu)," *ZTHXL*, 1: 236.

139. Zhou, "Wode zaxue: shiqi," *ZZRQJ*, 5: 437.

140. Morse, "The Search for Japan's National Character and Distinctiveness," p. 106.

141. Zhou, "Wode zaxue: shisi," *ZZRQJ*, 5: 432–33.

142. Zhou, "Wode zaxue: shiwu" (My miscellaneous learning: fifteen), *Kukou gankou*, *ZZRQJ*, 5: 434.

143. Zhou, "*Yuanye wuyu*" (*Tōno monogatari*), *Ye du chao*, *ZZRQJ*, 2: 569.

144. Ronald Morse, Translator's Introduction to Yanagita, *The Legends of Tōno*, p. 27.

145. On Yanagita's involvement with the new literary establishment in the late 1890s, see Morse, "The Search for Japan's National Character and Distinctiveness," pp. 19–30. His essays have been described as "the greatest example of that form written in Japan since the Restoration" (Kato, *A History of Japanese Literature*, p. 130).

146. Yanagita, *The Legends of Tōno*, p. 7.

147. Zhou, "*Yuanye wuyu*," *ZZRQJ*, 2: 471.

148. Morse, "The Search for Japan's National Character and Distinctiveness," p. 152, notes that by the time he came to write *Tōno Monogatari*, Yanagita had read books by Frazer and Lang.

149. Lang, *Ritual, Myth and Religion*, 1: 264.

150. Yanagita, *The Legends of Tōno*, p. 8.

151. Morse, "The Search for Japan's National Character and Distinctiveness," pp. 124–48.

152. Zhou, "*Yuanye wuyu*," *ZZRQJ*, 2: 473.

153. Zhou sources Haddon's remarks to the concluding chapter of *A History of Anthropology*.

154. Morse, "The Search for Japan's National Character and Distinctiveness," p. 63. I have not so far been able to find evidence of personal contact between Yanagita and Zhou in Chinese sources.

155. Ibid., pp. 52–53.

156. This translation of *jōmin*, fuller than Morse's "common man," is from Harootunian, "Disciplining Native Knowledge and Producing Place," p. 110; see Morse, "The Search for Japan's National Character and Distinctiveness," pp. 96–101.

157. Morse, "The Search for Japan's National Character and Distinctiveness," p. 98.

158. Harootunian, "Disciplining Native Knowledge and Producing Place," p. 110.

159. Zhou, "Wode zaxue: shisi," *ZZRQJ*, 5: 432.

160. Harootunian, "Disciplining Native Knowledge and Producing Place," p. 112.

161. Zhou, "Yu youren lun guomin wenxue shu" (Letter to a friend about national literature), *Yu tian de shu*, ZZRQJ, 2: 336. The friend to whom the letter was addressed was Mu Mutian (1900–1971).

162. See McDermott, "Emperor, Elites and Commoners," for a discussion of the history and function of the community pact.

163. Duara, *Rescuing History from the Nation*, p. 210.

164. Kinkley, *Odyssey of Shen Congwen*, pp. 122–23.

165. Zhou, "Xila shenhua er" (Greek myths, two), *Ye du chao*, ZZRQJ, 2: 518–19.

166. The preface to this translation is included in *Lichun yiqian*, ZZRQJ, 4: 623–25, titled "Xila shenhua yinyan" (Introduction to the Greek myths). See also C. H. Wang, "Chou Tso-jen's Hellenism," p. 18.

167. Zhou, "Mingzhi wenxue zhi zhuiyi" (Recollections of Meiji literature), *Lichun yiqian*, ZZRQJ, 4: 540.

168. Ibid., p. 541.

169. Rimer, *Modern Japanese Fiction and Its Traditions*, pp. 6–7.

170. Matsumoto, *Motoori Norinaga*, pp. 43–44; de Bary, *Sources of Japanese Tradition*, 1: 172–73.

171. Motoori Norinaga, "Ashiwake obune"(Small boat through the reeds), cited in Matsumoto, *Motoori Norinaga*, p. 45.

172. Ibid., 49.

173. Rimer, *Modern Japanese Fiction and Its Traditions*, pp. 138–40.

174. Kato, *A History of Japanese Literature*, p. 186.

175. Zhou, "Dongjing sance ji" (i.e., "Tōkyō sansaku ki" [An account of strolls around Tokyo]), *Kucha suibi*, ZZRQJ, 3: 30. This essay, named after the subtitle of *Hiyorigeta*, includes Zhou's translations of parts of the first and second sections of the work.

176. Ibid. The quotation was from Kafū's *Edo geijitsu ron* (On the arts of Edo).

177. Ching-mao Cheng, "Zhou Zuoren di Riben jingyan," p. 890.

178. The passage, from Kafū's article "An Appreciation of *ukiyo-e*," included in his *Edo geijitsu ron*, appears among other places in Zhou, "Huai Dongjing," ZZRQJ, 4: 54.

179. The translation of the sentence beginning "everything" is from Edward Seidensticker, *Kafu the Scribbler*, p. 72.

180. Zhou, "Huai Dongjing," ZZRQJ, 4: 54.

181. Zhou, "Dongjing sance ji," ZZRQJ, 3: 32–33; Nagai, *Nagai Kafū*, p. 197.

182. Zhou, "Paixie" (*Haikai*), ZTHXL, 1: 240.

183. Rimer, *Modern Japanese Fiction and Its Traditions*, p. 15.

184. Zhou, "Laonian" (Old age), *Feng yu tan*, ZZRQJ, 3: 267–70.

185. Rimer, *Modern Japanese Fiction and Its Traditions*, p. 205.

186. Ibid., citing George B. Samson's translation of Kenkō's "Essays in Idleness," in *Anthology of Japanese Literature*, ed. Donald Keene (New York, 1955), p. 232.

187. Zhou, "Laonian," *ZZRQJ*, 3: 269.

188. Kato, *A History of Japanese Literature*, p. 32; See also Irokawa, *Culture of the Meiji Period*, chap. 4, for a discussion of the place of poetry composed in Chinese, including Chinzan's, in the oppositional "People's Rights" movement.

189. Lu Yan, "Beyond Politics in Wartime: Zhou Zuoren, 1931–1945." Yan is referring to Poshek Fu's *Passivity, Resistance and Collaboration*. Yan's article is a good introduction to the sources and issues involved. My thanks to Rana Mitter for sending me a copy of the article.

190. For the text of the poem, see *Nianpu*, p. 315. See also Wollf, *Chou Tso-jen*, p. 78.

191. Lu Xun made the comments in a letter to Cao Juren, cited in *Nianpu*, p. 315.

192. Zhou, "Guanyu zheng bing" (On the question of a military draft), *Kan yun ji*, *ZZRQJ*, 2: 258.

193. See Zhou, "Qi wen jiu wu" (Abandoning civilian life and taking up arms), *Ku cha suibi*, *ZZRQJ*, 3: 78–81. See also the discussion in Qian, *Fanren di bei'ai*, pp. 124–30.

194. See Zhou, "Riben de guankui" (A personal view of Japan), *Ku cha suibi*, *ZZRQJ*, 3: 92–100; the title of the second article, "Riben guankui zhi er," was changed to "Riben de yi shi zhu" (Japan: food, clothing and housing) when it was included in *Ku zhu za ji*, *ZZRQJ*, 3: 514–22; "Riben de guankui zhi san" (A personal view of Japan, pt. III), *Feng yu tan*, *ZZRQJ*, 3: 385–93.

195. Zhou, "Riben zhi guankui zhi si" (A personal view of Japan, pt. IV) was not published until after the war; see *Zhitang yiyou wenxuan*, *ZZRQJ*, 5: 702–10.

196. Zhou quotes Watsuji in his essay "Riben de renqing mei" (Japanese sensibilities and their beauty), *Yu tian de shu*, *ZZRQJ*, 2: 339–41, written in 1925. See Watsuji, *Climate and Culture*.

197. Zhou briefly mentions the meetings with Watsuji in an essay mourning Shimazaki Tōson (1872–1943), "Daoqi Tengcun xiansheng," *Yaotang zawen*, *ZZRQJ*, 4: 239–41.

198. The phrase is from Robert N. Bellah, "Japan's Cultural Identity: Some Reflections on the Work of Watsuji Tetsuro," *Journal of Asian Studies* 24, no. 4 (Aug. 1965): 573; cited in LaFleur, "A Turning in Taisho," p. 235.

199. Watsuji, *Climate and Culture*, p. v.

200. Ibid., pp. 1–17.

201. Harumi Befu, "Nationalism and *Nihonjinron*," p. 109.

202. Zhou, "Difang yu wenyi," (Place and literature), *Tan long ji*, *ZZRQJ*, 1: 8.

203. "While we do not endorse the writing of parallel prose and regulated verse by our contemporaries, yet we most certainly do not ignore the possibility of the two kinds of parallelism of meaning and sound found in Chinese characters. We feel that the development of parallel prose and regulated verse are necessities of fate, and not wholly under the control of men" (Zhou, "Guocui yu ouhua" [National essence and Europeanization], *Ziji de yuandi*, *ZZRQJ*, 1: 11).

204. Zhou, "Guanyu mingyun" (About destiny/fate), *Ku cha suibi* (Yuelu shushe edition), p. 109. I am using this edition, since this article was for some reason omitted from *ZZRQJ*. The article of this title found in *Ku cha suibi, ZZRQJ*, 3: 75, should be titled "Guanyu mingyun zhi er" (About destiny/fate, pt. II), which is how it appears in the Yuelu shushe edition of *Ku cha suibi*, pp. 114–18. According to *Nianpu*, pp. 696–97, "Guanyu mingyun" first appeared in the Literary Supplement to *Dagongbao*, no. 148 (April 21, 1935) and "Guanyu minyun zhi er" in issue no. 154 (June 2, 1935).

205. Zhou, "Guanyu mingyun," *Ku cha suibi* (Yuelu shushe ed.), pp. 110–11.

206. Ibid., pp. 112–13. According to *Nianpu*, p. 341, the unnamed critics who attacked the reading of *Zhuangzi* and the *Wenxuan* included "Lu Xun and others." See Lu Xun, "'Gan jiu' yi hou: shang/xia" (After "Response to the Old," pts. I and II), *Zhun feng yue tan, LXQJ*, 5: 328–35. "Guanyu mingyun" elicited accusations that (as could be expected of someone whose historical moment had passed), Zhou was indulging in mysticism or superstition. His response to his critics covers much of the same ground as the first essay. See "Guanyu mingyun zhi er," *Ku cha suibi* (Yuelu shushe), pp. 114–18.

207. Zhou, "Jie yuan dou" (Beans for tying affinities), *Gua dou ji, ZZRQJ*, 4: 134.

208. Watsuji, *Climate and Culture*, p. 118.

209. Sakai, "Modernity and Its Critique."

210. LaFleur, "A Turning in Taishō," p. 235.

211. Watsuji, *Climate and Culture*, p. 202.

212. Ibid., p. 207.

213. Zhou, "Riben guankui zhi san," *ZZRQJ*, 3: 386.

214. Zhou, "Riben guankui zhi si," *ZZRQJ*, 5: 706.

215. Maruyama, "The Ideology and Dynamics of Japanese Fascism."

216. Dong Bingyue, "Zhou Zuoren de 'fu ni' yu wenhuaguan."

217. Zhou, "Yingxiong chongbai" (Hero worship), *Ku cha suibi, ZZRQJ*, 4: 126.

218. Zhou, "Ziji de yuandi," *ZZRQJ*, 2: 5–6.

219. Zhou, "Guanyu Wang Nüe'an" (About Wang Nüe'an [Wang Jichong]), *Feng yu tan, ZZRQJ*, 3: 311–15.

220. Zhou, "Yue Fei yu Qin Kui" (Yue Fei and Qin Kui), *Ku cha suibi, ZZRQJ*, 4: 120–21.

221. In a letter to the editor of *Cosmic Wind* written in August, Zhou said that he had too many dependents to be able to leave Peking and so would have to resign himself to "living in bitterness." In 1966 Zhou expanded on this in a letter to Xu Xu (1908–80) published in the Hong Kong journal *Biduan* (see *Zhitang shuxin*, p. 421–22). In all, he had ten dependents: his wife, his mother, Lu Xun's first wife, his daughter and two grandchildren, and "my younger brother's abandoned wife, that is my wife's younger sister, with two sons and a daughter." Zhou bitterly reflected that

this "explanation" would merely prove that "my intentions were weak, that I did not have the willpower to cast aside my family, sacrifice others, and save myself." On Zhou Jianren's marriage to Hata Nobuko's sister Yoshiko in 1914, see Huang Qiaosheng, *Dujin jiebo*, pp. 202–3.

222. Qian, *Fanren de bei'ai*, pp. 152–53; Gunn, *Unwelcome Muse*, pp. 152–56. Lu Yan, "Beyond Politics in Wartime," pp. 9–10, reports evidence that Zhou was persuaded by key underground workers to take up a position in the puppet regime. Qian, *Fanren de bei'ai*, p. 169, notes that Zhou probably had contacts with both Guomindang and Communist agents.

223. Zhou, "Bianjie" (Explanations in self-defense), *Yaowei ji*, ZZRQJ, 4: 221–23; and "Bu bianjie shuo: shang" (Against explanations in self-defense, pt. I), ZTHXL, 2: 420–24.

224. Lu Yan, "Beyond Politics in Wartime," p. 10. For the transcripts of Zhou's trial, see Nanjing shi dang'an guan, *Shenxun Wangwei hanjian bilu*.

225. Gunn, *Unwelcome Muse*, p. 160.

226. Zhou, "Zhongguo de sixiang wenti" (Problems of Chinese thought), *Yaotang zawen*, ZZRQJ, 4: 170.

227. Zhou, "Han wenxue de qiantu," *Yaotang zawen*, ZZRQJ, 4: 182.

228. Zhou, "Yu ji si" (The Temple of Yu's footprint), *Yaowei ji*, ZZRQJ, 4: 315, 318.

229. Zhou, "Shizi yu Rusheng" (Sons of Buddha and students of Confucius); and "Daode mantan" (Digressions on morality), *Yaotang zawen*, ZZRQJ, 4: 219, 197.

230. Zhou, "Wode zaxue: shisi," ZZRQJ, 5: 432.

231. Zhou, "Zai tan paiwen" (More on *haibun*), *Yaowei ji*, ZZRQJ, 4: 356.

## Chapter 3

1. Hu Shi, *Wushinian lai Zhongguo wenxue*, p. 150. Hu's comments on the new literature were very sketchy, and the bulk of his essay is devoted to literature of the preceding fifty years.

2. Yang Mu, "Zhou Zuoren lun," p. 143.

3. Pollard, *A Chinese Look at Literature*.

4. Lynn, "Orthodoxy and Enlightenment," pp. 217–23.

5. Zhou, "Di'er jiang: Zhongguo wenxue de bianqian," ZZRQJ, 5: 327–28.

6. Zhou, "Tan Rujia" (Talking about Confucians), *Ku zhu za ji*, ZZRQJ, 3: 245.

7. Graham, *Disputers of the Tao*, p. 3.

8. Ibid., 13–22; DeWoskin, "Early Chinese Music," p. 190.

9. DeWoskin, "Early Chinese Music," p. 191. A. C. Graham (*Chuang-tzu*, p. 18) notes that "although Chuang-tzu shares the general tendency of Confucians and Daoists to think of Heaven as an impersonal power . . . his attitude has a strong element of numinous awe, a sense of man's littleness before an incomprehensible power . . . while he does not believe in a personal God, he does think of Heaven and the Way

as transcending the distinction between personal and impersonal." Moreover, Heaven, the Way, and man are "all part of a cosmos constituted by the *qi* (energy)" which has the place in Chinese cosmology accorded to "matter" in the Western.

10. DeWoskin, "Early Chinese Music," pp. 191–92.

11. Van Zoeren, *Poetry and Personality*, pp. 7–8.

12. DeWoskin, "Early Chinese Music," p. 194.

13. Van Zoeren, *Poetry and Personality*, p. 12.

14. Ibid., pp. 56–59.

15. Ibid., p. 95. The Preface is translated in full in the context of an invaluable discussion and exegesis in ibid., pp. 80–115.

16. Ibid., pp. 108–11.

17. Ibid., pp. 52–54. Van Zoeren suggests that in the fourth century B.C.E., under the impact of criticisms from proto-Daoist thinkers, Confucians became interested in the notion of a self that could be so completely remade that it did what was right spontaneously.

18. On this last point, see Kang-i Sun Chang, "Chinese 'Lyric Criticism' in the Six Dynasties."

19. Ibid.

20. Van Zoeren, *Poetry and Personality*, pp. 106–8. Van Zoeren quotes from the "Way of Heaven" (*Tiandao*) chapter in the *Zhuangzi*: "What is valuable about talk is intentions [*yi*]. Intentions have something with which they are concerned, but what the intentions are concerned with cannot be passed on in words." Strictly speaking, according to Graham (*Chuang-tzu*, p. 258), this chapter, not being one of the seven Inner Chapters of the *Zhuangzi* text, should not be attributed to Zhuangzi himself but to the syncretist school. On the interchangeability of *yi* and *zhi*, see Van Zoeren, *Poetry and Personality*, p. 73.

21. Cf. the following passage in the seminal "Qiwulun" (The sorting that evens things out) chapter of the *Zhuangzi*: "Pleasure in things and anger against them, sadness and joy, forethought and regret, change and immobility, idle influences that initiate our gestures—music coming out of emptiness, vapour condensing into mushrooms—alternate before it [i.e., the heart, the organ of thought] day and night and no one knows from which soil they spring. Enough! The source from which it has these morning and evening, is it not that from which it was born?" (Graham, *Chuang-tzu*, pp. 50–51). Shortly afterward, the problem is raised of the relationship between the "heart" and the emotions and where the "true overlord" (*zhen zai*) among them is to be found. It would seem therefore that the Confucian and Daoist positions we have been talking about share common ground on the "naturalness" of the emotions. The differences, as we have already seen from DeWoskin, are over the question of whether and how to transform them.

22. Van Zoeren, *Poetry and Personality*, p. 53.

23. Bol, *"This Culture of Ours,"* p. 28.

24. Zhou, "Diyi jiang: guanyu wenxue zhi zhu wenti" (First lecture: some questions pertaining to literature), *Zhongguo xin wenxue de yuanliu,* ZZRQJ, 5: 325.

25. Zhou, "Lun xiao shi" (On the "small poem"), *Ziji de yuandi,* ZZRQJ, 2: 32–33.

26. Zhu, "Xu" (Preface), in idem, *Shi yan zhi bian,* p. v.

27. Zhu, *Shi yan zhi bian,* p. 33.

28. Ibid., p. 36. I have used the translation of Lu Ji's "Descriptive Poem on Literature" [*Wen fu*], in Owen, *Readings in Chinese Literary Thought,* pp. 73–181. The quotation occurs on p. 130.

29. Owen, *Readings in Chinese Literary Thought,* p. 130.

30. Zhu, *Shi yan zhi bian,* p. 36.

31. Ibid., pp. 38–40.

32. Owen, *Readings in Chinese Literary Thought,* p. 131. The reference to Ming and Qing critics is also Owen's.

33. Zhu, *Shi yan zhi bian,* pp. 43–44.

34. Graham, *Chuang-tzu,* p. 25.

35. James Liu, *Language-Paradox-Poetics,* p. 56.

36. Zhu, *Shi yan zhi bian,* p. 44.

37. Pollard, *A Chinese Look at Literature,* pp. 12, 11.

38. Ibid., p. 11.

39. In formulating this idea I am indebted to Owen, "Introduction," *Readings in Chinese Literary Thought,* pp. 3–8.

40. Zhou, "Diyi jiang," ZZRQJ, 5: 316–17.

41. Zhou, "Xu" (Preface), *Tan long ji,* ZZRQJ, 1: 3–4.

42. This Graham explicates as follows in *Chuang-tzu* (p. 49): "It is natural for differently constituted persons to think differently; don't try to decide between their opinions, listen to Heaven who breathes through them."

43. Zhou, "'Cao mu chong yu' xiao yin" (Minor preface to "Plants, Trees, Insects, and Fish"), *Kan yun ji,* ZZRQJ, 2: 159.

44. Zhou, "Yan ci" (Condolences), *Yu tian de shu,* ZZRQJ, 2: 278; "Chong kan Yuan Zhonglang ji xu" (Preface to the republication of Yuan Zhonglang's collection), *Ku cha suibi,* ZZRQJ, 3: 49.

45. Zhou, "Diyi jiang," ZZRQJ, 5: 324.

46. Ibid.

47. Zhou, "'Cao, mu, chong, yu' xiao yin," ZZRQJ, 2: 158–59.

48. Ibid., p. 159.

49. Ibid., p. 160.

50. There is an ironic twist in the use of insects and fish in the title: See *Zhongwen da cidian,* where the phrase *chong yu* is glossed as a sarcastic reference to scholarly research on trivial philological matters.

51. Zhou, "'Cao, mu, chong, yu' xiao yin," p. 160.

52. According to *Ziliao*, the dates of composition and publication, respectively, are as follows: (1) "Jinyu" (Goldfish), Mar. 31, 1930, Apr. 17, 1930 (*Yishi bao*); (2) "Shizi" (Lice), Apr. 5, 1930, Apr. 30, 1930 (*Weiming*); (3) "Shuili de dongxi" (Denizens of the water), not known, May 12, 1930 (*Luotuo cao*); (4) "Guanyu bianfu" (About bats), July 23, 1930, Aug. 4, 1930 (*Luotuo cao*); (5) "'Cao mu chong yu' xiao yin" (Small preface to "Grass, Trees, Insects, and Fishes"), Oct. 6, 1930, Oct. 13, 1930 (*Luotuo cao*); (6) "Liangzhu shu" (Two trees), Dec. 25, 1930, Mar. 10, 1931 (*Qingnian jie*); (7) "Anshanzi" (= Japanese *kagashi*; i.e., Scarecrows), Oct. 11, 1931 (first published in *Kan yun ji*, 1932); (8) "Xiancai geng" (Amaranth stalks), Oct. 26, 1931 (first published in *Kan yun ji*). This differs from the order in which they appear in *Kan yun ji*: "Preface," "Goldfish," "Lice," "Two Trees," "Amaranth Stalks," "Denizens of the Water," "Scarecrows," "About Bats." Zhou himself claimed to have written "Goldfish" on Mar. 11, 1930. See Zhou, "Xie 'Jinyu' de yueri" (The date of composition of "Goldfish"), *JWW*, 2: 363.

53. Zhang Juxiang (*Nianpu*, p. 279) also believes that Zhou was responding to the establishment of the League.

54. Zhou, "Jinyu" (Goldfish), *Kan yun ji*, *ZZRQJ*, 2: 160–61.

55. Ibid., p. 162.

56. Lynn, "Orthodoxy and Enlightenment," p. 219. The text used here is Yan Yu, *Canglang shihua jiaoshi*, ed. Guo Shaoyu.

57. On the Zhuangzian dimension of the *Canglang shihua*, see Lynn, "Orthodoxy and Enlightenment," pp. 228–29.

58. Yan Yu, "Shi bian," section 1, in idem, *Canglang shihua*.

59. Ibid., section 4. Thus, Han, Wei, and Jin poetry is first-order Enlightenment and its practitioners resemble the adherents of the Linji school (which favored sudden Enlightenment), whereas students of poetry after the Tali reign era (766–79) are like the adherents of the Caodong sect (which preferred the *kōan* method).

60. Zhang Jian, *Canglang shihua yanjiu*, p. 16.

61. Yan Yu, "Shi bian," section 4, in idem, *Canglang shihua*.

62. Ibid.

63. My translation of *danghang* as "plying one's proper trade" and *bense* as "showing the true colors" modifies James Liu, *Chinese Theories of Literature*, p. 38. Gong Pengcheng, *Shishi bense yu miaowu* (pp. 93–97), explains that *bense* originally referred to the distinctive clothing obligatory for members of particular trades (*hang*) in Sui and Tang times; *danghang* meant "up to professional standards." When the terms began to be applied to literature and art in Song times, they referred to styles and genres. As an example of this usage, Gong (p. 97) quotes from Chen Houshan's *shihua*, "Tuizhi [Han Yu] took prose (*wen*) for *shi* poetry, and Zizhan (Su Shi) took *shi* poetry for *ci* poetry. Just like the dance of Lei Dashi in the Imperial School of Arts,

although it was at the acme of artistry, their work has to be considered as stylistically incorrect (*fei bense*)."

64. Owen, *Readings in Chinese Literary Thought*, pp. 407–8, shows that *cai* was the term used in popular poetics to mean "materials"; I follow him here in using it rather than the more commonly seen "talent."

65. James Liu, *Chinese Theories of Literature*, p. 39; Owen, *Readings in Chinese Literary Thought*, p. 211.

66. Owen, *Readings in Chinese Literary Thought*, p. 47. See also Liu's comments on the passage in *Chinese Theories of Literature*, p. 120.

67. Lynn, "Orthodoxy and Enlightenment," p. 227; Zhang Jian, *Canglang shihua yanjiu*, p. 24.

68. Owen, *Readings in Chinese Literary Theory*, pp. 410–11.

69. On Owen's attitude to Yan Yu, see Lynn's review of *Readings in Chinese Literary Thought*, pp. 47–52.

70. Yan Yu, "Shibian," section 5, in idem, *Canglang shihua*.

71. Zhang Jian, *Canglang shihua yanjiu*, pp. 24–25.

72. Gong, *Shishi bense yu miaowu*, p. 116.

73. *Xingqu* "appears to refer to a kind of ineffable feeling or mood inspired by the poet's contemplation of Nature" (James Liu, *Chinese Theories of Literature*, p. 39).

74. For Zhang Jian (*Canglang shihua yanjiu*, pp. 34–36), this points to a contradiction in the text: if Meng Haoran (689–740) and Wang Wei's (701–61) work epitomized *xingqu*, then why are they not also considered to have "entered the spirit"? In answer, he concludes that there is no reason to assume an internal relationship between the two categories.

75. Yan Yu, "Shibian," in idem, *Canglang shihua*, 3: 7–8. In translating some of these terms, I have followed Robertson, "'. . . To Convey What Is Precious.'"

76. Zhang Jian, *Canglang shihua yanjiu*, 27. In addition to Robertson's work, see also Owen's chapter (pp. 299–357) on Sikong Tu in *Readings in Chinese Literary Thought*, which is most useful, notwithstanding his irritated description of the work as "at worst, a poetics of Oz."

77. Robertson, "'. . . To Convey What Is Precious,'" p. 333.

78. Ibid., p. 328.

79. Ibid., p. 353n23.

80. Pauline Yu, *The Reading of Imagery*, p. 199 and *passim*.

81. Ibid., p. 185.

82. Ibid., pp. 206–16.

83. Owen, *Readings in Chinese Literary Thought*, pp. 256–58.

84. See Pauline Yu (*The Reading of Imagery*, pp. 190–96) on Li Bai and Du Fu's control of imagery.

85. Ibid., p. 199.

86. Ibid., p. 186.

87. Owen, *The High Tang*, p. xv. Owen notes (p. 109) that Li Bai's poetry was inimitable because its goal was to embody a unique personality; moreover, whereas Li Bai saw the literary past as a vast collection of lines from which he could borrow unabashedly, Tu Fu saw it as a series of powerful voices (p. 141).

88. Lynn, "Orthodoxy and Enlightenment," pp. 224–25. The quotation occurs in Yan Yu, *Canglang shihua*, section 4, "Shi ping" (Evaluations), 24: 171.

89. Lynn, "Alternate Routes to Self-realization," pp. 317–18.

90. Ibid., pp. 319–20.

91. Lynn, "Orthodoxy and Enlightenment," pp. 229–37; Yoshikawa, *Five Hundred Years of Chinese Poetry*, pp. 137–76; Wu Hongyi, *Qingdai shixue chutan*, pp. 34–53.

92. Lynn, "Orthodoxy and Enlightenment," p. 231.

93. Wing-Tsit Chan, "The Ch'eng-Chu School of Early Ming," p. 34.

94. Julia Ching, "Introduction," p. 12.

95. The brothers were Yuan Zongdao (Boxiu; 1560–1624), Yuan Hongdao (Zhonglang; 1568–1610), and Yuan Zhongdao (Xiaoxiu; 1570–1624). The middle brother, Hongdao, was the most important. The standard English-language reference is Chih-p'ing Chou, *Yuan Hung-tao and the Kung-an School*. See also the entries on Yuan Hongdao in Goodrich and Fang, *Dictionary of Ming Biography*, and Nienhauser et al., *Indiana Companion*.

96. Lynn, "Alternative Routes to Self-realization," p. 329; Guo Shaoyu, *Zhongguo wenxue piping shi*, pp. 568–71.

97. Yoshikawa, *Five Hundred Years of Chinese Poetry*, pp. 78–84. It has been suggested that Yoshikawa's view that the *wenren* were free from connections with politics or philosophy may have been unduly colored by his interest in Tokugawa culture. See Atwell, "Afterword," p. 193. We have here an intriguing glimpse into an instance of the mutual construction and appropriation of culture by Chinese and Japanese intellectuals in the twentieth century.

98. Zhou, "*Jindai sanwen* chao xin xu" (New preface to *Jindai sanwen*), *Tianma Yearbook*, 1934 (1st ed.); *Zhitang shuhua*, 1: 105.

99. Zhou, "Du wan Ming xiaopin xuanzhu" (On reading selected and annotated *xiaopin* of the late Ming), *Yishi bao*, May 6, 1937, in *Zhitang shuhua* 1: 428.

100. Wang Ji (1498–1583) developed the intuitive tendency in Wang Yangming's thinking. His differences with Wang's other prominent follower, Qian Dehong (1496–1574), who emphasized moral cultivation, are recorded in the *Instructions for Practical Living* (*Chuanxi lu*) compiled by Wang Yangming's followers. A translation of this can be found in Chan, *A Sourcebook in Chinese Philosophy*, pp. 686–91.

101. Huang Tsung-hsi, *Records of Ming Scholars*, p. 165.

102. K. C. Hsiao, "Li Chih"; de Bary, "Individualism and Humanitarianism in

Late Ming Thought," pp. 195–96; Ch'ien, "Chiao Hung and the Revolt Against Ch'eng-Chu Orthodoxy," p. 289.

103. Zuo Dongling, *Li Zhi yu wan Ming wenxue sixiang*, p. 187.

104. See Chih-p'ing Chou, *Yuan Hung-tao and the Kung-an School*, pp. 44–48.

105. Zhou, "Di'er jiang," *ZZRQJ*, 5: 331.

106. See entry for Ricci in Goodrich and Fang, *Dictionary of Ming Biography*, s.v.

107. Zhou, "Di'er jiang," *ZZRQJ*, 5: 332. I have used Chih-p'ing Chou's translation in *Yuan Hung-tao and the Kung-an School*, p. 44.

108. Chih-p'ing Chou, *Yuan Hung-tao and the Kung-an School*, pp. 118, 70.

109. Zhou, "Disan jiang," *ZZRQJ*, 5: 337.

110. Chou Chih-p'ing, *Yuan Hung-tao and the Kung-an School*, p. 84.

111. Zhou, "Chong kan Yuan Zhonglang ji xu," *ZZRQJ*, 3: 44.

112. Zhou, "Di'er jiang," *ZZRQJ*, 5: 335.

113. Owen, *Readings in Chinese Literary Thought*, pp. 257–58.

114. Chinese commentators did not agree among themselves on how the properties of stimulus relate to categories of appeal. For a helpful discussion, see Pauline Yu, *The Reading of Imagery*, pp. 57–67.

115. Zhou, "Yang bian ji xu" (Preface to *Yang bian ji*), *Tan long ji*, *ZZRQJ*, 1: 29–31.

116. Ode number 6 in the Zhou Nan section of the *Shijing*.

117. Zhou, "Tan 'tantan *Shijing*'" (Talking about "talks on the *Shijing*"), *Tan long ji*, *ZZRQJ*, 1: 99–101.

118. As Pollard suggests (*A Chinese Look at Literature*, p. 78), the words *yuxiang* and *huiwei* are drawn directly from the aesthetics of indirectness and evocativeness, the "meaning and flavor" that remain after the words are done.

119. Pauline Yu, *The Reading of Imagery*, pp. 177–182, 215.

120. Zhou, "Meihua caotang bitan deng" (Conversational scribblings from the Plumflower Thatched Hut and so on), *Feng yu tan*, *ZZRQJ*, 3: 354.

121. Zhou, "Tao'an mengyi xu" (Preface to *Recollections of Tao'an's Past Dreams*), *Zexie ji*, *ZZRQJ*, 1: 137.

122. Zhou, "Difang yu wenyi," *ZZRQJ*, 1: 8–11.

123. Ibid., p. 9.

124. Ibid.

125. Ibid.

126. Ibid., p. 10.

127. Ibid.

128. Zhou, "Jiu meng" (Old dreams), *Ziji di yuandi*, *ZZRQJ*, 2: 83–85.

129. Ibid., pp. 83–84.

130. Ibid., p. 83.

131. Ibid., p. 84.

132. Yuan Hongdao, "Xu Chen Zhengfu huixin ji" (Preface to Chen Zhengfu's 'Intuition' Collection), in *Yuan Hongdao ji jianjiao*, juan 10, vol. 1, pp. 463–65. See also the discussion and full translation in Pollard, *A Chinese Look at Literature*, pp. 79–80, and the discussion in Chaves, "The Panoply of Images," p. 345, both of which I have consulted to great profit.

133. Chaves, "The Panoply of Images," p. 345.

134. Ch'ien, *Chiao Hung*, pp. 77–78.

135. Ibid., p. 78.

136. Ibid., p. 79. Cf. Huang Tsung-hsi, *Records of the Ming Scholars*, p. 176, on Wang Gen: "He taught that the daily activity of the common people was the Dao, and he pointed in illustration of this to the unfailing naturalness of domestic servants in the midst of their every activity."

137. De Bary, "Individualism and Humanitarianism," p. 200.

138. Chih-p'ing Chou, *Yuan Hung-tao and the Kung-an School*, pp. 105–12.

139. Zhou, "Yuan Yuan he chang ji" (Collection of poetry exchanged by the two Yuans), *Yaowei ji*, ZZRQJ, 4: 298–99.

140. Zhou, "Qing jia lu" (Qing jia records), *Ye du chao*, ZZRQJ, 2: 524–25.

141. Pollard, *A Chinese Look at Literature*, p. 133, quotes the relevant passage as "Observe the patterns in the sky (*t'ien wen*) to discover the seasons' changes."

142. Chaves, "The Panoply of Images," p. 345.

143. Zhou, "Li Weng yu Sui Yuan" (Li Weng [Li Yu] and Sui Yuan [Yuan Mei]), *Ku zhu zaji*, ZZRQJ, 3: 441–44.

144. See the entries on Li Yu and Yuan Mei in Hummel, *Eminent Chinese of the Ch'ing Period*, and Nienhauser et al., *Indiana Companion*.

145. Zhou, "Li Weng yu Sui Yuan," ZZRQJ, 3: 442.

146. Ibid., ZZRQJ, 3: 441, 443.

147. Ch'ien, *Chiao Hung*, p. 76. See also Wang Yangming, "Inquiry on the Great Learning," in Chan, *A Sourcebook of Chinese Philosophy*, pp. 659–61. Wang held that "the great man regards Heaven and Earth and the myriad things as one body," feels commiseration for other humans and animals, and even feels regret over broken tiles and stones.

148. Identified variously as Mind (*xin*), nature (*xing*), and the principle of Heaven (*tian li*). See Ch'ien, *Chiao Hung*, pp. 79–86.

149. Zhou, "Li Weng yu Sui Yuan," ZZRQJ, 3: 443.

150. Ibid.

151. Clunas, *Superfluous Things*, p. 171.

152. Ibid., pp. 88–89.

153. Ibid., p. 190n55.

154. Zhou, "Li Weng yu Sui Yuan," ZZRQJ, 3: 442.

155. Chih-p'ing Chou, *Yuan Hung-tao and the Kung-an School*, pp. 21–23.

156. Clunas, *Superfluous Things*, p. 62. Referring to menial crafts, Zhang commented, "There is nothing under the sun which is not sufficient of itself to ennoble someone; it is simply that people will consider them as 'menial.'"

157. Zhou, "Chong kan Yuan Zhonglang ji xu," *ZZRQJ*, 3: 44.

158. Ibid.

159. Zhou, "Bense," *Feng yu tan*, *ZZRQJ*, 3: 277–79. To my knowledge, this is Zhou's only discussion of *bense*.

160. Pollard, *A Chinese Look at Literature*, pp. 62–64.

161. Tu, "Neo-Confucianism and Literary Criticism in Ming China," p. 553.

162. Ching-yi Tu, "T'ang Shun-chih," in Nienhauser et al., *Indiana Companion*, s.v.

163. Tu, "Neo-Confucianism and Literary Criticism in Ming China," pp. 550–56.

164. Tang Shunzhi, "Da Mao Lumen zhi xian er" (Second reply to Magistrate Mao Lumen [Mao Kun; 1512–1601]), in Guo Shaoyu et al., *Zhongguo lidai wenxue lunzhu jingxuan*, 2: 294–95.

165. Ibid., p. 295.

166. Gong, *Shishi miaowu yu bense*, p. 126.

167. Zhou, "Bense," *ZZRQJ*, 3: 277.

168. See Wu Hongyi, *Qingdai shixue chutan*, pp. 113–16.

169. Pauline Yu, "Canon Formation in Late Imperial China," p. 96.

170. Gong, *Shishi bense yu miaowu*, p. 130.

171. Ibid., p. 129n45; Pauline Yu, "Canon Formation in Late Imperial China," p. 96.

172. Gong, *Shishi bense yu miaowu*, p. 129n45.

173. Qian's views are quoted at some length in Che, "Not Words but Feelings."

174. Wu Hongyi, *Qingdai shixue chutan*, pp. 121–22.

175. See Che, "Not Words but Feelings," p. 59.

176. Yoshikawa, *Five Hundred Years of Chinese Poetry*, pp. 188–89.

177. Wu Hongyi, *Qingdai shixue chutan*, pp. 61–65.

178. Ibid., p. 108.

179. Ibid., p. 122.

180. Ibid., pp. 136–38.

181. Thus he said: "Sikong Tu's 'It does not inhere in any single word / Yet the utmost flair is obtained' is the theory of personal emotion and nature (*xing qing*). Yang Xiong's (53 B.C.E.-C.E 18) 'Read a thousand *fu* poems and then you can write one' is the theory of learning. The two are complementary" (cited in ibid., p. 176). I have taken the translation of Sikong Tu's phrase *bu zhuo yi zi / jin de fengliu* from Owen, *Readings in Chinese Literary Thought*, p. 326.

182. Wu Hongyi, *Qingdai shixue chutan*, pp. 167–76; Lynn, "Orthodoxy and Enlightenment," pp. 240–57.

183. For a painstaking discussion of the meaning of *shenyun*, see Lynn, "Orthodoxy and Enlightenment," pp. 246–53. Lynn (p. 253) concludes that *shenyun* is a

catch-all term in Wang's criticism referring to personal tone, intuitive cognition, and intuitive control or various combinations of the three. Wu Hongyi (*Qingdai shixue chutan*, p. 170) equates *shenyun* and *qingyuan* (pure and distant) through the following abbreviated quotation from Wang: "Poetry is to express one's personal nature, but to be worthy of esteem, it must be pure and distant . . . the summation of this marvel lies in *shenyun*" (translation from Lynn, "Orthodoxy and Enlightenment," p. 248) But, unlike previous scholars including Guo Shaoyu, Wu (pp. 171–73) also considers *shenyun* to include the notions of enlightenment associated with Yan Yu and Sikong. I prefer Wu's interpretation because it is less restricted to formal considerations than those of the other scholars he quotes.

184. See Ch'ien, *Chiao Hung*, pp. 241–78. I am not attributing the archaist view to Yan Yu in this instance because of his assertion that "poetry is to tell one's inborn nature" in the context of his discussion of *miaowu*.

185. See Wu Hongyi, *Qingdai shixue chutan*, pp. 184–85; Siu-Kit Wong, "T'an-lung lu," in Nienhauser et al., *Indiana Companion*, s.v.; Zhang Jian, *Ming Qing wenxue piping*, p. 168.

186. Wu Hongyi, *Qingdai shixue chutan*, pp. 29–31.

187. Tu Lien-che, "Hao I-hsing," in Hummel, *Eminent Chinese of the Ch'ing Period*, s.v. Zhou was impressed with this aspect of Hao's learning; see his "Ji haicuo" (Records of *haicuo* [a type of seafood]), *Feng yu tan, ZZRQJ*, 3: 273–77.

188. Zhou, "Bense," *ZZRQJ*, 3: 277.

189. Ibid.

190. Ibid., pp. 277–78.

191. Ibid., p. 278.

192. Ch'ien, *Chiao Hung*, pp. 218, 231; idem, "Neither Structuralism nor Lovejoy's History of Ideas: A Disidentification with Professor Ying-shih Yu's Review as a Dis-course," pp. 65–66. The review referred to in the title of Ch'ien's article is Ying-shih Yu, "The Intellectual World of Chiao Hung Revisited: A Review Article."

193. Zhou, "Bense," *ZZRQJ*, 3: 278.

194. Ibid.

195. Ibid., p. 279.

196. Gong, *Shishi bense yu miaowu*, pp. 110–11. Wang Jide classified *Pipa ji* as an example of the northern style, which he contrasted with the later *Xiangnang ji* (Perfumed brocade bag).

197. Ch'ien, *Chiao Hung*, p. 76.

198. Ibid.

199. Wilson, *Genealogy of the Way*, p. 103.

200. Ch'ien, *Chiao Hung*, p. 188.

201. See the discussion in ibid., pp. 180–94.

202. Zhou Zhenfu, "Bense," in idem, *Wenzhang lihua*, pp. 117–20.

203. Ibid., p. 118 The source of the quotation from Huang Zongxi is not given.

204. Zhou, "Chun zai tang zawen" (Miscellaneous essays of Chun zai tang [Yu Yue]), *Yaowei ji*, *ZZRQJ*, 4: 311–15.

205. Since the early 1930s was a period when *xiaopin* and *sanwen* essay writing flourished to the extent that "how to" books for would-be writers became very popular, Zhou may have wanted to reiterate the need for independent thinking rather forcefully. But this circumstance alone cannot account for his stance. See Yu Shusen, "Xiandai sanwen lilun niaokan," pp. 13–15.

206. Zhou, "Bense," *ZZRQJ*, 3:279.

207. Zhou, "Chun zai tang zawen," *ZZRQJ*, 4: 312.

208. Ibid., p. 313.

209. Hao Yixing, "Bense."

210. Ch'ien, *Chiao Hung*, p. 258. Ch'ien (pp. 253–65) provides an illuminating discussion of how the different attitudes to reading of Zhu Xi and Lu Xiangshan (1139–93) exemplified their differently structured conceptions of the self.

211. Wu Hongyi, *Qingdai shixue chutan*, p. 119.

212. Zhou, "Riji yu chidu" (Diaries and letters), *Yu tian de shu*, *ZZRQJ*, 2: 272.

213. Zhou, "Diwu jiang: Wenxue geming yundong" (Fifth lecture: the movement for literary revolution), *Zhongguo xin wenxue de yuanliu*, *ZZRQJ*, 5: 358–59.

## Chapter 4

1. Zhou, "Moxuyou xiansheng zhuan xu" (Preface to *Moxuyou xiansheng zhuan*), *Biance* 1, no. 3 (Mar. 1932), *ZTSH*, 2: 936–38. The passage Zhou quotes is translated as follows in Graham, *Chuang-Tzu*, pp. 48–49: "That hugest of clumps of soil [i.e. the universe, according to Graham, p. 49] blows out breath, by name the 'wind.' Better if it were never to start up, for whenever it does ten thousand hollow places burst out howling, and don't tell me you have never heard how the hubbub swells! The recesses in mountain forests, the hollows that pit great trees a hundred spans round, are like nostrils, like mouths, like ears, like sockets, like bowls, like mortars, like pools, like puddles. Hooting, hissing, sniffing, sucking, mumbling, moaning, whistling, wailing, the winds ahead sing out AAAH!, the winds behind answer EEEH!, breezes strike up a tiny chorus, the whirlwind a mighty chorus. When the gale has passed, all the hollows empty, and don't tell me you have never seen how the quivering slows and settles!"

2. Zhou, "Yu Fei Mingjun shu shiqi tong" (Seventeen letters to Fei Ming), letter no. 16, *Zhou Zuoren shuxin*, *ZZRQJ*, 5: 146.

3. Zhu Guangqian, "Yu tian de shu."

4. Zhou, "Meiwen" (Belles lettres), *Tan hu ji*, *ZZRQJ*, 1: 201.

5. See Kang-i Sun Chang, "Chinese 'Lyric Criticism' in the Six Dynasties." Wu

Hongyi (*Qingdai shixue chutan*, p. 5) has noted that Qing *shihua* (personal comments on poetry) and the portmanteau category of *biji* were often indistinguishable.

6. Pollard (*A Chinese Look at Literature*, p. 106) comments that Zhou never discusses the English essay in any detail and concludes: "As it was almost indecent to mention Chinese literature except as an afterthought during the May Fourth period, [Zhou's] pretension to familiarity with the English essay is understandable, but fortunately it was soon discarded."

7. Agreeing with English critics who found that Lang's writing lacked depth and staying power, Zhou argued that Lang's multifaceted erudition brought its own stamp and flavor to his work; see "Xisu yu shenhua" (Custom and myth), *Ye du chao*, ZZRQJ, 2: 477–78.

8. Alexander Kuprin (1870–1938). Zhou had translated this piece in his *Dian di* collection (Pollard, *A Chinese Look at Literature*, p. 105).

9. Li Zhi, "Tongxin shuo" in Guo Shaoyu et al., *Zhongguo lidai wenxue lunzhu jingxuan*, 2: 332; see Billeter, *Li Zhi*, pp. 250–54. For a useful discussion of the semantic and textual antecedents of the expression *tongxin*, see Zuo Dongling, *Li Zhi yu wan Ming wenxue sixiang*, pp. 160–66.

10. Li Zhi, "Tongxin shuo," in Guo Shaoyu et al., *Zhongguo lidai wenxue lunzhu jingxuan*, 2: 332.

11. Hsiao, "Li Chih," p. 811, citing Li Zhi's second letter in reply to Geng Dingxiang (1524–96). For a discussion of Li's philosophical dispute with Geng and the text of this letter, see Billeter, *Li Zhi*, pp. 123–34.

12. Hsiao, "Li Chih," p. 811.

13. Li Zhi, "Tongxin shuo," in Guo Shaoyu et al., *Zhongguo lidai wenxue lunzhu jingxuan*, 2: 333.

14. Ibid.

15. Zuo Dongling, *Li Zhi yu wan Ming wenxue sixiang*, pp. 210–15.

16. Ibid., pp. 191–92.

17. Zhou, "Wenyi piping zahua" (Miscellaneous thoughts on literary criticism), *Tan long ji*, ZZRQJ, 1: 4.

18. Ibid., p. 5.

19. Ibid.

20. Zhou's quotation "da jiang yu ren yi gui ju, bu neng yu ren qiao," is a paraphrase of *Mencius*, 7B.5.

21. Zhou, "Wenyi piping zahua," ZZRQJ, 1: 5.

22. Ibid.

23. Ibid., p. 6.

24. Zhou, "Ziji de yuandi jiu xu" (Old preface for *In My Own Garden*), *Tan long ji*, ZZRQJ, 1: 23–25.

25. Ibid., p. 24.

26. Ibid., pp. 24–25.

27. McDougall, *The Introduction of Western Literary Theories into China, 1919–1925*, pp. 239–48; Gálik, *The Genesis of Modern Chinese Literary Criticism*, pp. 88–93.

28. Guo's article "Piping—xinchang—jiancha" (Criticism, appreciation, examination), published in *Chuangzao zhoukan* (Creation monthly) in October 1923, took exception to Zhou's assertion in "*Ziji di yuandi jiu xu*" that criticism was "subjective appreciation rather than objective examination" (McDougall, *Introduction of Western Literary Theories*, p. 240). Gálik (*The Genesis of Modern Chinese Literary Criticism*, p. 90) suggests that Cheng's article "Zhuguandi yu keguandi" (Objective and subjective), published in the first issue of *Creation Monthly*, may have been written in response to Zhou's "Wenyi piping zahua" (Miscellaneous thoughts on literary criticism).

29. Cheng Fangwu, "Jianshe di piping lun" (On constructive criticism), *Shiming* (The mission), Shanghai, 1927, cited in Gálik, *The Genesis of Modern Chinese Literary Criticism*, p. 80.

30. Zhou, "Yinian de zhangjin" (My progress over the past year), *Yu tian de shu*, *ZZRQJ*, 2: 343.

31. Ibid.

32. On Zhang (Carsun Chang), see Boorman et al., *Biographical Dictionary of Republican China*, s.v. Chang Chia-sen; Hao Chang, "New Confucianism and the Intellectual Crisis of Contemporary China"; and Jeans, *Democracy and Socialism in Republican China*.

33. Furth, "Intellectual Change, 1895–1920," p. 372.

34. Zhou's comments were made in a speech published under the title "The Question of Religion" ("Zongjiao wenti") on May 15, 1921, in *Young China* (*Shaonian Zhongguo*). See *Nianpu*, p. 113. For the text, see *JWW*, 1: 338–42. Since Zhou had been hospitalized since March, the speech must have been made earlier. However, Zhou allowed it to be published just days before he began writing the series of letters from the Biyun Temple to Sun Fuyuan in which he began to resolve his mental struggle over being unable to reconcile the many kinds of thinking he found attractive. Some of the arguments and examples about the relationship between literature and religion he formulated here were repeated in his talks on the origin of modern Chinese literature.

35. Jeans, *Democracy and Socialism in Republican China*, p. 3. On Zhang's activities after his return to China in 1922, see ibid., pp. 62–63.

36. See Gálik, *The Genesis of Modern Chinese Literary Criticism*, pp. 129–41.

37. Ibid., pp. 131–32.

38. Ibid., 142–65.

39. It is unlikely that Zhou and Lu Xun had much, if any, contact. Lu Xun's account of his association with *Yusi* suggests that he was not present at its founding meeting. It also makes clear that he became involved at Sun Fuyuan's request. See

"Wo yu *Yusi* de shizhong" (My involvement with *Yusi* from beginning to end), *San xian ji* (Three Leisures Collection), *LXQJ*, 4: 164–75. See *Nianpu*, p. 177.

40. Zhou, "*Yusi* fakan ci" (Publication announcement of *Yusi*), *JWW*, 1: 623.

41. Ibid.

42. Lee, *Voices from the Iron House*, p. 151.

43. For Lu Xun's ripostes to his attackers, see his "Xu yan" (Preface), *San xian ji* (Three leisures collection), *LXQJ*, 4: 6.

44. Amintendranath Tagore, *Literary Debates in Modern China*, p. 124, describes the League as coming to dominate intellectual life in China. With the contemporary scholarly reassessment of twentieth-century Chinese literary history, Tagore's judgment may be seen as somewhat overstated. However, the League had branches in Peking and Tokyo, with sub-branches in Nanjing and Guangzhou, and attracted nearly 300 writers, "amounting to a sizeable proportion of writers and critics in China at that time," according to McDougall and Kam, *The Literature of China in the Twentieth Century*, p. 25.

45. Zhou, "Xu" (Preface), *Zexie ji* (Water plantain collection) *ZZRQJ*, 1: 131. The book was subtitled "the third little book from the Bitter Rain Studio (*ku yu zhai xiao shu zhi san*)" by Shanghai Beixin shuju, its publishers. The publishers may have wanted to retroactively establish *Ziji de yuandi* and *Yu tian de shu*, both of which they had also published, as the first and second in a series. Zhou's *Yongri ji* (Endless days) collection was published as the fourth in the series. Information taken from *Ziliao*, pp. 818–30.

46. Zhou, "Pengshang" (Meeting with harm), *Zexie ji*, *ZZRQJ*, 1: 176–77.

47. Ibid., p. 177.

48. Zhou, "Ku yu" (Bitter rain), *Zexie ji*, *ZZRQJ*, 1: 149–50.

49. Ibid., pp. 149–52.

50. Zhou, "Xianhua size" (Four idle digressions), *Zexie ji*, *ZZRQJ*, 1: 180–81.

51. Zhou, "Tian zu" (Natural feet), *Tan hu ji*, *ZZRQJ*, 1: 212–13. The essay is dated August 1921.

52. For an example of such a view, see Amitendranath Tagore, *Literary Debates in Modern China*, p. 61.

53. Zhou, "Liangge gui" (Two demons), *Tan hu ji*, *ZZRQJ*, 1: 334.

54. Ibid., pp. 334–35.

55. Zhou, "Shan zhong zaxin—liu" (Miscellaneous letters from the mountains—number six), *Yu tian de shu*, *ZZRQJ*, 2: 356.

56. See *Zhou Zuoren shi quanbian jianzhu*, pp. 280–87, for the verses and some of the many responses they elicited. See also Wolff, *Chou Tso-jen*, pp. 78–80.

57. Qian, *Fanren de bei'ai*, p. 97.

58. Bauer, "The Hidden Hero."

59. Qian, *Fanren de bei'ai*, p. 91. Other writers associated with the journal were Yu Pingbo, Xu Zuzheng (1895–1978), Liang Yuchun (1905–32), and Xu Yunuo (1893–1958), according to *Nianpu*, p. 280.

60. *"Luotuo cao fakan ci"* (Inaugural statement of *Camel Grass* journal), cited in Qian, *Fanren de bei'ai*, p. 91.

61. Sima Changfeng, *Zhongguo xin wenxue shi*, juan 2, p. 145.

62. Zhou, "Houji" (Afterword), *Ye du chao* (Notes from night reading), ZZRQJ, 2: 607.

63. Zhou, "Yu Yu Pingbojun shu sanshiwu tong (yi)" (Thirty-five letters to Yu Pingbo, no. 1), *Zhou Zuoren shuxin*, ZZRQJ, 5: 128.

64. Zhou, *"Tao'an mengyi xu"* (Preface to the *Recollections of Tao'an's Past Dreams*), *Zexie ji*, ZZRQJ, 1: 139.

65. Zhou, *"Zaban ji ba"* (Colophon to [Yu Pingbo's] *A Table Laid with Sweets and Nuts*), *Yongri ji*, ZZRQJ, 1: 499.

66. Zhou, *"Yan zhi cao ba"* (Colophon to [Yu Pingbo's] *Yan zhi cao*), *Yongri ji*, ZZRQJ, 1: 501.

67. See their *"Xuyu sanwen,"* in Yu Shusen, *Xiandai zuojia tan sanwen*, pp. 14–16.

68. Zhu Ziqing, "Lun xiandai Zhongguo di xiaopin sanwen" (On the modern Chinese *xiaopin* essay), in Yu Shusen, *Xiandai zuojia tan sanwen*, p. 46. This essay was dated July 31, 1928, and was undoubtedly written in response to Zhou's *"Zaban ji ba"* which is dated May 26, 1928.

69. Yu Shusen, "Xiandai sanwen lilun niaokan," pp. 15–17. Yu's sources, contained in the body of the book, are Zhou's preface to *Tao'an mengyi*; Lu Xun's "Xiaopinwen de weiji" (The crisis of the *xiaopin wen*); and Fang Fei's "Xiandai suibi zhi chansheng" (The production of the modern informal essay). He notes that the article by Feng Sanmei titled "Xiaopin wen yu xiandai shenghuo" (The *xiaopin wen* and contemporary life) appeared in October 1928 in the first issue of *Dajiang yuekan* (Big river monthly).

70. Hsia, *A History of Modern Chinese Fiction*, p. 132.

71. Lin Yutang, *A History of the Press and Public Opinion in China*, p. 127.

72. Lin Yutang, *"Renjian shi* fakan ci" (Inaugural statement of *This Human World*), in Yu Shusen, *Xiandai zuojia tan sanwen*, pp. 95–96.

73. Hsia, *A History of Modern Chinese Fiction*, 131–34.

74. Zhou, "'Zhongguo xin wenxue daxi. sanwen yiji' bianxuan ganxiang" (Thoughts on editing the *Compendium of Modern Chinese Literature: Essays*, vol. 1), *Xin xiaoshuo* 1, no. 2 (Feb. 15, 1935), and JWW, 2: 404. The general editor of the *Compendium* was Zhao Jiabi (1908– ).

75. Lu Xun, "Xiaopin wen de weiji" (The crisis of the *xiaopin wen*), *Nanqiang beidiao ji*, LXQJ, 4: 574–77.

76. See Lee, *Voices from the Iron House*, pp. 173–89.

77. A Ying, "Xiaopin wen tan" (On the *xiaopin wen*), in Yu Shusen, *Xiandai zuojia tan sanwen*, pp. 72–77.

78. Zhou, "Cangying," *Zexie ji*, ZZRQJ, 1: 131–34. A Ying ("Xiaopin wen tan," in Yu Shusen, *Xiandai zuojia tan sanwen*, p. 74) gives its date of publication in *Xiaoshuo yuebao* as 1922.

79. A Ying, "Xiaopin wen tan," in Yu Shusen, *Xiandai zuojia tan sanwen*, p. 76.

80. Zhou, "Feng yu tan xiao yin" (Small preface to *Talks in Wind and Rain*), *Feng yu tan*, ZZRQJ, 3: 259–60.

81. Partha Chatterjee, *Nationalist Thought and the Colonial World*, p. 17.

82. See the interesting discussion in Lydia Liu, *Translingual Practice*, pp. 133–43.

83. Chih-p'ing Chou, *Yuan Hung-tao and the Kung-an School*, p. 146.

84. Lin Yutang, "Lun xiaopin wen bidiao" (On the literary tone of *xiaopin wen*), in Yu Shusen, *Xiandai zuojia tan sanwen*, p. 111.

85. Ibid., p. 113.

86. Lin Yutang, "Xiaopin wen zhi yixu" (The inherited business of *xiaopin wen*), in Yu Shusen, *Xiandai zuojia tan sanwen*, p. 119.

87. Taylor, *Sources of the Self*, p. 211.

88. Zhou, "Zaban ji ba," ZZRQJ, 1: 499.

89. Zhou, "'Zhongguo xin wenxue daxi: sanwen yi ji' daoyan," (Preface to *Compendium of New Chinese Literature: Essays, the first collection*), in Yu Shushen, *Xiandai zuojia tan sanwen*, p. 249. Zhou's preface is dated August 1935.

90. Ibid., p. 251.

91. Ibid., p. 252. I have not identified the source of this quotation.

92. Zhou, "Wode zaxue: ershi" (My miscellaneous learning: twenty), *Kukou gankou*, ZZRQJ, 5: 443. As will be clear from the discussion which follows, in translating *yi* as "intention," I am following Van Zoeren.

93. Ching-mao Cheng, "Zhou Zuoren de Riben jingyan," p. 885.

94. See Legge, *Mencius*, 5A.iv, for the phrase *yi yi ni zhi, shi wei de zhi*.

95. Van Zoeren, *Poetry and Personality*, p. 73.

96. *Zhuangzi*, chap. 26 ("Waiwu"), cited in ibid., pp. 162–63.

97. Van Zoeren, *Poetry and Personality*, p. 196.

98. Gunn, *Unwelcome Muse*, pp. 151–71; idem, *Rewriting Chinese*, p. 119.

99. Ch'ien, *Chiao Hung*, pp. 86–92.

100. Ibid., p. 90.

101. Taylor, *Sources of the Self*, p. 396.

102. Ibid., pp. 401–10.

103. Gálik, *The Genesis of Modern Chinese Literary Criticism*, pp. 72–85.

104. Ching-mao Cheng, "Zhou Zuoren de Riben jingyan," pp. 881–83. Cheng identifies the four basic components in Shirakaba ideology as (1) Tolstoyan humanitarianism, (2) European humanism as developed since the Renaissance (in

Taylor's terms, the "affirmation of ordinary life"), (3) Christian universal love, (4) Western liberal democratic, individualistic, and utopian thinking. Shirakaba influence is visible in "A Literature of Man" in the questions treated: mankind's evolution, the discovery of "man," an evolutionary view of literature, the soul and the body, animal nature and human nature, relations between parents and children and love, desire and morality; in phraseology; in concepts such as the will of mankind, human and inhuman life, and morality; in the authorities cited: Jesus, Tolstoy, Dostoyevsky, Turgenev, Blake, and Whitman. Finally, Cheng says, Zhou's diaries of the time show the extent of Shirakaba influence on him.

105. Zhou, "Ren de wenxue," *Yishu yu shenghuo*, ZZRQJ, 3: 564.

106. Ibid., p. 567.

107. Ibid., p. 572.

108. Zhou, "Zixu" (Preface), *Yishu yu shenghuo*, ZZRQJ, 3: 559.

109. Zhou, "Jiaoxun di wuyong" (The uselessness of moral instruction), *Yu tian de shu*, ZZRQJ, 2: 337.

110. Zhou, "Xiao he yu Xin cun (xia)" (The stream and the New Village [movement], pt. II), ZTHXL, 2: 393.

111. Pollard, *A Chinese Look at Literature*, p. 120.

112. For a useful selection, see *Ziliao*, pp. 313–98.

113. See Yamamoto and Yamamoto, "Religion and Modernization in the Far East"; and Lutz, *Chinese Politics and Christian Missions*.

114. Wolff, *Chou Tso-jen*, p. 61. In "Guanyu fei zongjiao" (On opposing religion), *Tan hu ji*, ZZRQJ, 1: 331–32, written in 1927, Zhou refers to his opposition to the 1922 movement.

115. Shu Wu, "Ziwo, kuanrong, youhuan." Shu (p. 66) comments that Zhou seems to have intentionally diluted the impact of the conflict in his works so much that he (Shu) had been unaware of it until he read an article by the Japanese scholar Ozaki Fumiaki, "Yu Chen Duxiu fen dao yang biao de Zhou Zuoren" (Zhou Zuoren's decisive parting of ways with Chen Duxiu [Japanese title not given]) in *Riben xuezhe yanjiu xiandai wenxue lunwen xuancui* (Choice distillation of research articles by Japanese scholars on modern literature), ed. Ito Takemaru, Liu Boqing, et al. (n.p.: Jilin University Press, 1987). Zhou's intervention in the movement is covered in Qian, *Fanren de bei'ai*, pp. 26–31.

116. Yamamoto and Yamamoto, "Religion and Modernization in the Far East," p. 138.

117. Qian, *Fanren de bei'ai*, p. 27.

118. Ibid.; Shu, "Ziwo, kuanrong, youhuan," p. 67.

119. Zhou, "Zhuzhang xinjiao ziyouzhe de xuanyan" (Manifesto advocating freedom of religious belief), JWW, 1: 395.

120. Qian, *Fanren de bei'ai*, p. 28.

121. Zhou, "Gu jin zhong wai pai" (The ancient-modern-Chinese-foreign school), *JWW*, 1: 403, cited in Qian, *Fanren de bei'ai*, p. 28.

122. Text as cited in Qian, *Fanren de bei'ai*, p. 28. The first part of the quotation is from Zhou, "Sixiang yapo de liming" (The dawn of the oppression of thought), carried in *Chenbao*, Apr. 11, 1922, *JWW*, 1: 408–9. I have been unable to positively identify the source for the part following the ellipses.

123. Qian, *Fanren de bei'ai*, p. 76n48.

124. Zhou, "Xinjiao ziyou de taolun—zhi Chen Duxiu" (The discussion on freedom of religion—to Chen Duxiu), *JWW*, 1: 407, cited in Qian, *Fanren de bei'ai*, p. 30.

125. See Goldman, *Literary Dissent in Communist China*.

126. Chow Tse-tsung, *The May Fourth Movement*, p. 324.

127. As random examples, see "Tiji" (Foreword), *Gua dou ji, ZZRQJ*, 4: 3; "Dunyin zalu" (Miscellaneous notes of Dunyin [Feng Ban]), *Feng yu tan, ZZRQJ*, 3: 279–82.

128. Zhou, "Qingpu Zijue (i.e., Kiyoura Shishaku) zhi teshu lijie" (The special understanding of Viscount Kiyoura), *Tan hu ji, ZZRQJ*, 1: 398. Zhou had seen Kiyoura's comments in a newspaper report.

129. Ibid., p. 399.

130. Hashikawa, "Japanese Perspectives on Asia," pp. 342–43.

131. Zhou, "Xin jiu yixue douzheng yu fugu" (The struggle between old and new medicine and archaism), *Yongri ji, ZZRQJ*, 1: 508–10.

132. Boorman et al., *Biographical Dictionary of Republican China*, s.v. Chang Shih-chao.

133. Zhou, "Zuxian congbai" (Ancestor worship), *Tan hu ji, ZZRQJ*, 1: 186–88.

134. Zhou, "Fa-bu-er *Kunchong ji*" (Fabre's *Insect Life*), *Ziji de yuandi, ZZRQJ*, 2: 59.

135. Zhou, "Wode zaxue: jiu" (My miscellaneous learning: nine), *Kukou gankou, ZZRQJ*, 5: 425–26. Cf. *Analects*, 17.9, where Confucius lists as a reason for studying the *Odes*: "From them we become largely acquainted with the names of beasts and plants."

136. Zhou, "Cangying," *Zexie ji, ZZRQJ*, 1: 132.

137. Ibid., p. 133.

138. Zhou, "Shanzhong za xin—er," (Miscellaneous letters from the mountains—two), *Yu tian de shu, ZZRQJ*, 2: 350.

139. Zhou, "Dongjing zhi shudian" (Tokyo bookshops), *Gua dou ji, ZZRQJ*, 4: 57.

140. Robinson, *The Modernization of Sex*, p. 3.

141. Ibid., p. 24.

142. Ibid., p. 21.

143. Zhou translates a passage on the topic in his "He-li-si ganxiang lu chao" (Copied from Ellis's *Impressions and Comments*), *Yongri ji, ZZRQJ*, 1: 488–89.

144. Wolff, *Chou Tso-jen*, p. 41.

145. Rowbotham and Weeks, *Socialism and the New Life*.

146. Ellis, *Impressions and Comments*, p. 139. Zhou quotes almost exclusively from *Affirmations* and the three volumes of *Impressions and Comments* (1913–24), for bibliographic details of which, see "He-li-si ganxiang lu chao," *ZZRQJ*, 1: 492. Given the Bergsonian impulse in Ellis's thinking, it is not out of place to recall Leo Lee's comment that Bergson's philosophy "fits nicely into a familiar framework of Chinese cosmological thinking which focuses on the metaphysical qualities of the *qi*" including the "varieties [of *qi*] found in Neo-Confucianism" (Lee, "In Search of Modernity," p. 119). However, I believe that Zhou would have been skeptical about Bergson, not least because of the support such ideas could give to the forces of reaction in China.

147. Robinson, *The Modernization of Sex*, p. 29.

148. Ibid., pp. 30–31.

149. See Zhou, "He-li-si de hua" (Ellis's words) and "Shenghuo de yishu" (The art of living) in *Yu tian de shu*, *ZZRQJ*, 2: 320–22 and 322–24, respectively. The source is Ellis's essay "St. Francis and Others," in *Affirmations*, pp. 220–221.

150. Zhou, "Shenghuo de yishu," *ZZRQJ*, 2: 322–23.

151. Zhou, "Shanghai qi" (Shanghai style), *Tan long ji*, *ZZRQJ*, 1: 67–68.

152. Rowbotham and Weeks, *Socialism and the New Life*, pp. 168–70.

153. For some of the implications of this, see Alison M. Jaggar, "Human Biology in Feminist Theory," pp. 78–89.

154. De Bary, "Individualism and Humanitarianism," pp. 197–98. For a translation of Li Zhi's "Fufulun" (Discourse on husband and wife), see Billeter, *Li Zhi*, pp. 229–30.

155. Ellis, *Affirmations*, p. 224.

156. Robinson, *The Modernization of Sex*, p. 34. Ellis's eugenicist ideas should be seen in the context of a social reformist discourse which linked women's control over their bodies through birth control and access to abortion to racial progress. See Rowbotham and Weeks, *Socialism and the New Life*, pp. 174–78.

157. Zhou, "Weixie lun" (On obscenity), *Ziji de yuandi*, *ZZRQJ*, 2: 60–62.

158. See Dikotter, *The Discourse of Race in Modern China*, pp. 169–73.

159. Robinson, *The Modernization of Sex*, p. 39.

160. Ellis, "The Significance of War," chap. in *My Confessional*, p. 65.

161. Ellis (*Affirmations*, p. 79) praised Nietzsche thus: "From first to last, wherever you open his books, you light on sayings that cut to the core of the questions that every modern thinking man must face." What he most appreciated was Nietzsche's rejection of unthinking obedience to received morality. But he distinguished (p. 68) between a "middle period" from 1876 to 1883 in Nietzsche's work, which produced his best thinking, and the subsequent period in which "his thinking became intem-

perate, reckless, desperate"(p. 70), and he "grew to worship cruel strength" (p. 73). *Zarathustra*, written between 1883 and 1885, thus falls into Nietzsche's "last period."

162. Ellis, *Affirmations*, p. 227.

163. See the following in *Ziji di yuandi*, in ZZRQJ, 2: "Meng" (Dreams), on Schreiner, pp. 92–95; "Jiehun di ai" (Married love), on Stopes, pp. 87–89; "Ai di chuangzao" (The creation of love), on Yosano, pp. 89–92; Zhou, "'Zhencao lun' yiji" (Notes on the translation of [Yosano's] "On Chastity"), *JWW*, 1: 269.

164. See, e.g., the following in *Ziji di yuandi*, ZZRQJ, 2: "Ertong di shu" (Children's books), pp. 78–80; "Wanju" (Toys), pp. 76–78; "Ertong ju" (Children's plays), pp. 73–75. See also "Kongde xuexiao jinian ri de jiu hua" (Old words on the Comte School Memorial Day), *Ku zhu za ji*, ZZRQJ, 3: 550–51.

165. Zhou, "An de chuntian" (My spring; i.e., *Ora ga haru*), *Ziji de yuandi*, ZZRQJ, 2: 71–73.

166. Zhou, "Geyong ertong de wenxue" (In praise of children's literature), *Ziji de yuandi*, ZZRQJ, 2: 68–70.

167. Zhou, "Wode zaxue: shiyi" (My miscellaneous learning: eleven), *Kukou gankou*, ZZRQJ, 5: 428.

168. Zhou, "Guanyu Yu Lichu," *Bingzhu tan*, ZZRQJ, 3: 139–143; idem, "Han wenxue di chuantong" (Chinese literary traditions), *Yaotang zawen*, ZZRQJ, 4: 164.

169. Zhou, "Dushu de jingyan" (My reading experiences), *Yaotang zawen*, ZZRQJ, 4: 189.

170. Zhou, "Du *Chutan ji*" (Reading *The First Lake Collection*), *Yaotang zawen*, ZZRQJ, 4: 248.

171. Zhou, "Wenyishang de Eguo yu Zhongguo" (Russia and China in terms of literature), *Yishu yu shenghuo*, ZZRQJ, 3: 609.

172. Bloom, "On the Matter of the Mind."

173. As my use of the term "restructured Neo-Confucianism" at the beginning of the paragraph makes clear, my debt here in this summing up is to Edward Ch'ien. It should be evident that this was the starting point for discussion within late Ming discourse, not a conclusion.

174. Cascardi, *The Subject of Modernity*, p. 5.

175. Ibid., pp. 61 and 1–71 *passim*.

176. See ibid., p. 51, for a reference to Niklas Luhmann's theory of social differentiation, which he sources to Niklas Luhmann, "The Individuality of the Individual" in *Reconstructing Individualism*, ed. Thomas C. Heller, Morton Sosna, and David E. Wellbery (Stanford: Stanford University Press, 1986).

177. Hsiao, "Li Chih," p. 810.

178. Chow, *The Rise of Confucian Ritualism in Late Imperial China*.

179. Polachek, *The Inner Opium War*, esp. pp. 63–99, 225–35.

180. Dirlik, "Reversals, Hegemonies, Ironies." Dirlik lists Mao and Gandhi as promoters of alternative modernities. Although on one commonsense level I would agree with him, I would nonetheless clearly differentiate the two: Mao's opposition was framed in Marxist categories, reflecting Marxism's function as an internal critique of modernity, but one that never resolved the problem of the nation-state. Gandhi's view of modernity as destructive of man's capacity for truth was far more radical, notwithstanding his attempt to find an anchor for his vision of community within the nation-state.

## Chapter 5

1. Bol, "*This Culture of Ours,*" pp. 108–36.

2. On Han Yu's desire to use *guwen* as a weapon against heterodoxy, see Yu-shih Chen, *Images and Ideas in Chinese Classical Prose*, pp. 8–11.

3. Hartman, *Han Yu and the T'ang Search for Unity*, p. 155 and *passim*; McMullen, "Han Yu: An Alternative Picture."

4. Schwartz, *In Search of Wealth and Power*, pp. 64–72.

5. Zhou, "Tiji," *Gua dou ji, ZZRQJ*, 4: 4.

6. For example, in late 1921 in the preface to a volume of Eastern European short stories, Zhou wrote that the spirit of sympathy with "insulted and suffering" individuals and peoples he had felt as a student in Tokyo still ran deep. He hoped China would produce specialists in their literatures as well as in the Western European ones. See Zhou, "Xiandai xiaoshuo yicong diyi ji xuyan" (Preface to vol. 1 of the Modern Fiction in Translation series), *ZTSH*, 2: 1324. Of the thirty stories in this volume, eighteen were translated by Zhou Zuoren, nine by Lu Xun, and three by Zhou Jianren.

7. Zhou, "Sixiangjie de qingxiang" (Intellectual trends), *Tan hu ji, ZZRQJ*, 1: 236.

8. Zhou, "Guorong yu guochi" (National honor and national humiliation), *JWW*, 1: 348.

9. Zhou, "Guanyu ertong de shu" (About children's books), *Tan hu ji, ZZRQJ*, 1: 367–69.

10. Zhou, "Jingda Zheng Zhaogong xiansheng" (A respectful reply to Mr. Zheng Zhaogong), *JWW*, 1: 526.

11. Zhou, "Tichang guohuo de xinli" (The psychology of promoting national products), *JWW*, 1: 524.

12. Zhou, "Ping *Ziyou hun*" (Criticizing *Soul of Freedom*), *Tan hu ji, ZZRQJ*, 1: 371.

13. At first reading, this sentence seems to be making the shocking suggestion that it is permissible to caricature Jews (presumably because they deserve it). I think, however, that Zhou considered the Jews a special case on the grounds that they were not nationals of a particular country. In a later article, Zhou described medieval European beliefs that Jews killed Christians (as detailed in Chaucer's tale of Sir

Hugh) as a "barbaric superstition" that had "given rise to many tragedies." In fact, "in certain half-civilized parts of Europe such as Hungary and Russia, up to recent times, the belief that Jews make sacrifices of Christian children has led to many anti-Jewish acts of murder" (Zhou, "Cong Youtairen dao Tianzhujiao" [From Jews to Catholicism], *Tan hu ji, ZZRQJ,* 1: 327–30). But if Zhou did mean to condone anti-Semitism, we can only surmise that, tragically, his suspicion of capitalism may have left him open to the anti-Semitic construct linking Jews and money, which was pervasive in the 1920s and 1930s.

14. Zhou, "Ping *Ziyou hun," Tan hu ji, ZZRQJ,* 1: 372.

15. Tang Jiyao (1881–1927) was a Yunnan-based warlord and politician. See Boorman et al., *Biographical Dictionary of Republican China,* s.v. T'ang Chi-yao.

16. Zhou, "Ping *Ziyou hun," ZZRQJ,* 1: 373.

17. Zhou, "Wenxingchu de yuyan" (Astrological predictions), *Tan hu ji, ZZRQJ,* 1: 242.

18. Zhou, "Du *Jinghua bi xue lu"* (On reading *Record of Blood Shed in Righteous Death in the Capital* [by Lin Shu]), *Yu tian de shu, ZZRQJ,* 2: 385. Here Zhou is reiterating a point he made in July 1923: "I am not a nationalist, but if someone should advocate militarism, the use of armed force against foreign [enemies], I would support it as logical and reasonable because all along China has suffered through not having any real strength" (Zhou, "Hai buru junguozhuyi" [Militarism would be better], *JWW,* 1: 510).

19. Zhou, "Du *Jinghua bixue lu," ZZRQJ,* 2: 385.

20. Zhou, "Wenxingchu de yuyan," *ZZRQJ,* 1: 242.

21. Sheridan, "The Warlord Era," p. 315.

22. Waldron, *From War to Nationalism,* p. 5. It is beyond the scope of this study to engage with the revisionist thesis put forward in this work that nationalism should not be seen as a cause but as an effect produced by events.

23. Zhou, "Yuandan shi bi" (Trying out my writing brush to mark the new year), *Yu tian de shu, ZZRQJ,* 2: 344.

24. Ibid., p. 345.

25. Ibid., p. 345. The term I have translated as "anti-Manchu struggle" is *guangfu,* which refers broadly to restoration of a status quo ante. I believe Zhou is alluding here to the period during which the anti-Manchu Guangfu hui (Restoration society) was active. The society, which had a predominantly Zhejiangnese membership, included Cai Yuanpei, Zhang Binglin, and the woman martyr Qiu Jin (1879?–1907). Qiu Jin's gruesome execution in Shaoxing (which forms the background of Lu Xun's story "Medicine") shocked the Tokyo-based Zhejiang community. See "Xu Xilin shijian" (The Xu Xilin affair), *ZTHXL,* 1: 198–201.

26. Zhou, "Zixu er" (Second preface), *Yu tian de shu, ZZRQJ,* 2: 267. It is significant that Zhou chose to include "Yuandan shi bi" in this collection, one of the

themes of which is Zhou's self-reflection and self-fashioning, rather than in *Talking of Tigers*, which contains a large number of polemical pieces.

27. See, e.g., his angry responses to Japanese suggestions that the Chinese ought to restore the Qing dynasty: "Jieshao Riben ren de guailun" (Introducing the strange comments of the Japanese), *JWW*, 1: 656–58; and "Zai jieshao Riben ren de miulun" (Further introducing Japanese fallacies), *JWW*, 1: 694–95. More noteworthy is "Riben de renqingmei" (Japanese sensibilities and their beauty), *ZZRQJ*, 2: 339–41.

28. See, e.g., an article by Zhou written in 1920, "Qin Ri pai" (The pro-Japanese faction), *Yu tian de shu*, *ZZRQJ*, 2: 193.

29. Zhou, "Ribenren de haoyi" (The good intentions of the Japanese), *Tan hu ji*, *ZZRQJ*, 1: 385–87; "Zai tan *Shuntian ribao*" (More on the *Shuntian Daily*), *Tan hu ji*, *ZZRQJ*, 1: 387–89.

30. Zhou, "Tongyuan de yaojiao" (Incriminations of a copper coin), *Tan hu ji*, *ZZRQJ*, 1: 279–80.

31. Zhou, "Zhina yu wo" (Shina and dwarves), *Tan hu ji*, *ZZRQJ*, 1: 401–3.

32. Zhou, "'Ribenren de guailun' shu hou" (Written after "Strange Comments of the Japanese"), *JWW*, 1: 659.

33. Zhou, "Duiyu Shanghai shijian zhi ganyan" (My response to the Shanghai incident), *JWW*, 1: 714.

34. In January 1925, Zhou translated a *kyōgen*, and in March he translated Kenkō's *Essays in Idleness* (*Nianpu*, pp. 185, 190).

35. Zhou, "Beijing de hao sixiang" (Smart thinking in Peking), *JWW*, 2: 198.

36. *Mencius* 1A6.

37. Zhou, "Houji" (Afterword), *Tan hu ji*, *ZZRQJ*, 1: 433.

38. Zhou, "Nanbei" (North and south), *Tan hu ji*, *ZZRQJ*, 1: 266.

39. Ibid., p. 267.

40. Zhou, "Xinnian tongxin" (New year letter), *JWW*, 2: 302.

41. Zhou, "Bihu dushu lun" (Reading behind closed doors), *Yongri ji*, *ZZRQJ*, 1: 524.

42. Zhou, "Yanshi xueji" (Record of my study of the works of Yan Yuan [1635–1704] by Dai Wang [1837–73]), *Ye du chao*, *ZZRQJ*, 2: 482.

43. Ibid., 483.

44. Eastman, "Nationalist China During the Nanking Decade," p. 146.

45. Zhou, "Xiyang ye you chouchong" (The West also has bedbugs), *JWW*, 2: 388.

46. Eastman, "Nationalist China During the Nanking Decade," p. 134.

47. On the basic similarity of Nationalist and Communist nation-building goals, see Esherick, "Ten Theses on the Chinese Revolution."

48. Zhou, "Shizi jiekou de ta" (The tower at the crossroads), *Yu tian de shu*, *ZZRQJ*, 2: 307–9.

49. Ibid., p. 309.

50. See Min, *National Polity and Local Power*, pp. 137–79.

51. Zhou, "Weite xiao xue zhi yijian" (An opinion in support of primary education), *JWW*, 1: 119. Intriguingly, the article was drafted by Zhou as a letter to the head of the local county assembly and published in a Zhejiang newspaper in January 1912, signed by Lu Xun and Zhou Jianren but not by Zhou Zuoren. Without more information, it is useless to speculate on the reasons for this.

52. Duara, *Rescuing History from the Nation*, pp. 177–204.

53. Chesneaux, "The Federalist Movement in China," p. 134.

54. Zhou, "Difang yu wenyi," *ZZRQJ*, 1: 8.

55. Ibid., p. 11.

56. Zhou, "Baoding Dingxian zhi you" (A trip to Baoding in Dingxian), *Ku cha suibi, ZZRQJ*, 3: 88.

57. Wright, "From Revolution to Restoration," pp. 525–26.

58. Zhou, "'Xiaohe' he xincun" ("The Stream" and the New Village [movement]), *ZTHXL*, 2: 383–87.

59. Zhou, "Yu youren lun guomin wenxue shu," *ZZRQJ*, 2: 336.

60. Zhou, "Guizudi yu pingmindi" (Elite and popular), *Ziji de yuandi, ZZRQJ*, 2: 11–13.

61. Zhou, "Wenxue de guizuxing" (The aristocratic nature of literature), *JWW*, 2: 296. This was the text of a speech published in January 1928 in which Zhou spelled out his opposition to "revolutionary literature."

62. Ibid., p. 299.

63. Zhou, "Wenxue tan" (Literary reflections), *Tan long ji, ZZRQJ*, 1: 70.

64. Zhou, "*Ying'er shahai yinyan*" (Introduction to *Infanticide*), *Yusi*, Sept. 7, 1928; cited in *Nianpu*, p. 265.

65. See, e.g., Zhou, "Changnü lizan" (In praise of prostitution), *Kan yun ji, ZZRQJ*, 2: 150–53.

66. Zhou, "E quwei de duhai" (The harmfulness of the degradation of taste/flavor), *JWW*, 1: 451.

67. Zhou, "Waihang de anyu" (Comments from a layman), *Tan hu ji, ZZRQJ*, 1: 285–86.

68. Zhou, "Fulu yi: Lun baguwen" (Appendix 1: *Baguwen*), *Zhongguo xin wenxue de yuanliu, ZZRQJ*, 5: 363.

69. Ibid., p. 362.

70. Ibid., p. 364.

71. Ibid., p. 365.

72. Ibid., pp. 365–66.

73. Ibid., p. 362.

74. Zhou, "Tan ce lun" (Remarks on questions and themes), *Feng yu tan*, *ZZRQJ*, 3: 292–94.

75. Ibid., p. 292.

76. Ibid., p. 294. *Xiucai*: Ming/Qing term for a successful candidate in the imperial examinations at the county level.

77. "In sum, I wish to propose that *baguwen* become a subject for research. This is the crux of what I have to say, the rest can be considered as so much superfluous nonsense. Second, my suggestions certainly cannot all be reduced to irony and satire, although I have put things so indecorously" (Zhou, "Fulu yi: Lun baguwen," *ZZRQJ*, 5: 366).

78. Lu Xun, "Guanyu xin wenzi" (On the new writing system), *Qiejieting zawen*, *LXQJ*, 6: 160.

79. Zhou, "Hanzi gaige de wo jian" (My views on the reform of Chinese characters), *JWW*, 1: 480–82. The article appeared in 1922 in *National Language Monthly* (*Guoyu yuekan*), no. 7. This was a special issue on the reform of Chinese characters. In 1917 Zhou became one of four members of a research group on the reform of the written language, along with Qian Xuantong, Ma Yuzao, and Liu Wendian (1889–1958). However, according to Zhou's memoirs, the group never met for research. See "Wusi zhiqian" (Before the May Fourth Movement), *ZTHXL*, 2: 373.

80. This may have been part of a general cosmopolitan current of thought regarding the desirability of a universal written language. Elsewhere Zhou described this idea as "frankly, nothing more than an ideal." A universal language would have to be in the same relationship to the various systems of national languages as a unified national language with its dialects (Zhou, "Guoyu gaizao de yijian" [My opinions on reform of the national language], *Yishu yu shenghuo*, *ZZRQJ*, 3: 605).

81. Zhou, "Hanzi gaige de wo jian," *JWW*, 1: 480.

82. Ibid.

83. Zhou, "Guoyu gaizao de yijian," *ZZRQJ*, 3: 598.

84. Zhou, "Han wenxue de qiantu," *ZZRQJ*, 4: 181.

85. Zhou, "Guocui yu ouhua" (National essence and Europeanization), *Ziji de yuandi*, *ZZRQJ*, 2: 9.

86. See the discussion of the *Critical Review* group in Lydia Liu, *Translingual Practice*, pp. 246–56.

87. Ibid., pp. 254–55.

88. Zhou, "Guocui yu ouhua," *ZZRQJ*, 2: 9.

89. Ibid.

90. The word Zhou used here is *wenzi*, which could mean "writing system" (in the sense of script) or more broadly, "written language" in the sense of style, phraseology. Either reading is possible here.

91. Ibid., 9–10.

92. Zhou, "Guocui yu ouhua," *ZZRQJ*, 2: 10.

93. The letters Zhou wrote to Sun Fuyuan during his convalescence at the Biyun Temple in the Western Hills mention that he found some relief from his mental distress in Buddhist sutras, even as he decried the degenerate behavior of the monks; see Zhou, "Shanzhong za xin" (Miscellaneous letters from the Mountains), *Yu tian de shu*, *ZZRQJ*, 2: 347–58.

94. Benedict Anderson, *Imagined Communities*, p. 26.

95. Bakhtin, "The Bildungsroman and Its Significance in the History of Realism."

96. Ibid., p. 42.

97. Ibid., p. 25.

98. Ibid., p. 27.

99. Ibid., p. 28.

100. Wu Hongyi, *Qingdai shixue chutan*, p. 122.

101. Lu Xun brought up the distinction between eye and ear in an oblique attack on *quwei* (and no doubt Zhou) in 1934. In the preface to a collection of previously published articles, he noted that each work was accompanied by the pen-name under which it had first appeared. When the articles had first come out, his multitude of pen-names had caused some "literary figures" who "did not use their sense of vision to read with but merely relied on their sense of smell to become afraid of their own shadows. Moreover, their sense of smell has not evolved at the same rate as the rest of their bodies so that when they saw the name of a new author, they suspected it was me" (Lu Xun, "Qian ji" [Preface], *Zhun feng yue tan*, *LXQJ*, 5: 190).

102. Bakhtin, "The Bildungsroman and Its Significance in the History of Realism," p. 28.

103. Ibid., p. 34.

104. Ibid.

105. Ibid., p. 43.

106. Ibid., p. 46.

107. Ibid., p. 52.

108. Ibid., pp. 52–53.

109. Quoted in Berlin, *Vico and Herder*, pp. 179–80.

110. Partha Chatterjee, "A Response to Taylor's 'Modes of Civil Society.'"

111. Ibid., pp. 127–28.

112. Ibid., pp. 128–29.

113. Ibid.

114. Shen remarked that he "would rather fail out of the technical limits of the short story than succeed within them" (see Nieh, *Shen Ts'ung-wen*, p. 124).

115. Shen, "Duanpian xiaoshuo" (On short stories), *SCWWJ*, 12: 126; cited in David Wang, *Fictional Realism in 20th Century China*, p. 203.

116. David Wang, *Fictional Realism in 20th Century China*, p. 206.

117. Ibid., p. 210.

118. Ibid., p. 202.

119. Grant, *Realism*, pp. 49–50.

120. Ibid., pp. 52–53.

121. David Wang, *Fictional Realism in 20th Century China*, p. 210.

122. Ibid., p. 205.

123. Ibid., p. 1.

124. Shen, "Cong xianshi xuexi" (Learning from reality), *SCWWJ*, 10: 301. This essay is a retrospective view of his career written in 1946, but possibly revised in 1983 before appearing in *SCWWJ*.

125. Kinkley, *The Odyssey of Shen Congwen*, pp. 191–209.

126. Shen, "Cong xianshi xuexi," *SCWWJ*, 10: 299.

127. Ibid., p. 301.

128. Ibid., p. 309.

129. Shen, "Zhishi" (Knowledge), *SCWWJ*, 6: 292–97.

130. Shen, "Quiet," trans. William McDonald, in *Imperfect Paradise*, p. 78.

131. Wang Zengqi, "Zixu" (Preface), in idem, *Wanfanhua ji*, pp. 1–5.

132. Wang Zengqi, "Xiaoshuo sanpian: Qiu yu; Milu; Mai qiuyin de ren" (Three anecdotes: Praying for rain; Lost; The earthworm-seller), in idem, *Wanfanhua ji*, pp. 182–96.

133. Wang Zengqi, "Zixu," in idem, *Wanfanhua ji*, p. 3.

134. Wang Zengqi, "Xiaoshuo sanpian," in idem, *Wanfanhua ji*, p. 196.

135. However, Ah Cheng claimed to have been deeply impressed by reading Wang Zengqi's pastoral celebration of innocence, childhood, and love in "Shoujie" (The Initiation), written in 1980 (Ah Cheng, *Xianhua xianshuo*, pp. 187–88).

136. For the reactions of one such critic, see Zeng Zhennan, "Yicai yu shen wei."

137. L. Yang, *Chinese Fiction of the Cultural Revolution*, is an important study that substantiates many of the hitherto vague charges against this body of fiction.

138. Gang Yue's article "Surviving (in) the 'Chess King,'" written ten years after the novella's first publication, traces the trajectory of this process.

139. Ibid., p. 572.

140. See Huters, "Speaking of Many Things," which links Ah Cheng's "metaphysical" ideal of chess to the earlier abstraction of National Essence.

141. Yue, "Surviving (in) the 'Chess King,'" p. 578.

142. Ibid., pp. 583–88. On "Chess King" as a reversal of the cannibal banquet, see Catherine Yeh, "Roots Literature of the 1980s."

143. Yue, "Surviving (in) the 'Chess King,'" pp. 589–90.

144. Han, "Wenxue de gen."

145. Han, "Ba ba ba."

146. This is the reading of Liu Zaifu; cited in Lee, "On the Margins of Chinese Discourse," p. 209.

147. Han, "Kefu xiaoshuo yuyanzhong de xuesheng qi."

148. See Schneider, *Ku Chieh-kang and China's New History*, p. 266.

149. Han, *Maqiao cidian*. I am indebted to my student Julia Lovell for bringing this work to my attention.

150. Two accounts from the perspective of literary studies are Jing Wang, *High Culture Fever*, and Zhang Xudong, *Chinese Modernism in the Era of Reforms*.

151. The term "mastermind" is from Ling, "From Social Criticism to Cultural Criticism," p. 2.

152. Ibid.

153. Ibid., pp. 18–26.

154. Ibid., p. 26.

155. Ibid., p. 25.

156. Woei, "Mankind and Nature in Chinese Thought," p. 146. In what follows I have relied heavily on Woei, without, I hope, distorting too much her exceptionally erudite reading of Li.

157. Ibid., p. 150.

158. Ibid., pp. 153–54, introduces these ideas followed by a chronological account of Chinese thinking from early Confucianism to Mao (pp. 154–74).

159. Ibid., p. 175.

160. Ling, "From Social Criticism to Cultural Criticism," 21–26.

161. Zhou, "Mingling yu yinghuo" (Corn earworms and fireflies), *Feng yu tan*, ZZRQJ, 3: 294.

162. Thus Ling ("From Social Criticism to Cultural Criticism," p. 25) denies the possibility of separating Chinese tradition from its feudal content, for "What is Chinese tradition without its feudal tyranny?"

163. See Zhao, "Chinese Intellectuals Quest for National Greatness"; and Xu, "From Modernity to Chineseness."

164. Here I have borrowed the words, although not the whole context, of David Wang's discussion of Shen (*Fictional Realism in 20th Century China*, p. 218).

# Works Cited

## Works of Zhou Zuoren

The edition of Zhou Zuoren's works cited in the text is the five-volume *Zhou Zuoren quanji* 周作人全集 (Complete works of Zhou Zuoren) (Taipei: Landeng wenhua chuban, 1982; reprinted—1993), abbreviated in the notes as *ZZRQJ*. In the following description of the contents of each volume, the year of original publication is indicated for each title. Although the inclusion of Zhou's lecture notes on European literature, his joke collections, and his essays on children's literature makes this a well-rounded collection, it cannot be said to be complete. In choosing the materials for his essay collections, Zhou omitted many writings. There is as yet no complete edition (全集) of Zhou's works published in Mainland China. However, several of Zhou's essay collections have been reissued by the Yuelu shushe 岳麓書社 publishers in Changsha, Hunan; these volumes contain subject indexes and errata lists. In this respect they are superior to *ZZRQJ*. Other valuable collections have been published in China, including one of Zhou's uncollected works. Mention should be made of a recent ten-volume compilation of Zhou's works, *Zhou Zuoren wenlei bian* 周作人文類編. As the title indicates, the distinction between Zhou's previously collected and uncollected materials has been dispensed with. These collections are listed below, after the contents of *ZZRQJ*.

## *Zhou Zuoren quanji*

### VOLUME 1

*Tan long ji* 談龍集 (Talking about dragons). 1927.
*Zexie ji* 澤瀉集 (Water plantain collection). 1927.
*Tan hu ji shang xia* 談虎集上，下 (Talking of tigers), 2 vols. 1928.
*Yongri ji* 永日集 (Endless days collection). 1929.

### VOLUME 2

*Ziji de yuandi* 自己的園地 (In my own garden). 1923; enl. ed., 1928.
*Kan yun ji* 看雲集 (Gazing at clouds collection). 1932.
*Yu tian di shu* 雨天的書 (Rainy day book). 1925, 1933.
*Ku cha an xiaohua ji* 苦茶庵笑話集 (Joke collection from the Bitter Tea Studio).
　　1933.
*Ye du chao* 夜讀抄 (Notes from night reading). 1934.

### VOLUME 3

*Ku cha suibi* 苦茶隨筆 ("Bitter tea": casual notes). 1935.
*Bingzhu tan* 秉燭談 (Talks by candlelight). 1936.
*Feng yu tan* 風雨談 (Talks in wind and rain). 1936.
*Ku zhu za ji* 苦竹雜集 (Miscellaneous notes of bitter bamboo). 1936.
*Yishu yu shenghuo* 藝術與生活 (Art and life). 1926, 1936.

### VOLUME 4

*Gua dou ji* 瓜豆集 (Melons and beans collection). 1937.
*Yaotang zawen* 藥堂雜文 (Miscellaneous writings of the Medicine Studio). 1944.
*Yaowei ji* 藥味集 (Taste of medicine collection). 1942.
*Shufang yijiao* 書房一角 (A corner of my study). 1945.
*Lichun yiqian* 立春以前 (Before spring). 1945.

### VOLUME 5

*Guoqu di gongzuo* 過去的工作 (My past work). 1945.
*Zhou Zuoren shuxin* 周作人書信 (Correspondence of Zhou Zuoren). 1933.
*Ertong wenxue xiaolun* 兒童文學小論 (Essays on children's literature). 1932.
*Ertong zashi shi* 兒童雜事詩 (Poems on random subjects for children). 1932.
*Zhongguo xin wenxue de yuanliu* 中國新文學的源流 (On the origins of China's new
　　literature). 1934.

*Kukou gankou* 苦口甘口 (Bitter and sweet). 1944.

*Ouzhou wenxue shi* 歐洲文學史 (History of European literature). N.d.

*Zhitang yiyou wenxuan* 知堂乙酉文選 (Zhitang's writings of 1945). 1959.

## Other Works of Zhou Zuoren

"Daoyan" 導言 (Preface). In *Zhongguo xin wenxue da xi: sanwen yi ji* 中國新文學大系：散文一集 (Compendium of new literature, vol. 6, essays, first collection), ed. Zhao Jiabi 趙家璧, 1: 1–14. Shanghai: Liangyou, 1935.

*Zhitang huixiang lu* 知堂回想錄 (Zhitang's reminiscences). 2 vols. Hong Kong: San Yu Stationery and Publishing, 1970.

*Zhou Zuoren jiwai wen* 周作人集外文 (Zhou Zuoren's uncollected works). Vol. 1, 1904–25; vol. 2, 1926–48. Ed. Chen Zishan 陳子善 and Zhang Tierong 張鐵榮. Haikou: Hainan guoji xinwen chuban zhongxin, 1995.

*Zhitang jiwai wen: sijiu nian yihou* 知堂集外文：四九年以後 (Zhitang's uncollected writings: after 1949). Ed. Chen Zishan 陳子善. Changsha: Yuelu shushe, 1988.

*Zhou Zuoren shi quanbian jianzhu* 周作人詩全編淺注 (Poetry of Zhou Zuoren: fully edited and annotated). Ed. Wang Chongsan 王仲三. Shanghai: Xuelin chubanshe, 1996.

*Zhitang shuhua* 知堂書話 (Zhitang's notes on books). 2 vols. Comp. Zhong Shuhe. Fully revised and reset. Haikou: Hainan chubanshe, 1997.

*Zhou Zuoren wen lei bian* 周作人文類編 (Writings of Zhou Zuoren arranged in subject categories). Comp. Zhong Shuhe 鍾叔河. 10 vols. Changsha: Hunan wenyi chubanshe, 1998.

## Secondary Sources

Ah Cheng 阿城 (Zhong Acheng 鍾阿城). "Qiwang" 棋王 (The chess king). *Shanghai wenxue* 1984, no. 7: 15–35.

———. *Xianhua xianshuo: Zhongguo shisu yu Zhongguo xiaoshuo* 閑話閑說：中國世俗與中國小說 (Digressions on idle tales: common customs and fiction in China). Taipei: Shibao wenhua, 1994.

Anderson, Benedict. *Imagined Communities: Reflections on the Origin and Spread of Nationalism.* Rev. ed. London: Verso, 1991.

Anderson, Marston. *The Limits of Realism: Chinese Fiction in the Revolutionary Period.* Berkeley: University of California Press, 1989.

Atwell, William S. "Afterword." In Yoshikawa Kōjirō, *Five Hundred Years of Chinese Poetry, 1150–1650,* pp. 191–96. Princeton: Princeton University Press, 1989.

Avineri, Shlomo. *Hegel's Theory of the Modern State.* Cambridge, Eng.: Cambridge University Press, 1972.

A Ying 阿英 (Qian Xingcun 錢杏村). "Xiaopin wen tan" 小品文談 (On *xiaopin wen*). In *Xiandai zuojia tan sanwen* 現代作家談散文 (Modern writers on the essay), ed. Yu Shusen 余樹森, pp. 72–77. Tianjin: Baihua wenyi chubanshe, 1986.

Bakhtin, M. M. "The Bildungsroman and Its Significance in the History of Realism (Towards a Historical Typology of the Novel)." In idem, *Speech Genres and Other Late Essays*, pp. 10–59. Trans. Vernon W. McGee. Austin: University of Texas Press, 1986.

Bauer, Wolfgang. "The Hidden Hero: Creation and Disintegration of the Ideal of Eremetism." In *Individualism and Holism: Studies in Confucian and Taoist Values*, ed. Donald J. Monro, pp. 157–97. Ann Arbor: Center for Chinese Studies, University of Michigan, 1985.

Bauman, Zygmunt. *Modernity and the Holocaust*. Cornell Paperbacks. Ithaca, N.Y.: New York: Cornell University Press.

Bayly, C. A. *Imperial Meridian: The British Empire and the World, 1780–1830*. London: Longman, 1989.

Befu, Harumi. "Nationalism and *Nihonjin ron*." In *Cultural Nationalism in East Asia: Representation and Identity*, ed. idem, pp. 107–35. Berkeley: University of California, Institute of East Asian Studies, 1993.

Berlin, Isaiah. *Vico and Herder: Two Studies in the History of Ideas*. New York: Viking Press, 1976.

Berman, Marshall. *All That Is Solid Melts into Air: The Experience of Modernity*. New York: Simon & Schuster, 1982.

Bhaba, Homi K. *Nation and Narration*. London: Routledge, 1990.

Billeter, Jean-François. *Li Zhi: philosophe maudit (1527–1602)*. Geneva: Librairie Droz. 1979.

Bloom, Irene. "On the Matter of the Mind: Metaphysical Basis of the Expanded Self." In *Individualism and Holism: Studies in Confucian and Taoist Values*, ed. Donald J. Monro, pp. 293–332. Ann Arbor: Center for Chinese Studies, University of Michigan, 1985.

Bol, Peter K. *"This Culture of Ours": Intellectual Transitions in T'ang and Sung China*. Stanford: Stanford University Press, 1992.

Boorman, Howard, et al., eds. *Biographical Dictionary of Republican China*. 5 vols. New York: Columbia University Press, 1967.

Brennan, Timothy. "The National Longing for Form." In *Nation and Narration*, ed. Homi K. Bhabha, pp. 44–70. London: Routledge, 1990.

Brook, Timothy. *The Confusions of Pleasure: Commerce and Culture in Ming China*. Berkeley: University of California Press, 1998.

Calhoun, Craig. *Critical Social Theory: Culture, History and the Challenge of Difference*. Twentieth-Century Social Theory. Oxford: Blackwell, 1995.

Carrère d'Encausse, Helene, and Stuart R. Schram. *Marxism and Asia: An Introduction with Readings*. London: Allen Lane, The Penguin Press, 1969.

Cascardi, Anthony J. *The Subject of Modernity*. Cambridge, Eng.: Cambridge University Press, 1992.

Chan, Wing-tsit. "The Ch'eng-Chu School of Early Ming." In *Self and Society in Ming Thought*, ed. Wm. Theodore de Bary, pp. 29–51. New York: Columbia University Press, 1970.

Chan, Wing-tsit, trans. and comp. *A Sourcebook in Chinese Philosophy*. Princeton: Princeton University Press, 1963; Princeton paperback edition, 1969.

Chang, Hao. *Chinese Intellectuals in Crisis: The Search for Order and Meaning, 1890–1911*. Berkeley: University of California Press, 1987.

———. "Intellectual Change and the Reform Movement, 1890–1898." In *The Cambridge History of China*, vol. 11, *Late Ch'ing, 1800–1911, Part II*, ed. John K. Fairbank and Kuang-ching Liu, pp. 274–338. Cambridge, Eng.: Cambridge University Press, 1980.

———. "New Confucianism and the Intellectual Crisis of Contemporary China." In *The Limits of Change: Essays on Conservative Alternatives in Republican China*, ed. Charlotte Furth, pp. 276–302. Harvard East Asian Series, 84. Cambridge, Mass.: Harvard Unviersity Press, 1976.

Chang, Sun Kang-i. "Chinese 'Lyric Criticism' in the Six Dynasties." In *Theories of the Arts in China*, ed. Susan Bush and Christian Murck, pp. 215–24. Princeton: Princeton University Press, 1983.

Chatterjee, Margaret. *Gandhi's Religious Thought*. Notre Dame, Ind.: University of Notre Dame Press, 1983.

Chatterjee, Partha. *Nationalist Thought and the Colonial World: A Derivative Discourse?* London: Zed Books, 1986.

———. *The Nation and Its Fragments: Colonial and Postcolonial Histories*. Princeton Studies in Culture/Power/History. Princeton: Princeton University Press, 1993.

———. "A Response to Taylor's 'Modes of Civil Society.'" *Public Culture* 3, no. 1 (Fall 1990): 119–32.

Chaudhuri, K. N. *Asia Before Europe: Economy and Civilisation of the Indian Ocean from the Rise of Islam to 1750*. Cambridge, Eng.: Cambridge University Press, 1990.

Chaves, Jonathan. "The Panoply of Images: A Reconsideration of the Literary Theories of the Kung-an School." In *Theories of the Arts in China*, ed. Susan Bush and Christian Murck, pp. 341–64. Princeton: Princeton University Press, 1983.

Che, K. L. "Not Words but Feelings—Ch'ien Ch'ien-i (1582–1664) on Poetry." *Tamkang Review* 6, no. 1 (Apr. 1975): 55–75.

Chen Xiaomei. *Occidentalism: A Theory of Counter-discourse in Post-Mao China*. Oxford: Oxford University Press, 1995.

Chen, Yu-shih. *Images and Ideas in Chinese Classical Prose: Studies of Four Masters.* Stanford: Stanford University Press, 1988.

Cheng, Ching-mao (Zheng Qingmao 鄭清茂). "The Impact of Japanese Literary Trends on Modern Chinese Writers." In *Modern Chinese Literature in the May Fourth Era*, ed. Merle Goldman, pp. 63–88. Cambridge, Mass.: Harvard University Press, 1977.

————. "Zhou Zuoren di Riben jingyan" 周作人的日本經驗 (Zhou Zuoren's Japanese experience). In *Zhongyang yanjiu yuan di'erjie guoji hanxue huiyi lunwen ji* 中央研究院第二屆國際漢學會議論文集 (Proceedings of the Second International Conference on Sinology, Academia Sinica), Taipei, Taiwan, ROC, Dec. 29–31, 1986, pp. 869–900. Taipei: Zhongyang yanjiu yuan, 1989.

Cheng, Wah-kwan. "*Vox populi*: Language, Literature and Ideology in Modern China," Ph.D diss., University of Chicago, 1989.

Chesneaux, Jean. "The Federalist Movement in China, 1920–1923." In *Modern China's Search for a Political Form*, ed. Jack Gray, pp. 96–137. London: Oxford University Press, 1969.

Cheung, Chiu-yee (Zhang Zhaoyi 張釗貽) *Nicai yu Lu Xun sixiang fazhan* 尼采與魯迅思想發展 (Nietzsche and the development of Lu Xun's thought.) Hong Kong: Qingwen shuwu, 1987.

Ch'ien, Edward T. *Chiao Hung and the Restructuring of Neo-Confucianism in the Late Ming.* New York: Columbia University Press, 1986.

————. "Chiao Hung and the Revolt Against Ch'eng-Chu Orthodoxy: The Left-Wing Wang Yang-ming School as a Source of the Han Learning in the Early Ch'ing." In *The Unfolding of Neo-Confucianism*, ed. Wm. Theodore de Bary et al., pp. 271–301. New York: Columbia University Press, 1975.

————. "Neither Structuralism Nor Lovejoy's History of Ideas: A Disidentification with Professor Ying-shih Yu's Review as a Dis-course." In *Ming Studies* 31 (Spring 1991): 42–86.

Ching, Julia. "Introduction." In Huang Tsung-hsi, *The Records of Ming Scholars*, trans. Julia Ching. Honolulu: University of Hawaii Press, 1987.

Chou, Chih-p'ing. *Yuan Hung-tao and the Kung-an School.* Cambridge, Eng.: Cambridge University Press, 1987.

Chou, I-fu 周億孚. "Zhou Zuoren zhuzuo kao" 周作人著作考 (On Zhou Zuoren's literary works). *Zhuhai xuebao* 6 (1973): 75–117.

Chow, Kai-wing. *The Rise of Confucian Ritualism in Late Imperial China: Ethics, Classics, and Lineage Discourse.* Stanford: Stanford University Press, 1995.

Chow, Rey. *Woman and Chinese Modernity: The Politics of Reading Between East and West.* Minnesota: University of Minnesota Press, 1991.

Chow Tse-tsung. *The May Fourth Movement: Intellectual Revolution in Modern China.*

Cambridge, Mass.: Harvard University Press, 1960; reprinted—Stanford: Stanford University Press, 1967.

Clunas, Craig. *Superfluous Things: Material Culture and Social Status in Early Modern China*. Chicago: University of Illinois Press, 1991.

Cole, James H. *Shaohsing: Competition and Cooperation in Nineteenth Century China*. Association of Asian Studies Monograph, no. 44. Published for the Association of Asian Studies. Tucson: University of Arizona Press, 1986.

de Bary, Wm. Theodore. "Individualism and Humanitarianism in Late Ming Thought." In *Self and Society in Ming Thought*, ed. Wm. Theodore de Bary and the Conference on Ming Thought, pp. 145–247. New York: Columbia University Press, 1970.

de Bary, Wm. Theodore, ed. *Self and Society in Ming Thought*. New York: Columbia University Press, 1970.

——. *Sources of Japanese Tradition*. 2 vols. New York: Columbia University Press, 1958.

——. *The Unfolding of Neo-Confucianism*. New York: Columbia University Press, 1970.

Denton, Kirk, ed. *Modern Chinese Literary Thought: Writings on Literature, 1893–1945*. Stanford: Stanford University Press, 1996.

Devji, Faisal Fatehali. "Hindu/Muslim/Indian." *Public Culture* 5, no. 1 (Fall 1992): 1–18.

DeWoskin, Kenneth. "Early Chinese Music and the Origin of Aesthetic Terminology." In *Theories of the Arts in China*, ed. Susan Bush and Christian Murck, pp. 187–214. Princeton: Princeton University Press, 1983.

Dikötter, Frank. *The Discourse of Race in Modern China*. Stanford: Stanford University Press, 1992.

Dirlik, Arif. "Reversals, Ironies, Hegemonies: Notes on the Contemporary Historiography of Modern China." *Modern China* 22, no. 3 (July 1996): 243–84.

Dong Bingyue 董炳月. "Zhou Zuoren de 'fu ni' yu wenhuaguan" 周作人的「附逆」與文化觀 (Zhou Zuoren's 'betrayal' and cultural outlook). *Ershiyi shiji* 13 (Oct. 1992): 95–102.

Dorson, Richard M. "The Eclipse of Solar Mythology." In *Myth: A Symposium*, ed. Thomas A. Seboek, pp. 25–63. Bloomington: Indiana University Press, 1958; reprinted—Midland Books Edition. Bloomington: Indiana University Press, 1965.

Duara, Prasenjit. *Culture, Power, and the State: Rural North China, 1900–1942*. Stanford: Stanford University Press, 1988.

——. *Rescuing History from the Nation: Questioning Narratives of Modern China*. Chicago: University of Chicago Press, 1995.

Eagleton, Terry. *The Ideology of the Aesthetic*. Oxford: Basil Blackwell, 1990.

Eastman, Lloyd E. "Nationalist China During the Nanking Decade, 1927–37." In *Cambridge History of China*, vol. 13, *Republican China, 1912–1949*, pt. II, ed. John K. Fairbank and Albert Feuerwerker, pp. 116–67. Cambridge, Eng.: Cambridge University Press, 1986.

Ellis, Havelock. *Affirmations*. Boston: Houghton Mifflin, 1916.

———. *Impressions and Comments*. 3 vols. London: Constable, 1913–24.

———. *My Confessional*. London: John Lane, 1934.

Elman, Benjamin. *From Philosophy to Philology: Intellectual and Social Aspects of Change in Late Imperial China*. Cambridge, Mass.: Council on East Asian Studies, Harvard University, 1984.

Esherick, Joseph. "Ten Theses on the Chinese Revolution." *Modern China* 21, no. 1 (Jan. 1995): 45–76.

Foot, Philippa. "Nietzsche's Immoralism." *New York Review of Books*, June 13, 1991, pp. 18–22.

Foucault, Michel. *The Archeology of Knowledge and the Discourse on Language*. Trans. A. M. Sheridan Smith. New York: Pantheon Books, 1972.

Fu, Poshek. *Passivity, Resistance, and Collaboration: Intellectual Choices in Occupied Shanghai, 1937–1945*. Stanford: Stanford University Press, 1993.

Furth, Charlotte. "Culture and Politics in Chinese Conservatism." In *The Limits of Change: Essays on Conservative Alternatives in Republican China*, ed. C. Furth, pp. 22–53. Harvard East Asian Series 84. Cambridge, Mass.: Harvard University Press, 1976.

———. "Intellectual Change: From the Reform Movement to the May Fourth Movement." In *Cambridge History of China*, vol. 12, *Republican China, 1912–1949*, Part I, ed. John K. Fairbank, pp. 322–405. Cambridge, Eng.: Cambridge University Press, 1983.

———. "The Sage as Rebel: The Inner World of Chang Ping-lin." In *The Limits of Change: Essays on Conservative Alternatives in Republican China*, ed. idem, pp. 113–50. Cambridge, Mass.: Harvard University Press, 1976.

Furth, Charlotte, ed. *The Limits of Change: Essays on Conservative Alternatives in Republican China*. Harvard East Asian Series 84. Cambridge, Mass.: Harvard University Press, 1976.

Gálik, Marian. *The Genesis of Modern Chinese Literary Criticism (1917–1930)*. London: Curzon Press, 1980.

Gluck, Carol. *Japan's Modern Myths: Ideology in the late Meiji Period*. Princeton: Princeton University Press, 1985.

Goldman, Merle. *Literary Dissent in Communist China*. Cambridge, Mass.: Harvard University Press, 1967; New York: Atheneum, 1971.

Goldman, Merle, ed. *Modern Chinese Literature in the May Fourth Era*. Harvard East Asian Series 89. Cambridge, Mass.: Harvard University Press, 1977.

Goodrich, L. Carrington, and Chao-ying Fang, eds. *Dictionary of Ming Biography.* New York: Columbia University Press, 1976.

Goody, Jack. *The East in the West.* Cambridge, Eng.: Cambridge University Press, 1996.

Gong Pengcheng 龔鵬程. *Shishi bense yu miaowu* 詩史本色與妙悟 (*Bense* and marvelous enlightenment in the history of the *shi* poem). Taipei: Taiwan xuesheng shuju, 1986.

Graham, A. C. *Chuang-tzu: The Inner Chapters.* London: Unwin Hyman, 1986.

——. *Disputers of the Tao: Philosophical Argument in Ancient China.* La Salle, Ill.: Open Court, 1989.

——. "Language." In Graham, *Chuang-tzu: The Inner Chapters,* pp. 25–26. London: Unwin Hyman, 1986.

Grant, Damian. *Realism.* The Critical Idiom, 9. London and New York: Methuen, 1970; 1985.

Greenfeld, Liah. *Nationalism: Five Roads to Modernity.* Cambridge, Mass.: Harvard University Press, 1992.

Gunn, Edward. *Rewriting Chinese: Style and Innovation in Twentieth Century Chinese Prose.* Stanford: Stanford University Press, 1991.

——. *Unwelcome Muse: Chinese Literature in Shanghai and Peking, 1937–1945.* New York: Columbia University Press, 1980.

Guo Shaoyu 郭紹虞. *Zhongguo wenxue piping shi* 中國文學批評史 (History of Chinese literary criticism). Hong Kong, n.d.; reprinted—Taipei: Wen shi zhe chubanshe, 1990.

Guo Shaoyu 郭紹虞 et al., comps. *Zhongguo lidai wenxue lunzhu jingxuan* 中國歷代文學論著精選 (Collection of theoretical writings on Chinese literature through the ages). 3 vols. Taipei: Hua zheng shuju, 1991.

Han Shaogong 韓少功. "Ba ba ba" 爸爸爸 (Da da da). *Renmin wenxue* 1985, no. 6: 83–102.

——. "Kefu xiaoshuo yuyanzhong de 'xuesheng qiang'" 克服小說語言中的「學生腔」 (Overcome "student accents" in the language of fiction). *Beifang wenxue* 1983, no. 1: 66–70.

——. *Maqiao cidian* 馬橋辭典. Beijing: Zuojia chubanshe, 1997.

——. "Wenxue de 'gen'" 文學的「根」 (The roots of literature). *Zuojia* 1985, no. 4: 2–5.

Hao Yixing 郝懿行. "Bense" 本色. Section in "Bilu" 筆錄 (Notes), in *Shai shu tang ji* 曬書堂集 (Collection of the Book Sunning Studio), *juan* 6. N.p.: Dong lu ting, 1884.

Harootunian, H. D. "Disciplining Native Knowledge and Producing Place: Yanagita Kunio, Origuchi Shinobu, Takata Yasuma." In *Culture and Identity: Japa-*

*nese Intellectuals During the Interwar Years*, ed. J. Thomas Rimer, pp. 99–127. Princeton: Princeton University Press, 1990.

Hartman, Charles. *Han Yu and the T'ang Search for Unity*. Princeton: Princeton University Press, 1986.

Hashikawa, Bunso. "Japanese Perspectives on Asia: From Dissociation to Co-prosperity." In *The Chinese and the Japanese*, ed. Akira Iriye, pp. 328–55. Princeton: Princeton University Press, 1980.

Hay, Stephen N. *Asian Ideas of East and West: Tagore and His Critics in Japan, China and India*. Cambridge, Mass.: Harvard University Press, 1970.

He Degong 何德功. *Zhongri qimeng wenxue lun* 中日啓蒙文學論 (On Chinese and Japanese literature of Enlightenment). Riben yanjiu boshi congshu. Beijing: Dongfang chubanshe, 1995.

Hegel, Friedrich. *The Philosophy of History*. Trans. J. Sibree. New York: Dover, 1956.

Henderson, John B. *The Development and Decline of Chinese Cosmology*. New York: Columbia University Press, 1984.

Hevia, James. *Cherishing Men From Afar: Qing Guest Ritual and the Macartney Embassy of 1793*. Durham, N.C.: Duke University Press, 1995.

Hockx, Michel. *A Snowy Morning: Eight Chinese Poets on the Road to Modernity*. Leiden: Research School Center for Non-Western Societies, 1994.

————. "The Literary Association (Wenxue yanjiu hui, 1920–1947) and the Literary Field of Early Republican China." *China Quarterly*, no. 153 (March 1998): 49–81.

Hsia, C. T. *A History of Modern Chinese Fiction*. 2d ed. New Haven: Yale University Press, 1971.

————. "Obsession with China: The Moral Burden of Modern Chinese Literature." In idem, *A History of Modern Chinese Fiction*, 2d ed., Appendix 1, pp. 533–54. New Haven: Yale University Press, 1971.

————. "Yen Fu and Liang Ch'i-ch'ao as Advocates of New Fiction." In *Chinese Approaches to Literature from Confucius to Liang Ch'i-ch'ao*, ed. Adele Austin Rickett, pp. 221–57. Princeton: Princeton University Press, 1978.

Hsiao, K. C. "Li Chih." In *Dictionary of Ming Biography*, ed. L. Carrington Goodrich and Chaoying Fang, s.v. New York: Columbia University Press, 1976.

Hu Menghua 胡夢華 and Wu Shuzhen 吳淑貞. "Xuyu sanwen" 絮語散文 (Essays of outpouring). In *Xiandai zuojia tan sanwen* 現代作家談散文 (Modern writers on the essay), ed. Yu Shusen 余樹森, pp. 14–16. Tianjin: Baihua wenyi chubanshe, 1986.

Hu Shi 胡適. "An Autobiographical Account at Forty." In *Two Self-portraits: Liang Ch'i-ch'ao and Hu Shih*, ed. Li Yu-ning, pp. 151–88. New York: Outer Sky Press, 1992.

————. "Daoyan" 導言 (Preface). In *Jianshe lilun ji* 建設理論集 (Towards a constructive literary theory). Vol. 1 of *Zhongguo xin wenxue da xi* 中國新文學大系

(Compendium of new literature), ed. Zhao Jiabi 趙家璧, pp. 1-32. Shanghai: Liangyou, 1935.

———. *Hu Shi wencun* 胡適文存 (Works of Hu Shi), series 1. Shanghai: Yadong, 1930.

———. *Hu Shi zuopin ji* 胡適作品集 (Hu Shi: collected works), vol. 8, *Wushi nian lai zhi Zhongguo wenxue* 五十年來之中國文學 (Chinese literature over the past fifty years). Taipei: Yuanliu chuban, 1986.

Hua, Shiping. *Scientism and Humanism: Two Cultures in Post-Mao China (1978–1989)*. Albany: State University Press of New York, 1995.

Huang, Philip C. C. "Liang Ch'i-ch'ao: The Idea of the New Citizen and the Influence of Meiji Japan." In *Transition and Permanence: Chinese History and Culture. A Festschrift in Honor of Dr. Hsiao Kung-ch'uan*, ed. David C. Buxbaum and Frederick T. Mote, pp. 71–102. Hong Kong: privately printed, 1972.

Huang Qiaosheng 黃喬生. *Dujin jiebo: Zhoushi san xiongdi* 度盡劫波周氏三兄弟 (Through the cataclysm: The three brothers Zhou). Beijing: Qunzhong chubanshe, 1998.

Huang Tsung-hsi. *The Records of Ming Scholars*. Ed. and trans. by Julia Ching with the collaboration of Chaoying Fang. Honolulu: University of Hawaii Press, 1987.

Hummel, Arthur W., ed. *Eminent Chinese of the Ch'ing Period*. 2 vols. Washington, D.C.: U.S. Government Printing Office, 1943; reprinted—Taipei: SMC Publishing, 1991.

Hung, Chang-tai. *Going to the People: Chinese Intellectuals and Folk Literature, 1918–1937*. Cambridge, Mass.: Harvard University Press, 1985.

Huntington, Samuel P. "The Clash of Civilizations." *Foreign Affairs* 72, no. 3 (1993): 22–49.

Huters, Theodore. "Lives in Profile: On the Authorial Voice in Modern and Contemporary Chinese Fiction." In *From May Fourth to June Fourth: Fiction and Film in Twentieth Century China*, ed. Ellen Widmer and David Der-wei Wang, pp. 269–94. Harvard Contemporary China Series, 9. Cambridge, Mass.: Harvard University Press, 1993.

———. "Speaking of Many Things: Food, Kings, and the National Tradition in Ah Cheng's 'The Chess King.'" *Modern China* 14, no. 4 (Oct. 1988): 388–418.

Hyman, Stanley Edgar. "The Ritual View of Myth and the Mythic." In *Myth: A Symposium*, ed. Thomas A. Seboek, pp. 136–53. Bloomington: Indiana University Press, 1958; Midland Books Edition. Bloomington: Indiana University Press, 1965.

Ichiko Chuzo. "Political and Institutional Reform, 1901–1911." In *The Cambridge History of China*, vol. 11, *The Late Ch'ing*, pt. II, ed. John K. Fairbank and Kuang-chi Liu, pp. 375–415. Cambridge, Eng.: Cambridge University Press, 1980.

Inden, Ronald. *Imagining India*. Oxford: Blackwell, 1990.

Irokawa Daikichi. *The Culture of the Meiji Period*. Ed. Marius B. Jansen. Princeton: Princeton University Press, 1985.

Jaggar, Alison M. "Human Biology in Feminist Theory: Sexual Equality Reconsidered." In *Knowing Women: Feminism and Knowledge*, ed. Helen Crowley and Susan Himmelweit, pp. 78–89. Cambridge, Eng.: Polity Press in association with the Open University, 1992.

Jansen, Marius. *China in the Tokugawa World*. Cambridge, Mass.: Harvard University Press, 1992.

Jeans, Roger B., Jr. *Democracy and Socialism in Republican China: The Politics of Zhang Junmai (Carsun Chang), 1906–1941*. Lanham, Md.: Rowman and Littlefield, 1997.

Johnston, Georgia. "The Whole Achievement in Virginia Woolf's *The Common Reader*." In *Essays on the Essay: Redefining the Genre*, ed. Alexander J. Butrym, pp. 148–58. Athens: University of Georgia Press, 1989.

Karatani, Kōjin. *The Origins of Modern Japanese Literature*. Ed. Brett de Bary. Durham, N.C.: Duke University Press, 1993.

Kato, Shuichi. *A History of Japanese Literature: The Modern Years*. Trans. Don Sanderson. Tokyo: Kodansha International, 1983.

Kinkley, Jeffrey. *The Odyssey of Shen Congwen*. Stanford: Stanford University Press, 1985.

LaFleur, William R. "A Turning in Taishō: Asia and Europe in the Early Writings of Watsuji Tetsurō." In *Culture and Identity: Japanese Intellectuals During the Interwar Years*, ed. J. Thomas Rimer, pp. 234–56. Princeton: Princeton University Press, 1990.

Lang, Andrew. *Myth, Ritual and Religion*. 2 vols. London: Longmans, Green, 1887.

Larson, Wendy. *Literary Authority and the Modern Chinese Writer: Ambivalence and Authority*. Durham, N.C.: Duke University Press, 1991.

Lee, Leo Ou-fan. "In Search of Modernity: Some Reflections on a New Mode of Consciousness in Twentieth Century Chinese History and Literature." In *Ideas Across Cultures: Essays on Chinese Thought in Honor of Dr. Benjamin I. Schwartz*, ed. Paul A. Cohen and Merle Goldman, pp. 109–35. Cambridge, Mass.: Harvard University Press, 1990.

———. "On the Margins of the Chinese Discourse: Some Personal Thoughts on the Cultural Meaning of the Periphery." *Daedalus* 120, no. 2 (Spring 1991): 207–26.

———. *The Romantic Generation of Modern Chinese Writers*. Cambridge, Mass.: Harvard University Press, 1973.

———. "Tradition and Modernity in the Writings of Lu Xun." In *Lu Xun and His Legacy*, ed. Leo Ou-fan Lee, pp. 3–31. Berkeley: University of California Press, 1985.

———. *Voices from the Iron House: A Study of Lu Xun*. Bloomington: Indiana University Press, 1987.

Legge, James, trans. *The Works of Mencius*. New York: Dover, 1970.

Lenin, V. I. "Imperialism, the Highest Stage of Capitalism." In *Lenin on Politics and Revolution*, ed. James E. Connor, pp. 111–48. Pegasus Books. Indianapolis and New York: Bobbs-Merrill, 1968.

Li Jie 李劼. "Zuowei Tang Jihede de Lu Xun, zuowei Hamulete de Zhou Zuoren" 作爲唐。吉訶德的魯迅和作爲哈姆雷特的周作人 (Lu Xun as Don Quixote and Zhou Zuoren as Hamlet). *Zhongguo yanjiu yuekan*, Sept. 1996, pp. 20–31.

Li Tuo 李陀. "Yixiang de jiliu (tigang)" 意象的激流(提綱) (A surging current of imagery: outline). N.p., n.d. Obtained in Prof. Leo Ou-fan Lee's Seminar in Modern Chinese Literature, Winter 1989, University of Chicago. Photocopy.

Lin, Yu-sheng. *The Crisis of Chinese Consciousness: Radical Iconoclasm in the May Fourth Era*. Madison: University of Wisconsin Press, 1979.

Lin Yutang. *A History of the Press and Public Opinion in China*. Published for the Institute of Pacific Relations by Humphrey Milford. London: Oxford University Press, 1937.

Ling, Mu. "From Social Criticism to Cultural Criticism: A Study of Chinese 'Culture Craze' and Li Zehou." Paper presented at the annual meeting of the Association for Asian Studies in Los Angeles, April 25–28, 1993. Photocopy.

Link, Perry. *Mandarin Ducks and Butterflies: Popular Fiction in Early Twentieth Century Chinese Cities*. Berkeley: University of California Press, 1981.

Liu, James J. Y. *Chinese Theories of Literature*. Chicago: University of Chicago Press, 1975.

———. *Language—Paradox—Poetics: A Chinese Perspective*. Ed. Richard John Lynn. Princeton: Princeton University Press, 1988.

Liu, Lydia. *Translingual Practice: Literature, National Culture, and Translated Modernity—China, 1900–1937*. Stanford University Press, 1995.

———. "Translingual Practice: The Discourse of Individualism Between China and the West." *positions* 1, no. 1 (Spring 1993): 160–93.

Liu Xuyuan 劉緒源. *Jiedu Zhou Zuoren* 解讀周作人 (Reading Zhou Zuoren). Shanghai: Shanghai wenyi, 1994.

Lu Xun 魯迅 (Zhou Shuren 周樹人). *Dawn Blossoms Plucked at Dusk*. Trans. Yang Hsien-yi and Gladys Yang. Beijing: Renmin chubanshe, 1976.

———. *Lu Xun quanji* 魯迅全集. 16 vols. Beijing: Renmin wenxue, 1982.

———. *Lu Xun: Selected Works*. 4 vols. Trans. Yang Hsien-yi and Gladys Yang. 2d ed. Beijing: Foreign Languages Press, 1980.

Lutz, Jessie Gregory. *Chinese Politics and Christian Missions: The Anti-Christian Movements of 1920–28*. Notre Dame, Ind.: Cross Cultural Publications, 1988.

Lynn, Richard John. "Alternative Routes to Self-realization in Ming Theories of Poetry." In *Theories of the Arts in China*, ed. Susan Bush and Christian Murck, pp. 317–40. Princeton: Princeton University Press, 1983.

———. "Orthodoxy and Enlightenment: Wang Shih-chen's Theory of Poetry and Its Antecedents." In *The Unfolding of Neo-Confucianism*, ed. Wm. Theodore de Bary et al., pp. 217–69. New York: Columbia University Press, 1975.

———. Review of *Readings in Chinese Literary Thought*, by Stephen Owen. *China Review International* 1, no. 2 (Fall 1994): 43–57.

Mao, Zedong. "On New Democracy." In *Selected Works of Mao Tse-tung*, 2: 339–84. Peking: Foreign Languages Press, 1967.

Maruyama, Masao. "The Ideology and Dynamics of Japanese Fascism." In idem, *Thought and Behaviour in Japanese Politics*, ed. Ivan Morris, pp. 25–83. Oxford: University of Oxford Press, 1963.

Matsumoto, Shigeru. *Motoori Norinaga, 1730–1801*. Cambridge, Mass.: Harvard University Press, 1970.

McDermott, Joseph P. "Emperor, Elites, Commoners: The Community Pact Ritual of the Late Ming." In *State and Court Ritual in China*, ed. Joseph P. McDermott, pp. 299–351. Cambridge, Eng.: Cambridge University Press, 1999.

McDougall, Bonnie S. *The Introduction of Western Literary Theory into Modern China*. Tokyo: Centre for East Asian Cultural Studies, 1971.

McDougall, Bonnie S., and Louie Kam. *The Literature of China in the Twentieth Century*. London: Hurst and Co., 1997.

McMullen, David. "Han Yu: An Alternative Picture" *HJAS* 49, no. 2 (1989): 603–57.

Min, Tu-ki. *National Polity and Local Power: The Transformation of Late Imperial China*. Harvard-Yenching Monograph Series 27. Cambridge, Mass.: Council on East Asian Studies, Harvard University, 1988.

Momose, Hiromu. "Fang Tung-shu." In *Eminent Chinese of the Ch'ing Period*, ed. Arthur Hummel, 1: 238–40. Washington, D.C.: Government Printing Office, 1943.

Morse, Ronald. "The Search for Japan's National Character and Distinctiveness: Yanagita Kunio (1875–1962) and the Folklore Movement." Ph.D. diss., Princeton University, 1975.

Nagai Kafū 永井荷風. *Nagai Kafū, 1879–1959* 永井荷風. Ed. Ozawa Nobuo 大澤信夫. Tokyo: Chikuma shobō, 1992.

Najita, Tetsuo. *Japan: The Intellectual Foundations of Modern Japanese Politics*. Chicago: University of Chicago Press, 1974.

Nandy, Ashis. *The Intimate Enemy: Loss and Recovery of Self Under Colonialism*. Delhi: Oxford University Press, 1983.

———. *Traditions, Tyranny and Utopias: Essays in the Politics of Awareness*. Delhi: Oxford University Press, 1987.

Nanjing shi dang'an guan 南京史檔案館. *Shenxun Wangwei hanjian bilu* 審訊汪僞漢奸筆錄 (Trial proceedings of the Wang Jingwei puppet regime traitors). Nanjing: Jiangsu guji chubanshe, 1992.

Ng, Mau-sang. *The Russian Hero in Modern Chinese Fiction.* Hong Kong: Chinese University Press; New York: SUNY, 1988.

Nieh, Hua-ling. *Shen Ts'ung-wen.* Twayne's World Author Series. New York: Twayne, 1972.

Nienhauser, William H., Jr., ed. *The Indiana Companion to Traditional Chinese Literature.* 2d rev. ed. Taipei: Southern Materials Center, by arrangement with Indiana University Press, 1988.

Nietzsche, Friedrich. *Thus Spake Zarathustra.* Trans. R. J. Hollingdale. London: Penguin, 1969.

Okakura, Kakasu (Kakazo) (Okakura Tenshin). *The Ideals of the East, with Special Reference to the Art of Japan.* London: John Murray, 1903.

Owen, Stephen. *The Great Age of Chinese Poetry: The High Tang.* New Haven: Yale University Press, 1981.

————. *Readings in Chinese Literary Thought.* Harvard-Yenching Institute Monograph Series, 30. Cambridge, Mass.: Council on East Asian Studies, Harvard University, 1992.

Pagden, Anthony. *Lords of All the World: Ideologies of Empire in Spain, Britain and France, c. 1500– c. 1800.* New Haven: Yale University Press, 1995.

Pinker, Stephen. *The Language Instinct: The New Science of Language and Mind.* New York: Wm. Morrow, 1994; Harmondsworth, Eng.: Penguin Books, 1995.

Plaks, Andrew. *The Four Masterworks of the Ming Novel.* Princeton: Princeton University Press, 1987.

Polachak, James M. *The Inner Opium War.* Harvard East Asian Monographs, 151. Cambridge, Mass.: Council on East Asian Studies, Harvard University, 1992.

Pollard, David E. *A Chinese Look at Literature: The Literary Values of Chou Tso-jen in Relation to the Tradition.* Berkeley: University of California Press, 1973.

————. "Chou Tso-jen: A Scholar Who Withdrew." In *The Limits of Change: Essays on Conservative Alternatives in Republican China,* ed. Charlotte Furth, pp. 332–56. Harvard East Asian Series 84. Cambridge, Mass.: Harvard University Press, 1976.

————. "Translation and Lu Xun: The Discipline and the Writer." Chinese University of Hong Kong Professorial Inaugural Lecture Series 13. *Chinese University Bulletin,* Supplement 21. 1991?

Pusey, James Reeve. *China and Charles Darwin.* Harvard East Asian Monographs, 100. Cambridge, Mass.: Council on East Asian Studies, Harvard University, 1983.

Qian Liqun 錢理群. *Fanren di bei'ai: Zhou Zuoren zhuan* 凡人的悲哀～周作人傳 (The sorrows of an ordinary man: the biography of Zhou Zuoren). Taipei: Yeqiang, 1991.

————. *Zhou Zuoren lun* 周作人論 (On Zhou Zuoren). Shanghai: Renmin, 1991.

Ricoeur, Paul. "Civilizations and National Cultures." In idem, *History and Truth*, pp. 271–84. Trans. Charles A. Kelbley. Evanston, Ill.: Northwestern University Press, 1965.

Rimer, J. Thomas. *Modern Japanese Fiction and Its Traditions: An Introduction.* Princeton: Princeton University Press, 1978.

Robertson, Maureen. "'. . . To Convey What is Precious': Ssu-k'ung Tu's Poetics and the *Erh-shih-ssu Shih Pin.*" In *Transition and Permanence: Chinese History and Culture. A Festscrift in Honor of Dr. Hsiao Kung-ch'uan,* ed. David C. Buxbaum and Frederick T. Mote, pp. 323–57. Hong Kong: privately printed, 1972.

Robinson, Paul. *The Modernization of Sex: Havelock Ellis, Alfred Kinsey, William Masters and Virginia Johnson.* New York: Harper and Row, 1976.

Rowbotham, Sheila, and Jeffrey Weeks. *Socialism and the New Life: The Personal and Sexual Politics of Edward Carpenter and Havelock Ellis.* London: Pluto Press, 1977.

Rudolph, Lloyd, and Susanne Rudolph. *The Modernity of Tradition.* Chicago: University of Chicago Press, 1966.

Said, Edward. *Orientalism.* New York: Random House, 1978; Vintage Books, 1979.

Sakai, Naoki. "Modernity and Its Critique: The Problem of Universalism and Particularism." In *Postmodernism and Japan,* ed. Masao Miyoshi and H. D. Harootunian, pp. 93–122. Durham, N.C.: Duke University Press, 1989.

Sautman, Barry. "Sirens of the Strongman: Neo-Authoritarianism in Recent Chinese Political Theory." *China Quarterly* 129 (Mar. 1992): 72–100.

Schipper, Kristoffer. *Le Corps taoïste: corps physique, corps social.* Paris: Librairie Artheme Fayard, 1987.

Schneider, Laurence. *Ku Chieh-kang and China's New History: Nationalism and the Quest for Alternative Traditions.* Berkeley: University of California Press, 1971.

Schwarcz, Vera. *The Chinese Enlightenment: Intellectuals and the Legacy of the May Fourth Movement of 1919.* Berkeley: University of California Press, 1989.

Schwartz, Benjamin. *In Search of Wealth and Power: Yen Fu and the West.* Cambridge, Mass.: Harvard University Press, 1964; reprinted—New York: Harper Torchbooks, 1969.

Seidensticker, Edward. *Kafū the Scribbler.* Stanford: Stanford University Press, 1965.

Shen Congwen 沈從文. *Shen Congwen wenji* 沈從文文集. Ed. Shao Huaqiang 邵華強 and Ling Yu 凌宇. 12 vols. Guangzhou: Huancheng; Hong Kong: Sanlian, 1982–85.

Sheridan, James E. "The Warlord Era: Politics and Militarism Under the Peking Government, 1916–28." In *Cambridge History of China,* vol. 12, *Republican China,*

*1912–1949, Part 1,* ed. John K. Fairbank, pp. 284–321. Cambridge, Eng.: Cambridge University Press, 1983.

Shiba, Yoshinobu. "The Formation of the East Asian Maritime Economy." Lecture Series. Faculty of Oriental Studies, University of Cambridge, May 1997.

Shih, Vincent Y., trans. *The Literary Mind and the Carving of Dragons.* Bilingual ed. Taipei: Chung Hwa, 1970.

Shimada Kenji. *Pioneer of the Chinese Revolution: Zhang Binglin and Confucianism.* Trans. Joshua Fogel. Stanford: Stanford University Press, 1990.

Shu Wu 舒蕪. "Nüxing de faxian: Zhitang funü lun lüeshu" 女性的發現～知堂婦女論略述 (The discovery of the female sex: a brief account of Zhitang's theories on women). *Zhongguo shehui kexue* 1988, no. 6: 129–52.

———. "Zhou Zuoren gaiguan" 周作人概觀 (Survey of Zhou Zuoren). 2 parts. *Zhongguo shehui kexue* 1986, no. 4: 89–115; no. 5: 187–214.

———. "Ziwo, kuanrong, youlu: liangtiao lu" 自我。寬容。憂患。兩條路 (Self, tolerance, suffering: two roads). *Dushu* 1989, no. 4: 65–73.

Sima Changfeng 司馬長風. *Zhongguo xin wenxue shi* 中國新文學史 (A history of China's new literature). Enl. ed. Banqiao, Taiwan: Luotuo chubanshe, 1987.

Smith, Antony D. "Opening Statement: Nations and their Pasts," *Nations and Nationalism* 2, no. 3 (1996): 358–65.

Spence, Jonathan. *The Search for Modern China.* New York: Norton; London: Hutchinson, 1990.

Stokes, Eric. *The English Utilitarians and India.* Oxford India Paperbacks. Delhi: Oxford University Press, 1990.

Tagore, Amitendranath. *Literary Debates in Modern China, 1918–1937.* Tokyo: Centre for East Asian Cultural Studies, 1967.

Tagore, Rabindranath. *Nationalism.* London, 1917.

Taine, Hippolyte. "Author's Introduction to This Translation." In idem, *A History of English Literature.* Trans. H. Van Laun. New York: Holt and Williams, 1872.

Tambiah, Stanley Jeyaraja. *Magic, Science, Religion and the Scope of Rationality.* Cambridge, Eng.: Cambridge University Press, 1990.

Tang, Xiaobing. *Global Space and the Nationalist Discourse of Modernity: The Historical Thinking of Liang Qichao.* Stanford: Stanford University Press, 1996.

Taylor, Charles. *Sources of the Self.* Cambridge, Mass.: Harvard University Press, 1989.

Thomas, William. Introduction to *The History of British India,* by John Stuart Mill. Classics of British Historical Literature. Chicago: University of Chicago Press, 1976.

Tort, Patrick. "L'Introduction a l'anthropologie darwinienne." In Tort, *Marx et le problème de l'ideologie,* pp. 117–46. Paris: Presses universitaires de France, 1988.

———. *La Pensée hiérarchique et l'évolution: les complexes discursifs.* Paris: Aubier, 1985.

Tu, Ching-i. "Neo-Confucianism and Literary Criticism in Ming China: The Case of T'ang Shun-chih (1507–1560)." *Tamkang Review* 15, nos. 1–4 (Autumn 1984–Summer 1985): 547–60.

Van Zoeren, Steven. *Poetry and Personality: Reading, Exegesis, and Hermeneutics in Traditional China*. Stanford: Stanford University Press, 1991.

Vickery, John B. *The Literary Impact of the Golden Bough*. Princeton: Princeton University Press, 1973.

Waldron, Arthur. *From War to Nationalism: China's Turning Point, 1924–1925*. Cambridge, Eng.: Cambridge University Press, 1995.

Wang, C. H. "Chou Tso-jen's Hellenism." *Renditions* 7 (Spring 1977): 5–28.

Wang, David Der-wei. *Fictional Realism in Twentieth-Century China: Mao Dun, Lao She, Shen Congwen*. New York: Columbia University Press, 1992.

———. *Fin-de-siècle Splendor: Repressed Modernities of Late Qing Fiction, 1848–1911*. Stanford University Press, 1997.

Wang Fansen 王汎森. *Zhang Taiyan di sixiang jian lun qi dui Ruxue chuantong di chongji* 章太炎的思想兼論其對儒學傳統的衝擊 (Zhang Taiyan's thought and his attack on Confucian learning). Taipei: Shibao, 1985, 1992.

Wang, Jing. *High Culture Fever: Politics, Aesthetics and Ideology in Deng's China*. Berkeley: University of California Press, 1996.

Wang, John C. Y. "Lu Xun as a Scholar of Traditional Chinese Literature." In *Lu Xun and His Legacy*, ed. Leo Ou-fan Lee, pp. 90–103. Berkeley: University of California Press, 1985.

Wang Zengqi 汪曾棋. *Wanfanhua ji* 晚飯花集. Beijing: Renmin wenxue, 1985.

Watson, Burton, trans. *The Tso Chuan: Selections from China's Oldest Narrative History*. New York: Columbia University Press, 1989.

Watsuji, Tetsuro. *Climate and Culture: A Philosophical Study*. Trans. Geoffrey Bownas. Tokyo: Japanese National Commission of UNESCO and Ministry of Education, 1961; reprinted—Classics of Modern Japanese Thought and Culture Series. New York: Greenwood Press, 1988.

*Wenxue yundong ziliao xuan* 文學運動資料選. 3 vols. Shanghai: Shanghai jiaoyu, 1979.

White, Hayden. "Foucault Decoded: Notes from Underground." In idem, *Tropics of Discourse: Essays in Cultural Criticism*, pp. 230–60. Baltimore: Johns Hopkins University Press, 1978.

Wilson, Thomas A. "Genealogy and History in Neo-Confucian Sectarian Uses of the Confucian Past." *Modern China* 20 (Jan. 1994): 3–33.

———. *Genealogy of the Way: The Construction and Uses of the Confucian Tradition in Late Imperial China*. Stanford: Stanford University Press, 1995.

Woei, Lien Chong. "Mankind and Nature in Chinese Thought: Li Zehou on the Traditional Roots of Maoist Voluntarism." *China Information* 11, no. 2/3 (Autumn/Winter 1996–97): 138–75.

Wolff, Ernst. *Chou Tso-jen.* Twayne's World Authors Series. New York: Twayne, 1971.

Wong, Siu-kit. *Early Chinese Literary Criticism.* Hong Kong: Joint Publishing, 1983; reprinted—Taipei: Bookman Books, 1990.

Wong, Young-tsu. *Search for Modern Nationalism: Zhang Binglin and Revolutionary China, 1869–1936.* Hong Kong: Oxford University Press, 1989.

Wright, Mary C. "From Revolution to Restoration: The Transformation of Kuomintang Ideology." *Far Eastern Quarterly* 14, no. 4 (1955): 515–23.

Wu Fuhui 吳福輝. "Dalu wenxue de Jing Hai chongtu gouzao" 大陸文學的京海沖突構造 (The structure of the clash between the Peking and Shanghai schools in mainland literature). *Shanghai wenxue* 1989, no. 10: 71–77.

Wu Hongyi 吳宏一. *Qingdai shixue chutan* 清代詩學初探 (A preliminary exploration of Qing poetics). Taipei: Taiwan xuesheng shuju, 1986.

Wu Yixia et al. 吳一霞, eds. *Guwen guan zhi* 古文觀止. Xi'an: Shaanxi renmin, 1990.

Xu, Ben. "From Modernity to Chineseness: The Rise of Nativist Cultural Theory in Post-1989 China." *positions: east asia cultures critique* 6, no. 1 (Spring 1998): 203–37.

Yamamoto, Tatsuro, and Sumiko Yamamoto. "Religion and Modernization in the Far East, Part Two, The Anti-Christian Movement in China, 1922–1927." *Far Eastern Quarterly* 12, no. 2 (Feb. 1953): 133–47.

Yan Jiayan 嚴家炎. *Zhongguo xiandai xiaoshuo liupai shi* 中國現代小說流派史 (A history of the schools of modern Chinese fiction). Beijing: Renmin wenxue, 1989.

Yan, Lu. "Beyond Politics in Wartime: Zhou Zuoren, 1931–1945." *Sino-Japanese Studies* 11, no. 1 (Oct. 1998): 6–12.

Yan Yu 嚴羽. *Canglang shihua jiaoshi* 滄浪詩話較釋 (*Canglang shihua:* annotated edition), ed. Guo Shaoyu 郭紹虞. Taipei: Liren shuju, 1983.

Yanagita, Kunio. *The Legends of Tōno.* Trans. Ronald Morse. Tokyo: Japan Foundation, 1975.

Yang, Lan. *Chinese Fiction of the Cultural Revolution.* Hong Kong: Hong Kong University Press, 1998.

Yang Mu 楊牧 (C. H. Wang). *Wenxue de yuanliu* 文學的源流 (The origins of literature). Taipei: Hongfan shudian, 1984.

———. "Zhou Zuoren lun" 周作人論 (On Zhou Zuoren). In idem, *Wenxue de yuanliu* 文學的源流 (The origins of literature), pp. 143–47. Taipei: Hongfan shudian, 1984.

Yeh, Catherine V. "Roots Literature of the 1980s: May Fourth as a Double Burden." Paper presented at International Conference on The Burdens of the May Fourth Cultural Movement, Charles University, Prague, August 1994.

Yeh, Michelle. "Introduction." In *An Anthology of Modern Chinese Poetry*, ed. and trans. M. Yeh, pp. xxiii–l. New Haven: Yale Univesity Press, 1992.

Yeh, Wen-hsin. *The Alienated Academy: Culture and Politics in Republican China*. Harvard East Asian Monographs, 148. Cambridge, Mass.: Council on East Asian Studies, Harvard University, 1990.

Yoshikawa, Kōjirō. *Five Hundred Years of Chinese Poetry*. Trans. John Timothy Wixted. Princeton: Princeton University Press, 1989.

Yu, Pauline. "Canon Formation in Late Imperial China." In *Culture and State in Chinese History: Conventions, Accommodations, Critiques*, ed. Theodore Huters, R. Bin Wong, and Pauline Yu, pp. 83–104. Irvine Studies in the Humanities. Stanford: Stanford University Press, 1997.

———. *The Reading of Imagery in the Chinese Poetic Tradition*. Princeton: Princeton University Press, 1987.

Yu Shusen 余樹森. *Xiandai zuojia tan sanwen* 現代作家談散文 (Modern writers on the essay). Tianjin: Baihua wenyi chubanshe, 1986.

———. "Xiandai sanwen lilun niaokan: dai xu" 現代散文理論鳥瞰(代序) (By way of a preface: an overview of modern theories on the essay). In idem, *Xiandai zuojia tan sanwen* 現代作家談散文 (Modern writers on the essay), pp. 1–24. Tianjin: Baihua wenyi chubanshe, 1986.

Yu, Ying-shih. "The Intellectual World of Chiao Hung Revisited: A Review Article." *Ming Studies* 25 (Spring 1988): 24–66.

Yuan Hongdao 袁宏道. *Yuan Hongdao ji jianjiao* 袁宏道集箋校 (The complete works of Yuan Hongdao, annotated). Ed. Qian Bocheng 錢伯城. 3 vols. Shanghai: Guji chubanshe, 1981.

Yue, Gang. "Surviving (in) the 'Chess King': Towards a Post-revolutionary Nation-Narration." *positions: east asia cultures critique* 3, no. 2 (Fall 1995): 564–94.

Zeng Zhennan 曾鎮南. "Yicai yu shenwei: du A Cheng de zhongpian xiaoshuo Qiwang" 異彩與深味～讀阿城的中篇小說棋王 (Radiant splendor and profound intimations: reading A Cheng's novella "The Chess King"). *Shanghai wenxue* 1984, no. 10: 77–80.

Zhang Jian 張健. *Canglang shihua yanjiu* 滄浪詩話研究 (Research into the *Canglang shihua*). Taipei, 1966; reprinted—Taipei: Wunan tushu, 1986.

———. *Ming Qing wenxue piping* 明清文學批評 (Ming and Qing literary criticism). Taipei: Guojia, 1983.

Zhang Juxiang 張菊香. *Zhou Zuoren nianpu* 周作人年譜. Tianjin: Nankai daxue chubanshe, 1985.

Zhang Juxiang 張菊香 and Zhang Tierong 張鐵榮, eds. *Zhou Zuoren yanjiu ziliao* 周作人研究資料 (Research materials on Zhou Zuoren). 2 vols. Tianjin: Tianjin renmin, 1986.

Zhang Ruoying 張若英 (Qian Xingcun 錢杏村), ed. *Zhongguo xin wenxue yundong ziliao* 中國新文學運動資料 (Materials on the history of China's New Literature movement). Shanghai: Guangming shuju, 1934; facsimile reprint—Shanghai: Shanghai shuju, 1982.

Zhang Taiyan 章太炎 (Zhang Binglin 章炳麟). *Zhang Taiyan quanji* 章太炎全集 (Complete works of Zhang Taiyan). Shanghai: Renmin, 1985.

———. *Zhang Taiyan zhenglun xuanji* 章太炎政論選集 (Selected political works of Zhang Taiyan). Ed. Tang Zhijun 湯志鈞. Beijing: Zhonghua shuju, 1977.

———. *Zhangshi congshu* 章氏叢書 (Collected works of Zhang Binglin). Hangzhou: Zhejiang Tushuguan, 1917–19.

Zhang Xudong. *Chinese Modernism in the Era of Reforms: Cultural Fever, Avant-garde Fiction and the New Chinese Cinema.* Durham, N.C.: Duke University Press, 1997.

Zhao Jiabi 趙家璧, ed. *Zhongguo xin wenxue daxi* 中國新文學大系 (Compendium of China's new literature). 10 vols. Shanghai: Liangyou, 1935–36. Facsimile reprint—Shanghai: Wenyi chubanshe, 1981.

Zhao, Suisheng. "Chinese Intellectuals Quest for National Greatness and Nationalistic Writing in the 1990s." *China Quarterly* 152 (Dec. 1997): 725–45.

*Zhongwen da cidian* 中文大辭典. 10 vols. Taipei: Zhongguo wenhua yanjiusuo, 1962–68.

Zhou Zhenfu 周振甫. *Wenzhang lihua* 文章例話 (Systematic exemplification of elements of prose). Beijing, n.d.; reprinted—Taipei: Pugongying, n.d.

Zhu Guangqian 朱光潛. "*Yu tian di shu*" 雨天的書 (The *Rainy Day Book*). *Yiban* 1, no. 3 (Nov. 5, 1926). Reprinted in *Zhou Zuoren yanjiu ziliao* 周作人研究資料 (Research materials on Zhou Zuoren), ed. and comp. Zhang Juxiang 張菊香 and Zhang Tierong 張鐵榮, pp. 315–20. Tianjin: Renmin, 1986.

Zhu Ziqing 朱自清. "Lun xiandai Zhongguo de xiaopin sanwen" 論現代中國的小品散文 (On the modern Chinese *xiaopin* essay). In *Xiandai zuojia tan sanwen* 現代作家談散文 (Modern authors on the essay), ed. Yu Shusen 余樹森, pp. 43–48. Tianjin: Baihua wenyi, 1986.

———. *Shi yan zhi bian* 詩言志辨 (An analytical study of *shi yan zhi*). Taipei: Taiwan kaiming shuju, 1964; reprinted—1982.

Zuo Dongling 佐東岭. *Li Zhi yu wan Ming wenyi sixiang* 李贄與晚明文藝思想 (Li Zhi and the late Ming aesthetics). Tianjin: Tianjin renmin, 1997.

# Character List

A Cheng　阿城
ai guo bao en　愛國報恩
An Lushan　安祿山
Atarashiki mura　新村

bagu wen　八股文
ba Rumen dakai fangjin Chan wei lai
　把儒門打開放進禪味來
baihua　白話
baihua sanwen　白話散文
baihua wenxue　白話文學
Bai Juyi　白居易
Baima　白馬
baixing riyong　百姓日用
baokuo guominxing de quanbu　包括
　國民性的全部
baotian tianwu　暴殄天物
beizhuang　悲壯
benlaide zhidi xingse　本來的質地
　形色
bense　本色
benti sixiang　本體思想

benzhuo　笨拙
bidiao　筆調
biecai　別材
biequ　別趣
bihuo　筆禍
biji　筆記
bi/xing　比/興
Bing Xin　冰心
Biyong　辟雍
bu zhuo yi zi jin de feng liu　不著一
　字盡得風流

Cai Yuanpei　蔡元培
can shi　參詩
cao mu chong yu　草木蟲魚
ce lun　策論
chang　長
Chen Duxiu　陳獨秀
Chen Houshan　陳后山
Chen Zhengfu (Suoxue)　陳正甫
　(所學)
Chenbao　晨報

cheng　誠
Cheng Fangwu　成仿吾
Cheng Hao　程顥
Cheng Yi　程頤
chengyi　誠意
Chikamatsu　近松
chōnin　町人
chuanqi　傳奇
chunwang　春王
ci　詞
ciqu　詞曲
cun xing　存性

da　達
da wo　大我
Dai Wang　戴望
danghang　當行
daoli　道理
daotong　道統
daoxue　道學
datong　大統
dawo　大我
dayoushi　打油詩
Deng Zhongxia　鄧中夏
diding　地丁
di'erge guxiang　第二個故鄉
difangzhuyi　地方主義
difang zizhi　地方自治
diji quwei　低級趣味
dingfa　定法
Dingxian　定縣
di zhi zi　地之子
Du Fu　杜甫
Duan Chengshi　段成式
Duan Qirui　段祺瑞
duchuang　獨創
dunwu　頓悟
du shan qi shen　獨善其身
du shu xingling buju getao　獨抒性
　靈不拘格套

Er Cheng quan shu　二程全書

Fan Yin (Xiaofeng)　范寅 (嘯風)
Fang Bao　方苞
Fang Dongshu　方東書
Fang Fei　方非
fang yan gao lun　方言高論
Fei zongjiao da tongmeng　非宗教大
　同盟
Feng Ban (Dunyin)　馮班 (頓吟)
Feng Sanmei　馮三昧
Feng Wenbing (Fei Ming)　馮文炳
　(廢名)
Feng Shu (Mo'an)　馮舒 (默庵)
Feng Yuxiang　馮玉祥
feng hua yue xue　風花月雪
fengqu　風趣
fengtu (Jp: fūdo)　風土
fengzhi　風致
fu　賦
Fu Shan (Qingzhu)　傅山 (青竹)
Fu Sinian　傅斯年
fude　賦得
fugu　復古
Fukuzawa Yukichi　福沢論吉
fuqiang　富強

gaige wenti　改革文體
ganjue　感覺
ganqing　感情
ganxiang xiao pian　感想小篇
gao　高
Gao Bing (Tingli)　高棅 (廷禮)
Geng Dingxiang　耿定向
Genji monogatari　源氏物語
Genzhai xushuo　艮齋續說
Gesheng liu Hu xuesheng zonghui
　各省留滬學生總會
Getian　葛天
gewu　格物

gong rong gong cun　共榮共存

gu　古

Gu Jiegang　顧頡剛

gu jin zhong wai　古今中外

Gu Xiancheng (Jingyang)　顧憲成
　(涇陽)

Gu Yanwu　顧炎武

Guan Zidong　關子東

Guangfu hui　光復會

gui　鬼

Gui Youguang　歸有光

guocui (Jp: kokusui)　國粹

guocuizhuyi　國粹主義

guojiazhuyi　國家主義

guominxing　國民性

Guo Moruo　郭沫若

guoxue (Jp: kokugaku)　國學

guoyu　國語

guoyu de wenxue wenxue de guoyu
　國語的文學文學的國語

guwen　古文

haibun　俳文

haikai　俳諧

haiku　俳句

Han Shaogong　韓少功

Hanxue shangdui　漢學商兌

Han Yu (Tuizhi)　韓愈 (退之)

Hanyu　漢語

Hanzi　漢字

haohua　豪華

Hao Yixing　郝懿行

Hara (Sen) Kōdō　原(善)公道

Hata Nobuko　羽太信子

Hata Yoshiko　羽太芳子

*Hiyorigeta*　日和下駄

Hu Shi　胡適

huaji　滑稽

Huang Zongxi　黃宗義

Huang Zunxian　黃遵憲

huiwei　回味

huo wenxue　活文學

Inui Shigeko　乾榮子

*Ishi-gami mondō*　石神問答

Ji Yun　紀昀

jia　家

Jiang Guangci　蔣光慈

Jiang Shaoyuan　江紹原

Jianhu　鍵湖

jianshi　見識

jian xiu　漸修

Jiao Hong　焦竑

jiaohua　教化

jiaohuai　教壞

Jiao Xun (Litang)　焦循 (理堂)

jiaqu　佳趣

jiezhi　節制

Jin Shengtan　金聖歎

*Jinghua bixue lu*　京華碧血錄

Jingling　竟陵

Jingpai　京派

jingshi　經世

*Jinhua lun*　進化論

jinti sanwen　近體散文

Jippensha Ikku　十返舍一九

jiuliu baijia　九流百家

jōmin　常民

kami　神

Kang Youwei　康有爲

kanji　漢字

kaozhengxue　考證學

Kiyoura Keigo　清浦奎吾

Kobayashi Issa　小林一茶

kokkeibon　滑稽本

konnyaku　蒟蒻

Kuaiji　會稽

Kuga Katsunan　陸羯南

Kuriyagawa Hakuson　廚川
　白村
Ku yu zhai　苦雨齋
kyōgen　狂言

laiyuan　來源
Lanting　蘭亭
li　理
Li Bai　李白
Li Ciming (Yueman)　李慈銘
　(越縵)
Li Dazhao　李大釗
Li Jinfa　李金髮
Li Jinxi　黎錦熙
Li Sancai　李三才
Li Shizeng　李石曾
Li Xiaofeng　李小峰
Li Yu　李漁
*Li Yueman riji chao*　李越縵日記鈔
Li Zhi　李贄
Liang Qichao　梁啓超
Liang Shiqiu　梁實秋
Liang Shuming　梁漱溟
liangzhi　良知
liansheng zizhi　聯省自治
*Liaozhai zhiyi*　聊齋志異
lijiao　禮教
Lin Shu　林紓
lishi minzu　歷史民族
lisu　禮俗
Liu Bannong (Fu)　劉半農 (復)
Liu Dabai　劉大白
Liu Wendian　劉文典
Liu Xianting (Jizhuang)　劉獻廷
　(繼莊)
Liu Xie　劉勰
Liu Zongyuan　劉宗元
Lu Ji　陸機
Lu Xiangshan　陸象山
lun shi ru lun Chan　論詩如論禪

*Lunyu*　論瑜
*Luotuo cao*　駱駝草

Ma Yuzao　馬裕藻
Mao Kun (Lumen)　茅坤 (鹿門)
Mao Xihe (Qiling)　茅西河 (奇齡)
Masaoka Shiki　正岡子規
Matsuo Bashō　松尾芭蕉
Mei Guangdi　梅光迪
mei quwei　沒趣味
meiwen　美文
*Meizhou pinglun*　每周評論
Meng Haoran　孟浩然
menglong　朦朧
miaowu　妙悟
*Minbao*　民報
*Mingliao xijiyou*　冥寥子記遊
mingshi pai　名士派
minguo zhengnian　民國正年
mingyun　命運
minzuzhuyi　民族主義
Miyake Setsurei　三宅雪嶺
mono (no) aware　物哀
Mori Ōgai　森鷗外
Motoori Norinaga　本居宜長
Mou Ting (Moren)　车庭 (默人)
Moxuyou xiansheng zhuan　莫須有
　先生傳
Mu Mutian　穆木天
Mushakōji Saneatsu　武者小路篤
Muzha　木柵

Nagai Kafū　永井荷風
Naitō Konan　内藤湖南
Natsume Sōseki　夏目淑石
Nihonjinron　日本人論

Oka Senjin　岡千仞
Okakura Tenshin　岡倉天心
Ōnuma Chinzan　大沼枕山

Ouyang Xiu 歐陽修

paiwai 排外
Pei Du (Jingong) 裴度 (晉公)
piaoyi 飄逸
pingdan tanhua 平淡談話
pingdan ziran 平淡自然
Pingshui 平水
Pipa ji 琵琶記
pu 樸
Pu Songling 蒲松齡

Qian Dehong 錢德洪
qian gu buke momie zhi jian 千古不
　可磨滅之見
qian gu zhi yan 千古之眼
qianhou qizi 前後七子
Qian Qianyi 錢謙益
Qian Xuantong 錢玄同
Qian Xun (Nianqu) 錢恂
　(念劬)
qijie 氣節
qijue 奇崛
qing 情
qing yu zhi 情與知
qingbo 輕薄
qinglang 清朗
qingqu 情趣
qingse 清澀
qingxin liuli 清新流麗
qingyi 情意
qingyuan pingdan 清遠平淡
Qiu Jin 秋瑾
qiwan 淒婉
qiwei 氣味
qi wen gong xinshang yi yi xiang yu xi
　奇文共欣賞疑義相與析
Qiwulun 齊物論
qu 曲
quwei 趣味

rakugo 落語
Re feng 熱風
ren 仁
rendao 人道
ren de shenghuo 人的生活
ren de wenxue 人的文學
Renjian shi 人間世
ren jie di ling 人杰地靈
renqing wuli 人情物理
renqing wuse 人情物色
rensheng de wenxue 人生的文學
rensheng riyong 人生日用
renwu zhidu dili fengsu zhi lei 人物
　制度地理風俗之類
riyong renshi 日用人事
Rujia 儒家
Rujiao 儒教
rushen 入神

sanwen shi 散文詩
satuo 灑脫
senryū 川柳
Sentetsu sōdan 先哲叢談
Shaoxing 紹興
Shedi 射的
shen 深
Shen Congwen 沈從文
Shen Jianshi 沈兼士
shenke 深刻
shenqie 深切
Shen Shiyuan 沈士遠
shenxing 神性
Shen Yinmo 沈尹默
shenyun 神韻
shi 詩
Shiga Shigetake 志賀重昂
shihua 詩話
shijiao 詩教
shijiezhuyi 世界主義
Shijing 詩經

shijing　詩境

Shikitei Sanba　式亭三馬

Shimazaki Tōson　島崎藤村

Shirakaba　白樺

shisu　世俗

shitie shi　式帖詩

*Shitaya sōwa*　下谷叢話

shi wai you shi　詩外有詩

shi wei　詩味

Shiwubao　時務報

shi yan zhi　詩言志

shi yuan qing er qimi　詩緣情而
　綺靡

Shi Zhecun　施蟄存

Shōtetsu　正徹

*Shuihu zhuan*　水滸傳

Shun　舜

shuo　說

*Shuowen jiezi*　說文解字

shuqing shi　抒情詩

Sikong Tu　司空圖

Sima Guang　司馬光

Sima Qian　司馬遷

si wenxue　死文學

sixiang geming　思想革命

Song Lao (Muzhong)　宋勞 (牧仲)

su　俗

su di　素地

Su Shi (Zizhan, Dongpo)　蘇軾
　(子瞻, 東坡)

suibi　隨筆

Sun Fuyuan　孫伏園

Suzuki Miekichi　鈴木三重吉

*Taibai*　太白

*Tan long lu*　談龍錄

Tan Yuanchun　譚元春

Tang Jiyao　唐繼堯

Tang Shunzhi　唐順之

Tang Xianzu　湯顯祖

Tang Zixi (Geng)　唐子西(庚)

Tanizaki Jun'ichirō　谷崎潤一朗

Tao Qian (Yuanming)　陶潛(淵明)

tian li　天理

tian wen　天文

tiekuo　帖括

Togawa Shūkotsu　戶川秋骨

Tokugawa Mitsukuni　德川光邦

Tongchengpai　桐城派

tongda　通達

Tongmenghui　同盟會

tong wen tong yu　同文同語

tongxianghui　同鄉會

tongxin　童心

tongxin zhe zhen xin ye　童心者眞
　心也

tongzi zhe ren zhi chu ye tongxin zhe
　xin zhi chu ye　童子者人之初也
　童心者心之初也

*Tōno mongatari*　遠野物語

Torii Ryūzō　鳥居龍藏

Tu Long　屠隆

tu zhi li　土之力

Uchida Roan　內田魯庵

ukiyo-e　浮世繪

Wang Bo　王勃

Wang Gen　王艮

Wang Ji　王畿

Wang Jide　王驥德

Wang Jingwei　汪精衛

Wang Jizhong (Siren)　王季重
　(思任)

Wang Shizhen (Yuyang, Yishang)
　王士禎 (漁洋, 貽上)

Wang Tiaowen (Wan)　汪荍文 (琬)

Wang Yangming　王陽明

Watsuji Tetsurō　和辻哲朗

weixin　維新

weiyuti 娓語體

wen 文

wenjian 聞見

Wen Lugong (Yanbo) 文潞公
(彥博)

wenming 文明

*Wenxuan* 文選

wenyan 文言

*Wenxue gailiang chuyi* 文學改良
芻議

wenxue geming 文學革命

*Wenxue geming lun* 文學革命論

Wenxue yanjiu hui 文學研
究會

wen yi zai dao 文以載道

wenzi 文字

Wuhuai 無懷

Wu Rulun 吳汝綸

wuli renqing 物理人情

wu quwei 無趣味

wuxian 無限

Wu Yue 吳越

Xia Suiqing (Zengyou) 夏穗卿
(曾佑)

xiandai de qixi 現代的氣息

xiang 香

xiangfeng 鄉風

*Xiang nang ji* 香囊記

xiangtu de qiwei 鄉土的氣味

xiangtu yishu 鄉土藝術

xiangxia ren 鄉下人

xiangyue 鄉約

xianshi bidiao 閑適筆調

xiantan shuoli bidiao 閑談說理
筆調

xiantan ti 閑談體

xianzhe yulu 賢者語錄

Xiao Chunu 蕭楚女

Xiao he 小河

Xiao Maoting (Yingshi) 蕭茂挺
(穎士)

xiaopin sanwen 小品散文

xiaowo 小我

Xie Fangde 謝枋德

xin 心

Xin chao she 新潮社

xing (inspired, heightened) 興

xing (nature) 性

xing qu 興趣

xing wei 興味

xingling 性靈

xingling liulu 性靈流露

xin jing 心境

*Xinmin congbao* 新民叢報

*Xin qingnian* 新青年

*Xin sheng* 新生

xiong hun 雄渾

xiti zhongyong 西體中用

xiucai 秀才

xiuci fangfa 修辭方法

Xu Wei (Wenchang) 徐渭 (文長)

xuanyan shi 玄言詩

*Xueheng* 學衡

xungen 尋根

xuyu sanwen 絮語散文

ya 雅

Yamamoto Yūzō 山本有三

Yan Fu 嚴復

Yan Yuan 顏元

Yan Zhitui 顏之推

Yanagi Muneyoshi 柳宗悅

Yanagita Kunio 柳田國男

yang bagu 洋八股

yangcheng guomin longtong de sixiang
養成國民籠統的思想

Yang Weizhen 楊維楨

Yang Wenhui 楊文會

Yao 堯

Yao Nai　姚鼐

Yazhouzhuyi　亞洲主義

ye　業

yi (intention, meaning)　意

yi (oneness)　一

yi (righteousness)　義

Yihetuan　義和團

*Yijing*　易經

yilao　遺老

yili　義理

yilun sanwen　議論散文

yinyong qingxing　吟詠情性

yixiang　意象

yiyi　意義

yi yi ni zhi shi wei de zhi　以意逆志
　是爲得之

yiyuande　一元的

yongwu　詠物

Yosa Buson　与謝蕪村

Yosano Akiko　与謝野晶子

Yoshida Kenkō　吉田兼好

you bieze　有別擇

You Tong (Xitang)　尤侗 (西堂)

youxuan (Jp. yūgen)　幽玄

Youyang zazu　酉陽雜俎

yuan (affinity)　緣

yuan (distance, aloofness)　遠

Yuan Mei　袁枚

yuanyin　原因

Yu Pingbo　俞平伯

Yu Zhengxie (Lichu)　俞正燮
　(理初)

Yu Yue　俞樾

Yuan Zhongdao (Xiaoxiu)　袁中道
　(小修)

Yuan Zongdao (Boxiu)　袁宗道
　(伯修)

*Yucheng xinwen*　禹誠新聞

Yue Fei　岳飛

yuefu　樂府

*Yuewei caotang biji*　閱微草堂筆記

*Yue yan*　越諺

Yuezhong　越中

Yun Daiying　惲代英

Yushan　虞山

*Yusi*　語絲

yuxiang　餘香

*Yuzhou feng*　宇宙風


zagan　雜感

zaxue　雜學

Zeng Guofan　曾國藩

Zhang Binglin (Taiyan)　章炳麟
　(太炎)

Zhang Dai (Zongzi)　張岱 (宗子)

Zhang Erqi　張爾歧

Zhang Junmai　張君勱

Zhang Ru'nan　張汝南

*Zhangshizhai wenji*　章實齋文集

Zhang Shizhao　章士釗

Zhang Xuecheng　章學誠

Zhang Zhidong　張之洞

Zhang Zuolin　張作霖

Zhao Hengti　趙恆惕

*Zhao hua xi shi*　朝花夕拾

Zhao Zhiqian　趙之謙

Zhao Zhixin　趙執信

Zhedong　浙東

zhengjiao　政教

zhengzong　正宗

zhenjie　貞節

zhen qing hua　眞情話

zhen quan　眞詮

zhen xiang　眞相

zhen zai　眞宰

zhi　知

*Zhijiang ribao*　之江日報

Zhina tong　支那通

Zhitang　知堂

zhiyi　志意

*Zhongguo qingnian* 中國青年

zhonghou 重厚

zhongxiao 忠孝

zhongyong 中庸

zhong yu di 忠於地

Zhou Dunyi 周敦頤

Zhou Jianren 周建人

Zhou Shuren 周樹人

Zhu Xi 朱熹

Zhu Zhiyu (Shunshui) 朱之瑜 (舜水)

Zhu Ziqing 朱自清

zhuo 拙

ziran wuru 自然悟入

*Zizhi tongjian* 資治通鑑

Zongshedang 宗社黨

zui you wenxue yiwei de 最有文學意味的

# Index

Harvard East Asian Monographs
(* out-of-print)